Nutrition,
National Development,
and Planning

The MIT Press
Cambridge, Massachusetts, and
London, England

**Nutrition,
National Development,
and Planning**

Edited by
Alan Berg
Nevin S. Scrimshaw
David L. Call

Proceedings of
an International Conference
held at Cambridge, Massachusetts,
October 19-21, 1971

Library of Congress Cataloging in Publication Data

International Conference on Nutrition, National Develop-
   ment, and Planning, Massachusetts Institute of
   Technology, 1971.
   Nutrition, national development, and planning.

   1. Nutrition–Congresses. 2. Economic development
–Congresses. 3. Nutrition policy–Congresses.
I. Berg, Alan D., ed. II. Scrimshaw, Nevin S., ed.
III. Call, David L., 1932-   ed. IV. Title.
[DNLM: 1. Developing countries–Congresses. 2. Nu-
trition–Congresses. 3. Nutrition disorders–
Congresses. 4. Social planning–Congresses. QU 145
I605n 1971]
TX345.I56 1971   641.1   73-4799
ISBN 0-262-02092-0

Contents

Preface

This book reports the proceedings of the International Conference on Nutrition, National Development, and Planning held at the Massachusetts Institute of Technology from October 19 to October 21, 1971. The purpose of this conference was to explore the place of large-scale nutrition programs in planning for national development, particularly in the developing countries and among low-income groups. The participants included nutritionists, economists, development planners, and national and international administrators. Papers and discussion focused on two main issues: (1) problems of nutrition per se, as they affect both the individual and the nation, and the most feasible means of alleviating the problems; (2) the integration of nutrition planning into an overall national development program in nations with limited economic resources.

The participants included 35 from Asia, 38 from Latin America, 24 from the United Kingdom and Europe, 14 from Africa, 8 from the Middle East, 11 from Canada, and 209 from the United States. An attempt was made to represent as many as possible of the groups and institutions working in areas related to the conference theme.

The plan of the book follows the conference program: Part I: The Effects of Nutrition on the Individual; Part II: The Role of Nutrition in National Development; Part III: Diagnosis of Food and Nutrition Problems and Establishment of Priorities; Part IV: Determinants of Malnutrition and Alternative Nutrition Intervention Programs; Part V: A Conceptual Approach to National Nutrition Program Planning; and Part VI: Case Studies. Except for the last section, the keynote paper is followed by four to six shorter panel papers commenting on the theme elaborated in the principal paper. Each session concluded with a general floor discussion, which appears in the book in condensed and edited form.

An important purpose of the conference was to stimulate nutritionists and development specialists to talk to each other, to share information on mutual tasks, and to search for ways to jointly advance the goal of national development through improving the nutritional and health status of a nation's population—not simply on humanitarian grounds but for pragmatic economic reasons as well. The participants agreed that unless the two disciplines do join forces, in planning and in implementation, neither will fully achieve its goals. As is always the case, many more issues were raised than solved. But the conference was a fruitful beginning and may constitute a foundation for continuing dialogue and accomplishment.

The conference was initiated by the Committee on International Nutrition Programs, Food and Nutrition Board, National Academy of Sciences. We were assisted in developing the plans by a committee consisting of Mr. Sol Chafkin, Dr. Martin Forman, Dr. Derrick Jelliffe, Mr. Mogens Jul, Dr. Michael Latham, Dr. Arthur Mosher, Dr. Robert Muscat, Dr. Merrill Read, Dr. Roberto Rueda-Williamson, Dr. Lester Tepley, Dr. Douglas Wilson, and Mr. John Hurley. Support for the conference was provided by the U.S. Agency for International Development; the U.S. National Institutes of Health through the Joint Malnutrition Panel of the U.S.–Japan Cooperative Medical Science Program; the World Bank; and the Association for the Aid of Crippled Children. Participating agencies included the Ford Foundation, UNICEF, WHO, FAO, UNIDO, and UNESCO.

The editors also wish to thank Janice Young of M.I.T., Ann Watkins of the Brookings Institution, and C. Frederick Bentley II and his administrative staff at M.I.T. for their valuable assistance. They acknowledge with appreciation the work of Ruth D. Kaufman, who edited the manuscript.

Alan Berg, Senior Editor
Nevin S. Scrimshaw
David L. Call

April 1972

Contributors

Benjamin Barg
Chief, New Technologies Section
Office for Science and Technology
United Nations

Moisés Béhar
Director, Instituto de Nutrición de
Centro America y Panama
Guatemala City

Maaza Bekele
Head, Social Services Department
Planning Commission Office
Office of the Prime Minister
Imperial Ethiopian Government
Addis Ababa

J. M. Bengoa
Chief, Nutrition Unit
World Health Organization
Geneva

Alan Berg
Senior Fellow, the Brookings
Institution, Washington, D.C.,
and
Belding Scholar, Association for the
Aid of Crippled Children, N.Y.
Visiting Professor, M.I.T.

David L. Call
Professor of Food Economics
Graduate School of Nutrition
Cornell University
Ithaca, New York

Joaquín Cravioto
Chairman, Department of Nutrition
Hospital Infantil de México
Mexico City

Elsa R. De Licardie
Hospital Infantil de México
Mexico City

Fanny Ginor
Economic Advisor, Bank of Israel
Jerusalem
Senior Lecturer, Tel-Aviv University

Derrick B. Jelliffe
Director, Caribbean Food and
Nutrition Institute
Kingston, Jamaica

Leonard Joy
Fellow, Institute of Development
Studies
University of Sussex
Sussex, U.K.

Mogens Jul
Director, Danish Meat Products
Laboratory, Copenhagen
Protein Advisory Group
United Nations

Karl Eric Knutsson
Head, Department of Social
Anthropology
University of Stockholm

Uwe Kracht
Marketing Research Manager,
International
The Quaker Oats Company
Chicago

L. Křikava
Head, Division of Metabolism
and Nutrition
Institute of Human Nutrition
Prague

Michael C. Latham
Professor of International Nutrition
Cornell University
Ithaca, New York

F. James Levinson
Department of Agricultural
Economics
Cornell University
Ithaca, New York

P. Mahadevan
Animal Production Service
FAO
Rome

P. Malek
Institute of Human Nutrition
Prague

Wilfred Malenbaum
Professor of Economics
University of Pennsylvania
Philadelphia

Richard K. Manoff
Chairman, Richard K. Manoff Inc.
New York

J. Mašek
Director, Institute for Clinical
and Experimental Medicine
Prague

John W. Mellor
Professor of Agricultural Economics
Cornell University
Ithaca, New York

Asok Mitra
Secretary, Planning Commission
New Delhi

Robert Muscat
Chief, Near East-South Asia
Planning Division
Agency for International
Development
Washington, D.C.

Robert R. Nathan
President, Robert R. Nathan
Associates
Washington, D.C.

Amorn Nondasuta
Principal Medical Officer
Department of Health
Bangkok

Mohamed A. Nour
Assistant Director-General, FAO
Near East Regional Office
Cairo

Toshio Oiso
Director, National Institute of
Nutrition
Tokyo

Saburo Okita
President, Japan Economic
Research Center
Tokyo

Sadao Orita
Chief, Nutrition Section
Ministry of Health and Welfare
Tokyo

Jaime Paez-Franco
Director of Nutrition
Colombian Institute of Family
Welfare
Bogotá

V. Ramalingaswami
Director, All-India Institute of
Medical Sciences
New Delhi

Roberto Rueda-Williamson
Regional Nutrition Adviser
Pan American Health Organization
Washington, D.C.

F. T. Sai
Director of Medical Services,
Ghana
Accra

Nevin Scrimshaw
Professor and Head
Department of Nutrition
and Food Science
Massachusetts Institute of Technology
Cambridge, Massachusetts

In Sang Song
President, Korean Development
Association
Seoul

Carl E. Taylor
Professor and Chairman, Department
of International Health
School of Hygiene and Public Health
The Johns Hopkins University
Baltimore, Maryland

Jerome B. Wiesner
President, Massachusetts Institute
of Technology
Cambridge, Massachusetts

Douglas Wilson
Senior Analyst
Office of Management and Budget
Washington, D.C.

Part I

The Effects of Nutrition
on the Individual

1 The Effect of Malnutrition on the Individual

Joaquín Cravioto,
Chairman, Department of Nutrition
Hospital Infantil de México

Elsa R. De Licardie
Hospital Infantil de México
Mexico City

In recent years, nutrition as a public policy issue has become a major topic of discussion for an increasing number of persons and bodies concerned with social, political, and economic development. Actually, nobody denies that nutrition is an important factor in the life of the individual from the time of conception to the time of death. Intake of a diet adequate in quantity and quality has been recognized, since the early days of pediatrics, as a prerequisite for the optimal growth and development of the child. Nonetheless, when one moves from the individual to the community as a whole, the need for maximizing insufficient resources forces those responsible for planning and operating development programs to question the priority of malnutrition vis-à-vis other problems. Berg [1] has indicated that the central point for the planner in developing countries is to decide if malnutrition is such an important obstacle to national development as to justify rerouting resources now earmarked for other needs. In the presence of limited resources good planning demands that each disease, each damage, must be ranked against every other need. Some specific aspects of this comparison are (1) the magnitude of the problem; (2) how vulnerable are its proximal and distal causes to the means available for its prevention and treatment; and (3) what are the implications of its presence and its sequelae for the continuous development of the community (historical transcendency).

The intent here is to summarize our knowledge on the physical and mental sequelae of malnutrition with emphasis on how malnutrition affects the capacity of an individual to make a meaningful contribution to society. Because, either alone or more often in combination with infectious disorders, protein-calorie malnutrition constitutes one of the main causes of death and disease in the world population, our review is restricted to this particular form of nutritional inadequacy.

At the community level, protein-calorie malnutrition is a man-made disorder characteristic of the lower segments of society, particularly of the preindustrial societies, where the social system (consciously or unconsciously) creates malnourished individuals generation after generation through a series of social

Supported in part by grants from Association for the Aid of Crippled Children, New York, the Nutrition Foundation, Inc., the Van Ameringen Foundation, the Monell Foundation, and the Hospital Infantil de México.

mechanisms among which limited access to goods and services, limited social mobility, and restricted experiential opportunities at crucial points in life play a major role.

At the individual level, the term *protein-calorie malnutrition* is a generic name used in the medical literature to group the whole range of mild to severe clinical and biochemical signs present in children as a consequence of a deficient intake and/or utilization of foods of animal origin, accompanied by variable intakes of rich carbohydrate foods. Kwashiorkor and marasmus are the names given to the two extreme clinical varieties of the syndrome. The appearance of one or another of these nutritional disorders is related to the age of the child, time of full weaning, time of introduction of food supplements to breast milk, caloric density and protein concentration of the supplements actually given, and frequency and severity of infectious disorders during weaning.

Although its incidence varies from place to place, the syndrome presents the same basic characteristics of clinical and biochemical pathology. The regional variations observed are generally associated with other concomitant nutritional deficiencies, the pattern of weaning, and the infectious pathology prevalent in the area.

The interaction of the effects produced by the societal factor and the individual factor is what ultimately results in malnutrition. Taking low weight gain in early infancy as the single most characteristic sign of protein-calorie malnutrition, Figure 1 was constructed as a flow diagram to illustrate several pathways through which this complex of interrelations may result in malnutrition in infancy.[2] Starting with a low level of modern technology, which results in limited income and the expenditure of almost all the available energy (time available to be converted to consumption goods) for the procurement of the bare necessities of life, one is confronted with reduced purchasing power and with the absence of reserves and surpluses. At least two pathways can derive from this point to produce low weight gain in infants. The first is direct, and proceeds from insufficient investment in sanitary modifications of the environment to the persistence of traditional conceptions of health and disease. [3,4] These prescientific conceptions include incorrect ideas on the role of food in the production of disease, which translate into practices that, within the limits set by the purchasing power of the family, determine the pattern of distribution of available food within the family; the net result is a reduction in the type and amount of food that the infant is allowed to consume. This ultimate step would be the last link of the

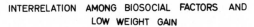
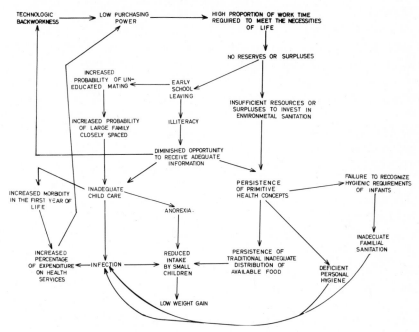

Figure 1. Interrelation among Biosocial Factors and Low Weight Gain

chain producing low weight gain. Indirect branching may occur when primitive conceptions on health result in lack of awareness of the hygienic requirements of the child, and lead through a chain of unsanitary conditions in the home to poor cleanliness of the mother and other members of the household in direct contact with the infant, who is then exposed to a higher risk of infections that either directly or indirectly may produce low weight gain.

A second major pathway proceeds from lack of reserves or surpluses to pressures for early school-leaving as an attempt to increase the purchasing power of the family unit. The consequences of school dropout are high illiteracy and diminished opportunities for obtaining adequate information, which in turn reinforce technological backwardness and the persistence of primitive conceptions of health and disease. Early school dropout also results in the conferral by society of adulthood status and role to a group of individuals at an earlier age than would be the case had they remained students. This situation may lead to an increased chance of marrying at a younger age and to an equally uneducated spouse, thus multiplying the likelihood of a larger family, inadequate child care, illness, and malnutrition. The increased morbidity in turn would translate into increased expenditures on health services, thus aggravating the effect of low purchasing power.

Clearly many other pathways may be identified, all of them resulting in a reinforcement of opportunities for the persistence of a way of life which drastically reduces the chances of an adequate development of technological and educational competence. Malnutrition becomes just one of the expressions of the interactions of social variables capable of influencing nutritional and health practices.

In examining the possibility that malnutrition may result in suboptimal functioning of the individual it becomes necessary to consider the role of food and feeding along several dimensions. The first one, which may be called a physiological dimension, has as a unit of measurement the *nutrient,* and its function is to provide chemical substances to the organism for its growth, maintenance, and metabolic regulation. The second dimension of food may be considered as psychophysical. Its unit of measurement is the *foodstuff,* which through its organoleptic characteristics would provide the organism with a variety of stimuli (texture, color, aroma, taste, temperature). In this context a foodstuff presented at the table in two different kitchen preparations having the same nutrient and calorie content would in fact be considered as two different foods by the individual. Finally, the third food dimension may be considered as psychosocial in nature, and its unit of measurement is the *mealtime.* The function of food along this line is, on the one hand, to aid in symbol formation through the values that family and society attach to food, such as: a form of reward or punishment; an experience attached to a gratifying or ungratifying person; and an identifying characteristic of an ethnic or subcultural group. On the other hand, the mealtime provides opportunities to demonstrate, clarify, and practice role and status at the family level and at the community level. Who is waited on first? Who sits at the place of honor at the table? Who receives the best part of a dish? Who moderates conversation at the table?

Given thus the fact that human malnutrition is a consequence of a malfunctioning society, and that food is something more than nutrients and calories, it appears as a corollary that the evaluation of its role as a cause of suboptimal performance of the individual can be done only through the longitudinal study of infants at risk and of an appropriate control population over a long period of time. The information available from cross-sectional studies is not enough to settle the main question. Nevertheless, even in the absence of the final answer, there is plenty of suggestive evidence that individuals who were severely malnourished, particularly in early infancy, have performance levels below those to be expected according to their social class. It is not implicit in this statement that lack of nutrients per se is the responsible factor for the suboptimal functioning.

Size

Since the classical studies of Jackson and Stewart [5] published in 1920, it has been established that malnutrition produced in animals during the suckling period results in permanent reduction of ultimate size. The reports of McCance, [6] Platt, [7] Pratt, [8] and Dobbing [9] among many others leave no doubt that in a variety of animal species malnutrition imposed during the rapid phase of growth, when the rate of protein synthesis and the rate of cell division are at their maximum, decelerates body growth and changes the structure of some organs. The transiency or permanency of the damage is a function of time and duration.

For the human, as so frequently happens, our information on the later effects of early malnutrition is fragmentary and scanty, with as yet no clear-cut conclusions. For animal research, all that is required is the definition of severity of malnutrition, type, duration, and age of onset. Thus adequate controls can be run, and in a relatively short period of observation the problem can be solved. Human malnutrition, on the other hand, does not occur in isolation and many of the nonnutritional factors that accompany or contribute to its appearance may independently influence growth and development. Therefore, the presence of malnutrition conjointly with other potential conditions of risk for maldevelopment makes it difficult to determine the contribution that inadequate nutrient intake per se may be making to the inhibition of growth and development, especially among populations where differences in the level of nutrient consumption are generally associated with other profound differences in familial characteristics and environmental circumstances related directly or indirectly to social disadvantage.

The association between adult stature and socioeconomic status is well known, [10] and recently Naeye et al. found that infants of poor mothers, in New York City, were at delivery 15 percent smaller than infants of nonpoor mothers. [11] Most of the few published studies on the effect of early malnutrition on physical growth in humans are handicapped by our lack of information about the genetic potential of the children under observation and by the scarcity of data on the adequacy of the diet and health care received by the children in their home environment after discharge from hospital. The results obtained under these circumstances in several ethnic groups (Bagandan, Peruvian, Chilean, South African Coloured) show that previously malnourished children do not attain, at least for several years, the weight, height, and bone age of children of the same ethnic background but of a higher social class. [12-16]

Considering that children from a higher social class may be nutritionally above average and may also be genetically different, Garrow and Pike [17] decided to compare the growth of previously malnourished Jamaican children with the growth of their siblings or close relatives. Using a matched-pair technique it was found that the index cases examined 2 to 8 years after discharge from hospital were slightly taller and heavier than their siblings, who, in the opinion of the authors, had never been severely malnourished.

Since, on the one hand, no relationship has been found between the severity of malnutrition on admission to hospital and the degree of somatic deficiency years later, or between length of stay in hospital and degree of catch-up in growth; and, on the other hand, there is a weak, not statistically significant relation between age on admission and size at follow-up, the apparent discrepancy of results obtained when comparing previously malnourished children with siblings or with higher class natives can be interpreted as suggesting that the severe acute episode of malnutrition that throws the child into hospital has little influence on subsequent growth after discharge. But chronically malnourished infants, with or without an acute episode of superimposed deficiency, would not reach for many years the norms of growth of their ethnic class.

In support of the above suggestion are the findings of Ashworth, [18] who studied for a sufficiently long period the growth rates of 8 children recovering from protein-calorie malnutrition. Compensatory growth was very rapid at the beginning of recovery, but when the expected weight for height was reached, food intake fell abruptly by 30 percent and growth rates dropped to a level comparable with those of normal children of that height and weight. Accordingly it can be expected that, if height for age was markedly low on admission, stunting will be present at least for several years, even if home conditions are favorable to meet the requirements for rapid growth. Since it has been calculated that a child needs 81 Kcal to form 10 g of new tissue containing 1.7 g/protein and 2.5 g/fat, a reasonable conclusion is that under present conditions it may be very difficult for children to receive at home a diet adequate to enable them to reach their full growth potential.

It seems clear that the extent of permanent stunting due to early malnutrition depends on many factors. The importance of attaining full physical growth can be illustrated by Thomson's study, [19] which documented that in primigravidae in Aberdeen (excluding those over 29 years of age, in whom the matter is more complex) short stature is associated with a greatly increased liability to delivery by caesarean section, and of perinatal deaths due to birth trauma. There were 43.6 caesarean sections per thousand mothers of less than 60 inches of stature, and only 4.2 per thousand when stature was equal to 62 inches. Similarly, perinatal deaths due to birth trauma rose from 2.7 per thousand in infants from mothers with heights around 64 inches to 8.6 in infants from mothers of only 60 inches or less.

Mental Performance

The association between malnutrition in preschool children and low levels of mental performance has been amply documented in several regions of the world where malnutrition is highly prevalent. A direct association between deficits in height and weight of malnourished children and retardation in psychomotor, adaptive, language, and social-personal behavior, as measured by the Gesell, Cattell, or Bayley techniques, has been reported. [15, 20-23]

Studies of mental performance of kwashiorkor patients during the period of rehabilitation have shown that, as children recover from malnutrition, developmental quotients increase in most cases. The magnitude of the increment varies in direct relation to the age at which the children suffered the disease. Therefore, with successful treatment, the difference between chronological and mental age progressively diminishes in all children except those who are sticken by severe malnutrition below the age of 6 months. [24] Research conducted in infants recovering from nutritional marasmus has also disclosed that basal intelligence and psychomotor activity, as judged by the Bayley scales, remain severely retarded despite apparent somatic recovery. [25] These studies extend the results found in children recovered from kwashiorkor and point out the fact that both extremes of chronic severe protein-calorie malnutrition behave in similar ways, giving a marked retardation in mental development, which is present even after physical and biochemical rehabilitation have occurred. [26, 27]

The effect of added stimulation during the initial recovery has been recently reported. [28] Two groups of severely malnourished children were evaluated during their recovery by the Griffiths scale. One group, paired for sex and age, was situated in an environment where there were pictures, drawings, toys, and music, and where nurses played with the children and sang to them, establishing a good emotional relationship. The nonstimulated group stayed in a place with similar dimensions but with no decorations, and without toys and music. The medical and dietetic treatment was the same for both groups. The initial difference in developmental quotients was not significant. Both groups increased their mental performance in a significant and almost parallel form, and only toward the end of the observation period (4 months) did the stimulated group show higher quotients, resulting basically from a drop in the performance level of the nonstimulated group. Both groups remained below the values expected for their age; the interesting fact was that the greater deficit occurred, as was the case among Roblés et al.'s Mexican children, in the area of language and communication.

Another approach to assessing the persistence of mental lags in malnutrition has been the study of survivors several years after discharge from a hospital. Four such studies have been published. The first is a report on the follow-up of 36 Serbian children who had been hospitalized for severe malnutrition when they were between 4 and 24 months of age. [29] Their level of intelligence was evaluated when they were between 7 and 14 years old, using a modification of the Binet-Simon scale. The mean IQ level was 88, which is significantly lower than the figure of 93 found in a group of normal children of unskilled workers. It is interesting that one-third of the fathers of the children rehabilitated from malnutrition were either professionals or army officers, and the rest were skilled or unskilled workers. In relation to the IQ distribution, one-half of the 39 rehabilitated children showed IQs below 90, with 6 children not scoring above 70. These frequencies are in contrast with those found in the general population of Serbian children in which 32 percent had IQ scores above 110. The weight deficit on admission to the hospital and the IQ at school age showed a significant association.

The second study was done in Indonesia [30] in a group of children 5 to 12 years old whose nutritional status at the age of 2 to 4 years was known. When tested with the Goodenough and Wechsler techniques, the children who had been previously malnourished and who had shown signs of vitamin A deficiency in the preschool years had significantly lower intelligence scores than the children who were regarded as healthy during the 2-year to 4-year age period. The IQs derived from the total Wechsler scale were 77 ± 2.3 and 68 ± 2.7, respectively, for 33 children considered as healthy in the preschool period and the 12 children who at that time were diagnosed as malnourished and showing vitamin A deficiency. The group of 19 school-age children whose diagnosis at the preschool age was malnutrition without vitamin A deficiency had a mean IQ of 73 ± 3.3. The difference between normal and malnourished, with or without vitamin A deficiency, is significant at the 0.01 level of confidence. According to the authors, the intellectual development as well as the physical development of the children could be predicted with a high degree of accuracy on the basis of their nutritional status during the preschool years.

The third study is the follow-up of a group of Indian children who had been treated for kwashiorkor. [31] The ages at the time of admission into the hospital were between 18 and 36 months. At the time of follow-up the children were between 8 and 11 years of age. Each index case was matched for age, sex, religion, caste, socioeconomic status, family size, birth order, and educational background of the parents, with three children who had never been hospitalized for malnutrition. All control children also belonged to the same class in school as the index case. The results of the mental tests showed a significant difference between groups not only in intelligence but also in level of intersensory adequacy. The younger age group gave the maximal differences. Subsequently, at the 1971 Asian Nutrition Conference (report in press) the author (Srikantia) showed that the mothers of kwashiorkor children were less competent than those of the controls.

The fourth report describes a study carried out in a group of Mexican school-age children who had suffered severe protein-calorie malnutrition before their 30th month of life. [32] In an attempt to reduce the influence of environmental variables, a group of siblings of similar age and sex were also examined; the difference in age between the index child and his sibling never was more than 3 years. The Wechsler Intelligence Scale for Children was administered to both groups. As expected, the results showed that the environment in which children at risk of malnutrition live is highly effective in reducing mental competence. Children developing in this milieu have a high probability of scoring in the low range of values in intelligence tests as well as in other types of tests related to basic mechanisms for learning. It is important to emphasize that the presence of an episode of severe malnutrition early in life increased the chances of scoring in the very low range of values. The distribution of total IQ illustrates the differences found between rehabilitated children and siblings. Thus, while 9 of the 37 siblings had quotients below 70, 18 survivors of malnutrition were in this range. In contrast only 4 survivors scored above 90, while 10 siblings obtained these values.

Learning

In further assessment of the mental development of school-age children who
experienced severe malnutrition early in life, a series of investigations compared the performance of children who were hospitalized because of the
severity of the syndrome before the age of 30 months, and a group of their
siblings. It was assumed that selecting a comparable group from within the
sibship to which the malnourished child belongs is probably the best procedure, in a cross-sectional study, to control familial and social circumstances
which in themselves may be conducive to impaired development. In order to
minimize the differences found between index cases and controls, which can
represent the residual effect of recent long-term hospitalization, only children
who had been out of the hospital at least 30 months were included. The
sibling closest in age to the index case was included in the comparison group.

Mental performance on a variety of tests related to basic learning mechanisms has been evaluated in index cases and siblings in a series of sessions,
while maintaining high motivation during the administration of the stimuli.

In a first study, [33] the developmental course of auditory-visual equivalence was studied in 39 index cases and in 39 siblings. One of the reasons for
selecting auditory-visual competence was the report of Birch and Belmont [34] who have shown that this form of intersensory integration—
besides having a clear-cut developmental course in normal children during the
first school years—can be effectively used to differentiate good readers from
poor readers. The child's ability to integrate auditory and visual stimuli was
studied by an equivalence method. The children were asked to identify visual
dot patterns corresponding to rhythmic auditory patterns; that is, the task
explored the ability to equate a temporally structured set of auditory stimuli
with a spatially distributed set of visual ones.

The siblings in the low urban social class had scores below those of children
of the same age but of a better socioeconomic status. The improvement in
auditory-visual competence with age was obvious for all social classes and for
urban and rural environments. The difference in performance is shown by the
slope of the lines relating achievement score to age.

When the performance age-by-age of siblings and index cases is contrasted it
becomes apparent that the children recovered from severe malnutrition were
well below their siblings in auditory-visual integration, and well below the
expected values for their social class. To illustrate that this difference in
ability was not due to a few extreme cases affecting the mean value of the
group, the cumulative percentage of 7-year-old index cases and siblings was

compared. The lag in development of auditory-visual competence of the index cases was evident.

In a second study, [32] the visual-kinesthetic intersensory integration, an ability closely related to learning to write, was explored by a method of equivalence in the perception of geometric forms. The kinesthetic sense modality in this context refers to the sensory inputs obtained through passive arm movement. Such motion entails sensory input from the wrist, elbow, and shoulder joints and from the arm and shoulder muscles as its principal components. In this test, kinesthetic information is provided by placing the child's preferred arm behind a screen and, with the arm out of sight, passively moving it through a path describing a geometric form. [35]

It was evident that, age by age, the children recovered from severe early malnutrition had significantly lower performance levels than their siblings. With respect to the proportions of index cases and siblings making errors in the identification of either identical or nonidentical geometric forms at ages 5 to 7, significant differences in accuracy of judgment always are in favor of the siblings. Similar findings have been reported by Champakam and coworkers [31] in India. The data from the siblings in our study and in the matched controls of the Indian group show that the lag in a mechanism basic for learning to write that is present in the children rehabilitated from early severe malnutrition is greater than the lag which could be expected as an effect of the low social class.

There is a tendency to view the human organism as an agent that processes information. Humans live primarily in a visual world, and, logically, we expect more elaboration and more uses of visual information than of information from other sense modalities. Consequently, reading and writing have become primary tools in our society.

Learning to read has as an essential prerequisite the ability to distinguish simple visually presented figures. However, the ability to make gross discriminations among visually perceived figures, although it is a necessary component ability, does not constitute a sufficient refinement of perceptual skill for the task of reading. In addition to making gross discriminations, if a child is to learn to read he must also respond to more differentiated aspects of the figural percept such as angular properties and spatial orientation.

The child's failure to respond to the spatial orientation of a visual form can result in his confusing a number of letters in the Roman alphabet that are identical in form but distinguishable by their spatial positioning. Letters such as b, p, d, and q, or N and Z, W and M, all represent equivalent shapes, with the distinction among them depending upon the child's ability to respond simultaneously to shape and to orientation in visual space.

Birch and Lefford, [36] in order to obtain information on features of increased differentiation in visual perceiving, have constructed a visual discrimination task that provides information not only on gross discrimination ability but also on response to spatial position and to differences in angular symmetry. It is known that children with significant mental subnormality are incapable of making a discrimination requiring that they (1) respond selectively to aspects of the whole figure; (2) take into account spatial orientation with respect to a coordinate system; (3) separate complex visual wholes into their component subwholes; or (4) reconstruct a pattern from its elements. For this reason, visual perception of forms was explored in children recovered from severe malnutrition as a means of assessing their readiness to learn to read. Their achievement was compared with that of siblings who had not suffered severe malnutrition.

The performance of both groups on the recognition of geometric two-dimensional forms showed that as age increased from 5 to 10 years the mean number of errors committed progressively diminished. Again the performance level, although low for both groups of children, was significantly lower for the previously malnourished children until age 9, when both siblings and recovered children achieved similar levels of performance. When the children were tested for their ability to analyze geometric forms, the mean number of errors committed also decreased as age advanced. A sharp difference was found again to be in favor of the siblings.

The studies using matched controls or siblings as comparison groups suggest that it is not only general environmental deprivation but also factors closely related to the event of early severe malnutrition that are contributing to a further depression of intellectual performance and learning.

Based on the demonstration that the adequate integration of information deriving from the sense avenues constitutes one of the major functions of the cerebral cortex, the development of intersensory liaisons in the kinesthetic-visual, kinesthetic-haptic, haptic-visual, and auditory-visual modalities have been explored by the equivalence method in Guatemalan, Mexican, Indian, and Philippine school-age children who have had variable degrees of risk of malnutrition during their preschool-age period. [31, 37-40]

In communities whose children had been at great risk of malnutrition, those of shorter stature, age by age, showed poorer intersensory development than taller children. Analysis of various factors related to environmental and familial background supported the view that height differences among these school-age children can be regarded as an indirect indicator of previous malnutrition. In a comparison group of urban upper-class school children, intersensory development was more advanced and no relationship was found between neurointegrative adequacy and height.

These studies of neurointegrative adequacy in four different cultural groups may be significant because they seem to indicate that functional lags can occur at the mild-moderate degrees of protein-calorie malnutrition associated with stunted growth, and are not limited to the extremely severe cases represented by kwashiorkor and marasmus.

All the information available leads one to conclude that the existence of an association between protein-calorie malnutrition in infancy and retardation in mental development has been established beyond reasonable doubt. However, it must be emphasized that the fact of such an association provides strongly suggestive but by no means definite evidence that the lack of nutrients per se directly affects intellectual competence.

At least two possibilities should be considered in an effort to define a causal linkage between insufficient nutrient intake and subnormal mental functioning. The simplest hypothesis would be that nutrient deficiency directly affects intellect by producing central nervous system (CNS) damage. In favor of this explanation is the fact that increase of cell cytoplasm with extension of axons and dentrites (one of the processes associated with the growth of the brain in early life) is largely a process of protein synthesis. From the microspectrographic investigation of the regenerating nerve fibers it has been estimated that protein substance increases more than 2,000 times as the apolar neuroblast matures into the young anterior horn cell. In experimental animals specific amino acid deficiencies can cause structural and functional lesions of the CNS. [41] Inhibition of protein synthesis in the brain, produced by puromycin, is accompanied by loss of memory in mice. [42] Delays in myelination, and reductions in cell number and in cell distribution in the brain, caused by interference with adequate nutrition in early life have been amply documented. [9, 43-48] Preliminary findings of reduction in brain size, and even in cell number, in children who died with severe malnutrition have been reported from Chile, [49] Mexico, [50] and Uganda. [51]

The second hypothesis states that malnutrition in human infants may contribute to intellectual inadequacy through at least three possible indirect mechanisms:

1. **Loss of learning time.** Since the child was less responsive to his environ-

ment when malnourished, at the very least he had less time in which to learn and had lost a certain number of months of experience. On the simplest time basis, therefore, he would be expected to show some developmental lags.

2. Interference with learning during critical periods of development. Learning is by no means simply a cumulative process. A considerable body of evidence indicates that interference with the learning process at specific times during its course may result in disturbances in function that are both profound and of long-term significance. Such disturbance is not merely a function of the length of time the organism is deprived of the opportunities for learning. Rather, what appears to be important is the correlation of the experiential opportunity with a given stage of development—the so-called critical periods of learning. It is possible that exposure to malnutrition at particular ages may in fact interfere with development at critical points in the child's growth course and so cause either abnormalities in the sequential emergence of competence or a redirection of developmental course in undesired directions.

3. Motivation and personality changes. It should be recognized that the mother's response to the infant is to a considerable degree a function of the child's own characteristics of reactivity. One of the first effects of malnutrition is a reduction in the child's responsiveness to stimulation and the emergence of various degrees of apathy. Apathetic behavior in its turn can reduce the value of the child as a stimulus and diminish the adult's responsiveness to him. Thus, apathy can provoke apathy and so contribute to a cumulative pattern of reduced adult-child interaction. If this occurs it can have consequences for stimulation, for learning, for maturation, and for interpersonal relations, the end result being significant backwardness in performance on later more complex learning tasks. It has been reported in experimental animals that small, but statistically significant, differences in the size of the cerebral cortex can be obtained by manipulation of the stimulatory aspects of the environment. [52]

Regardless of whether or not insufficient nutrient intake per se can cause mental subnormality, it is evident that children who have survived the severe forms of malnutrition show alterations in intellectual performance and learning ability which clearly imply a higher risk of failure to profit from school exposure. The child who lags in the performance of basic mechanisms related to fundamental skills such as reading and writing will be ill prepared for the learning tasks required of him when he enters school. If he is behind when he enters, he may never have an opportunity to match the performance of his mates. If the initial impression he gives is of a child who cannot fully benefit from the learning experiences provided by the school, the behavior of his teachers toward him will reflect their expectations of his performing below par, thus reinforcing the probability of inadequate performance.

In a preindustrial society where staying in school imposes a real sacrifice on the parents and other members of the household, the demand for leaving school to contribute to the familial purchasing power may be a social mechanism that prevents the child from being classed as backward, giving him instead the role of a victim whose sacrifice is necessary, almost indispensable, for the survival of the family group. It is conceivable that through this mechanism the self-esteem of these individuals may be sustained, since the self concept—the individual as he is known to himself—is the result of the reactions that other persons have to his behavior, and of the expectations that those others hold about the ways he will behave. To remain in school can lead to a series of failures that will create a negative self-image, which in turn will lead the individual to define himself as incompetent. To abandon school, on the other hand, is to conform to the expected pattern of behavior, to take the role and status of a victim, avoiding without trying a series of continuous failures. Motivation to complete the number of school years constituting the national norm would be markedly reduced under these circumstances.

It has been observed that children who are malnourished in infancy, or who belong to families where food is not abundant, tend to develop anxiety about food. It is understandable that if a child is worried about what or when will he eat next time, his attention and motivation for learning will be reduced, limiting his probabilities for profiting from the school experience. Even if the child has good mental equipment, if his motivation is low he will not learn early what the school expects of him, and he may be forever handicapped or he may be another member who could not progress because his sacrifice was needed by his society.

It is apparent that children who survived a severe episode of chronic malnutrition run a higher risk of failing to profit from the cumulative knowledge available to their socioeconomic group. Survival from severe malnutrition may constitute the event that starts a developmental path characterized by psychologically defective functioning, school failure, and subsequent subnormal adaptive functioning. At the familial and societal levels the ultimate result of this chain of events is what in an ecological sense could be called a "spiral" effect. A low level of adaptive functioning, lack of modern knowledge, social custom, infection, or environmental insufficiency of foodstuffs produces malnutrition, resulting in a large pool of survivors who come to function in suboptimal ways. Such survivors themselves run more risk of being the victims of their poor socioeconomic environment, since they are less effective than otherwise would be the case in their social adaptations. In turn, they will choose mates of similar characteristics and may rear children under conditions and in a fashion fatally programmed to produce a new generation of malnourished individuals.

It is obvious from the unequal distribution of malnutrition among the various socioeconomic groups of society that its consequences interact with the negative impact of all the other factors, present in those subsegments of the population, that interfere with the optimal functioning of the individual. It is apparent that many questions, particularly those related to a causal relationship between nutrient deficiency and mental development, remain to be answered, but the available knowledge leaves no doubts about the strong association between the antecedent of severe malnutrition in infancy and suboptimal performance at school age. It is also obvious that the consequences of early malnutrition will be greatest when, after rehabilitation, the child continues to live in an environment in which both social and nutritional circumstances are poor and hostile to his growth and development.

References

1. Berg, A. Priority of nutrition in national development. In *Amino-acid Fortification of Protein Foods.* N. Scrimshaw and A. Altschul, eds. Cambridge, Mass.: M.I.T. Press, 1971.

2. Cravioto, J., H. G. Birch, E. R. De Licardie, and L. Rosales. The ecology of infant weight gain in a preindustrial society. *Acta Paediat. Scand.* 56:71, 1967.

3. Cravioto, J., L. Rivera, J. L. Pérez-Navarrete, J. Gónzalez, A. Vilchis, R. Arrieta, and E. Santibañez. The popular concept of communicable disease. *Bol. Ofic. Sanit. Panamericana* 53:136, 1962.

4. Rosales, L., C. L. Quintanilla, and J. Cravioto. "Operación Nimiquipalg" III: Epidemiología popular de las enfermedades prevalentes en el medio rural de Guatemala, C. A. *Guatemala Pediat.* 4:59, 1964.

5. Jackson, C. M., and C. A. Stewart. The effects of inatition in the young upon ultimate size of the body and of the various organs in the albino rat. *J. Exp. Zool.* 30:97, 1920.

6. McCance, R. A. Food, growth and time. *Lancet* 2:621, 1962.

7. Platt, B. S., C. R. C. Heard, and R. J. C. Steward. Experimental protein-calorie deficiency. In *Mammalian Protein Metabolism,* Vol. 2. H. N. Munro and J. B. Allison, eds. New York: Academic Press, 1964, Chap. 21.

19   The Effect of Malnutrition on the Individual

8. Pratt, C. W. M., and R. A. McCance. Severe undernutrition in growing and adult animals, VI. Changes in the long bones during the rehabilitation of cockerels. *Brit. J. Nutr.* 15:121, 1961.

9. Dobbing, J. Vulnerable periods in developing brain. In *Applied Neurochemistry*. A. N. Davidson and J. Dobbing, eds. Oxford and Edinburgh: Blackwell, 1969.

10. Richardson, S. A. Psychological and cultural deprivation in psychobiological development: psychological aspects. In *Deprivation in Psychobiological Development*. Panamerican Health Organization, Science Publication No. 134, 1966, 55 pp.

11. Naeye, R. L., M. M. Diener, W. S. Dellinger, and W. A. Blanc. Effects on prenatal nutrition. *Science* 166:1026, 1969.

12. MacWilliam, K. M., and R. F. A. Dean. The growth of malnourished children after hospital treatment. *East Afr. Med. J.* 42:297, 1965.

13. Krueger, R. H. Some long-term effects of severe malnutrition in early life. *Lancet* 2:514, 1969.

14. Graham, G. G. Effect of infantile malnutrition on growth. *Fed. Proc.* 26:139, 1967.

15. Monckeberg, F. Effect of early marasmic malnutrition on subsequent physical and psychological development. In *Malnutrition, Learning, and Behavior*. N. S. Scrimshaw and J. E. Gordon, eds. Cambridge, Mass.: M.I.T. Press, 1968.

16. Suckling, P. V., and J. A. H. Campbell. A five-year follow-up of Coloured children with kwashiorkor in Capetown. *J. Trop. Pediat.* 2:173, 1957.

17. Garrow, J. S., and M. C. Pike, *Lancet* 1:1, 1967.

18. Ashworth, A. *Brit. J. Nutr.* 23:835, 1969.

19. Thomson, A. M. The later results in man of malnutrition in early life. In *Calorie Deficiencies and Protein Deficiencies*. R. A. McCance and E. M. Widdowson, eds. London: Churchill, 1968, p. 289

20. Robles, B., J. Cravioto, L. Rivera, L. Vega, and J. L. Pérez-Navarrete. Influencia de ciertos factores ecológicos sobre la conducta del niño en el medio rural mexicano. Paper presented at IX Reunión, Asociación de Investigación Pediátrica, Cuernavaca, México, 1959.

21. Cravioto, J., and B. Robles. The influence of malnutrition on psychological test behavior. In *Mild-Moderate Forms of Protein-Calorie Malnutrition*. G. Blix, ed. Bastad and Goteborg: Swedish Nutrition Foundation, 1962, p. 115.

22. Geber, M., and R. F. A. Dean. The psychological changes accompanying kwashiorkor. *Courier* 6:3, 1956.

23. Barrera-Moncada, G. *Estudios sobre Alteraciones del Crecimiento y del Desarrollo Psicológico del Síndrome Pluricarencial (Kwashiorkor)*. Caracas, Venezuela: Editora Grafos, 1963.

24. Cravioto, J., and B. Robles. Evolution of motor and adaptive behavior during rehabilitation from kwashiorkor. *Amer. J. Orthopsychiat.* 35:449, 1965.

25. Pollitt, E., and D. Granoff. Mental and motor development of Peruvian children treated for severe malnutrition. *Revista Interamericana de Psicología* 1:93, 1967.

26. Bothe-Antoun, E., S. Babayan, and J. K. Harfouche. Intellectual development relating to nutritional status. *J. Trop. Pediat.* 14:112, 1968.

27. Chase, H. P., and H. P. Martin. Undernutrition and child development. *New Eng. J. Med.* 282:933, 1970.

28. Yatkin, U. S., and D. S. McLaren. The behavioral development of infants recovering from severe malnutrition. *J. Ment. Def. Res.* 14:25, 1970.

29. Cabak, V., and R. Najdavic. Effect of undernutrition in early life on physical and mental development. *Arch. Dis. Child.* 40:532, 1965.

30. Liang, P. H., T. T. Hie, O. H. Jan, and L. T. Giok. Evaluation of mental development in relation to early malnutrition. *Amer. J. Clin. Nutr.* 20:1290, 1967.

31. Champakam, S., S. G. Srikantia, and C. Gopalan. Kwashiorkor and mental development. *Amer. J. Clin. Nutr.* 21:844, 1968.

32. Cravioto, J., E. R. De Licardie, C. Piñero, M. Lindoro, M. Arroyo, and E. Alcalde. Neurointegrative development and intelligence in school children recovered from malnutrition in infancy. Paper presented at the Seminar on Effects of Malnutrition on Growth and Development, Golden Jubileum Nutrition Research Laboratories of India, Hyderabad, India. September 27-28, 1969.

33. Cravioto, J., and E. R. De Licardie. Infant malnutrition and later learning. Paper presented at the Symposium on Dysnutrition in the Seven Ages of Man, University of California Program for Continuing Education, 1969.

34. Birch, H. G. and L. Belmont. Auditory-visual integration in normal and retarded readers. *Amer. J. Orthopsychiat.* 34:852, 1964.

35. Birch, H. G., and A. Lefford. Intersensory development in children. *Monogr. Soc. Res. Child Develop.* 28: serial 89, 1963.

36. Birch, H. G. and A. Lefford. Visual differentiation, intersensory integration and voluntary motor control. *Monogr. Soc. Res. Child Develop.* 32: serial 110, 1967.

37. Cravioto, J., E. R. De Licardie, and H. G. Birch. Nutrition growth and neurointegrative development: an experimental and ecologic study. *Pediatrics* 38:319, 1966.

38. Cravioto, J., C. Espinosa-Gaona, and H. G. Birch. Early malnutrition and auditory-visual integration in school-age children. *J. Spec. Educ.* 3:75, 1967.

39. Guthrie, H. A., G. M. Guthrie, and A. Tayag. Nutritional status and intellectual performance in a rural Philippine community. *Philippine J. Nutr.* 22:2, 1969.

40. Cravioto, J., H. G. Birch, and E. R. De Licardie. Influencia de la desnutrición sobre la capacidad de aprendizaje del niño escolar. *Biol. Med. Hosp. Infantil* (Méx.) 24:217, 1967.

41. Scott, E. B. Histopathology of amino acid deficiencies, VII Valine. *J. Exp. Molec. Pathol.* 3:610, 1964.

42. Flexner, L. B., E. Stellar, G. de la Haba, and R. B. Roberts. Inhibition of protein synthesis in brain and learning and memory following puromycin. *J. Neurochem.* 9:595, 1962.

43. Dobbing, J. The influence of early nutrition on the development and myelination of the brain. *Proc. Roy. Soc. Med.* 159:503, 1964.

44. Dobbing, J. The effect of undernutrition on myelination in the central nervous system. *Biol. Neonat.* 9:132, 1965/1966.

45. Winick, M. and A. Noble. Cellular response in rat during malnutrition at various ages. *J. Nutr.* 89:300, 1966.

46. Winick, M., I. Fish, and P. Rosso. Cellular recovery in rat tissues after a brief period of neonatal malnutrition. *J. Nutr.* 95:623, 1968.

47. Chase, P. H., J. Dorsey, and G. M. Mckhan. The effect of malnutrition on the synthesis of a myelin lipid. *Pediatrics* 40:551, 1967.

48. Culley, W. J., L. Yuan, and E. T. Mertz. The effect of food restriction and age on rat brain phospholipid levels. *Fed. Proc.* 25:674, 1966.

49. Winick, M. Malnutrition and brain development. *J. Pediat.* 74:667, 1969.

50. Ambrosius, K. D. El comportamiento del peso de algunos organos en niños con desnutrición de tercer grado. *Bol. Med. Hosp. Infantil* (Méx.) 13:47, 1951.

51. Brown, R. E. Decreased brain weight in malnutrition and its implications. *East Afr. Med. J.* 42:584, 1965

52. Rosenweig, M. R., D. Krech, E. L. Bennett, and J. F. Zollman. Variation in environmental complexity and brain measures. *J. Comp. Physiol. Psychol.* 55:1092, 1962.

2 Nutrition, Planning, and Development

Maaza Bekele
Head, Social Services Department
Planning Commission Office
Imperial Ethiopian Government
Addis Ababa

It is only during the last two decades that the problem of nutrition has been given significant attention at either the national or international levels. For thousands of years the peoples of earth have either survived on the fruits of the earth, or have died in times of famine, or have migrated to greener pastures. But over the past two hundred years, within the context of a rapid increase in world population, the disappearance of most of the world's empty spaces, and the institutionalization of a world economy, two-thirds of the human race have become exposed to varying degrees of poverty and want, while the remainder have become harbingers of plenty—a plenitude which has permitted waste in the face of want. Call it what you will—underdeveloped, developing, or Third World—here are the economic conditions that have perpetuated undernutrition and a devastating degree of malnutrition.

The facts about the economic conditions producing malnutrition are beginning to emerge after about two decades of study. We are now told that the world—in particular its less developed areas, where the staple food is usually one of the common cereals (rice, maize, wheat, and in the case of Ethiopia, teff)—is facing a "protein crisis" and that international action to avert this crisis is urgently needed. The improvement of nutritional standards has become one of the goals of the Second United Nations Development Decade. The Food and Agriculture Organization (FAO), the United Nations International Children's Emergency Fund (UNICEF), and the World Health Organization (WHO) have instituted the Protein Advisory Group (PAG). Universities in western countries are sponsoring research at home and abroad in an effort to come to grips with the problem of malnutrition. In Ethiopia, for instance, the Ethiopian Nutrition Institute (ENI), established in 1962 with the assistance of the Swedish government, has attempted to survey the dietary habits of typical groups in the country and is continuing to study the effects of malnutrition in the society at large while trying to develop an infant supplementary weaning food, "Faffa." It appears that the alarm has now been sounded.

Dr. Cravioto's paper, which is based on available experimental data concerning the effects of severe chronic malnutrition on individual children in a variety of settings, is yet another important contribution to the growing body of literature on this subject. The findings are indeed alarming in that they suggest that the conditions prevailing in developing countries (as illustrated in his Figure 1) can lead inevitably to the steady degeneration, mentally and physically, of large numbers of human beings. It should, however, be noted that the evidence is not yet conclusive, particularly as regards brain damage, since the nutrition factor has not been clearly isolated. It is still not possible to say that there were no other contributory factors to the mental and physical decline in the cases cited, as Dr. Cravioto himself acknowledges (see p. 15). It should also be noted that nearly all the studies conducted were of cases of "severe, chronic protein-calorie malnutrition" manifested for the most part in typical marasmus and kwashiorkor patients. The effects of general undernutrition are not the subject of intensive investigation, and it is open to debate whether the more important problem is not the latter, at least in certain parts of the developing world.

In Africa, where precise data on infant mortality and morbidity are not readily available, it is difficult to estimate what percentage of the child population is suffering from protein-calorie malnutrition (PCM). Dr. Fred Sai has made a brave guess, on the basis of surveys carried out largely in Ghana, that as many as 40 or 50 percent of children under 5 years of age can be passing through a protein-calorie deficiency at any given point in time. [1] These are indeed "terrifying statistics," particularly if this deficiency can result in irreparable damage to body and mind. Preliminary results of the ENI's 1966 survey of 6 small Ethiopian villages, [2] where a 10 to 20 percent sample of families with children under 10 years of age was taken, indicate that the average calorie intake (unweighted) was 1,890 as against a possible requirement of 2,170 per capita, a clear indication that there are significant shortfalls.

Nutritionists have therefore concluded that improvement of the diet of the average family, and in particular the most vulnerable groups—infants, young children, and pregnant and lactating mothers—should be given high if not first priority in national development plans. They argue that the quality of human life will be enhanced, the productivity of the worker will be increased, and, since fewer children will die of malnutrition, the investments already made in them will not be wasted. In this highly persuasive argument they are now being supported by men of influence. A. H. Boerma, the Director General of FAO, [3] in his address to the first Asian Congress of Nutrition, strongly endorsed the World Food Congress' plan for the "humanization of the whole development process." Mr. Ernst Michanek, Director General of the Swedish International Development Authority (SIDA), has also come out in strong support of the U.N. development strategy in respect to nutrition. Indeed he poses the very important question, "Should not the provision of a nutritionally high standard food in sufficient amount constitute a *basic human right* for the individual and consequently a basic obligation of the modern society?" [4] And Mr. Robert McNamara, president of the World Bank, placed nutrition first among the basic problems of development as he addressed the Board of Governors of the World Bank Group last September. [5] Both Mr. Michanek and Mr. McNamara seem to agree that the problem of malnutrition can be solved at "comparatively little cost": Mr. Michanek says that the problem is principally one of organization, of distribution of food and knowledge; Mr. McNamara tells us that research has provided the necessary information "both to recognize the importance and implications of the nutrition problem, and to take the requisite action to deal with it."

It would seem that we are now being asked to conclude that giving high priority to raising nutritional standards is a task for the development planners of the developing world. But what, realistically speaking, can the planner do in a developing country to interrupt the vicious circle of poverty in which hundreds of millions of people, old and young, are trapped? He generally has at his command very limited resources, which must be so allocated and utilized as to make the quickest possible impact on the development process, while at the same time laying the foundation for sustained development in the future. It is only in this way that he can ensure increasing opportunities for people to improve the quality of their lives. In a sense his concerns are similar to those of the nutritionist (and to all the other specialists who have an equally just claim to a share of the country's resources). Therefore the planner must put the nutrition problem into a wider context, in particular as it relates to the possibility of providing food for a growing population. This means that he must establish a scale of priorities. Terrible choices have to be made and a delicately balanced development program has to be worked out.

Perhaps it is fair to say that a major concern of the peoples of the developing world is to get *enough to eat*. This means *producing* more food, which also usually means increasing the yield of all types of crops under a variety of growing conditions. Population in the developing world is growing at an average annual rate of about 2 percent. Up to the end of the century, very little can be done to make an appreciable dent in this curve. Given the existing population structure, the most efficiently run family planning program will not begin to significantly decrease fertility until after one or two generations; at least this appears to be the case in Ethiopia. [6] Berg and Muscat claim that improved nutrition would result in lower fertility; [7] but there must be a time lag. Undoubtedly, declining deaths among children will eventually reassure the peasant whose basic concern has been to produce an adequate supply of farm labor. Therefore, national development plans must give high priority to increasing the supply of food.

This does not mean that attention should not be paid to improving the quality of such food as can be made available. But the stark reality is that the only tested innovations that will increase yield at bearable costs are in the use of fertilizers on *cereals.* No significant breakthrough in raising the yields and reducing the production costs of *pulses,* the cheapest source of protein, has so far been made. Thus, it is almost inevitable that priority must continue to be given to cereal production until such time as research and successful pilot projects prove that production of pulses can be as profitable to farmers as cereal production.

One might ask why not increase the production of meat and fish, particularly since they are the most important sources of protein? But how much meat can a farmer afford to buy when he lives in an economy where the average annual per capita income is often less than U.S. $100? One or two feast days a year is generally the maximum he and his family will expect. Besides, where cattle are the only source of income, it can safely be assumed that few if any will be slaughtered for home consumption.

Preindustrialized countries cannot change these conditions overnight. The development of an agriculturally based economy is of necessity a relatively slow process. It involves transforming the traditional sector through carefully managed innovations and integrating it into the more modern, monetized sector. This in turn implies the establishment of all the necessary physical and socioeconomic infrastructure: land reform; a marketing system (internal and external); the building of roads and transportation services to facilitate the movement of people and goods; a safe water supply; the establishment of an adequate education and communication system as well as health facilities. These services are of vital importance in the development effort. They create the conditions for increased earnings and therefore better nutrition.

We must also remember that exports of primary commodities including minerals still constitute between 80 and 90 percent of the total exports of African countries. [8] This fact necessarily dictates the agricultural policy of many countries, since it is these exports that bring the foreign exchange needed to finance the country's total development program. The U.N. Conference on Trade and Development (UNCTAD) has been endeavoring since

1964 to alter the terms of trade between the developed and developing countries, and it is interesting to note that the president of the World Bank has now added his voice to the proposal that not only should developing countries begin to manufacture goods for export at competitive prices, but that the developed nations must make the necessary adjustments in their own production patterns and reduce the tarriff barriers so as to admit the products of developing countries. This in turn will mean greater employment opportunities in the developing countries and thus enhance their ability to produce and consume more and better food.

But these basic structural changes will take time to organize, perhaps the greater part of the Second Development Decade. In the meantime, what are the prospects of improving the nutritional level of the peasant farmer and the low-income urban dweller whose families are the most seriously endangered? New inputs organized through the "package type" approach to smallholder cultivators, such as is being attempted in the Ethiopian highlands, [9] will enable some farmers to significantly increase their yields, improve their storage and marketing procedures, and thus raise their incomes. A concerted effort to educate the farmer's wife in the improved preparation of foods can ensure that, on a small portion of the farm, the peas, beans, and lentils, traditionally part of the diet, will continue to be cultivated, at least for home use. But it seems almost inevitable that most farmers will continue to produce the more profitable cereals. It should also be realized that only a limited number of farmers each year can be reached and offered the requisite assistance.

The low-income urban dweller will be able to afford only the less expensive carbohydrates until such time as increased industrial output makes it possible to pay higher wages. It has been estimated by Berg and Muscat [7] that supplementary food, sufficient to provide a balanced diet for young children, can be made available at a cost of U.S. $8.00 per child per year (a figure quoted in Mr. McNamara's address [5]). But it is interesting to note that the money available from internal revenue in the national Ethiopian budget for the current fiscal year is also U.S. $8.00 per capita. It is no wonder then that it is proving extremely difficult to sell the weaning food, Faffa, at 10 U.S. cents per unit of 300 grams (enough for 3 days for one child) to low-income urban families. Marketing surveys seem to suggest that it is the middle-income group, already better fed, that is able to afford Faffa, and this despite the fact that about one-fifth of the production costs are subsidized.

It can be deduced that the malnutrition-undernutrition problem has its roots in the world economic situation, and it is not as easily soluble as we are being persuaded to believe. It is only through the process of development (a process that is still painfully slow for some) that the underfed, malnourished people of the world can reach the point where they will be able to afford better nutrition. Dr. Cravioto is warning us once again that before this point is reached it might be too late for millions who may never be able to realize their full potential.

What then is the alternative? The planning and executing agencies in developing countries can do their utmost to ensure that all available knowledge, particularly of intermediate technology, is applied to the problem of food and nutrition; that production is speeded up as fast as possible; that such food resources as exist are properly stored, marketed, and distributed; that the health services are as efficiently run as possible and expanded as quickly as possible. But all this effort, although it will improve the situation somewhat, will not attack the problem at its roots. This can be done only at the level of the world community, where hard decisions will have to be taken on methods and measures of equalizing the opportunity to live the richer, fuller life to which each individual member of mankind is entitled.

References

1. Sai, F. T. Nutrition as a priority in national development. In *Proceedings of the 1971 Dag Hammarskjold Seminar on Nutrition as a Priority in African Development.* Uppsala: The Dag Hammarskjold Foundation, July 1971.

2. Ethiopian Nutrition Institute. Survey of six villages of lower income families to give a "model" picture of calorie intake. Unpublished paper, 1966.

3. Boerma, A. H. Keynote address to the First Asian Congress on Nutrition, Hyderabad, India, January 28, 1971.

4. Michanek, E. Opening speech at the 1971 Dag Hammarskjold Seminar on Nutrition as a Priority in African Development, Uppsala, Sweden, July 1971.

5. McNamara, R. Address to the Board of Governors of the World Bank Group, Washington, D.C., Spetember 27, 1971.

6. Bekele, Maaza, and L. Bondestam. Ethiopia: a case study on the interrelations of population with economic and social development. Paper prepared for the Population Conference, Accra, December 1971. At two levels of fertility (the lower assumes an effective FPP over the 30-year period 1968-98) there is a difference of only 5% in the actual population by 1998.

7. Berg, A., and R. Muscat. Nutrition and development. The view of the planner. Paper prepared for United Nations Panel to Formulate a Strategy Statement on the Protein Problem Confronting the Developing Countries, New York, May 3-7, 1971. *Amer. J. Clin. Nutr.* 25:186, 1972.

8. Economic Commission for Africa. *Africa's Strategy for Development.* E/CN.14/493/ Rev. 1. Addis Ababa, June 1971.

9. Nekby, B. *CADU: An Ethiopian Experiment in Developing Peasant Farming.* Lund, Sweden: Berlingska Boktryckeriet, 1971.

3 Malnutrition: Macrolevels and Microlevels

Karl Eric Knutsson
Head, Department of Social Anthropology
University of Stockholm

The Need to Simplify Complexities

I would like to open my comments by summarizing briefly some of my own attitudes to the problems we are discussing, in the hope that it will clarify what I may say later. Basic to the perspective in which I view nutrition is that it cannot be looked at as a separate sector of social reality which can be studied and acted upon in isolation. On the contrary, as Dr. Cravioto repeatedly points out, nutrition (and thereby malnutrition) is an integral aspect of the total context of our social and cultural reality. To understand it completely requires a thorough knowledge of the complexity of its surroundings. And it is here that the social scientists ought to tell us what are the *actual* interrelations between problems of malnutrition and its social environment in a given situation. We ought to request not only information, but information of a quality that will make it possible to understand, and later on to attack, the problems of malnutrition not only in the technical or scientific sense but also from the inside—that is from the point of view of the people who suffer from them. Without this kind of understanding much, not to say most, of our brilliant work in laboratories and research institutes will be useless, because we will not be able to communicate with the people we want to assist.

So much about the obvious need to look at the complex environment of malnutrition. But equally important, in order to be able to establish priorities and formulate practical programs for the fight against malnutrition, we cannot go on forever talking about complexity. We need also to simplify. But here again is a danger. We should remember that any subdivision of the problems of malnutrition—into malnutrition and individual, and family, and community, and traditional knowledge, and subsistence economy, and so on—is the result of an analytical operation aimed at facilitating the interpretation of our information. Our various modes of subdividing and thereby simplifying the problems of malnutrition, in other words, reflect our way of thinking about them, but may not necessarily reflect reality. There is indeed a frustrating dilemma here. We need to simplify in order to be able to act, but the action will be useless or detrimental if we have not an adequate and realistic conception of the complexity and integratedness of the problem—an insight which, in its turn, tends to inhibit action. This again demonstrates the necessity of intensive, broad-spectrum field research on malnutrition in the many different types of local communities where people face the problems.

Only in this way can we achieve a familiarity and understanding on which realistic simplification and thereby pragmatic approaches can be founded.

A Stage of Awareness Reached

A second factor contributing to my comments on Dr. Cravioto's paper is the conviction that we now, after several decades of research and various kinds of applied nutrition programs, have reached a stage of international and national awareness of the seriousness of the problem of malnutrition and its implications for other development efforts. This conference is one indication of that awareness, which has been generated to a great extent by the kind of research that Dr. Cravioto and his colleagues have done.

But if this is so, it must have important implications for all of us who have been engaged in promoting the awareness, whether we be nutritionists, biochemists, social scientists, or other experts. We ought to tell ourselves and others that we now have enough information to act. Increasingly we ought to formulate our contributions with a view to narrowing the distance to policy-makers and planners and jointly working out plans for attacking the problems of malnutrition that are open to attack at the moment.

Social scientists, for example, should discard some of their purely academic ambitions and careers—including sometimes the hunger for publication—and instead join in the work of identifying malnutrition in its social environment, formulating and executing pilot programs, and finally designing campaigns to implement those programs that survive the tests of feasibility. In my view, social scientists have hitherto not understood or taken the responsibility for their part of this job.

I want to stress that it will continue to be important to investigate and demonstrate the effects of malnutrition on the individual. I think, however, that our first duty now, preparing for a phase of wider application and action, is to identify areas for action and create means and instruments for attack. If we fail to do this I fear that we will soon confront a dangerous situation. People in positions of decisionmaking and resource allocation may be aware of the terrible effects of malnutrition and the necessity to do something. However, if they are not convinced that significant, practical results can be achieved, they may well choose to allocate—against their own preferences—resources to other sectors which may be less critical for development, but where instruments and organizational models exist to guarantee results.

The Macrolevels of Malnutrition

Among the many important insights in Dr. Cravioto's paper is the view that malnutrition should be looked upon not as something static but rather as a process, the process of malnourishing, just as so-called underdevelopment to a great extent ought to be looked upon as the end result of processes of under-developing. Some malnutrition is without doubt such an end effect of dominant processes within the global economic system, which nutritionists unfortunately cannot do much about. However, this macrodimension of the problems of malnutrition should not be left out as completely as has generally been the case.

Furthermore, when we state that malnutrition cannot be looked at in isolation we ought also to recognize the relationship between processes responsible for malnutrition and national political systems. Dr. Cravioto hints at this when he states that "protein-calorie malnutrition is a man-made disorder characteristic of the lower segments of society, particularly of the preindustrial societies, where the social system consciously or unconsciously creates malnourished individuals. . . ." If this is so, the problem of malnutrition cannot be fully solved except when the overall political goal is the welfare in general of those "lower segments of society." But apart from the statement quoted, Dr. Cravioto's paper is rather typical of the reluctance among nutritionists, as well as many others, to touch the political aspects of the question of malnutrition.

We have been stressing the fact that any nation, any political system, any community wants to have children and adults who are well nourished and healthy. Perhaps we have felt that viewing and discussing in political terms the continuous malnourishment of what Dr. Cravioto terms the lower segments of society would jeopardize work with other important aspects of the syndrome. To me this reluctance on the part of the nutritionist to touch the more controversial aspects of malnutrition is dangerous. We cannot discuss improved nutrition as a way to optimize the ability of individual human beings and whole generations to function, in terms of capacity for learning and working, if we do not also put the question: optimal for what goal, and in which system?

A third aspect of the process of malnutrition which is not stressed enough is the often negative relation to economic development. The introduction of a cash crop, for instance, many times means a decrease in the variety and thereby the richness of the diet, because of reductions in the cultivation of food plants and also because of the channeling of a large proportion of the new income into nonfood sectors of the household budget.

Increasing productivity in agriculture through improved technology represents another situation that can lead to intensified nutritional stress on all those who are made landless or jobless in the process of improving efficiency. Migrations to towns and cities and the transformation of the peasant into a wage-earner constitute still another context in which problems of malnutrition may be aggravated. Although time and space limitations prevent me from giving any concrete evidence, one point should be stressed here. If malnutrition to such a large extent is an unintended side effect of economic development, then development should be planned in such a way that the risks of generating or increasing malnutrition are avoided or at least minimized.

Malnutrition on the Microlevel

What then can be done with the problems of malnutrition on the level of the local community, the microlevel? After all it is here that people live and that the fight against malnutrition has to be fought. Or is this a meaningless question as long as development on the macrolevels cannot be controlled? Is the only alternative perhaps to wait and hope that politicians will cooperate to improve the global trade situation and reform national political and economic goals so that malnutrition as an aspect of maldevelopment can be attacked more efficiently?

I say no because I firmly believe that the understanding of the kind of damage that malnutrition causes in the individual and the community that he belongs to, and finally the whole of his society, can be a forceful instrument in influencing political goals and development planning. In other words, it is only through understanding the effects of malnutrition on the microlevel that we can hope to achieve changes in those larger structures and systems in which and by which processes of malnutrition are generated and sustained.

I want to add a second no because I am convinced that if we analyze carefully the microprocesses of malnourishing, or as Dr. Cravioto terms them, "the pathways leading to malnutrition," it will be possible to plan and execute immediate, meaningful, and efficient action to prevent and cure some of the grave effects of malnutrition among those especially vulnerable. As this will be the topic for many of the deliberations during this conference I shall not go into further details here, but will conclude with a comment which I believe partly explains the difficulties encountered in translating our understanding of malnutrition into practical, large-scale programs. Dr. Cravioto, quoting Alan Berg, suggests that the explanation may be found in a situation where many important development goals compete for limited resources. This is of course true. But I do not think that it gives the whole answer to why nutrition has fared so badly in this competition; to a great extent I think that many of us who have worked in the field of nutrition bear that responsibility. We have not emphasized the need to distinguish between the macrolevels and the microlevels of malnutrition. Most of us have shown a tendency to focus our interests, our information, and our plans for action on the individual and the local community level. And we have perhaps given rather rosy pictures of what can be done on those levels to prevent and cure malnutrition. Instead of trying to understand those who in their work and thinking must direct most of their attention to the macrolevels, we have been critical of what we have taken as signs of lack of interest and understanding.

The result of this discrepancy has been inevitable—lack of communication and even open negativism, not because nutritionists and planners have had different sets of values, but because they have viewed and discussed nutrition in two very different contexts and on two very different levels without really knowing that they have done so. A simple remedy to this situation should be to specify carefully the possibilities for and the restrictions on action that each level and each context contain. Once we do this it would not be impossible to jointly design, planners and nutritionists together, limited but meaningful programs which, for acceptable costs, will make it possible to attack some of the pathways leading to malnutrition on the local community level. And at the same time we could, again nutritionists and planners together, establish and promote improved nutrition as one of the goals for the organization of international trade as well as for national political and development work.

Each of these two levels represents a different time perspective, a different approach, a different way of thinking. But they do not represent conflicting contexts or interests. On the contrary, in order to avoid the effects of malnutrition on the individual we have to work on both the macrolevel and the microlevel.

4   The Effect of Malnutrition
on the Individual: Cellular
Growth and Development

V. Ramalingaswami
Director
All-India Institute of Medical Sciences
New Delhi

Dr. Cravioto, who originally triggered serious inquiry into the relationship between nutrition, somatic growth, and mental development, continues to enrich this area with significant studies. In discussing this presentation I would like to step back a little to consider some of the basic mechanisms of cellular reaction to protein deficiency.

As pointed out by Waterlow [1] several years ago, protein deficiency does not affect all organs at the same rate, nor are all cellular proteins affected at the same time and in the same way. There is a pattern in the biochemical response. Our studies of morphological sequences in nonhuman primates exposed to protein deficiency agree remarkably well with the biochemical sequences. [2, 3] Organs with high protein and high cell turnover bear the brunt of the body reaction in the early stages of protein depletion. The liver, the pancreas, and the salivary glands have a high rate of synthesis and secretion of proteins; the mucosa of the gastrointestinal tract, the bone marrow, and the lymphoid apparatus have a high rate of cell renewal. All these organs are affected early, and their involvement together is characteristic of protein deficiency in man or monkey. [4]

Our studies on the primate model of kwashiorkor initially, [5] and on the rat model subsequently, [6,7] revealed that a slowing down of cell generation time is a basic response to protein deficiency, whether one is dealing with a continuous cell renewal system such as the mucosa of the small intestine or a conditional cell renewal system such as the liver. There is evidence in these studies of a significant prolongation of the DNA synthetic phase, of the mitotic phase, and of the rate of flow of cells into mitosis in protein deficiency. Studies in other laboratories indicate similar events. [8] This impairment of DNA replication, coupled with the rapid degradation of cytoplasmic RNA and consequent reduction of protein biosynthesis, [9] constitutes the two-faced Janus-like reaction to protein deficiency. Cell replication is a complex process mediated through a sequentially regulated synthesis of specific RNA and protein molecules (disturbed in protein deficiency) at various phases of the cell cycle.

On the basis of these two basic cellular reactions, the pathobiological spectrum of protein deficiency becomes intelligible. Thus diminished protein synthesis in the liver and pancreas leads to hypoalbuminaemia, fatty liver, and zymogen granule depletion. An impairment of cell production leads to intestinal atrophy, marrow hypoplasia, arrested endochondral bone growth, and diminished production of antibody forming cells. The consequences of protein deficiency in terms of these two basic reactions are shown in a conceptual form in Figure 1, which indicates the spectrum of change.

Cosmos of Growth and Development

In the conceptual cosmos of development a cell first proliferates, which is growth; then it becomes particular, which is differentiation. The composite is development. [10] Each organ has its own timing sequences in its development, exquisitely related to the development of the whole organism, a concept initially presented by Von Baeher in 1828. Beneath growth and development lie a variety of biochemical and physiological vicissitudes of appearance, disappearance, and regulation of proteins of many types and functions. The intestine, for example, is a beautiful organ as it demonstrates growth and differentiation throughout the entire life cycle of the organism. Both these processes are affected in protein deficiency. Cell generation in the crypts slows down and the activity of lactase, an enzyme reflecting intestinal differentiation in the villus epithelial cells, diminishes in activity.

Cell proliferation starts at the moment of conception. It increases during

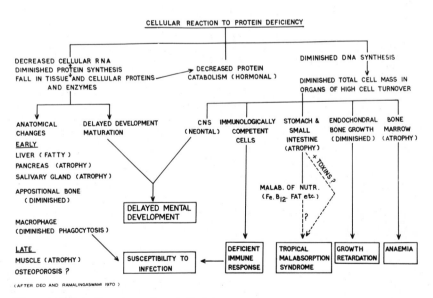

Figure 1. Cellular Reaction to Protein Deficiency

pregnancy and then gradually declines to a relatively steady state at the time of maturation with cell production and cell loss balancing each other. [11] Different organs have different rates of cell proliferation at different times during development. Some tissues such as the brain show early and rapid cell proliferation, reaching the final cell population much sooner than most other organs, which continue to engage in cell replication for a much longer time. In addition to genetic controls and hormonal regulation, the patterned accretion of proteins of many types which mediate growth and development must be sensitive to the supply of amino acid building blocks at the site of protein synthesis.

Protein nutrition can thus be an important regulatory influence during critical periods of cellular growth and differentiation. McCance [12] demonstrated in a series of classical experiments in animals that alterations in the plane of nutrition can have permanent consequences if imposed during a critical period of growth. The earlier the insult, the more marked the retardation in growth and less likely the recovery. Enesco and Leblond [13] and Winick and Noble [14] clarified the concept of growth in terms of increase in cell numbers and of cell sizes as a function of time during the growing period. Winick and Noble [15] went on to show that early malnutrition in the rat during the suckling period produces permanent effects on organ growth by curtailing cell division, resulting in organs with fewer cells. This work laid the foundation for intensive studies in recent years regarding the possibility of permanent defects of somatic growth and brain growth in animals and in undernourished populations. The current status of studies made so far in animals and man has been well reviewed by Winick [16] and Dobbing. [17] Winick, Rosso, and Waterlow [18] have shown that the cerebrum and cerebellum of children dying of marasmus had fewer cells. These studies have reinforced the hypothesis of Dobbing [17] that regions of the brain with rapid cell division are most vulnerable to the effects of malnutrition, and in view of the different regional growth patterns there are likely to be different regional effects of malnutrition on the brain. Acutely malnourished infants have low brain weights and low lipid content and a low number of cells in the brain.

Insofar as somatic growth is concerned, growth in the first 3 to 6 months after birth is generally satisfactory in most communities, whatever the nature of the environment. There are three critical phases of somatic growth in the life history of humans, and if severe and prolonged interruptions in growth occur at these phases there is likely to be persistence of growth deficit in later life. [19] The final phase of gestation is the first of these. WHO data from 37 countries on 2,300 births show consistently that in the less developed countries there is a widespread tendency toward low birth weight for gestational age. Thus average birth weights of viable newborn were lowest (2,700 g) in the Burmese and Indians of India and Malaya, somewhat higher (2,900 to 3,200 g) in Chinese and Japanese, and highest (3,400 g) in Caucasian neonates of the United Kingdom, Norway, and Sweden. [20] During development the mammalian organism passes through a number of critical periods, periods that never return. Failure to make the transition at the right time might thus be crippling. The fetus has been likened to a spaceman. [21] There is mounting evidence to indicate that it is neither a perfect parasite nor perfectly insulated and protected.

Mental Development
Dr. Cravioto's paper leads us a step further. It leaves little doubt that verbal and performance intelligence quotients are lower in children previously mal- nourished than in experimental controls. Other intersensory integration tests related to the acquisition of basic academic skills such as reading and writing also show that children who recovered from severe malnutrition were well below their controls in their performance. In interpreting these findings Dr. Cravioto exhibits great caution. There is a need to delineate more clearly the role of restrictions other than nutritional ones that go hand in hand in impoverished communities—restrictions in early experiences that can lead to impaired functions and limited perceptual experiences and maternal and social experiences; and meager environmental stimulation for verbal develop- ment and for experiences of affection and reward.

  We know that early influences play a most important part in converting genetic potentiality into phenotypic reality, and the latent potentialities of man have a better chance to emerge when the social environment is diverse and stimulating. [22] As Dubos puts it, featureless environments, drab uni- formity, and a narrow range of life experiences cripple intellectual growth. Diversity is vastly more important than efficiency. The use of siblings as controls reduces the play of nonnutritional variables in the results obtained on the mental development of previously malnourished infants. The use of infants of the same socioeconomic status and cultural background, whose parents have the same educational level and who have been exposed to a hospital environment for nonnutritional causes, would reduce these variables considerably. We still cannot make our measurements of mental development entirely culture-free. There is a need to adapt the tests developed in one culture to other cultures and also to establish their reliability and validity together with normal ranges in the local population.

Learning has been attributed to synaptic growth, and one of the key components of the central nervous system is the synapse, a specialized structure through which nerve cells make functional contact with their neighbors. Transmission of information at synapses is believed to be brought about in general by the release of special transmitter substances. Synaptosomes are metabolically competent; so are the nerve cells with huge amounts of rough surface endoplasmic reticulum and ribosomes. Although incapable of replication, nerve cells make protein for export down the axon. [23] It would be surprising indeed if the nerve cells and synapses were not affected by protein deficiency even after brain growth has ceased. On this basis I question the invulnerability of even the adult brain; Keys' volunteers did show disturbances in mental functioning when their caloric intake was reduced. [24] My colleague, Dr. S. Roy, has demonstrated significant ultrastructural alterations in axons and myelin in the peripheral nerves of our nonhuman primate kwashiorkor model. [25]

Even if we are unable in the present state of knowledge to disentangle the effects of malnutrition from other environmental deficiencies, the association between the nutrition-environment complex on the one hand and physical and mental growth and development on the other is beyond doubt. The practical lesson is clear that our attack must be along multiple fronts. Indeed the history of the spectacular improvement in the nutrition and health of the more affluent industrialized societies shows that the improvements have been effected not merely through direct nutritional programs but through a number of environmental changes affecting the totality of life. And here we come to the most crucial point of this conference—the adequacy of resources in developing countries to effect widespread simultaneous changes in agriculture, education, environmental sanitation, immunization, and fertility control, each of which is critically important. With severe limitations of resources, what strategies are the most appropriate in order that we may defend and protect human life as soon as it begins in the mother's womb up to the time it reaches adulthood?

References

1. Waterlow, J. C. Protein malnutrition and replenishment with protein in man and animals. In *International Symposium on Protein Metabolism.* Berlin: Springer, 1962, p. 90.

2. Ramalingaswami, V. Perspectives in protein malnutrition. *Nature* 201:546, 1964.

3. Deo, M. G., S. K. Sood, and V. Ramalingaswami. Experimental protein deficiency—pathological features in the rhesus monkey. *Arch. Pathol.* 80:141, 1965.

4. Ramalingaswami, V., and M. G. Deo. Experimental protein-calorie malnutrition in the rhesus monkey. In *Calorie Deficiencies and Protein Deficiencies.* London: Churchill, 1968, p. 265.

5. Deo, M. G. and V. Ramalingaswami. Reaction of the small intestine to induced protein malnutrition in rhesus monkeys—a study of cell population kinetics in the jejunum. *Gastroenterol.* 49:150, 1965.

6. Deo, M. G., M. Mathur, and V. Ramalingaswami. Cell regeneration in protein deficiency. *Nature* 216:499, 1967.

7. Verma, K., M. G. Deo, and V. Ramalingaswami. Interaction of X-radiation and malnutrition—a study of kinetics of cellular proliferation in the jejunum of protein deficient rats. *Amer. J. Pathol.* 61:341, 1970.

8. Hopper, A. F., R. W. Wannamacher, and P. A. McGovern. Cell population changes in the intestinal epithelium of the rat following starvation and protein depletion. *Proc. Exp. Biol. Med.* 128:965, 1968.

9. Munro, H. N. Metabolic regulation in relation to cell development. *Fed. Proc.* 29:1490, 1970.

10. Kretchmer, N. Developmental biochemistry—a relevant endeavor. *Pediatrics* 46:175, 1970.

11. Read, M. S. Nutrition and cell development: Introduction. *Fed. Proc.* 29:1, 1970.

12. McCance, R. A. Food, Growth and Time. *Lancet* 2:671, 1962.

13. Enesco, M. and C. P. Leblond. Increase in cell number as a factor in the growth of the organs and tissues of the young male rat. *J. Embryol. Exp. Morphol.* 10:530, 1962.

14. Winick, M. and A. Noble. Quantitative changes in DNA, RNA, and protein during prenatal and postnatal growth in the rat. *Develop. Biol.* 12:451, 1965.

15. Winick, M. and A. Noble. Cellular response in rats during malnutrition at various ages. *J. Nutr.* 89:300, 1966.

16. Winick, M. Fetal malnutrition. *Clin. Obstet. Gynaec.* 13:526, 1970.

17. Dobbing, J. Undernutrition and the developing brain—the relevance of animal models to the human problem. *Amer. J. Dis. Child.* 120:411, 1970.

18. Winick, M., P. Rosso, and J. C. Waterlow. Cellular growth of cerebrum, cerebellum and brain stem in normal and marasmic children. *Exp. Neurol.* 26:393, 1970.

19. Thomson, A. M. The evaluation of human growth patterns. *Amer. J. Dis. Child.* 120:399, 1970.

20. Rosa, F. W. International aspects of perinatal mortality. *Clin. Obstet. Gynaec.* 13:57, 1970.

21. Dawes, G. S. Chairman's closing remarks. In *Faetal Autonomy, a Ciba Foundation Symposium*. G. E. W. Wolstenholme and M. O'Connor, eds. London: Churchill, 1969, p. 316.

22. Dubos, R. Lasting biological effects of early influences. *Perspec. Biol. Med.* 12:479, 1969.

23. Whittaker, V. P. Subcellular fractionation techniques in the study of chemical transmission in the central nervous system. In *Control Processes in Multicellular Organisms*. G. E. W. Wolstenholme and J. Knight, eds. London: Churchill, 1970, p. 338.

24. Keys, A., J. Brozek, A. Henschel, O. Mickelsen, and H. L. Taylor. *Biology of Human Starvation*, vol. 2. Minneapolis: University of Minnesota Press, 1950, p. 819.

25. Roy, S., N. Sing, M. G. Deo, and V. Ramalingaswami. Ultrastructure of skeletal muscle and peripheral nerve in experimental protein deficiency and its correlation with nerve conduction studies. *J. Neurol. Sci.*, in press.

5   General Discussion

Chairman: **Dr. Bo Vahlquist** (University Hospital, Uppsala, Sweden); **Dr. Cravioto; Dr. Ramalingaswami; Dr. Fred Sai** (Ministry of Health, Ghana); **Dr. Dorothea Nicoll** (Massachusetts Council on Food, Nutrition, and Health); **Dr. Jibbe Joshi** (Food Research Laboratory, Nepal); **Dr. Hector Correa** (Ecuador; University of Pittsburgh); **Dr. Knutsson; Dr. Maaza Bekele; Dr. Derrick Jelliffe** (Caribbean Food and Nutrition Institute, Kingston, Jamaica)

Vahlquist   Dr. Cravioto very naturally focused strongly on the potential effects of early malnutrition on mental development, but he also mentioned more briefly the effects on physical development, saying that there are data enough to prove that nonprivileged groups of children will develop more slowly and gain more slowly in weight and height at least in the preschool period. That might imply to some listeners a possibility of catching up later on. Since there are good data indicating that the stunting, once started in the first two years of life, will be a permanent effect, would you like to comment on this.

Cravioto   I think there is evidence from many different places that, under present conditions, once an episode of severe malnutrition has caused stunted growth in height, catching up is very difficult if not impossible; and even under the best conditions the curves of growth run parallel after the first three years of life.

We have data showing that even just 15 days of malnutrition—the first 15 days of life—are enough to produce a distinct difference in height at the end of the third year of life. Of course we do not sell children or adults by pounds or by kilograms or by centimeters of stature, and it was even suggested about two years ago that reduced size might be a good thing because of the increasing number of people coming into the world. Unfortunately the work of A. M. Thomson and Sir Douglas Baird in Aberdeen disposes of this argument by showing that the probability of needing a caesarean section increases as the size of the mother, especially her height, is reduced; taking due account of such items as social class, birth order, age of mother, and so on, the difference in prenatal deaths due to birth trauma was 4 times greater in the shortest group as compared with the tallest group in the Aberdeen study (2.7 per thousand in infants from mothers with heights around 64 inches, and 8.6 in infants from mothers of only 60 inches or less).

This finding of a greater risk of death and a greater risk of needing a caesarean section, with all that it implies, convinces me that the short stature produced by malnutrition, within the context in which we have described malnutrition, is a relevant factor for the life of the individual.

Ramalingaswami I think that Dr. Cravioto's presentation this morning did have a salutary approach of great caution in interpreting the existing data. I think he was a bit more enthusiastic in his comment just now. I want to introduce a slightly discordant note here, referring to the great inherent ability of the organism to reverse, to come back, and to reconstitute cell cytoplasm. Here I am not talking about cell numbers. I am not even sure that cell numbers by themselves confer a biological inferiority, if cell size and cell synapses and interactions are well developed. However, that's a different question.

A great many of the effects of protein-calorie malnutrition on organ cell sizes are reversible. All of us, and I'm sure Dr. Cravioto himself, have undoubtedly seen the remarkable transformation in a child when he receives protein and calories; bone growth, for example, as we have seen in monkeys, comes back; the cells begin to function and lay down osteoid. This is one facet we ought to keep in focus, this great reversibility of at least the cytoplasmic content; and, of course, those organs that have the capacity to divide all through life will recover and divide normally.

Vahlquist One aspect which has been much discussed for a number of years is the trend in physical development; over the last century people have been getting considerably taller—in Sweden, adults are 10 centimeters taller today than they were a hundred years ago, and 15 centimeters is the difference for adolescents. Dr. Norio Shimazono has shown how this tendency to increased stature in Japanese adolescents and adults came to a sudden stop during and immediately after the war. I think that is one of the arguments for the effect of the environment, and especially the early environment, on physical development.

Sai I am happy that this conference has started with the question of the effects on the individual, because it is individuals and the way they feel that usually will make for a change. Unfortunately, and this has only recently occurred to me, in trying to make a case for nutrition activities in governmental planning, we forget that the ones whom we want to make the case to are the ordinary individuals. We state the problem as a need at the national level, at the community level, so the individual doesn't understand, doesn't get emotionally involved in it.

In public health practice we distinguish between needs and wants: wants are what the people ask of their politicians; needs are what scientists say the

people ought to want of their politicians—usually they don't. The politician is
the one who is going to make the decision, not the planner; and making the
planner feel that the decision is finally his is a wrong approach. It is all right
to make the planner aware of the situation, but we should go beyond that
and find out what will impel the people themselves to make the politicians
translate this particular want of theirs into action.

Emanating from this point, I want to sound a discordant note. I like science,
I like scientific niceties and minutiae, and what I am going to say should not
be taken as a criticism of science in any way. We seem to be in danger of
letting one bright spark in the nutrition game overshadow all the knowledge
that we have—I mean the emphasis that we are putting on malnutrition and
mental development. I cannot help feeling that if this particular chord is
played too strongly to the politician in the developing country, it may be
counterproductive.

It is not so long ago that people were making the African, for instance, feel
that he wasn't capable of the same level of intellectual development genetically as the white man. Now, if today we say that in Africa 50 to 60 percent of
the population are suffering malnutrition, 50 percent of them will die, so of
the adult population some 30 or 40 percent will have experienced malnutrition and have therefore suffered mental retardation and are incapable of full
mental development, it doesn't sound quite right to a politician. He will see it
as yet another way of the white man's saying he is inferior; and it will become
even more difficult to translate individual wants into national planning needs.
Nicoll I am very interested, in this day of conflict between the quality of life
and material values, that we are forced to try to frame the quality of human
existence in materialistic terms, to try to measure a decrease in IQ, in height,
in lifetime earning capacity in materialistic terms in order to sell to planners
the significance of nutrition. In every mother's breast is a need to feed her
child emotionally and physically, and it seems strange to me that we have to
reduce to these ridiculous materialistic terms the need to feed children.
Joshi Some ten to twenty years ago when the FAO nutrition officer came to
my country and made a case for nutritional improvement, one of the secretaries responded with a rebuff. These days people present concepts that they
would like to incorporate in the planning, but we are not in a position to
represent these development programs in layman's language, talking rather of
protein and amino acids and other difficult concepts.

In my country lots of children die in infancy; but nobody brings this into
the question, nobody has dared to represent the dying infant. If, instead of
speaking about protein, carbohydrate, and all these things, we could possibly

draw attention to the human aspect, the dying of the children, then I am sure planners and politicians would be more realistic in their attitudes to nutritional development programs.

Vahlquist One aspect of the effects of nutrition on the individual is the effect on the maternal-child unit. The World Health Organization recommends that maternal and child health services (MCH) be coupled together. This is an expression of the fact that the fate of the mother and the fate of the child are closely linked.

We are more and more realizing that malnutrition in the mother may influence the fetus. We have heard what Dr. Cravioto said about the low birth weights in nonprivileged groups, and there is the possibility that the mother who is malnourished and at the same time also has infections will not perform well during the lactation period. As a pediatrician I think it is correct to say that every factor which, in a developing country and in the poverty group, tends to shorten the breast-feeding period has very far-reaching nutritional consequences.

I am taking the opportunity to say this now because there may be a risk that, in discussing programs of various kinds, this question of protecting the mother both before delivery and during the lactation period in order to create an optimal situation for the child may not receive the attention that I and several others think it deserves.

Knutsson I have a question on Dr. Maaza Bekele's paper. We couldn't agree more that the primary solution to malnutrition problems must be found on the macro levels, on the level of world trade, world politics. But don't you think that the approach Dr. Vahlquist mentioned, the protection of the child and the mother, could be efficiently done at the same time as we try to work on the macro levels? It certainly is a very good goal to try, for example, to protect nutritionally the first year of infants in Ethiopia. You saw a conflict here that I don't see.

Maaza I don't see a conflict; I just see an impossibility. I agree completely with both you and Professor Vahlquist that the mother and child unit and the MCH services must be developed, that as many women as possible must be reached, and that the children must be protected in the first three years of life. I think, though, that doctors are notoriously inefficient in administration, and that the small amounts of money we can give them can be used more efficiently. But the services, at least judging from my own experiences in Ethiopia, cannot reach more than 10 to 15 percent of the population. This is the hard fact.

We can use the resources well and we can create another privileged group. But the urban population, people who are migrating into a city like Addis Ababa, which has grown 50 percent in the past ten years, cannot afford to buy adequate nutrition; and they can't afford to buy it because we don't have any industries in Addis Ababa that can provide the work that will provide the wherewithal. I refer back, then, to the cycles; we can do the two tasks together, but what we can do is infinitesimal compared to the problem.

Ramalingaswami   As to this argument about the macro and micro environment which has just been interestingly highlighted, we ought to do as much as we can at the macrolevel because we influence a very wide zone and vast numbers of people; but this is where some recent experience with disasters comes into the picture.

I refer to the situation in the Pakistani refugee camps in India, where abundant food grains have been provided on the basis of known caloric and protein needs and on the basis of the number of persons in each family, their ages, their sexes, and so on. And yet in the camps, there is a clear epidemic of malnutrition diseases, kwashiorkor and marasmus. There was food in the huts, fairly abundant in many places, and yet there were these listless children, 60 percent below their expected body weights.

What is the factor here? I don't mean to say that we shouldn't supply rations of sufficient amounts to the people. This is fine and in fact has done a lot of good. But that alone is not enough and in fact it might not accomplish the object we have in mind—to protect this biological continuum of the mother and the child, and this we see time and again. I therefore want to tilt the balance a little and plead for the micro environment; that is, to try to change the habits and attitudes of people in their homes. This we will do only by dealing with the totality of health as it affects the infants and children in the huts and in the dwellings. This should be the entering wedge. This should be the starting point of a revolution in education, of a change in patterns and habits and feeding and weaning and what have you in the community.

Therefore, I would emphasize rather strongly beginning to change the micro environment, and I want to add one more parameter to this. In the developing countries we need approaches by which we can save on capital investments and exploit the vast human resources. We want a human-intensive—I use the term human-intensive rather than labor-intensive—a human-intensive approach, an intermediate technology that would use these vast numbers of people to go into the homes of people and bring about a change through comprehensive health care.

Jelliffe First, I want to endorse Dr. Vahlquist's suggestion that the emphasis should be on the main biological unit, the mother-child unit, the two interrelated together all over the world, but especially in the two-thirds of the world where the problems are. I endorse this most wholeheartedly for various reasons. One is that the situation here is at the moment deteriorating especially in relation to lactation performance, and this is something that the nutritionists, the food planners, need to take full cognizance of.

As Dr. Cravioto has mentioned, the nutrition of the young girl later to become a mother is immensely important. We found in East Africa that many of the short mothers have what we believe to be nutritionally distorted pelves. This has a great impact on the mother and also on the baby during delivery.

If I may comment on the little argument which has developed here between Dr. Maaza and Dr. Knutsson, I think they are both right. I think that Dr. Knutsson is right because we have to give practical emphasis to the micro level, and also as nutritionists remember the macro level; but I agree with Dr. Maaza that this is impossible. It's impossible at the moment because the modes of delivering maternal and child health in developing countries are impossible. They are ludicrous. They have been imported from elsewhere and are being questioned even in the countries from which they have been imported. These models depend on expensive staff, on costly hospitals, on electronic gadgetry, and so forth.

Dr. Maaza is right that it is impossible at the present moment, but the impossibility can be overcome if one looks at the actual needs in this delivery system. Recently in Zagreb a meeting was held under the auspices of the International Union of Nutrition Sciences on this question of young child nutrition programs. By using newer knowledge, by applying it in an imaginative way, it is quite obvious that it is possible to reach a very large percentage of populations in many countries. This is not theory. It has been demonstrated at least on a small scale; for example, in Candelaria in Colombia there is an imaginative program based on the use of a limited number of highly trained people, mostly auxiliaries and volunteers, using uncomplicated methods, local foods, and the like.

Both speakers are correct and I think that their disagreements can be ironed out completely. By using our imaginations a system that is possible, feasible, practical, and realistic can be devised, I have no doubt.

Part II   **The Role of Nutrition
                           in National Development**

6 Nutrition and National Development

Benjamin Barg
Chief, New Technologies Section
Office for Science and Technology, U.N.

I

Most countries wish to accelerate their development with respect to certain
goals or objectives that they may have implicitly or explicitly identified. As
far as possible, most governments wish to exert as much control as feasible on
their national destinies and to further the progress of their societies. In the
context of the circumstances confronting a given country, various routes
present themselves for achieving such progress, the selection of which will
depend on many factors, internal and external, including the resources available for deployment for these purposes and the importance attached to a
particular goal. Some countries operate on the basis of rather generalized
goals, and adopt ad hoc policies for attempting their attainment. Other countries prefer more clearly defined goals, the formulation of related plans, and
the conscious selection of action programs from among the options available
to government. Probably most countries fall between these two categories.
Nutrition may be viewed within this perspective. On the one hand, the goals
of a country may be so general that nutrition as such is not identified as a
goal or even as a subset of a goal. On the other hand, nutrition may appear as
a derived or resultant condition arising from a particular goal or set of goals
being pursued by a country. The nutritional condition of the population in a
given country may be viewed as both a cause and an effect, and, as such, can
influence the way in which national goals are perceived.

The technical literature underscores the relationship between protein malnutrition and physical and mental well-being. [1-5] The studies point out not
only that physical growth and energy are adversely affected as the result of
poor nutrition but also that there is a possible link between malnutrition in
early life and reduced mental capability, impaired learning, and behavior.
Thus, a number of questions come into focus that relate to national development. To what degree does malnutrition really affect the adult's sustained
contribution to physical output and to production involving the use of his
intellectual abilities? If the phenomena are significant, will a country be
impeded in its development? Does improvement in the nutritional status of a
country's population essentially depend on the rate of increase in that country's national output? If, in the preadult years, a human suffers the prospect
of damage to his physical and mental development that may be irreversible,

This paper does not necessarily reflect the views of the above organization. The author
wishes to acknowledge with appreciation the assistance of Mr. Richard Longhurst.

how important is it to a country as a whole to reallocate its efforts and resources to prevent this situation's continuing or becoming worse? Furthermore, as malnutrition contributes to high death rates for infants, how critical is it for a country to take action to reduce poor nutrition in view of its effects on the rate of population growth and fertility rates?

Other similar questions may be posed but one conclusion is clear: at this time it is not possible to answer them definitively on the basis of available research findings. It is difficult to quantify with precision, in the present state of the art, the adverse effects of malnutrition on a society. It would, of course, be simplistic to suggest that protein malnutrition is the central reason for the lack of development within a developing country; many other factors—both singly and synergistically—play important roles within the complex process that is called national development. For example, there is no doubt that there is a strong synergism between the debilitating effects of malnutrition and social/environmental deprivation on the physical and mental development of children. Those who argue that malnutrition has been underrated or significantly overlooked in this cause and effect relationship with the developmental process are on very firm ground. To date, although information is becoming increasingly available about the importance of adequate protein nutrition in the diet of the populations of the developing countries, surprisingly little research effort has been directed to examining nutrition as such within the broad context of human resources development and its impact on the quantitative and qualitative progress of nations. This point is noteworthy in view of the resources that have been marshaled by governments, by international institutions, and by other groups for the stated purpose of contributing toward the improvement of the nutritional well-being of the populations in the developing countries.

Until recently, the increasing attention directed to nutrition has not been translated into sufficient concern to merit high priority programs within the schema of national development. There are many reasons for this. First, there has been and is a lack of widespread awareness about—perhaps sometimes even a lack of desire to examine—the implications of adverse nutritional status on populations, particularly in low-income groups. Second, the magnitude and severity of the problem of malnutrition among various population groups—especially groups at risk—has not been clear in many countries. Third, the use of aggregative per capita data dealing with supply and imputed consumption of edible protein and other needed nutritional inputs has tended to hamper rather than assist policymakers in determining the extent of nutritional need among various groups in their countries. Indeed there is an excessive reliance, in the absence of more refined survey data, on aggregative data. Fourth, concern about the implications of malnutrition for the future of the developing countries and their people has, for the most part, come from the specialists, the scientists, and the technical community and has not been widely articulated by or for politicians, planners, or government decision-makers who have not been involved. It bears emphasis that the problem of malnutrition, in large measure, has been defined essentially in *technical* terms. Efforts directed toward alleviating malnutrition were and are usually structured in relation to such areas as public health or food or agriculture. Because of the difficulties in communication from one discipline to another, and in particular from the natural and life sciences to the social sciences, a large chasm has evolved between those desirous of doing more with respect to alleviating malnutrition in their own societies, and those who control resources and influence political action within those countries. It was this thought that lay behind the following observation of the Secretary-General of the United Nations:

In the world today, there is a considerable body of scientific knowledge, as well as the necessary technology, that could be used to reduce the severity of protein malnutrition which affects hundreds of millions of people, particularly children. The principal need now is to find means of accelerating the way whereby scientific knowledge and technology is put to work for this purpose. Accordingly, the Secretary-General believes that at this time the protein problem must be regarded as more within the domain of economic and resource allocation, of political will and of priorities, than of being essentially defined in purely technical terms. Certainly much remains to be done to close certain gaps in scientific knowledge and in developing and adapting the necessary technology in various aspects of the protein problem. The scientific and technological obstacles and the work that must be pursued cannot be underestimated. However, over the next decade or two, the emphasis must be shifted if we are to ensure the pace of progress needed to combat protein malnutrition in so many countries throughout the world. [6]

II

Many of the approaches to national development or economic growth have either neglected to deal with human resources or have somehow implied that there would be an automatic upgrading of human resources development as ecomomic transformation takes place. The observation by Schultz [7] is most pertinent: "Investment in human beings has . . . seldom been incorporated in the formal care of economics, even though many economists, including Marshall, have seen its relevance at one point or another in what they have written." Over the last decade or so, increasing attention has been directed to the investment in human resources, in areas such as education [8-11] and in the provision of medical care to alleviate disease, [12-14] but very little has been written specifically about the role of nutrition. [5]

From a national standpoint, some interesting conceptual and policy implications arise in determining whether expenditures for nutritional purposes within the context of human resources development should be regarded as investment or consumption outlays. Traditionally, consumption expenditures have included outlays on such items as food, clothing, and shelter. An investment expenditure, however, implies a future stream of earnings or income that would be produced or returned by such investment, which could be of a social, economic, financial, material, or personal nature. In general, resources are diverted from investment to consumption at the cost of the future stream of income or returns that would have been generated by investment, unless the consumption outlays are accompanied by a high multiplier effect. Consumption may be beneficially affected through outlays to improve nutrition, both through the utility associated with more and better food and through reducing outlays on other consumption items such as costs of treating disease and infection. This change in the mix of consumption will in turn raise the utility associated with consumption.

The distinction between investment and consumption outlays may not be precise; in the national accounts, outlays deemed to be of a consumption nature in the governmental budget often, in fact, are of an investment character. Similarly, outlays on health and nutrition, from certain points of view, may be regarded as having a large investment component, whether these outlays facilitate the generation of future returns to those persons or to a society whose health and nutritional status has been improved. [15] An important investment aspect of expenditures to improve nutrition is the possible contribution made to current productivity (reduced materials wastage, less absenteeism, harder work by existing labor) or future productivity (improved physical and mental capacity of present and future generations, and better returns for educational outlays). The investment multiplier effect involved in health and nutrition outlays can be significant.

In examining outlays for ensuring nutritional well-being or alleviating malnutrition, a consideration of some significance is the purpose of such outlays. If the purpose is to reduce the incidence of disease and infection and lower the rate of infant mortality, it could be argued that resources deployed for nutrition purposes may be regarded as a means to an end. If, however, the purpose is to improve the well-being of the individual by enabling him to enjoy the opportunity—perhaps the human right—of a healthier and longer life, freer of the specter of physical and mental disabilities, then outlays on nutrition may be seen as an end in themselves. Though obvious, this is an important consideration in the political economy of nutrition and national development. In effect, there is a need to look behind certain of these questions and to inquire about the purpose of the state and the nature of its responsibilities to its citizens of all ages, present and future. At one end of the spectrum, improving human welfare may be *the* purpose of development effort and, if so, outlays to enhance nutritional status must be so perceived. At the other, improving the welfare of a country's citizens may be regarded as a necessary prerequisite to improving the opportunities for national development.[1] Most often, the motivation and underlying values of the relevant policymakers combine a "mix" of both of these perceptions. These perceptions will also influence the way cost-benefit analyses are structured in relation to outlays on nutrition activities.[2]

From the standpoint of national policy, there are many difficulties in ascertaining the trade-offs between various investment options dealing with human resources. In the first place, while many studies have been done in the general area of cost-benefit relationships, it is difficult to separate the actual from the full social cost in each situation and, similarly, to calculate the mix between the direct and the indirect benefits assumed to flow from various investment possibilities. At the heart of these difficulties are the quantitative estimates and weights of the qualitative returns anticipated from improvements in the

[1] Shaffer [16] has presented an interesting analysis: "While it is undeniable that the sum total of countless sensible expenditures on man (including expenditures for his education, health, proper nourishment, etc.) will tend, on the average, to have a beneficial impact upon his productivity, present and future, each of these expenditures individually and all of them in the aggregate consist of inseparable and indistinguishable parts of consumption and investment expenditures. The spender's motivation is essentially different from that of the investor in non-human capital. The return on the investment cannot be computed satisfactorily as both the amount of pure "investment" and the return to be allocated thereto are conjectural. And in society's allocation of productive resources for the advancement of economic and non-economic welfare, the question of the financial wisdom of any direct expenditure on man must be reduced to one of secondary importance. We have come to accept as axioms that health is preferable to illness, knowledge preferable to ignorance, freedom (whatever the term may mean) preferable to slavery, peace preferable to war, etc. Governmental expenditures bear no necessary relation to their economic profitability as investments."

[2] The view is sometimes expressed that the policy-makers' desire to allocate resources for programs in health or other human needs may be traced to a wish to be charitable rather than the belief that it is a good investment. [17]

nutritional status of a human being and the qualitative considerations for the society as a whole. The complexities involved in cost-benefit analyses in the health and nutrition field, and the underlying shortcomings in existing methodologies, necessitate a cautious approach, as well as a recognition that nutrition must be seen in its medical, environmental, cultural, and social milieu. In the second place, an overall appraisal of the social and economic costs to a country of maintaining the prevailing poor nutrition would provide a quantitative and qualitative benchmark against which to evaluate the returns that would flow to a country or to particular groups within a country if alternative nutrition programs were implemented.

III

The existing literature is not very helpful in providing deep insight into the relationship between nutrition and national economic development. The models of economic transformation that are available do not, for the most part, devote attention to the role that nutrition may play in the output of labor. In the classical view, labor is regarded as a capacity to undertake physical work involving little knowledge and skill, as a generally homogeneous factor of production with about an even endowment of manual input, and susceptible to the application of marginal productivity analysis. This view of labor has been fostered because of the failure to treat human resources explicitly as a form of capital and as the product of investment. [7] There is a wide range of models of economic development incorporating a variety of analytical frameworks and of explanations of national growth. For example, some writers seek to account for national growth in terms of a residual; in the case of an expansion in capital stock, the residual may be partially attributed to education. [18, 19]

 Some economic models[3] do not give explicit recognition to the quality of human resources while others[4] do take account, for instance, of labor, productivity, and the agricultural sector in low-income countries. Relatively little attention in general has been given to the changes that may take place in the quality of the labor force [10]—in particular through an improvement in the nutritional status of labor—and its subsequent influence on labor output and on the processes of economic transformation. Of course, there are many variables that affect the quantitative and a qualitative output of labor, but these too have often been included in the residual item, along with changes in

[3] For example, those of Harrod-Domar, Feldman, and Mahalanobis.
[4] For example, those of Lewis, Fei and Ranis, Jorgenson, and Mellor and Lele.

the effective application of technology. The residual item is used partially to explain growth and transformation itself.

Of particular note is the interesting effort of Correa to relate improved nutrition to economic growth. [20-22] His work examines work capacity and the effects thereon of increases in calorie consumption, and, as a derived result, its effects on the growth of total output. It points up the lack of precision and the nature of assumptions that must be made, in the light of existing knowledge. While progress has been made in developing concepts to measure changes in output that may be attributed to improvements in the productivity of labor, there is considerable difficulty in identifying the changes in output and in productivity that can be associated with improved nutritional status. Indeed, it would be useful, but difficult, to isolate the improvement in labor output that may be related to increased calorie intake as distinguished from improved nutrition. This is complicated by the calorie-protein requirements of labor at different age levels in various occupational groupings within each country. The OECD study by Turnham and Jaeger [23] is noteworthy in this regard. To make matters more complex, the output of labor—and increases in its productivity—are a function not only of physical energy utilized but also of the intellectual skill that labor is able to bring to bear on such output. The ability of labor to deal effectively with technology is indeed an important element in this context.

In low-income countries, in particular, the output of higher marginal returns for resources used in production will depend in large measure upon work efficiency, that is, productivity. Of course, the relationships and "mix" of the other factors of production must be fully taken into account, but it becomes apparent that nutrition as an aspect contributing to output and productivity has been seriously overlooked. For developing countries with careful decisions to be made regarding the use of their scarce resources, close consideration must be given to the possible contribution that an improved nutritional status of labor will make to future output and national growth, in comparison with the use of such resources elsewhere within the economy for other purposes. Similarly, resources directed to improvements in current productivity resulting from better nutrition may be accompanied by a high payoff, compared with their alternative deployment. The full extent of such an economic return must await valid empirical studies.

Another set of arguments suggests that nutrition must be viewed in a very broad economic context: malnutrition is really a phenomenon—indeed a characteristic or reflection—of underdevelopment, of poverty; and that improving nutrition as such is not an objective that can justify the allocation of scarce resources. Rather, policies must be pursued that will accelerate the rate of overall economic development and eliminate poverty. Furthermore, as the level of general economic development improves and policies are promoted to increase employment, the purchasing power available in the hands of consumers will rise, and it is argued that consequently there will be an enhancement in the nutritional status of the population at large as an increased amount of disposable income will be used, in part, for the purchase of foods containing a higher nutritional value. This line of reasoning appears to be held by many development planners and economists.

There is no doubt that malnutrition is a result of many contributing factors, ranging from sociocultural habits to insufficient food and imbalance in calorie-protein intake, and that the syndrome of poverty and underdevelopment includes a strong component of malnutrition. However, such a macro or general view of nutrition contains a number of weaknesses. First, in many developing countries, the highest rate of population growth is occurring in the subsistence, or near subsistence, groups. It has become increasingly apparent that, in many instances, the eradication of poverty has not followed improvements in the general level of national output and national income. Second, the vulnerable groups of the population at risk through malnutrition may not receive the necessary standard of nutritional intake to ensure that the legacy of malnutrition will be prevented. Third, there may often be a maldistribution of available nutritious foods among the individuals comprising the family unit. Fourth, improvements in purchasing power are not always accompanied by improvements in the nutritional quality of the foods purchased and subsequently consumed. It merits emphasis that the general progress of the economy as a whole may not be accompanied by improvements in nutritional status of those population groups particularly at risk.

Nutrition may have other effects on output. For example, decreased output can be related to an increased incidence of disease and infection among the labor force, with malnutrition a contributing cause of such ill health, resulting in increasing absenteeism from employment. There is an employment-effect of nutrition that merits some attention. [24] It may be argued that improved nutrition promotes a higher level of employment or a lower level of underemployment because workers are better able to perform than in an undernourished condition. Further, because of the suggested link between nutrition and mental development, the investment in the early years of life to ensure adequate protein consumption may stimulate higher employment rates in those activities involving a larger intellectual capability. More research could beneficially be undertaken on the income-creating and employment-creating effects of improved nutrition within the developing countries, especially in low-income economies. One may also hypothesize that an inadequate diet will result in low output by labor, causing higher underemployment or lower employment, which in turn will reduce the income of those in the labor force, decrease effective demand in the economy, and further worsen the nutritional status of workers and their families. There may be a negative multiplier nutrition effect. In formulating priorities for the allocation of nutritional resources the needs of workers cannot be overlooked, although the working adult may obtain a good part of his required protein—and minerals and vitamins—from the quantity of food consumed. And the nutritional needs of the very young may be viewed in the context of their later contribution to employment and income.

IV

A major national commitment in all countries is maintaining and enhancing the health of its people. The pursuit of this objective requires the continual allocation of resources and, it is hoped, a continual evaluation of the effectiveness and types of social and economic benefits resulting from these expenditures. There are good analyses of the interrelationships between malnutrition, infection, and disease, [1,4,5] and it is clear that inadequate nutrition will influence the nature and severity of the health problems confronting a country. The lower the general level of health, the higher the proportionate allocation of available national resources that will be required to improve the health of a people, if there is a national consensus supporting this goal.

In the developing countries there may be some ambivalence about the reasons for improving the level of health. In general terms, if the motivation is essentially humanitarian and there is a wish to enhance the general welfare of the people, then improving the health of the population is a goal in itself. On the other hand, improvement of health may be seen as a means of reducing the level of future expenditures that would otherwise be needed to repair the damage caused by poor health, infection, and disease, and of enabling a healthy population to make a more productive contribution to the country. Although these two positions overstate the motivation for undertaking and supporting health programs and although there are various definitions of a "healthy people," they do stimulate thought as to the purpose of improving nutrition or alleviating malnutrition within the public health context.

A major argument by some of those responsible for influencing and guiding the destiny of a country is that improving the nutritional situation or alleviating malnutrition is essential in order to enhance the "quality of life" of the population and to permit the fulfillment of individual and national aspirations. As such, nutrition is a most legitimate claimant on public health resources and efforts, and may be regarded as furthering a basic right of the human being. This line of thinking will have political pertinence to the extent that there exists among national leaders a conscious wish to improve the health and well-being of the country's population. At its heart lie humanitarian and welfare values and considerations, regard for the individual, and intuitive notions about the direction of a nation's development.

Proponents of another position, while acknowledging this "quality of life" or welfare argument, believe it much more important to emphasize the need for nutrition and good health from the standpoint of national output. They assert that, without a productive population, national output will never reach that point where an increasing percentage of resources will become available and may be deployed to improve further the health, well-being, and quality of life of a country's population. Indeed, national progress is made possible only through a healthy people. The impairment at an early age of the growth potential of a human being through malnutrition will provide a continuing drag on future output and national growth.

The degree of support for these public health objectives will depend upon the political leaders' views of their urgency and the time needed to achieve them. Few politicians will reject the "quality of life" or welfare position, but in deciding on the allocation of resources they may feel that it is a long-run—even an ultimate—objective and that more immediate demands for resources creating employment in agricultural or industrial development, or defense or transportation, must take priority. Intuitively, the planner or politician may feel that improving the level of health and nutrition of the working population by a certain percentage will incrementally justify the use of national resources if it will lead to a higher marginal level of national output. The planner, however, is a long way from having tools at his disposal to make such trade-off analyses on an explicit basis. In most cases, the politician and planner are more easily persuaded by economic rather than by noneconomic arguments, by a demonstration of the possible savings or economic benefits to be derived from certain outlays.

At present there is insufficient hard evidence on which to estimate the extent of the burden malnutrition places on the health infrastructure of the developing countries. The burden is quite likely substantial, because of the direct and indirect demands placed on the health delivery system and the great use made of institutions for treatment of patients suffering from malnutrition. [25] Resources being absorbed for treating malnutrition would not readily become available for other than public health purposes as they would probably be diverted to other health-related activities.

At the national level, there is considerable merit in trying to minimize or prevent the incidence of malnutrition rather than to remedy its impact. In many developing countries the public health impact of malnutrition may be so pervasive that it requires all the resources that may be obtained for curative purposes, leaving little else available for malnutrition prevention and nutritional enhancement programs. Wherever possible, concentrating on preventing malnutrition and enhancing nutrition will enable beneficial results to reach larger numbers of the population and in a more effective manner. This involves rational analyses of trade-offs between various strategies of action, and the clear delineation of priorities among various groups in the population. In this connection, activities designed to provide sufficient nutrition for the mental and physical development of infants and young children merit special attention, not only because of the demands placed on the health infrastructure by high illness and mortality rates among the young but also because of the continuing absorption of public health resources by survivors who have suffered from significant degrees of malnutrition.

V

Educational efforts are based, inter alia, on the assumption that children are endowed with the requisite intellectual capabilities to permit them to absorb knowledge and to learn. The implications suggested by the findings that malnutrition, particularly protein malnutrition, can have an adverse effect on mental development, learning, and behavior, are bringing into question the validity and widespread applicability of some of the basic assumptions underlying educational efforts. The results of these findings, as yet, are by no means exhaustive or all-encompassing because of the nature of experiments and research dealing with controlled and noncontrolled groups of children over a long time span.

A fundamental aim in development programs in almost all of the developing countries is to upgrade the quantity and quality of education. Success in educational efforts is often perceived as an indicator of national progress.

High explicit priority is accorded to education in low-income countries,[5] as reflected in the increases in related public expenditures. [9,26,14] Increases in public expenditures on education as a percentage of the budget and of national income, in 1960 and 1965 in all regions, are shown in Table 1. The magnitude of the increases in enrollment in the developing countries in the period 1960-1966 may be seen in Table 2.

If the learning potential of children can be impaired when they suffer, or have previously suffered, from protein malnutrition, then it may be suggested that (1) resources that have been deployed by governments and by the international community for educational activities in the developing countries may not achieve the desired results, and (2) a portion of these resources would be better deployed alleviating or eliminating protein malnutrition within the population groups at risk—in particular, the pregnant and lactating women and the infants and preschool children—so that the residual resources being utilized for further education would achieve a much higher rate of educational and social return. The evidence available so far hints that conditions contributing to the lack of educational return may be a combination of inadequate brain cell development (in utero and during the first 3 years of life under conditions of severe protein malnutrition), apathy, and disrupted behavior patterns. From the national point of view, more and urgent attention will be needed to determine the degree to which malnutrition—particularly severe malnutrition in the vulnerable groups of the population—can prevent a country from obtaining a desired national return for its expenditures on education. Indeed, one may perceive in the possible relationship between poor educational results and conditions of malnutrition a crucial fact about the dynamics of national development and the attainment of full individual and national potential. Also unknown to the full extent at this time is the relationship between adequate nutrition and the effectiveness of the educational process on older children, teenagers, and adults, thus including secondary, tertiary, and in-service training programs at all levels of a society.

As concern increases [4,22,23,27-29] about the possible impact of protein malnutrition on intellectual capability, the total educational effort in a society becomes a matter for critical review. As the relationship becomes

---

[5] Jolly [26] noted that "In Africa between 1950 and 1963, primary enrollments expanded nearly threefold, in Asia and Latin America they doubled, in contrast to Western Europe and North America where they increased respectively by only a quarter and a half. At secondary and higher levels in all continents of the Third World, expansion has been even more rapid, increasing between three and four times over the period, and in Africa, after independence, at an even faster rate."

Table 1. Public Expenditure on Education as a Percentage of the Budget and National Income, 1960 and 1965

	1960		1965		1960		1965	
	Percentage of budget	Number of countries*	Percentage of budget	Number of countries*	Percentage of national income	Number of countries	Percentage of national income	Number of countries
Africa	14.5	23	16.4	36	3.0	21	4.3	22
North America	15.6	10	17.6	18	3.9	15	4.1	14
South America	12.6	7	15.4	10	3.1	11	4.0	11
Asia	11.8	17	13.2	28	3.3	16	4.0	16
Europe and USSR	13.5	13	15.0	23	4.2	25	5.3	24
Oceania	10.4	4	15.7	10	3.7	2	4.4	2
World	13.5	74	15.5	125	3.6	90	4.5	89

Source: International Bank for Reconstruction and Development, *Education; Sector Working Paper.* Washington, D.C.: IBRD, 1971, p. 31. Figures derived from UNESCO questionnaire; see F. Edding *International Developments of Educational Expenditures 1950-1965* (Paris: UNESCO, 1966).
*Including territories.

Table 2. Enrollment Growth Rates by Educational Levels and Regions, 1960-1966

| | Number of Pupils (thousands) | | | | | | | | Percentage of increase 1960 - 66 | | | |
| | 1960/61 Academic year | | | | 1966/67 Academic year | | | | | | | |
	1st level	2nd level	3rd level	Total	1st level	2nd level	3rd level	Total	1st level	2nd level	3rd level	Total
Africa	18,931	2,115	192	21,238	26,748	3,893	334	30,975	+ 41	+ 84	+ 73	+ 45
Latin America	26,973	3,885	567	31,425	36,653	7,468	978	45,099	+ 36	+ 94	+ 72	÷ 45
Asia*	74,645	12,186	1,432	88,261	111,986	21,421	2,911	136,300	+ 50	+ 76	+103	+ 54
Developing Countries	120,549	18,186	2,191	140,924	175,387	32,782	4,223	212,374	+ 42	+ 80	+ 93	+ 51
World	248,486	63,927	11,174	323,587	311,700	96,713	19,992	428,405	+ 25	+ 51	+ 79	+ 32

Source: IBRD, *Education: Sector Working Paper*, p. 30. Figures obtained from UNESCO Office of Statistics.
*Excluding Japan, Mainland China, North Korea, and North Vietnam.

clearer and the educational disabilities of whole groups within a country—or whole groups of countries themselves—become more perceivable, the orientation of education may have to change. While the developing nations await the findings of ongoing studies, generations of the young will have moved through their country's educational system. And on the results produced by those educational systems will depend the nation's rate of progress in so many respects, including conditions affecting the quality of life of its citizens.

Those charged with justifying the allocation of resources and national effort to education usually point to the social returns of investment in education and to the higher earning potential of the educated. These analyses often contain a strong affirmation of faith in the value of the educational process. The introduction of nutritional well-being as a factor in evaluating present and future investment in education will significantly complicate these appraisals. A nation will have to determine the degree of risk it is willing to accommodate in using resources to educate undernourished or malnourished children who may be unable to benefit fully from educational effort.

VI

How important, then, is nutrition from the point of view of national development, and what sort of case can be made to justify a national commitment and the allocation of scarce resources to alleviate malnutrition and improve nutrition? The foregoing discussion of selected aspects of this question makes it apparent that the evidence on which to base the responses must be regarded at this time as suggestive and incomplete, but sufficiently indicative to merit significant attention and support.

Nations and peoples have suffered malnutrition for long periods, and many have survived. Over the long swings of history, some countries have declined and others prospered. Did nutrition play a role in the past development of nations and of peoples? Is survival, in a quantitative sense, a sufficient condition? Looking back over time, it is a fascinating but difficult challenge to attempt to weigh the interactions among nutrition, health, population growth, political and military power, agricultural and industrial development, intellectual accomplishments, and national growth. As for the present, and especially the future, nutrition must be appraised in terms of its importance for a nation and for an individual.

For a nation, nutrition is only one component in the condition or status of its people. For the individual, nutrition may be a limiting factor in his physical and mental development and in the attainment of his full potential. If a nation exists for and because of its people, then the interests and objectives of the state and of its citizens converge, above all, in the development of human resources. This assertion is at times ignored when the interests of the state are deemed to be more important, as for example in certain aspects of international relations. Of course, it could be argued that furthering the interests of the state in international affairs will ultimately contribute to the well-being of the individual. But this type of thinking often leads to a priority ranking that diverts politicians from a continuing concern for the fundamentals on which a society is built, particularly its human resources. Indeed, sometimes these fundamentals are taken for granted or viewed in a secular perspective, with their improvement, by definition, being seen as feasible only in the very long term. The time horizon of the politician is often rather short.

Notwithstanding the explicit recognition afforded to nutritional improvement by national and international institutions and organizations as well as in some legislation, nutrition has not captured the interest or the critical awareness of the political, planning, economics, and social science community. It is not only the relationship of nutrition and development that is at issue here, but also the time scale for achieving visible and identifiable results. Upgrading the nutritional status of a population or groups therein takes effort and financial resources. Of course, with sufficient interest and political will, nutrition can be improved in a variety of ways without necessarily increasing expenditures, for example, through more and better education on nutrition, changing food habits and related attitudes, and reorienting distribution systems. But, for lasting results, financial resources are required; they will be allocated to nutrition only if the ordering of national priorities through the political processes attributes sufficient importance to nutrition in competition with the many other objectives vying for support. Achieving a high priority for nutrition is difficult and elusive. Nutrition is not immediately quantifiable and it is diffuse—its improvement is reflected in various other characteristics of a population, including death rates, incidence of infection and disease, longevity, productivity, and intelligence. Unless the particular sector or subsector is identified and limited, it is difficult for the traditional planner or economist to justify to himself or to politicians the allocation of investments for wide-ranging, though important, objectives and to quantify the specific benefits.

Over the last two decades the populations of the developing countries have increased explosively, and conservative projections suggest a global population well over 6 billion by the end of the twentieth century, the majority of whom will be found in the developing countries. In comparison with the past, there is improved public health, lower death rates of infants and mothers, higher fertility rates, and, in general, sufficient food, all of which have contributed to this upsurge in population. Without questioning the moral desirability of alleviating malnutrition, in the minds of some politicians and social scientists there may be the notion, never candidly expressed, that in the light of these apparently inevitable population increases it is possible to make only a little dent in the nutrition problem, that whatever improvements may occur would have little political value and may only accelerate the population increase. This orientation is inadmissible in the latter part of the twentieth century, when man has learned how to increase the influence he has over his destiny. Of course, even in a Huxleyan brave new world, he will never be able to exercise limitless control. But by generating the political will to apply technology in a wise and humane way, the lot of man can be enhanced and the progress of nations promoted. With regard to population increase, little is known about motivation. In some countries religious, ideological, national prestige, or other considerations may be particularly relevant. One view is that:

the persistence of high mortality among infants and children is a major obstacle to family planning, as parents will not reduce the numbers of their children deliberately without greater assurance of their survival to adulthood. The reduction of malnutrition among infants and children thus emerges as a prerequisite for the fertility reduction without which the population explosion is assuming disastrous proportions. [6]

This theorem merits significant research. If population is going to continue to increase at a rapid rate in the developing countries, it is essential to make that population as productive as possible so that it can meet its own needs and aspirations. Nutrition, as suggested above, can contribute to increasing both the quantity and quality of output and productivity of labor. It may also have an employment-creating and income-creating effect. Furthermore, with larger populations, developing countries will need to be even more aware of the possible distortions in resource utilization that they may incur as a result of malnutrition.

The direct and indirect costs of malnutrition to the economy are often far more than would be required for prevention. To the direct increase in expenditures for medical care must be added the costs to society of rearing children who do not survive to a productive age, who having survived are less responsive to education, or who become constitutionally deficient adults. There is also an economic loss from absenteeism and reduced working capacity. The combined effect is to retard economic as well as social development. [6]

The experience with economic development performance over the last 20 years—in particular, during the First Development Decade of the 1960s—in the developing countries has been disappointing for many reasons, and new approaches and priorities are demanded. The dissatisfaction with old methodologies of development planning, policy, priorities, and evaluation must stimulate new ones. Nutrition is one area that merits the closest study and multi-disciplinary action.

There is a clear need for an expanded research effort in the broad field of nutrition and development, leading to a better conceptual framework. Deeper insight into the role of nutrition in national development will facilitate the formulation of policy in the broad field of nutrition, and the fashioning of tools for valid analyses of alternative courses of action. Relationships such as those between nutrition and productivity, education and employment, warrant considerable study, as do the investment and consumption implications of outlays on nutrition. Models of economic and social transformation need to take into account more explicitly the implications of the improvement in the quality of human resources in an economic system and to determine the importance attached to improvements resulting from improved nutrition. Valid methodologies are required in quantifying the macro and micro benefits presumed to flow from improved nutrition or reduced malnutrition in areas ranging from health to the technological capability of labor. The collection of more hard evidence on the human, clinical, labor, and educational aspects of nutrition is also critical. And the agenda for research can be expanded.

The case for national support for nutrition thus essentially rests on two bases—a welfare, or "quality of life," rationale and an economic rationale. The payoff of the first is qualitative and must be appraised in the light of the values in a society. The economic arguments also extend to the fields of education and health and focus on the benefits that a country may be forgoing, in spite of outlays in these fields, because of poor nutrition.

By making nutrition a national objective and identifying its relationship to national development, quantitatively and qualitatively, policy-makers are likely to obtain political commitment and interest, and thereby the resources and efforts, required for meaningful plans to be devised, evaluated, and implemented. As a consequence, the individual human being and each developing nation will gain.

References

1. Bengoa, J. M. Significance of malnutrition and priorities for its prevention. This volume, p. 103.

2. Cravioto, J., E. R. De Licardie, and H. G. Birch. Nutrition, growth and neurointegrative development: An experimental ecological study. *Pediatrics* 38:404, 1966.

3. Cravioto, J. and E. R. De Licardie. Mental performance in school age children; findings after recovery from early severe malnutrition. *Amer. J. Dis. Child.* 120:404, 1970.

4. Cravioto, J. and E. R. De Licardie. The effect of malnutrition on the individual. This volume, p. 3.

5. Scrimshaw, N. S. and J. E. Gordon. *Malnutrition, Learning and Behavior.* Cambridge, Mass.: M.I.T. Press, 1968.

6. United Nations. Strategy Statement on Action to Avert the Protein Crisis in the Developing Countries. Report of the Secretary-General, June 2, 1971. Doc. E/5018.

7. Schultz, T. W. Investment in human capital. *Amer. Econ. Rev.* 51:1, 1961.

8. Becker, G. S. *Human Capital: A Theoretical and Empirical Analysis with Special Reference to Education.* New York: Columbia University Press, 1964.

9. Hansen, W. Lee and B. A. Weisbrod. *Benefits, Costs and Finance of Public Higher Education.* Chicago: Markham, 1969.

10. Rabich, T. I. *Education and Poverty.* Washington, D.C.: Brookings Institution, 1968.

11. Selowsky, M. On the measurement of education's contribution to growth. *Quart. J. Econ.* 83:449, 1969.

12. Mushkin, S. J. Health as an investment. *J. Pol. Econ.* 70:129, 1962.

13. Rice, D. P. *Estimating the Cost of Illness.* Health Economics Series No. 6, PHS Publication 947-6. Washington, D.C.: GPO, 1966.

14. United Nations Educational, Scientific, and Cultural Organization. *International Yearbook of Education,* Vol. 31, 1969, p. 31.

15. Johnson, H. G. Towards a generalized capital accumulation approach to economic development. In *Residual Factors and Economic Growth,* Paris: OECD, 1964.

16. Shaffer, H. G. Investment in human capital: Comment. *Amer. Econ. Rev.* 51:1026, 1961.

17. Taylor, V. How much is good health worth? Rand Corporation paper P-3945. Santa Monica, California, 1969.

18. Correa, H. *The Economics of Human Resources.* Amsterdam: North Holland, 1963.

19. Denison, E. F. *Why Growth Rates Differ.* Washington, D.C.: Brookings Institution, 1967.

68   Benjamin Barg

20. Correa, H. Sources of economic growth in Latin America. *Southern Econ. J.,* No. 1, 17, 1970.

21. Correa, H. Nutrition, health and education. Ph.D. dissertation, Tulane University.

22. Correa, H., and G. Cummins. Contribution of nutrition to economic growth. *Amer. J. Clin. Nutr.* 23:560, 1970.

23. Turnham, D. assisted by I. Jaeger. The employment problem in less-developed countries. *Development Center Studies, Employment Series,* No. 1. Paris: OECD, 1970.

24. United Nations. *The Protein Problem.* Report of the Secretary-General, October 1, 1968. Doc. E/4592.

25. Cook, R. Is hospital the place for the treatment of malnourished children? *J. Trop. Pediat. Environ. Child Health* 17:15, 1971.

26. Jolly, R. Manpower and education. In *Development in a Divided World.* D. Seers and L. Joy, eds. Harmondsworth, England: Penguin, 1971.

27. United Nations. *Feeding the Expanding World Population: International Action to Avert the Impending Protein Crisis.* Report of the Advisory Committee on the Application of Science and Technology to Development, January 1968. Doc. E/4343/Rev. 1.

28. United Nations. *Increase in the Production and Use of Edible Protein. The Protein Problem.* Progress Report of the Secretary-General, June 2, 1971. Doc. E/5018.

29. Weisbrod, B. A. Education and investment in human capital. *Pol. Econ.* 70, Part 2, Supp., p. 106, 1962.

Additional References

Berg, A. Malnutrition and national development. *Foreign Affairs,* October 1967.

Berg, A. Nutrition as a national priority: Lessons from the India experiment. *Amer. J. Clin. Nutr.* 23:1396, 1970.

Berg, A., and R. Muscat. Nutrition and development: The view of the planner. Paper submitted to United Nations Panel to Formulate a Strategy Statement on the Protein Problem Confronting the Developing Countries, New York, May 3-7, 1971. *Amer. J. Clin. Nutr.* 25:186, 1972.

Buzzati-Traverso, A. Child malnutrition: Implications for education. Paper submitted to United Nations Panel to Formulate a Strategy Statement on the Protein Problem Confronting the Developing Countries, New York, 1971. UNESCO Doc. ROU/219.

Food and Agriculture Organization of the United Nations. The first quarter century, protein increases in a world of inequitable distribution. A background paper prepared for the occasion of FAO's 25th anniversary. Rome, 1970.

FAO/WHO/UNICEF Protein Advisory Group. Statement on the nature and magnitude of the protein problem and on the specific proposals in the ACAST report. Paper submitted to United Nations Panel to Formulate a Strategy Statement on the Protein Problem Confronting the Developing Countries, New York, 1971.

Fredericksen, H. Feedbacks in economic and demographic transition. *Science* 166:837, 1969.

International Bank for Reconstruction and Development. *Education. Sector Working Paper.* Washington, D.C., 1971.

Johnston, B. F. Agriculture and structural transformation in developing countries: A survey of research. *J. Econ. Lit.* 8:369, 1970.

Rosenberg, N. Neglected dimensions in the analysis of economic change. *Bull. Oxford Instit. Econ. Statistics,* February 1964.

Schertz, L. P. *The 40-Year War of the 20th Century.* U.S. Department of Agriculture Pub. No: 5177. Washington, D.C., 1967.

Schertz, L. P. The economics of protein strategies. FEDS Staff Paper 3, December 1970.

Schultz, T. W. *Food for the World.* Chicago: University of Chicago Press, 1945.

Selowsky, M. Infant malnutrition and human capital formation. Paper presented at the Research Workshop on Problems of Agricultural Development in Latin America, Caracas, Venezuela, May 1971.

Weisbrod, B. A. *Economics of Public Health.* Philadelphia: University of Pennsylvania Press, 1961.

Winick, M. Malnutrition and brain development. *J. Pediat.* 74:667, 1969.

The World Food Problem. Report of the President's Science Advisory Committee. Vol. 1. Washington, D.C., 1967.

7 Nutrition and
Economic Growth

John W. Mellor
Professor of Agricultural Economics
Cornell University, Ithaca, New York

There are two aspects of Mr. Barg's paper on which I would place somewhat
different emphasis. First, as a justification for improved nutrition I would
give primary place to its direct contribution to national welfare through an
enhanced quality of life, including improved physical and mental well-being.
We should not be reluctant to provide a humanistic rationale for what is after
all one of the fundamental objectives of economic development. I would thus
give little emphasis to measuring the effects of improved nutrition on economic output. [1] That is not to say such effects may not be substantial—
they are simply subordinate to the ultimate objective.

   Second, I see lack of income, not ineptness in allocating that income, as a
primary cause of malnutrition among the poor. For this reason a key means
of improving nutrition for the poor is their increased participation in economic growth. Increasing knowledge of the effects of malnutrition on human
welfare will strengthen the conviction that the costs of delay in providing
employment and income to the poor may be very high in the form of malnutrition and consequent physical and mental retardation. We need to change
our approach to growth so as to provide full employment to the poor if we
are to efficiently deal with their nutritional problems.

Improved Nutrition and Economic Growth
Currently dominant approaches to economic development have little place
for improved nutrition as either a short-run welfare objective or as a means of
achieving economic growth. Emphasis on high savings rates and direct allocation of physical resources to the production of capital goods have resulted in
slow growth in employment, slow growth in agricultural production, and
little participation of the poor in the growth process. Hence, there has been
neither the income nor the actual supply of food for improved nutrition of
the poor. Although these approaches to economic development do have
improved well-being as an ultimate objective, they emphasize deprivation now
in order to provide the base for a better life later. Naturally, it is the poor
who are deprived now. Studies of the mental and physical effects of extreme
malnutrition tell us that the long-run human welfare costs of such approaches
to economic development are much higher than previously thought.

   In a number of countries deprivation of the poor and extreme malnutrition
result from concentration of wealth in the hands of a few, who follow con-

sumption patterns which are capital or import intensive. As a result, little employment or purchasing power is made available to domestic low-income groups, and these groups cannot increase their expenditures for food. In these circumstances, nutrition programs may serve only as palliatives, adding to the stability of systems that will continue to deprive the poor of the means and the dignity of self-improvement.

Discouragement with the slow progress of economic development and simultaneous recognition of the long-run damage to the individual consequent to malnutrition have turned attention to faster means of improving nutrition. Direct delivery of food to the poor is attractive in this context. However, nutritional goals may be achieved with greater long-run efficiency by turning to substantially different processes of economic growth, which lay increased emphasis on production of food and other consumer goods, a larger employment component, and consequent greater increase in incomes of the poor. In an article in *International Affairs,* Uma Lele and I delineate an approach which would provide more food, either through domestic production or through imports, and a broad distribution of income to the laboring classes through higher levels of employment; both methods of course would offer opportunities for the poor to substantially improve their diets. [2] Scientific evidence of the effects of nutritional deprivation greatly strengthens the argument for such an approach to development.

Mr. Barg emphasizes how improved nutrition can increase the physical and mental productivity of the labor force. This argument loses its force if the supply of jobs cannot even match labor force growth, let alone begin to whittle down the existing stock of underemployed people. Raquibuz Zaman and I illustrated this point with a set of employment targets for Bangladesh. We made highly optimistic assumptions about intensification of food grain production, expansion of other agricultural production, and growth in manufacturing and public works. Nevertheless, total employment still equaled only 70 percent of the additions to the labor force in the subsequent 5-year period. [3] It is only when we succeed in increasing the rate of growth of employment opportunities that nutrition begins to become a limiting factor to total labor productivity. At that point, the very fact of having created employment and therefore having facilitated distribution of income means greater purchasing power and substantial improvement in the nutritional status of the poor.

The argument is similar with respect to mental development and education. Dropout rates in primary schools are high in many developing countries. Interviews suggest that neither the children nor the parents in many low-socioeconomic status rural families see employment opportunities available to them that will make use of primary level schooling.[1] The need is to expand the employment opportunities for workers with basic literary and calculating skills. An employment-oriented approach to development may provide that demand. It will also distribute more income to the poor and provide the purchasing power for improved diets.

Thus the findings of nutritionists constitute an additional powerful argument for more equity in the development process and for alternative means of achieving economic development. Unfortunately, the tragedy of the poor may be used to justify programs which at best provide them small palliatives and at worst allocate their benefits largely to the more well-to-do persons who control the economic and political system. Nutritionists can play an important role in documenting the need for changing the focus of development. They can also administer palliatives that allow old approaches and inequities to survive a little longer. I hope the former path is chosen.

The Nutritional Impact of Rising Incomes for the Poor

One of the arguments for massive special nutrition programs is that the poor will not efficiently use their increased incomes to ameliorate their nutritional problems. At least where the nutritional problem is one of caloric deficiency, this fear seems misplaced. It may also be misplaced with respect to protein deficiency. Analysis of Indian consumer survey data shows that the lower 20 percent in the income distribution scale spend 55 percent of increments to their income on food grains and 23 percent on other food, including 12 percent on milk, other livestock products, and fruits and vegetables. The total of incremental expenditure on food is 78 percent; and on food plus clothing it is 87 percent. [4] It is difficult to argue that a special national program operated through a large bureaucracy would channel as high a proportion of total expenditure to physically important needs. Even through the lower eight deciles of expenditure, over half of increments to income are spent on food.

The relative efficiency of food distribution programs may be substantially lowered because of the tendency for them to come under the control of the politically influential in rural areas and to be diverted to their purposes. Even if one has some question about how efficiently the poor spend their money, one can still question whether the political system will allocate it any more efficiently.

[1] Data being analyzed for an Occasional Paper, The demand for education by rural households in India as a function of local and regional employment opportunities. Cornell University-USAID Employment and Income Distribution Project, March 1973.

I have two objections, then, to massive food distribution programs. First, they may be inefficient in achieving their objectives. Second, there is danger of their being used to divert attention from the basic problem of insufficient income and food and toward ineffective but flashy palliatives. While 30 percent of the population in a low-income country may need major nutritional assistance, a nutrition program is likely to reach only a small proportion of them. It may make the rich feel good that they are doing something for the poor, when what is really needed is for the rich to go along with the kinds of development programs that will expand employment, incomes, and consumption of the lower income classes. However, the latter course very often involves much more substantial social, political, and economic change than the rich are willing to tolerate and certainly much more than is involved in most of the nutritional programs put forward.

Improving income distribution alone may not quickly solve the nutritional problem. That is why supplementary programs are needed to provide trained manpower and cheap sources of key nutrients. If such programs are to be effective they must be tailored to the specific situation, involve local people, and be efficiently administered by trained personnel. They may not be expensive in terms of physical resources, but neither are they as simple as the sloganeers imply.

Thus, improved nutrition should stand as a keystone in setting the objectives of national development policy, while specific nutrition programs play a modest but necessary role in the overall effort of achieving those objectives.

References

1. Call, David L., and Richard Longhurst. Evaluation of the economic consequences of malnutrition. Cornell Agricultural Economics Staff Paper No. 43, September 1971. This paper provides a substantial exposition of problems of measurement.

2. Lele, Uma J., and John W. Mellor. The economics and politics of employment oriented development. *Internat. Affairs* 48:20-32, 1972.

3. Mellor, John W., and M. Raquibuz Zaman. The special problem of employment in East Pakistan. Cornell Agricultural Economics Staff Paper No. 47, October 1971.

4. These data are drawn from a log-log inverse function fitted to NCAER consumer expenditure data for India. The calculations were made by Bhupendra Desai, Cornell University, and are reported more fully in a forthcoming paper by Desai as well as in Mellor, John W., and Uma J. Lele, Growth linkages of the new foodgrain production technologies. Occasional Paper No. 50. Cornell-USAID Income Distribution Research Project, 1971.

8 Nutrition and Population

Carl E. Taylor

Professor and Chairman,
Department of International Health
School of Hygiene and Public Health
The Johns Hopkins University, Baltimore

The relationship of nutrition and population is potentially one of the most important interactions in nutrition and development. We have few facts and the need for research is obvious. I will, however, try only to conceptualize the interaction in terms of possible areas of implementation of what we do know now. I am assuming that the conferees agree that in many countries population control is of the highest priority and the main question is how family planning can best be implemented.

A recurring problem in population planning is our chronic tendency to oversimplify. Death rates have fallen dramatically and we feel that birth rates should respond similarly. But we forget that there have been centuries of research on disease as compared with only a decade or so concentrated on fertility. We continue to look expectantly for simple answers—for the DDT of family planning. One of my favorite stories is of the population enthusiast speaking to a ladies club. He built up his argument dramatically to the point where he could say, "Do you know that somewhere in the world there is a woman having a baby every five seconds?" A little old lady in the front row jumped to her feet and exclaimed, "My goodness, why doesn't someone find that woman and make her stop!" The population problem is not that simple. We have to realize the complexity of our task and settle into the long, hard effort of finding fundamental answers as well as pursuing the immediately urgent process of providing basic services based on what we know now.

There is abundant evidence [1,2] that one of the best ways of promoting the health and nutrition of mothers and children is through family planning. It is well known that high parity and short interpregnancy intervals lead directly to malnutrition. In these comments, however, I will focus on the reverse interaction or the ways in which nutrition can be used to promote family planning.

Two major approaches have been proposed as practical ways of using better nutrition to reduce fertility. The first is the rather superficial approach of using food supplements as an incentive to promote family planning acceptance. In some field trials food supplements are given only if a couple can demonstrate that they are effectively practicing family planning. In the dramatic showcase atmosphere of the Ernakulum sterilization campaign in South India, for instance, a plastic bucket filled with rice was part of the incentive package, which also included a sari for the wife. Care must be exercised, however, because any element of coercion will eventually produce a backlash. To me it seems more promising to develop basic services in which the incentive is more indirect, such as simply providing combined services for nutrition and family planning. Some women will attend primarily because they want family planning, others because of the availability of nutritional supplements. We do not know the relative attracting power of such benefits, but it seems only reasonable that putting them together should produce a synergism of services. The same principle should apply to other activities for child and maternal care. The target group is those individuals who are already motivated but who need convenient and readily available services to make them get what they already recognize to be desirable. If this synergism is real we do not know its components or whether it is merely a matter of convenience; other considerations may enter in, such as the extent to which confidence in the person providing one type of services carries over to accepting advice on other matters for which motivation is lower. [3, 4]

The second basic approach recognizes that for many people the underlying motivation must be changed. [5,6] The concern is to remove fundamental blocks to family planning acceptance and produce a new orientation to family size. The target group here includes all those people whose behavior is resistant even though they might verbally respond in a KAP (Knowledge, Attitudes, and Practices Relating to Family Planning) survey that they believe family planning to be good. There are two components of nutrition activities that potentially might change basic motivation to use family planning. Although in field practice the services are combined, a distinction will be made here between programs designed to help children and those for mothers.

The simpler interaction is the linkage between women's services and family planning. The best evidence comes from the dramatically effective hospital postpartum programs. Almost nothing has been accomplished, however, in linking maternal care and family planning for rural populations. Even less has been done to improve maternal nutrition. In postpartum care the major influence of nutrition may be on lactation; and prolonged lactation increases the birth interval. [7] This effect may compensate for any possible biological increase in fecundity with better nutrition. A potentially more important relationship, which urgently demands research, is the effect of poor prenatal nutrition on the quality of offspring. It increasingly appears that the health of a child may be determined by the mother's nutrition during pregnancy. An urgent need in population planning is to learn how to improve the quality of the population while limiting quantity.

The second, and to me particularly interesting, interaction is between nutritional influences on child health and the parents' willingness to accept family planning. In many developing countries the high premium on male children really means that we are talking about the survival of sons. Demographic studies [8,9] have demonstrated that to ensure survival of one son, within present cultural and mortality constraints, village families really need to start with five children. For fifteen years I have been maintaining that parents cannot be expected to stop having children until they have assurance that those they already have will survive. Although many people now say this, little evidence has been presented for this common sense principle. The economists and planners rightly demand evidence. I will quickly summarize some findings that are beginning to come in:

1. Several demographic studies [10,11] show that a fall in death rates precedes a fall in birth rates by a period of 10 to 30 years.

2. Correlations between desired family size, acceptance of family planning, and child loss are now becoming available. Some findings showing associations have cropped up incidentally in other studies. Roger Bernard's International IUD Studies [12] include an interesting finding from Hong Kong (Table 1). About twice the percentage of women who had had three or four pregnancies and who had lost a child wanted more babies when compared with women with no child loss. Similarly, a study in Nigeria by Dr. Cunningham of our department compared two villages, Imesi Ile and Oke Messe. [13] Imesi Ile was where David Morley started his Under-Fives Program. [14] Excellent child care provided by nursing auxiliaries was the main point differentiating the two villages, which were otherwise remarkably alike and only eight miles apart (Table 2). Dramatic improvement in child mortality is evident, especially

Table 1. Influence of Child Loss on Women's Desire for More Children Among IUD Recipients in Hong Kong (1969-1970) (Pathfinder International IUD Program)

	Women without child loss		Women with child loss	
Parity	Number of women	% desiring more children	Number of women	% desiring more children
2	(394)	64.0	(1)	100.0
3	(400)	23.0	(13)	46.0
4	(324)	7.7	(28)	14.3
5 +	(334)	1.2	(71)	0

in the one-to-five age group (Table 3). But the important finding is that only half as many additional births were desired, four rather than eight, so that even though more children were surviving, the desired completed family size was 9.5 rather than 13 (Table 4). Hassan [15] from Cairo reported that a survey of nearly 2,700 Egyptian women showed that women with child death experience tended to postpone the use of contraception. He postulated that the untimely death of low parity children motivates couples to compensate for such loss.

Long-term prospective research conducted in the Punjab was designed to measure how much the utilization of family planning can be increased by

Table 2. Village Profiles: Imesi Ile and Oke Messi, 1967

	Imesi Ile	Oke Messi
Population	6,200	7,200
Person/house ratio	7.9	7.9
% of houses cemented	57	56
Water supply	Streams	Piped (since Dec.66)
Water coliform count	180/100 ML	90/100 ML
Staple foods	Yams, gari, eko, beans, rice	Yams, gari, amala, rice, eko
Cash crops	Yams, coca, kola, cotton	Rice, yams, cocoa, tobacco
School students	1,568	1,352
Seamstresses	24	47
Tailors	19	26
Palm wineries	16	29

Table 3. Birth Experience and Desire of Imesi Ile and Oke Messi Mothers by Weight-for-Age Status of Their Children, 1967 (N = 250)

	Child weight-for-age	Imesi Ile	Oke Messi
a. Mean number of babies born	Highs	5.5	4.2
	Lows	5.1	4.2
b. Mean number of live births	Highs	5.0	4.1
	Lows	4.8	4.0
c. Mean number of surviving children	Highs	3.8	2.8
	Lows	3.7	2.8
d. Mean number of additional births desired	Highs	4.1	7.9
	Lows	4.2	9.7
e. Calculated mean total births desired (a + d)	Highs	9.6	12.1
	Lows	9.4	13.9

Table 4. 1966-1967 Child Mortality at Imesi Ile and Oke Messi

	Imesi Ile	Oke Messi
Live births	262	368
Infant deaths	14	27
Infant mortality rate/1,000 live births	53	73
Child 1-5 population	905	1,023
Child 1-5 deaths	16	47
Child 1-5 mortality rate/1,000	18	46

combining it with minimum service packages of child care, women's services, and both child care and women's services in separate experimental groups of villages. [16] Auxiliary nurse midwives work according to clearly defined routines within a supervisory framework that can be expanded across rural India. In the past two years family planning utilization curves in all villages have been rising steadily with over 30 percent of couples on family planning, but we expect them to plateau at different levels according to the service packages provided. Nutrition, of course, is a major component of these services. In some villages the panchayats[1] have agreed to allocate to the village feeding centers food contributed by individual farmers at harvest time.

We already have evidence from our baseline surveys supporting the basic hypothesis that child survival motivation exerts its effect subconsciously. It has seemed apparent from talking with villagers that adults derive their expectations of survival from what happened to their brothers, sisters, and peers as they were growing up. A spontaneous shift to an expectation that children will survive would then normally require one generation. We think the lag can be shortened by using child health services deliberately to make awareness of child survival a direct and conscious reason for accepting family planning. In attitude questionnaires we asked whether child survival influenced the mother's thinking about family planning and only 10 percent said that it did. Supporting a subconscious awareness, however, are multiple cross-tabulations which show that people who recognize that more children are surviving now than thirty years ago also have significantly correlated patterns of response: they desire fewer children, fewer sons, refer less often to God's will as an explanation of demographic events, express greater approval of family planning, and even are more ready to accept permanent methods of family planning. In this field research we hope to be able to sort out the part that nutrition plays in this interaction.

[1] A panchayat is a council composed of five village elders or leaders.

Finally, perhaps the most important area requiring investigation is the changed attitude to the future that seems to follow better nutrition, more energy, and better prospects for survival of both adults and children. If parents come to see that they really can look forward to a future with a longer life span and that their children will survive with more than a flip-of-the-coin probability, then planning for the future becomes worthwhile. They must have more energy to carry out their plans, energy provided in large part by improved nutrition. Reaching right down to the roots of their beliefs, the demonstration that a dramatic cure can occur in a child with marasmus, whom the village spiritual healer had declared doomed because of the intrusion of an evil spirit, may help the villager to see that he can control his own future. Our work in the Punjab strongly suggests that such proposals for providing services can no longer be categorized as impossible and impractical. Our field demonstrations show that, by using auxiliaries, a package of services can be brought to the village home combining family planning, nutrition, and maternal and child care. This is feasible within the cost and manpower potential of a country such as India. The contribution of such micro research efforts is to demonstrate within the framework of national planning that the community and family can solve their own problems.

References

1. Rosa, F., and F. Gulick. A quantification of the impact of maternity care, including family planning, in infant-child mortality. Paper presented at WHO Meeting on Maternity-Centered Approach to Family Planning, New Delhi, July 27-28, 1971.

2. Wray, J. D. Population pressure on families: Family size and child spacing. *Reports on Population/Family Planning* (Population Council), No. 9, August 1971.

3. Taylor, C. E. Health and population. *Foreign Affairs,* April 1965, p. 475.

4. Taylor, C. E. Five stages in a practical population policy. *Internat. Development Rev.* 10:2, 1968.

5. Taylor, C. E. Population trends in an Indian village. *Scientific American* 223:106, 1970.

6. Taylor, C. E., and M. G. Hall. Health, population and economic development. *Science* 157:651, 1967.

7. Wyon, J. B., and J. E. Gordon. *The Khanna Study: Population Problems in the Rural Punjab.* Cambridge: Harvard University Press, 1971, p. 158.

8. May, D. A., and D. M. Heer. Son survivorship motivation and family size in India: A computer simulation. *Population Studies* 22:199-210, 1968.

9. Immerwahr, G. E. Survivorship of sons under conditions of improving mortality. *Demography* 4:710, 1967.

10. Heer, D., and D. O. Smith. Mortality level, desired family size and population increase. *Demography* 5:104, 1968.

11. Frederiksen, H. Determinants and consequences of mortality and fertility trends. *Public Health Reports* 81:715, 1966; Feedbacks in economic and demographic transition. *Science* 166:836, 1969.

12. Bernard, R. *Informal Report from the International IUD Program on 1970 Hong Kong Studies.* Boston: Pathfinder Fund, 1971.

13. Cunningham, N. An evaluation of an auxiliary based child health service in rural Nigeria. *J. Soc. Health, Nigeria* 3:21, 1969.

14. Morley, D. The under-five clinic. In *Medical Care in Developing Countries.* M. King, ed. Nairobi: Oxford University Press, 1966, chap. 16.

15. Hassan, S. S. Influence of child mortality on fertility. Paper presented to the Population Association of America at the annual meeting in New York, April 1966.

16. *India: Integration of Health and Family Planning in Village Sub-Centers.* Report on the Fifth Narangwal Conference, November 1970, Rural Health Research Center, Johns Hopkins University Projects, Punjab, India (published in India by the RHRC, 1971).

9 A Note on the Poor Nation Situation

Wilfred Malenbaum
Professor of Economics
University of Pennsylvania
Philadelphia

My observations on the role of health—a broader subject than the primary
focus of the present session—may be helpful in forming conclusions on the
possible role of nutrition in the economic development of poor nations.
These are still days of mounting concern about the race between population
growth and output growth in poor lands; this subject is directly relevant
to nutritional programs as well as to health programs. Emphasis leans toward husbanding resources for investment as against the consumption
emphasis usually associated with programs of nutrition and health; the classic
dichotomy between consumption (for today) and investment (for tomorrow)
needs to be reappraised with respect to important health and nutrition outlays. On these accounts, this conference should hear of the economic growth
possibilities associated with health inputs.

My research, directed to factors influencing output per man in poor lands,
until now has been confined to statistical analysis of data previously assembled for other purposes and generally for units below the national level—districts, regions, states, as against countries. Output data were associated with
fairly conventional independent input factors like land, capital, and labor as
well as with a wide range of health and education variables. The results
showed that health inputs were significantly associated with variations in
output. Without exception, this association was with health *facilities* rather
than with health *status.* That is, economic output variations associated with
health were found not with changes in morbidity, mortality, and similar
measures of a region's state of health, but rather with changes in sanitation
measures, in purified wells, in nurses per thousand people, in public health
outlays, and the like. The nature of these subnational data essentially pre-
cludes the possibility that these health facility changes are the result of output changes. One has to infer that the sequence from health input to economic output followed a motivational rather than some physical path.

The degree of statistical relationship of health input and economic output
(here measured by covariation percentages in input and output data) ranged
in different cases from less than 10 percent to about 40 percent. There is
some evidence in the data that these differences are associated with the
degree of homogeneity of the production process in the areas studied. In
particular, higher relationships might be anticipated where output is confined

to a single product or product group, where the production process is primarily the work of man rather than of complex machinery, and where labor is self-employed rather than hired on a wage-per-period basis. In poor lands, therefore, the health input and economic output relationship can be expected to be closer when the concern is with rural activities, especially agriculture and cottage industry.

These results have been published. [1] Comparable work on other data for Mexico, Egypt, and Syria is in process. But the subject warrants much more research effort, including particularly the collection of field data for areas and activities where health inputs are likely to be important. Preliminary plans for such research are being made for villages in India (at Gandhigram, Madurai District, and at Singur, near Calcutta) and in Nepal. Were these—and perhaps efforts in other relevant areas like the Appalachian regions of the United States—to add further support to the earlier suggestions that additional health facilities can motivate workers in economically backward areas to achieve greater output in small-scale activities like agriculture and home industry, it would hold great promise for national development in a very large part of the world.

This is particularly true because of our growing awareness of both the role of motivation in economic growth in poor lands and the real significance of greater rural output in that growth. These two matters deserve some elaboration. Much attention has already been given here to the increased recognition of the importance of the "residual factor" in economic expansion. Specifically, a number of scholars have discovered in research and analysis over the past decade or so that, for the world's rich countries (the United States, western Europe, the Soviet Union, Japan, and others) the growth of inputs of capital and labor alone fails by a large margin to account for the growth in national output. The residual is attributed to *quality* changes in contrast to *quantity* changes measured. By and large, quality factors account for at least half the total change in economic output. Moreover, the quality factors have become progressively more important with the continuation of economic progress. Thus, they may "explain" three-fourths or so of total output in the post-World War II years in the United States.

There has not been any satisfactory explanation of what is responsible for quality changes. Technological progress in new capital and more education and skills in new labor have been explored at length. These quality dimensions are obviously of great significance, but it is not clear to what extent their contribution has already been included (embodied) in the quantity measures. For it is also obvious that both technological progress and educational progress have accompanied capital and labor expansion. We are certain that, for growing rates of economic growth, only the quality inputs (*not correlated* with quantity) are of growing importance. The suggestion is that their causes go beyond education and technology.

New perspective on this matter comes from new evidence on what has been happening to economic expansion in poor countries, as against the rich lands which have provided the insights summarized in the preceding two paragraphs. Studies on some Latin American experience, [2] on the Philippine case, [3] and less systematically, on the record in India, [4] are enlightening. These are of necessity restricted; the record is simply too brief and the data too uncertain. But all three studies yield the following consistent results. First, the role of the residual—the quality inputs not correlated with quantity of inputs—is relatively smaller over the 15 to 20 years for which data are available than was true for early growth in today's rich lands. Second, and much more revealing, the relative importance of quality factors has *declined* over time (and as growth has progressed at slower rates). The record says that quality inputs in poor lands have not been able to keep abreast—let alone to lead—the expansion in quantity inputs. Man has been progressively less able to integrate the growing potential of the expanding labor and capital endowments of the world's poor lands.

These broad propositions find more specific support in the events within individual poor lands. Modern industrial capacity goes underutilized—perhaps progressively so. Rates of economic expansion decline. Labor is persistently underutilized, even as the need and scope for output of simple consumer goods expand. Regional differences in output per man exceed any measure of productivity differences. In sum, the economics manifest their limited capacity to integrate the material resources available to them. Still, modern and technologically advanced capital facilities are becoming of growing importance. Educated and skilled workers are increasing (although their unemployment rates expand). The relevant *quality* input is a capacity to lead in economic affairs. It is the motivation of a nation's work force toward persistent progress. It is the realization of a dissatisfaction with a long-persistent status quo. It is the determination to take action to change this status quo.

If health inputs operate on economic output through a motivational sequence, the need for new health inputs would thus seem clear. Moreover, and this is the second matter needing elaboration, the need and the prospect for such health inputs are especially great in rural areas. The evidence in many of today's poor countries is that an increasing proportion of the rural work force is being bypassed by the new modernity in small sectors of the economy—the modern enclaves with relatively few workers. Moreover, whatever the new capital inputs and the new technology and skills in these enclaves, they have not spread their output gains to the more backward remainder of the nation. There, unwarranted diversity of economic returns has persisted and has even intensified. Underemployment in rural areas, especially important in agriculture and handicrafts where workers are usually self-employed, could be expected to respond to a program of health inputs. There would be increased output (of goods for which there is both local need and demand) and increased productivity per man.

The evidence is also that the expanded output—total and per worker—in the modern components of the economy has increasingly confronted a restricted market, as a result of the limited spread of productivity gains from the small modern to the large traditional parts of the economy. Future expansion even in the modern capital-intensive area depends increasingly upon higher employment rates and higher productivity per member of the work force in the large, more backward parts of the economy where workers are primarily self-employed.

Health programs for such workers may well motivate the type of economic expansion that these nations need if they are to accelerate their progress. The direct gains in the large backward areas will provide the stimulus for expansion in the modern parts of the nation.

The new insights we have on the process of economic change in today's poor world—with the implications described in brief above—thus yield a new and exciting view of the promise that health inputs can offer for the economic expansion the poorer nations so urgently need. The major immediate tasks are to convert what must still be termed hypotheses and suggestions about the role of health into hard propositions. We need to try to define health facilities specifically, and to define more rigorous quantitative relationships. The priority need is for new research undertakings, in India and elsewhere.

The stress already given in this conference to the significance of improved nutrition for young children ties intimately into the important role of motivational change in economic development. It is certain that a society with a smaller percentage of adults with impaired mental capacities will be a society more likely to seek and achieve economic progress. The better and the sooner the nutritional effort, the more rapidly might societies gain through these motivational relationships. A somewhat different point emerges from the stress placed by our analysis on the development role of expanded output in the more backward rural areas and in small-scale activities generally. This is a framework that puts particular emphasis on greater output per person among the poorer parts of the population, increasing productivity of the poor at a more rapid rate. Whether as cause or as effect, such improvement in per capita product will be associated with expanded consumption of locally produced goods, and especially foodstuffs.

In this last production-consumption point, the distinction between health (and nutritional?) activities as *inputs* of the economic change process and their other characterization as *consequences* of the economic process itself is not emphasized. Such circularities abound in complex processes (for example, in the investment-output flows); but they need not be vicious circles. In general the input elements of health variables are significant *autonomous* factors in economies and societies at very low levels of per person output and income. The consequence element is a *derived* factor; it is more apparent as societies become richer. And it is the former, the input phenomenon, that our statistical studies should continue to measure. But both aspects need to be borne in mind. In particular, such circularity around the core of income change may shed some light on the question of the population growth consequences of health activities. If we recognize the central role of output change, it is more appropriate to consider changes in birth and death rates as functions of that variable and not of specific actions in the health (or nutrition) field. Health facilities as inputs operate toward output change, which in turn influences both the state of health and man's actions with respect to family size.[1] Involved here are such well-documented relationships as the income-elasticity functions and the sequence known as the demographic transition.

This matter warrants mention here, inasmuch as health and nutrition actions in poor areas have been held to be of major causal significance in population explosions. Output changes more nearly deserve that charge, although they obviously are precisely the objective toward which development actions are directed. The hope, the expectation, is that gains in output will (soon) proceed more rapidly than those in population. Also we will become increasingly aware of health actions that motivate output gains. At the least, those of us concerned with the economic development significance of these important

---

[1] Nutrition (and health) programs focused on young children seem to have a dramatic influence on death rates. This certainly goes beyond the text statement. However it is dramatic change in survival rates of young children that is generally credited with rapid downward adjustments in birth rates.

health fields ought not be deterred by accusations of some special responsibility for rapid rates of population growth.

Nor should we be deterred unduly by the difficulties of deriving favorable benefit-cost ratios for programs in health areas. The conceptual problem of designating both the benefit and the relevant cost flows is recognized. On the other hand, too little credit may be taken for the output contribution resulting from changes in motivation due to health facilities. But the point that must be stressed here is that we often exaggerate the benefit-cost ratio from alternative development actions, and notably from direct investment in modern industry. As our awareness of actual development performance increases, it is clear that alternative inputs, ex post facto, have shown only limited development gains. Thus, a new series of studies by the Organization for Economic Cooperation and Development (OECD) on industrialization in developing countries emphasizes the extent to which gains to industry were really transfers from domestic agriculture (and from agricultural exports). Some value added in modern enterprise turned out to be negative when account was taken of the difference between domestic prices and the world prices that might have pertained were some industry not encouraged. [5] Limited benefits have been associated with many of the accepted inputs of development. The new health inputs may well stand high in the rank of important growth inputs, seeming unfavorable benefit-cost ratios notwithstanding.

In the present world development scene, health activities may thus have a key role to play. The situation demands active new field research.

References

1. Malenbaum, Wilfred. Health and productivity in poor areas. In *Empirical Studies in Health Economics*. H. E. Klarman and H. H. Jaszi, eds. Baltimore: Johns Hopkins University Press, 1970, p. 31.

2. Bruton, H. J. Productivity growth in Latin America. *Amer. Econ. Rev.* 57:1099, 1967.

3. Williamson, J. G. Dimensions of postwar Philippine progress. *Quart. J. Econ.* 83:93, 1969.

4. Malenbaum, Wilfred. *Modern India's Economy*. Columbus, Ohio: Merrill, 1971, p. 117.

5. Little, Ian, Tibor Scitovsky, and Maurice Scott. *Industry and Trade in Some Developing Countries, A Comparative Study*. Paris: OECD, 1970. This volume deals with Argentina, Brazil, Mexico, India, Pakistan, the Philippines, and Taiwan. There is in the same OECD series a separate volume for each of these countries except Argentina.

**10 Planning Priorities in
Nutrition and Development**

Mohamed A. Nour
Assistant Director-General
FAO Near East Regional Office, Cairo

Dr. Barg has presented a lucid and painstaking study of a most complex subject. Some of the more striking facets brought out are as follows:

1. Nutrition is a young science, born of this century, and through its strikingly dynamic growth we have come to realize its multidimensional and multidisciplinary nature. Therefore, we should not allow policymakers and planners to view it from the technical angle alone.

2. Although there has been wide and deep research on nutrition, this research has not yielded significantly quantified results to facilitate decisive action by policymakers. In fact the widely scattered results might well lead to a sense of perplexity and confusion, turning us toward counterproductive avenues. Research results must be carefully integrated into the overall economic and social pattern of the society or country involved.

3. Because of its rather diffuse nature, nutrition has become, as it were, the baby of several foster parents. The doctor, the agriculturist, the sociologist, the economist, and the educator rightly wish, each from his own vantage point, to contain nutrition within his respective institutional domain. The policymaker and the planner find this an unappealing situation of nebulous dimensions; as a result meager resource funds are apportioned to nutrition and it is fragmented among executing units at different governmental ministries. Malnutrition, as a result, receives tangential attention. This continues to be the case until and unless the calamities of famine strike the nation.

Having been a policymaker once, I cannot overemphasize this point. Perhaps we could add that when malnutrition becomes a visible famine the government turns to international sources of aid and to ad hoc measures of relief from within. Under these depressing circumstances, the policymaker becomes agitated but the development planner remains inert. After all, this is outside the domain of his plans.

4. Dr. Barg tells us that nutrition can be viewed as a means or as an end—as a humanitarian goal or as an investment tool. He seems to prefer the tool approach to better attract the interest of planner-economists. As with education, one can hold that investment in nutrition is a long-term productive factor and not purely a consumptive drain upon the national economy. Presented thus, governments might listen more acutely. However, the issue at hand does not present a choice of alternative opposing arguments, but indeed it calls for a complementary wide-angled approach. After all, the ever rising expectations and awareness of people in the developing Third World cannot

be satisfied solely by an economic justification for the conquest of hunger and malnutrition; there is clearly a moral dimension.

Dr. Barg dissected and gave us a lucid diagnosis of this complex problem. However, he has left it open for us to suggest a prognosis and a choice of remedial measures. Further, we should take into consideration that malnutrition often varies in degree of severity from one part of a country to another. It varies in time and with levels of awareness as well. Malnutrition can develop as a result of crop failure, poverty, ignorance, or the duration of the period between the end of a cropping stage and the availability of the next crop. Each of these situations calls for specific package measures that involve a multiplicity of institutionally concerned bodies, necessarily coordinated—like the different parts of a vehicle—to develop motion that is unidirectional. So many questions thus present themselves, seeking answers.

1. How do we, at the national level, generate more interest, particularly within the concerned ministries, toward a coordinated approach?

2. How do we show more effectively the interest of nongovernmental organizations?

3. How can we draw upon, and even channel, the torrential resource of power lying latent within our idealistic youth? How do we motivate action from this massive sector of the population?

4. How best can we utilize our communication media—press and radio—and the village leaders, religious or otherwise?

5. Finally, how can we stimulate more interest and thought inside the centers of concentrated brainpower, particularly the national university, the writers' associations, and other similar centers, and persuade them to act and interact? Universities in developing countries have all too frequently remained ivory towers and status symbols. With an increasing awareness, and hopefully involvement, these institutions can and should constitute powerful instruments for sharpening and shaping public opinion, and thus increasingly influence government policy.

The single unifying theme implied by all these questions can be summed up in one phrase: participation at the national level.

This is one aspect. Another is that nutrition and food are inseparable sides of one coin. At the national level thinkers and politicians alike do not distinguish at all between the two. Further, there is no such thing as a farm policy separate from a food policy. Agriculture, food, and nutrition are closely interwoven. In this same context the Food and Agriculture Organization of the United Nations has contributed greatly to a clearer awareness of how food production is influenced by (and also is influencing) the state of nutrition in the world of today and tomorrow. I draw your attention to the truly outstanding address of the Director-General of FAO, delivered in May 1971 at the Eighteenth General Conference of the International Federation of Agricultural Producers (IFAP) held in Paris. The food situation, said Mr. A. H. Boerma, despite all the efforts in the last twenty-five years of FAO, IFAP, and other international and national bodies, is a very mixed one still containing distortions, imbalances, and injustices, and giving rise to deep unrest. If this scene were to be surveyed by a visitor from another planet—or if indeed it comes to be surveyed by future historians living in a more rational age—this visitor would probably conclude that, as far as the production and distribution of food are concerned, the world of today is mad. Boerma goes on to say that on the one side millions of people live in extreme poverty and without work; and on the other there is far too much food, and governments are paying huge sums of money to farmers to produce less while at the same time frantically encouraging medical research and refining medical care to combat and cure the sufferings brought by the calamities of overeating. The call in Mr. Boerma's message is for international agricultural adjustment; he asks that we face reality and responsibility, and he calls for a global strategy to conquer hunger and malnutrition.

While we should stress the need for adjustment of food quantity and quality, we should at the same time give careful attention and study to food habits at the national and even zonal levels within each country. Sometimes, through the powerful communications media of the developed world and particularly of the United States, we in the Third World are tempted to desert our traditional ways—adapted to our systems and environment—and ape the food habits of others. To quote a striking example, we have come to dogmatically believe that milk is good for us. However, recent research findings in this country are raising questions about this dogma. Dr. D. Paige and his colleagues described their preliminary findings, as reported in the *New York Times* of October 15, 1971, that nonwhite schoolchildren in Baltimore are strikingly more intolerant to milk sugar (lactose) than white children, in a ratio of 85 to 17, respectively. This intolerance, indicated in syndromes of bloating and diarrhea, is caused by a lactase enzyme deficiency. We could say, in a more jocular tone, that there is a negative correlation between white milk and black boys.

Coming back to national policy, we are urged to call for a *government will:* each nation to act in its own domain, and aggregately—indeed synergistically—at the global sphere against malnutrition and starvation. But where does a government in the developing world, with desperately meager resources, start and how does it proceed? I submit that the question of food and nutrition must be tackled at the grassroots level, in an integrated manner and upon a broad front.

The most acute problem, if we have to establish priorities, lies squarely in rural areas. Taking a global approach, according to International Labor Organization figures, the number of adult workers in the developing countries (not including China) is about 1 billion now, extrapolated to 1.25 billion by 1980. Of these, 100 million or so are unemployed now and an additional 250 million will be idle by 1980. Over 70 percent of these are and will be dwelling in rural areas. Although the problems of urban life and the stresses of massive migration from the village to the town merit serious attention, the pressure of figures alone argues for greater priority to a global strategy toward rural development. On a more positive note, the rural area is and will continue for decades to be the main source of national income. To combat malnutrition we need to place more money in the hands of the housewife, and this can result only from increasing job possibilities and incentives. We need a global strategy aimed at *an integrated rural development approach* with clear priorities accorded to breaking the vicious cycle that creates malnutrition—at the farm gate and within the village domain. What is advocated here is not a romantic dream or an individual's idea. Such attempts are already operational and showing promising results. To judge these experiments that are developing from the grassroots level, we need to make available our criteria of evaluation from the nutritional viewpoint.

I hasten to state once again that the problem is complex and involves specific features peculiar to specific countries or even regions within the same country. Therefore, the integrated rural development approach is but one developmental model that could be further tested and evaluated in the quest to reduce malnutrition and raise standards of living.

The planner and the policymaker of the Second Development Decade will rightfully think that our conference deliberations are neither clever nor unique unless we come forth with imaginative, realistic, and pragmatic guidelines indicating definite priorities for intervention now and follow-up action in the field of nutrition. The policy maker and the political leaders are confused and overwhelmed by the magnitude of the problem, as who is not? But we can make a start.

11   General Discussion

Chairman: **Mr. Alex Vamoer** (National Food and Nutrition Commission, Zambia); **Dr. Roger Revelle** (Harvard University); **Dr. Taylor**; **Dr. Cecile De Sweemer** (Belgium; Johns Hopkins University); **Dr. Mellor**; **Dr. Egbert deVries** (Netherlands; University of Pittsburgh); **Dr. Maaza Bekele**; **Dr. Correa**; **Dr. Sai**; **Dr. R. P. Chisala** (Secretary of Health, Malawi); **Dr. Fanny Ginor** (Bank of Israel, Jerusalem); **Dr. Walter Santos** (Brazilian Nutrition Society)

Revelle   Over the long term the most important problem in the world is to bring human populations to a stable equilibrium with their environment, and probably we can't support in the world more than about 10 billion people within the next century. If we are going to keep human populations down to this level, three times the present number, it's absolutely imperative that human beings limit their own fertility to a much greater extent than they are now doing; and I firmly believe that only well-nourished, healthy people will have the will, the self-confidence, and the hope for the future that will enable them to restrict the number of their children, which is an absolutely essential condition for any future for mankind.

One of the things mentioned at the beginning hasn't been touched by any of the panelists or the discussants. I think one of the nutrition problems in many less developed countries is food wastage. I don't mean by this the amount of food that is wasted because it is eaten by rats or bugs but the amount of food that is wasted in the human body because of malabsorption or poor digestion.

Several of us were in India in September 1971, and one of the things that came out very clearly was that rural Indians particularly—for a variety of reasons, one of them being the very poor quality of the water supply—carry a heavy load of intestinal parasites, worms, and various kinds of bacteria and protozoa, and these things are obviously living on the same food that the people live on; some estimates indicate that as much as 15 percent of the actual food intake among many people in poor countries may not go for human benefit. If this is the case, elimination of these parasites and reduction of this food waste would have a great many beneficial effects, including, of course, very considerable economic savings—perhaps in the Indian case two billion dollars a year, about 5 percent of the entire GNP. Moreover, if the food wastage were eliminated, it would allow a more varied and therefore a better diet. People wouldn't have to spend all of their meager food resources simply to get enough calories, because they would require fewer calories.

It would give an opportunity also for growing more nonfood crops and therefore facilitate the development of agro-industry and more employment, because both the nonfood crops and the more complicated crops like poultry and other animal proteins require a lot more labor per unit of output than the cereals do. So for a variety of reasons elimination of food wastage and improvement of nutrition might have a very significant economic payoff.

In support of what I am saying, nutrition surveys indicate that people actually eat about 200 or 300 calories more than the FAO-WHO standards indicate that they should for their weight and age. Here we have a wonderful example of the systems aspect of these nutrition problems: the interaction between public health measures and nutrition, and the interaction between both public health and nutrition and potentially increasing employment, which would in turn increase nutrition and improve public health by raising the incomes of the poorest classes. We are dealing with an extremely complex system, which has to be attacked not at only one point—the employment point or the nutrition point or the public health point—but in a systematic context.

Taylor   I certainly endorse what Dr. Revelle said. Perhaps it is just that everybody is taking it for granted, but I would broaden that to include not only the parasites in the bowels but also the total problem of infection as it relates to nutritional wastage; this includes the catabolic effects of any febrile condition. All of the information that we now have on the interaction of infection and nutrition seems to me to be a very important part of this whole equation.

Let me respond to another point—that economists say that economic development will automatically improve nutrition. Dr. Mellor said that by raising agricultural income through major social changes, better nutrition will result. At least this is the way I understood his thinking. Rather than going into specific programs to improve nutrition, he recommends some sort of a social revolution and change in land reform patterns as a way to improve food production and economic growth at the village level.

I disagree with this because of my experience with the Punjab villages. The economic development of those villages is one of the most fantastic occurrences, to my knowledge, anywhere: economic development is reaching right down through all the social and economic classes and is not limited to the upper groups. The interesting thing that I have observed in these Punjab villages is that, although the nutrition situation should have gotten better, on the basis of the standard economic argument, it is not working that way. Instead, the adults are moving toward the so-called high status, rich man's diet, which is nutritionally just as bad as it is anywhere in the world where bad nutritional patterns exist as part of an affluent system. Not only that, much more critical is the fact that we observe just as much, perhaps more, marasmus among children. It comes back to the argument that it really depends on what the mother does with the food that is available; we have to change the pattern of living in the village home, as has been brought out already. It is at that level that a specific nutrition program can begin to make an impact that will not automatically follow a general improvement in the food situation in those homes.

It is my feeling also that one of the ways to promote social revolution is to change the people; if they have more energy, if they emerge from this pattern of apathy, then the social changes that Dr. Mellor was speaking about—and which we all want—will result.

I have one other comment growing out of Dr. Barg's analysis of the investment versus consumption dilemma. It has seemed to me that one of the parts of this dilemma that needs to be very clearly understood is its relationship to the level of economic development. As I have seen the process occurring around the world, I have become more and more impressed with the probability that (and I don't think this necessarily fits with what Dr. Malenbaum said, but perhaps it does in some way that I don't understand economically) this investment use of nutrition is probably greatest at the lower socioeconomic levels. That is where we will see changes occurring in the productivity patterns and in attitude; as the economic level of the community rises, better nutrition becomes a consumption good rather than an investment good and finally gets to be a luxury and actually a negative, counterproductive type of economic drain perhaps. I think we have to look at it as a spectrum in which the maximum effects will be seen at the lowest economic development levels.

De Sweemer   Punjab, even before the Green Revolution, was considered by most Indian administrators as a surplus food area. During planning for the Green Revolution it was assumed that Punjab's production would help to solve the food problem in India. Nutrition was not foremost in the minds of planners with respect to Punjab, since they assumed there was no nutrition or food problem there. But workers in the Punjab villages do see a very real nutrition problem in the children under three years of age; we find between 5 and 10 percent of them are marasmus cases, depending on the season the prevalence measure is made.

Although the planning for the Green Revolution has been done very efficiently, the fact that a nutrition problem remains shows that there is a need for clarfiying the purpose of development and including nutrition as a specific goal.

Moreover, it is very clear that the Punjabi problem will not be solved solely by economic measures or by agricultural measures as such. It has been shown by A. Sorkin (The Green Revolution. *Growth and Change* 2:36, 1971) that, although most development programs have had the effect of leaving the poor behind, this has not been the case in Punjab. They have benefited proportionately from the development program but, because of the distortion of their value system and because of insufficient knowledge about nutrition, the nutrition problem in Punjab has not improved in recent years and might even have become worse.

Milk has become a cash crop, and therefore the main source of animal protein in Punjabi villages is very efficiently drained off to the cities. It so happens that most of the decision-makers live in the cities. They are very happy to get the milk and the eggs from the villages. One might wonder what policy changes would occur if some of them decided to live in the villages from March to June and found, as we have, that no amount of money can buy any milk or eggs. Then perhaps they would realize that there are problems even in the midst of one of the most marvelous development success stories in the world.

Mellor   I am always worried when I talk on this question that I may appear opposed to specific nutritional programs. I find that a very awkward position to be in, for obvious reasons, particularly with respect to specific programs such as child feeding.

The point I am trying to make is that when we are talking about the very poorest people in a society, perhaps in many countries the lower 20 or 30 percent of the population in income distribution, raising their incomes is likely to be a necessary condition of getting at the underlying nutritional health problem, but it may well not be a sufficient condition. What I am arguing is that the specific nutritional programs have to be seen as supplementary to doing something about the basic income problems of the lower income people.

Let me put the same thing in a little different way. What I have been arguing is that in dealing with the underlying problem of caloric deficiency—which, judging from at least some of the literature, is a problem to substantial numbers of people in the world—just getting income to them is a very efficient means of dealing with that. When they get more income, they spend a high proportion of it on food; that still may not solve the total nutritional problem, there may be some other supplements that are needed, and at that point such things as an educational program and a cheap protein program may be quite effective.

One of the other problems of dealing efficiently with the lowest income people is getting down to them. Very often where the lowest income people are not able to participate in the development process and are not getting increases in income and are not improving their material well-being through the development process, they may also be cut off from access to the special programs and thus the special programs may turn out to benefit only the lower-middle-income people. So there are some complicated interactions here. The main reason that I am pressing this very hard is because, unlike ten or fifteen years ago, we now understand that there are some alternatives with respect to the pattern of development we choose, and that the alternative of a high capital investment program and a postponement of consumption to some indefinite future time is not the only way to foster development. We have to choose up sides in a sense and decide what kind of path to follow; and I think that there is a lot of nutritional evidence for choosing the pattern that does create a good deal more employment and puts some income into the hands of the poor in the relatively short run.

This is really the basic point I am trying to make and it is certainly not in opposition to the specific nutritional program; it is an argument that increased income is a necessary condition for nutritional improvement.

Vamoer Dr. Mellor has raised a rather provocative question. It seems to assume that if you raise the income of the population, they necessarily spend more money on food. In some cases that's being done, but in other cases the additional income is spent on luxuries like radios, maybe bicycles, and other nonfoodstuffs.

deVries There is certainly an immediate relationship between food intake, the health of the people, and their capacity to work and make a contribution to society; at the same time, as Dr. Taylor said, unless family planning and child care are correlated with it, not very much is achieved. I think we learned that we have introduced in the developing countries a far too wide specialization of services that did not exist in the old days, when these services went through the community rather than through the person and they were integrated. I think we have to integrate the programs again. The second five-year plan of Zambia incorporated the idea of coordinating food and nutritional advice with community development, with health, with agricultural extension, and perhaps with other programs by a cross-training of people in the field and by thereafter operating in coordinated teams. That is the way we have to work because we have distorted the natural relationships by our Western specialized technical assistance procedures.

My second remark refers to the immediate effect on productivity of better food for laborers. There is an old, almost classic, example from Java in the thirties: frequent mistakes were made by laborers in the textile or metal industries because they were tired and did not have enough to eat; after a very good brunch was introduced at 10:30 in the morning, 40 percent of these mistakes were eliminated and productivity rose dramatically. While I am all for welfare rather than only economic development, I think unless you have high productivity you cannot achieve very much.

We are talking about preindustrial societies and about rural areas. In my view, differing from Dr. Maaza Bekele's, there is a new front open for migration—that is, to the cities. There are no more empty continents, but there are a few hundred cities absorbing millions and millions of people every year. I have the feeling that even worse than the famine conditions and the crop failures or the seasonal undernutrition in rural areas is the plight of the hundreds and hundreds of millions of people living in the shadowland between the rural areas and the urbanized, industrialized society, where the nutritional standards are deplorable and where it is most difficult to do anything because their productivity is almost nil and the old resources of the countryside and even the forests are gone for these people. They have no productive income. How do we deal with the perhaps 300 million people in the world who are in that status? From the point of view of human welfare perhaps that is the greatest nutrition problem.

Correa The main point I want to make is that economic development has failed in most of the countries as a solution to most socioeconomic problems. I think we have to find methods to bypass economic development. Economies, young economies have not been able to solve or even to tackle the problem of income redistribution. I know that in theory economic development that redistributes income will solve nutritional problems. Unfortunately in practice such a method of development is not achievable. We have to find ways that are agreeable and acceptable to the power structure in the country to solve the nutritional problem.

Sai I think Dr. Mellor is right only within certain very narrow limits. If the increased income comes in a situation where there is an abundance of food of the right quality and quantity, then the chances are it will be spent on food. In Ghana it was found that over a certain amount of income increase there was certainly an increase in the quantity of food entering the house, but that increase was almost completely absorbed by one staple. And if the staple happened to be casava, there was no improvement in nutrition.

Dr. Mellor said that the amount spent on food increased, and left us to deduce that therefore the quantity and quality of food coming into the family increased. We can't deduce that. Sometimes there are reactive increases in price when the economy improves in an area, so that the amount of actual food in quantity and quality may not be greater at all.

The relationship between increased egg production and good nutrition is something we should use. We have to try to make a paying business of nutrition. Let me give an example. All around West Africa today people are eating eggs and chicken. The output of chickens and eggs can be increased only if cereal production is increased. It is, therefore, necessary to increase cereal production and to establish feed-making institutions, in order to produce more chickens for those who are buying them so that those who are producing the cereals can have cash. Then we have really done something.

Chisala I am not a planner, nor am I a nutritionist, but my interest in this is that as an administrator I have to deal with both.

In this session we are talking about nutrition vis-à-vis the planning of development programs in a country. Now we in developing countries have to think of the battle we are waging against three deadly enemies: poverty, ignorance, and disease. To try and eliminate them is our basic objective. I accept that nutrition is very important, but only important insofar as it forms part of the general struggle to eliminate these three deadly elements. Therefore, in considering the role of nutrition we have to put it in the right perspective. We have to accept it as a concept within the overall planning of our basic health services, within the overall economic planning of a country. Unless we can do that, what we are really talking about is nutrition as a concept, as a scientific approach to a particular problem rather than as a practical contribution to economic development of the particular countries.

Ginor In reference to Dr. Mellor's suggestion about the change in the pattern of growth, I want to draw his attention to what happened: as long as the growth rate was the only objective, and planners and economists and government thought only of reaching the highest growth rate, we had in some countries a relatively high growth rate and growing unemployment. There has been a change in attitude and a recognition that the creation of jobs has to be one of the objectives. Why not consciously make nutrition another objective and find ways and means of solving the nutrition problem? Redistribution of incomes is not enough; much has to be done in education and also in making available the right foodstuffs and in enriching foods and carrying out various activities aimed at bringing about better nutrition.

Santos   In countries where average income is $250 or under, most of the people suffer from caloric deficiencies, total protein deficiencies, and many animal protein deficiencies. In countries with average individual income between $250 and $500, there is not usually a caloric problem but there is a continuing protein and animal protein shortage. Only where average income is $1,200 or over have the animal protein deficiencies been overcome. This shows a close correlation between the level of income and the nutrients a family can afford.

At the initial stage of development there is an increasing demand for food, and when the demand does not correspond to the increase in supply, there is a pressure that causes the price to increase. When prices rise, low-income groups become worse off. That is what Dr. Taylor observed in the Punjab, but the problems of kwashiorkor and other nutritional diseases there arose not because economic development had failed to improve the nutrition status but because the pattern of economic development was not right and was not followed by a redistribution of income. So in the initial stage of development the government should take steps to protect the low-income and other vulnerable groups.

Nutrition and Development: Carl E. Taylor
Joint Communiqué   John Mellor

An apparent polarization of views during the earlier discussion has led the two of us to intensive exploration of the issue of the relative balance that should be maintained in resource allocation between general economic development for agrarian societies and specific programs designed to improve nutrition and health.

It was not hard for us to reach agreement once we had each defined the specifics of what we considered appropriate program components—as so often happens in disagreement. In agreeing we may find ourselves in disagreement with many of the rest of the conference participants. We agree that package programs need to be developed both for general economic improvement of the village family and for combined nutrition, health, and family planning services. This help has to be generated in the village. For practical purposes and for the present, the economic program needs mostly male village workers reaching the men, while the nutrition, family planning, and health program needs mostly women workers reaching women.

John Mellor's Position
Economic development frequently excludes a substantial proportion of the population. The most serious incidence of malnutrition occurs in this group of very low-income people whose incomes are not increasing. The very social, political, and economic forces that often exclude the poor from participating in rising incomes are likely to exclude them from participation in special nutrition programs, particularly if those programs emphasize the delivery of food. Thus, without change in power structures, the programs justified by the tragedy of the poor may benefit only the rich. If those power structures are changed and the poor participate in economic growth, they will have higher incomes and will spend a high proportion of that added income on food, thereby solving much of the problem of caloric deficiency and possibly some of the protein problem as well. Integrated rural development schemes and increasing agricultural production combined with employment programs may be effective in meeting these objectives. Nutrition education programs would then operate in a favorable economic environment. Indeed, nutrition programs themselves may play a catalytic role in these same underlying processes.

Carl Taylor's Position
While we all agree that agricultural reform and development are important and desirable objectives, they cannot be expected to work automatically and

spontaneously to improve nutrition and health. The fact that they do eventually lead to better health is evident from the many clear demonstrations that the fall in death rates and growth in population have been more often related to such economic growth than to health programs. The evidence for this comes not only from European experience following the Industrial Revolution, but is even more clear in modern case histories such as Nepal. During the past thirty years Nepal's death rate has fallen so much that now one of the most serious population problems in the world crowds its hillsides. But there have been almost no health services reaching outside Kathmandu except for a malaria eradication program that has opened the Terai to mass migration from the crowded hills, with total decimation of the wonderful Terai jungle.

To permit this slow, spontaneous, and indirect evolution of privately financed nutrition and health services in the modern age is not only morally questionable but also an absolute mistake from the point of view of total development. We now have evidence that package programs for family planning, maternal and child health, and nutrition can reach village homes at reasonable cost. This is not mass distribution of food with all of the abuses to which such programs are often subjected. As with an agricultural extension program, it involves simple services by auxiliary workers who get village people to make the changes—and only those changes—in living habits that focus effort on producing a better life, especially for the poor. It has been clearly demonstrated in many countries that just having more money in the home, without knowledge of better nutrition, may lead to deterioration of nutritional status because people buy foods that they consider high social-status products but that are actually nutritionally atrocious. This health-nutrition-family planning integrated approach then would help make the best use of the family's economic improvement. Most important as a total development benefit is the increasingly clear demonstration that this integrated service package offers the best prospect of reducing the lag between reduction of the death rate and reduction of the birth rate and is thus the most practical move we can make now in resolving the population problem.

In summary, we agree that both agricultural and health package programs are necessary and complementary, and that the balance between them must be determined by local conditions.

Part III   Diagnosis of Food and
                                          Nutrition Problems and
                                          Establishment of Priorities

12 Significance of Malnutrition and Priorities for Its Prevention

J. M. Bengoa
Chief, Nutrition Unit
World Health Organization, Geneva

Introduction

When nutrition intervention programs were considered primarily as a welfare activity, planning was a relatively simple undertaking. Supplementary feeding programs, nutrition education, and little more were the foundations upon which the governments dealt with nutrition problems in developing countries. The reason for this was the assumption that the overall nutrition problems would be solved in the long run only through the improvement of standards of living. It was thought that what was required in the meantime was to protect the most vulnerable groups of the population, especially through the provision of additional foods to some members of the community.

Recently this simple approach, which is not without merit, has been challenged as being insufficient on three bases:

1. The standards of living are not improving at a substantial rate in developing countries, and the hopes for the future are limited.

2. Although some countries have had in recent years satisfactory rates of economic growth (but very unequally distributed), they have not had a corresponding improvement as far as nutrition is concerned. On the other hand, some countries of relatively moderate per capita income do not present significant nutrition problems.

3. Advances in agriculture, health, and food technology have opened the door to some nutrition intervention programs which can be contemplated within the socioeconomic development plans, without necessarily waiting for major development.

The new urgency and the scope of new possibilities have complicated the planning of nutrition programs to such a degree that at present we are suffering uncertainty and, to some extent, inertia. We recognize the need for an orderly methodology, based on appropriate criteria, which would permit the selection of best combinations of the many alternatives in a particular situation. We also realize that at present the precise criteria have not been defined and, even if defined, the data are not available in those countries where the problems may be most urgent. In this situation what is urgently needed are at least crude indicators that reflect the general nutritional situation as well as its social significance and that will help to establish priorities.

A further difficulty in the discussion of possible programs and objectives is the lack of precision in the use of terms. WHO and FAO have recently made an attempt to define nutrition terms and, from the comments that have been received, it is evident that there is a surprising lack of uniformity in the interpretation given to some even frequently used terms. [1]

An example is the "protein problem," which has been the subject of great international and national concern but with different meanings in many instances. Some people interpret the "protein problem" as an insufficient production of proteins on a worldwide basis; for others it means insufficient intake of proteins in some vulnerable groups of the population, due more to economic or cultural reasons than to a lack of availability in the market; for others the "protein problem" is only a facet of the total food supply problem, in which the lack or unequal distribution of sources of calories is the most important aspect; for others, finally—without exhausting the list—the "protein problem" is a clinical manifestation in young children in which the inadequacy of proteins is only a factor. Obviously, if the interpreted meanings differ, the proposed solutions will differ even more and major confusion will result; this is precisely the current situation.

For a public health worker, a nutrition problem is one that affects human health rather than a statistical estimate of local food availability. For example, a country with a surplus of food may still face malnutrition while another country with much more limited resources of food, but better distribution among the population, may have little or no malnutrition. Obviously if the food supply is grossly inadequate, malnutrition is unavoidable. A clear understanding of the meaning of our terms is essential to effective communication.

This paper will first highlight some pressing problems in the field of nutrition; special consideration will then be given to the nature, extent, and significance of protein-calorie malnutrition (PCM) and to the possible public health criteria for establishing priorities in the control of this condition.

Priorities

It is difficult to draw a precise line between good nutrition and malnutrition for there are many intermediate states between normal and pathological conditions. An important question is whether malnutrition is a single entity or a group of various diseases or conditions of independent character, as are infectious diseases. The answer is that malnutrition is in fact a group of problems, some in close association, but others completely independent.

In the booklet entitled *Control of Malnutrition in Man,* published by the American Public Health Association, [2], 30 nutritional diseases, mostly deficiency diseases, are described. Some of these occur all over the world;

others, frequently fatal, are uncommon; and still others are of scientific and academic interest but are of little importance in developing countries. For some that present major public health problems, measures for prevention are well established, although it may not be possible to implement them in all circumstances. For others our knowledge is not sufficiently well advanced to permit us to develop effective large-scale preventive measures.

From the point of view of geographical extent and prevalence, nutritional problems may be classified into three main groups: (1) those common to practically all the developing countries (protein-calorie malnutrition, nutritional anemia, endemic goiter, ariboflavinosis, and some dental problems); (2) those encountered in certain areas of developing countries (xerophthalmia and rickets); and (3) those limited only to specific areas (pellagra, beriberi, and scurvy).

From the international point of view the following four conditions deserve the highest priority (Figure 1): (1) protein-calorie malnutrition, because of its high mortality rate, its prevalence, and the irreversible physical and sometimes mental damage that can result; (2) xerophthalmia, because of its contribution to the mortality of malnourished children, its relatively wide extent, the dramatic irreversible damage (blindness) it causes, and the possibilities for its prevention; (3) nutritional anemias, because of their wide distribution, their contribution to mortality from many other conditions, and their repercussions on working capacity; and (4) endemic goiter, because of its wide distribution and the effectiveness and low cost of its prevention.

In some more limited areas of the world other nutritional problems, such as beriberi, pellagra, or rickets, may warrant a high priority, but on a worldwide basis the above mentioned seem the most important. [3] In the industrialized countries obesity is the most common form of malnutrition unless atherosclerosis is considered to be a nutritional disease.

It would be impossible within the limits of this presentation to discuss all nutrition problems and therefore, in view of the conspicuous importance of PCM and its socioeconomic implications, I shall limit the discussion to PCM as the central focus of the diversified nutritional problems in the world.

Nature, Extent, and Significance of PCM

Nature and Extent
The nature of PCM is complex. It covers not only the severe clinical forms known as (a) kwashiorkor, (b) nutritional marasmus, and (c) intermediate cases or "mixed forms," but also (d) moderate forms as well as (e) lasting

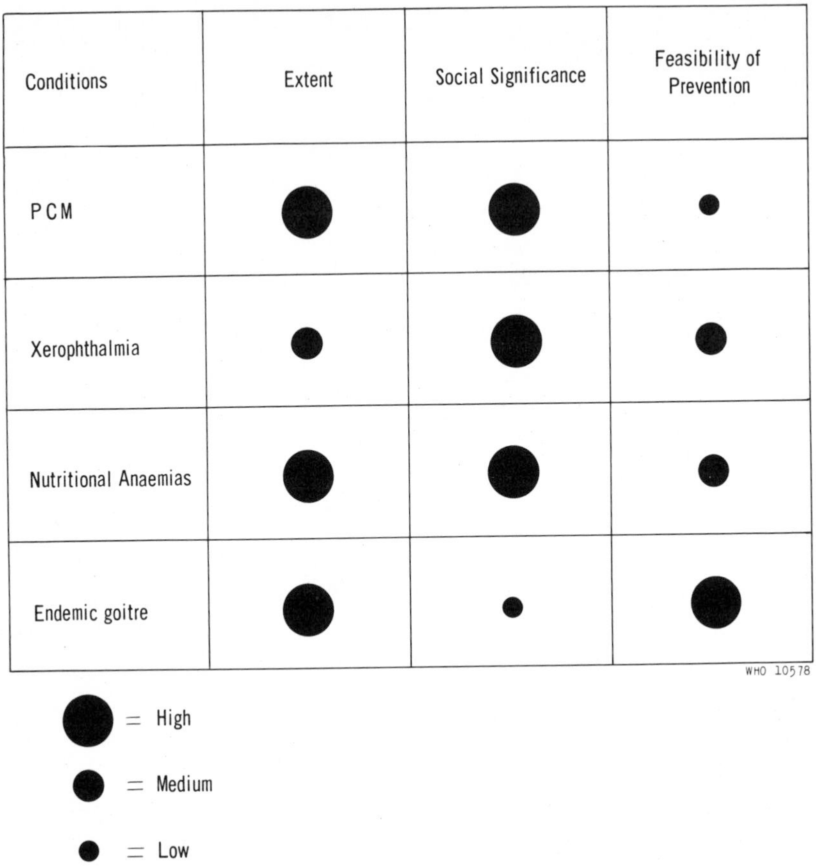

Conditions	Extent	Social Significance	Feasibility of Prevention
P C M	⬤	⬤	•
Xerophthalmia	●	⬤	●
Nutritional Anaemias	⬤	⬤	●
Endemic goitre	⬤	•	⬤

WHO 10578

⬤ = High

● = Medium

• = Low

Figure 1. Priorities among Nutritional Conditions

effects. Table 1 shows the main features of the above 5 PCM forms, as suggested by the Joint FAO/WHO Expert Committee on Nutrition, [4] with some small modifications.

The clinical picture of the three severe forms of PCM varies widely, reflecting a complex interrelationship of the causative factors. The actual features are influenced importantly by the age of weaning, the concurrent presence of infection, and perhaps the specific nature of the diet. There has been a tendency to overemphasize the importance of either protein or calorie deficiency alone, whereas in fact the two almost always occur together.

It is within the context of the above 5 forms of PCM that the extent of the problem will be discussed. The data, incomplete and scarce, are the results of

Table 1. Simplified Classification of PCM*

Categories	Body weight as % of standard	Body height	Edema	Deficit of weight for height
Kwashiorkor	80-60	Affected	+	+ +
Marasmus	< 60	Affected	0	+ +
Mixed forms (marasmic kwashiorkor)	< 60	Affected	+	+ +
Underweight child (moderate PCM)	80-60	Affected	0	Minimal
Nutritional dwarfing	< 60	Pronounced deficit	0	Minimal

*Adapted from the Joint FAO/WHO Expert Committee on Nutrition. *Eighth Report.* 1972.

community surveys carried out in children under 5 years of age during the last 4 years in 28 developing countries by different authors. [5]

Kwashiorkor. The characteristic feature of kwashiorkor is the presence of edema, and in field surveys edema is the main criterion for diagnosis, usually associated with other signs. Since kwashiorkor tends to be a relatively severe condition of short duration before recovery or death, the number of cases in the community at a given moment is apparently small. The surveys indicate that the point prevalence is in the range between 0.2 and 1.6 per 100 children under 5 years of age. The total number of kwashiorkor cases occurring in a given year is probably six or eight times higher. [6] The child with kwashiorkor usually dies if no medical attention is given; even in hospitals the mortality may be of the order of 20 to 30 percent. [5] There is an impression from data on hospital admissions that the number of cases of kwashiorkor is declining in many countries in comparison with admissions ten or twenty years ago; this requires confirmation from more accurate hospital data.

Nutritional marasmus. The other extreme of severe PCM is nutritional marasmus, characterized by gross loss of subcutaneous fat, muscle wasting, and frank growth retardation. No visible edema is present, and usually it is more chronic than kwashiorkor. In children under one year of age this is the most common form of PCM. In community surveys, the point prevalence has been found to be within the range of 1.2 and 6.8 percent of children under 5 years of age.

While in some areas of the world kwashiorkor has been more frequent than nutritional marasmus, it is becoming evident that a change is occurring in areas where early weaning is established, particularly in urban areas. [4] Chile, countries of the Middle East, and others are typical examples.

Mixed forms of severe PCM. Many severe forms are difficult to classify as kwashiorkor or nutritional marasmus. They are intermediate forms, with characteristics of both conditions. Moreover, a child with nutritional marasmus may develop kwashiorkor, and a child with kwashiorkor may present a picture of nutritional marasmus after losing edema following treatment.

Using as a criterion of this mixed form a weight deficit of more than 40 percent of the reference body weights (third degree of malnutrition in Gomez's classification) [7] the point prevalence in community surveys is within a range of 0.5 to 4.6 percent. In surveys where the combined prevalence of the three severe forms of PCM has been measured, it appears to be within a range between 0.2 and 7.6 percent, probably around 3 percent as an average.

Moderate forms of PCM. Comparative prevalence studies on moderate forms of PCM are even more difficult because of lack of uniformity in the clinical criteria to define them. Most of the surveys have used a weight deficit of 25 to 40 percent of the reference weight (second degree of malnutrition in Gomez's classification).

In the review of the literature mentioned above the moderate forms of PCM have been found to range between 4.4 and 43.1 percent, probably around 25 percent as an average. These children are at considerable risk of developing a more severe form of PCM should an infectious episode intervene. An unknown proportion of children in this category represent nutritional dwarfing, as discussed below, since the community studies have considered only weight for age and not weight for height. Table 2 shows, in summary form, the data available on the extent of the PCM problem.

Lasting effects of PCM. Studies on the prevalence of PCM should also include

Table 2. Prevalence of Severe and Moderate Forms of PCM (1966-1969)

Region	No. countries	Percentage of cases	
		Severe PCM	Moderate PCM
Africa	8	0.5 - 7.6	5.6 - 27.2
Latin America	12	0.5 - 4.1	4.4 - 32.0
Asia	4	1.4 - 2.9	16.0 - 43.1
Total and range extremes	24	0.5 - 7.6	4.4 - 43.1

the late effects of the condition, because of their great social significance, even when the effects may be irreversible. It is not always possible to make a clear distinction between the child who is *at present* malnourished and the child who was *in the past* malnourished and who now exhibits evidence of the lasting effects. Further, it may be even more difficult, without clinical trial, to distinguish between the child who has recovered from acute malnutrition and who is now subsisting on a marginal diet which prevents a catch-up in growth, and the child who has suffered permanent growth retardation as a result of acute malnutrition (nutritional dwarfing). The first would be expected to respond to improvement in diet; the second would not. The deficit in weight for height is minimal in these children, even in extreme cases of nutritional dwarfing.

The important point here is that many of the children in developing countries have at present lasting signs—particularly reflected by the pronounced deficit in height—of having been malnourished at one time or another. The number of children with signs of nutritional dwarfing is unknown.

The Public Health and Social Significance of PCM

The significance of a public health problem can be measured in terms of its effects on mortality and on the human and social development of the survivors. **Effects of malnutrition on mortality.** The severe forms of PCM contribute to the exceedingly high number of deaths in children under 5 years of age in developing countries. In Latin America, for instance, it may be estimated that the number of deaths due directly to malnutrition is at present of the order of 50,000 to 60,000 yearly. [8] It is certain that malnutrition is a contributing cause in a much larger number; exactly how many is not known.

The Inter-American Investigation of Mortality in Childhood, undertaken by the Pan-American Health Organization (PAHO), [9] found that 8 percent of deaths in children 6 months to 2 years have malnutrition as an underlying or main cause of death, and 41 percent as an associated cause (Figure 2).

There is at present an important decline in mortality in children under 5 years of age. This decline, as shown in Figures 3 and 4, is impressive in some countries and, unless carefully studied, may suggest that nutritional conditions are improving much more rapidly than is really the case. It is now well documented [10,11] that this decline is due more to specific public-health action preventing deaths than to any improvement in the standards of living, including general nutritional conditions in the country. The present situation in developing countries is very different from the situation of developed countries 30 or 50 years ago, where the drop in mortality was due mainly to

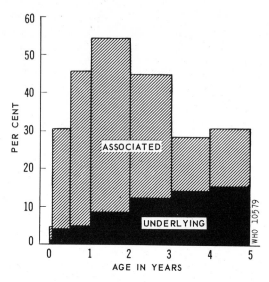

Figure 2. Percentage of Deaths of Children with Nutrition as Underlying or Associated Cause

the improvement in standard of living. [8] Mortality rates alone may not be a satisfactory criterion of the nutritional health of the community in these circumstances, particularly as mortality rates fall.

Effects of malnutrition on human and social development. The interaction of malnutrition and infections is intimately related to the high mortality in young children, which apparently is declining dramatically. In addition to the efforts in that direction, more attention should be paid to the survivors, handicapped biologically and socially because of incomplete recovery from previous severe and moderate episodes of malnutrition and infections. [12,13]

Figure 5 shows graphically a typical example of a mere survivor—a 2-year-old Latin American child from the poorer classes who has had 6 attacks of conjunctivitis, 5 of diarrhea, 10 infections of the upper respiratory passage, 4 attacks of bronchitis, measles followed by bronchopneumonia, and an episode of stomatitis. In 24 months this child has had nearly 30 attacks of illness and has had one infection or another for about 30 percent of his life. [14] In addition, his diet has been inadequate, with the result that each infection has led to a loss of weight from which he has never been able to recover completely. At 2 years of age he is almost a year behind in physical development. Thirty years ago a child with such a history would probably have died. Nowadays, he may well be surviving because of medical care during severe episodes.

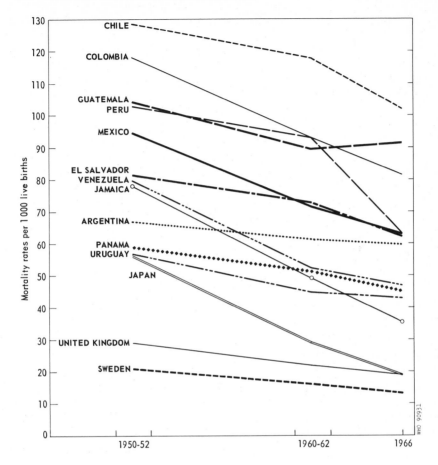

Figure 3. Infant Mortality Rates per 1,000 Live Births

In many parts of the world it is becoming common to see preschool children like him, of indefinite age, obviously physically underdeveloped, withdrawn, with an expression of indifference, and disinterested in the outside world.

A child 6 years old who at first sight may seem to be 3 years old because of physical underdevelopment clearly cannot be compared in behavior and learning capacity with a normal child of 6. Equally, he cannot be compared with a normal child of 3. He is another being altogether, with his own biological and behavioral characteristics, and it is difficult to assign a strict developmental age to him. [13] Scientific writers have recently begun to use terms for him which have great meaning. For example, it is said that malnutrition during the

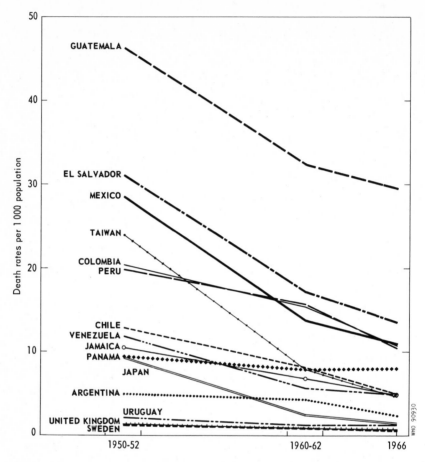

Figure 4. Death Rates in Children 1-4 Years per 1,000 Population of Same Age

first years of life "distorts the normal symmetry of size and body," [15] leads to a "perversion of development," [16] produces "a disharmonic and retarded development," [17] creates a "disproportionate child," [18] or is responsible for "lack of balanced growth." [19]

Difficulties in learning and in psychological and social adaptation should be considered in this context of survival. Between the child who has recovered completely and the survivor who has simply got by, there is an infinite number of intermediate stages. The possible repercussions on schooling performance have already been discussed elsewhere. [13, 15]

For the above reasons, neither the prevalence of existing malnutrition nor the mortality data demonstrate the true significance of the problem. In order

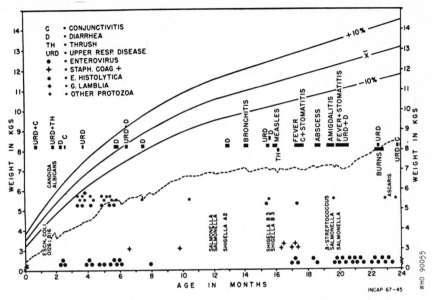

Figure 5. Weight and Infectious Diseases in a Guatemalan Village Child

to assess the social significance of PCM we should also include the proportion of the population with evident signs of incomplete recovery from past malnutrition. We must know whether these numbers are increasing or decreasing as mortality rates fall. Are we preventing death without improving life?

The need for a single indicator, or several, to assess the lasting effects of malnutrition in young children is a matter of urgency. It would be preferable to have a single indicator which would reflect, for a given community, the combined effect of a number of factors related to physical, functional, and social development. Such a single indicator should incorporate objectivity, feasibility, specificity, and sensitivity. I would suggest the possibility of using the height of children of 7 years of age as such a community indicator. The advantages, in principle and subject to some testing, would be that

1. The height of children 7 years old summarizes with objectivity the past history of the community in terms of nutrition (usually associated with other health problems).

2. Children of 7 years are entering school, which facilitates the task of measurement. The age of 5, or 6, years would be equally suitable, if this is the age of entrance into school.

3. Height represents a good indicator of physical development and in many respects it also reflects some parameters of functional development. Short

boys have a significant reduction in average hemoglobin, protein, and albumin
levels in comparison with control boys of the same geographical area, as has
been shown by Ronaghy et al. in Iran. [20]

4. There is also some evidence of a relationship between height and schooling
performance in low social groups. As Cravioto and De Licardie stated in their
paper, [21] "in communities whose children had been at risk of malnutrition,
those of shorter stature, age by age, showed poorer intersensory development
than taller children."

5. The index is sensitive, as suggested by the great differences among social
groups in a given country. In Costa Rica, for example, which is a country of
great homogeneity in racial origins, the percentile 50 of the height of boys 7
years old in urban areas is 118.7 cm. But the percentile 10 is 109.2 cm, and
the percentile 90 is 126.2 cm. [22] This range is apparently greater than can
be accounted for by genetic differences, but can be explained by environmental factors among which nutrition is the most important in this case. The
sensitivity of the index is shown also by the example of Japan, where the
height of 7-year-old boys increased from 112.3 cm in 1948 to 116.8 cm in
1963, paralleling improvements in the national diet and general health condition. [23]

6. The heights of children 7 years old are apparently closely correlated with
the socioeconomic index developed by the U.N. Research Institute for Social
Development, [24] as shown in Figure 6.

7. The selection of boys, instead of girls, is justified by the fact that they
seem more sensitive to environmental influences, at least as reflected in social
class. [25]

The advantages of using children of this age in evaluating nutritional status
has already been mentioned by Hundley et al. [26] and by Bengoa, Jelliffe,
and Perez. [27] Now that there is more interest in the lasting effects of malnutrition, it would be of great value to test if such an indicator, or some
other, or a combination of two or three, can provide the information that is
urgently required. It would be of great importance in assessing the significance of PCM in the community and in evaluation of nutrition intervention
programs in the prevention of PCM.

In summary, it can be said that the study of the nature, extent, and social
significance of PCM (and this study would be applicable to any other nutritional disease) requires an epidemiological approach comprehensive enough to
provide an understanding of the complexity of the problem, but simple
enough to enable such a study to be carried out with the usual limited re-

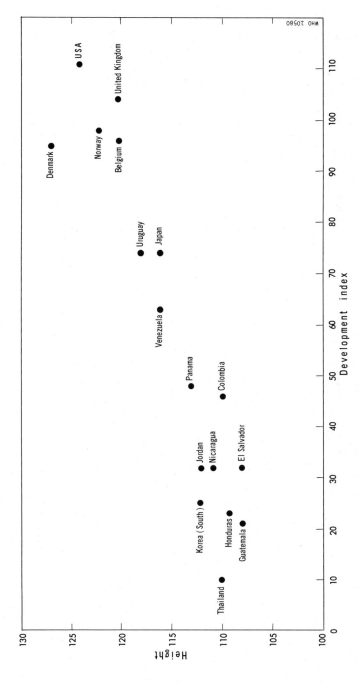

Figure 6. Correlation between Height of 7-Year-Old Boys and Socioeconomic Development Index for Different Countries

sources, in order to provide the minimum information needed for planning nutrition intervention programs.

Priorities for Food and Nutrition Intervention Programs in the Control of PCM

Discussion of priorities is an essential prerequisite to the development and implementation in the field of sound and realistic programs. But I agree with Dr. G. Ohlin, who stated in the 1971 Dag Hammarskjöld Seminar on "Nutrition as a Priority in African Development," "My non-expert contention is rather that there does not yet seem to be sufficient experience to recommend a strategy which ventures to put clear-cut priorities on all possible types of measures, nor is there sufficient uniformity of national conditions for such priorities to make much sense." [28]

Certainly all priority choices are necessarily based on assumptions and some degree of oversimplification—it would be impossible to identify all alternatives in priorities and goals. Malnutrition is a problem in which all causative factors are interrelated and impinge upon each other. In each stage of the natural history of malnutrition the major factor most subject to change must be identified if appropriate priorities are to be established. The soundness of any theoretical conclusion in a given country, at a given time and in a given political situation, can be tested only in practice.

Two illustrations may be useful in order to understand the chain of events in malnutrition.

First example: A child is malnourished and the history shows that the intake of protein is inadequate because there is insufficient protein available in his community. The insufficiency of protein reflects the lack of cattle (milk and meat) in the area due to inadequate pastures. Pastures are poor because of sparse rainfall and infertile soil. Hence the primary cause of the child's malnutrition is lack of water or soil infertility, and the obvious solution is to provide irrigation and to improve the soil through the use of fertilizers. But in this example there are some other alternatives that can interrupt the chain of events leading to the malnourished child without going necessarily to the primary cause. The lack of cattle in the area should not be considered as an insurmountable constraint in solving the protein shortage, since there are other means to overcome this immediate problem. For example, the increased production of legumes, the use of vegetable protein mixtures, or, in the final instance, supplementary feeding with donated food from outside the region may alleviate the situation.

Second example: A malnourished child, the seventh in a family, is ill and does not recover from repeated infectious diseases because the low income of the family does not permit the purchase of desirable foods that are on the market. The low income reflects the intermittent (periodic) unemployment of the father—unemployment due to his lack of skill for any job. This lack of skill in turn reflects his recent migration from a rural to an urban area, a migration that is attributable directly to the policy of the country on land tenure. Here, the primary cause of the child's malnutrition is a social cause, correctable only through political decision and action. Action necessary to alter social constraints may be even more difficult to take than action to correct physical conditions of the environment. However, here again there are possibilities for action, without awaiting the ultimate solution. A policy on employment and adequate income and family planning may be a satisfactory indirect intervention to improve the situation. Even the food received by the child might be sufficient if he was not condemned by his environment to frequent enteric and other infectious diseases. In this case means to improve environmental sanitation and personal hygiene, such as increased availabiltiy of water, could be decisive.

Epidemiologically, therefore, PCM is the result of the interaction of environment (including social structures), the agent (foods), and the host (the patient). This interaction is a dynamic process. [29,30] Logically, in the prevention of PCM we should look at the series of events in the environment, in the agent, and in the host that may be susceptible to correction. Therefore, three types of intervention should be considered: (1) action on the environment (physical and social); (2) action on the agent—programs designed to improve the quantity and quality of foods; and (3) action on the host—programs addressed to the human beings, in terms of promotion of better food habits, specific protection of special groups, and treatment and nutritional rehabilitation.

We shall try to develop these three concepts in the light of priorities at each level.

Action on the Environment
Ideally the aim of the intervention program should be to overcome the primary cause of malnutrition. The primary cause may be in some cases a clear-cut, well-defined problem related to the physical environment, social structure, agricultural practices, or natural disasters. In many instances, however, there are multiple primary causes which overlap, and it is difficult to identify a main primary cause or one which, if attacked in isolation, would markedly

influence the problem. In some cases the primary cause of malnutrition can be overcome if financial resources are available (physical environment, some natural disasters, etc.), but in others the ultimate solution requires profound changes in the behavior of the society (social changes). A primary cause—sometimes associated with the others—that has been relatively neglected is related to natural disasters and other events that may cause a sudden deterioration of nutritional status.

As already mentioned, one of the most important factors in explaining the high prevalence of malnutrition, as well as the great proportion of children biologically and socially handicapped, is the inadequate nutritional recovery between episodes of infection and malnutrition. Perhaps, in many instances, acute and frequent episodes of food shortages associated with infections are more important than chronically deficient diets in determining the current magnitude of malnutrition. That is, were it not for the acute episode, the chronic diet might barely suffice to maintain reasonable health; but it is not sufficient to permit recovery.

If this hypothesis is correct, high priority in the prevention of a primary cause of malnutrition should be given to predicting with some accuracy the probability of a sudden nutrition deterioration in the community. The report of the Swedish Nutrition Foundation on nutrition in times of disasters gives some clear orientation on warning systems. [31] The definition of some indicators in the fields of meteorology, socioeconomics, and epidemiology to predict such eventualities is urgently needed.

From the meteorological point of view, FAO has already established an early warning system for food shortages, which provides a monthly report. This is an excellent beginning. [32] From the report of March 1971, out of 35 countries for which information was available, 27 had food problems of an urgent character. Six countries were confronted with floods; 17 with droughts; 3 with cyclones; and 1 with a typhoon.

The study in Tanzania, by the University of Dar-es-Salaam in collaboration with the Colorado and Clark Universities in the United States and the University of Toronto in Canada, on the impact of droughts on the nutritional status of the population will be of great practical importance. [33] The study should provide the basis for a policy on reduction of drought loss, thus minimizing its effects on nutrition.

Floods are usually predictable; Roubault [34] states that, in view of the great amount of scientific information available and the research done during the last hundred years, *there are no more unpredictable floods.* While ultimately it may be possible to control flooding and harness the water for useful purposes, it may, in the meantime, be possible to minimize the impact of a flood through prompt relief action.

An economic crisis, with a sudden increase in unemployment or a sudden rise in the price of basic foods, may also signal the need for prompt action in the field of nutrition. It might also be useful to select indicators in the epidemiological field, particularly during epidemics of such diseases as diarrhea and measles.

The fact is that a sudden deterioration of nutritional status is usually predictable and frequently preventable. In view of the high cost and difficulties of obtaining a full recovery, after the event, of the population affected, it would be of great importance in terms of priorities to identify areas that are at present passing through a period of urgency as well as those passing through a predictable risk period.

Nutrition Intervention Programs Involving Foods

Different levels of action can be identified, ranging from food production to food fortification, all of them intended to improve the quantity or quality (or both) of food reaching the market. Identifying the point or points where the main factors should be interrupted is a crucial decision, generally taken at the central government level.

In developing countries, past concern may have centered on the total amount of food produced (measured as calories). However, a prime consideration must be decisions on the sources of these calories, for this determines the nutrient supply. In most of the developing countries, 2, 3, or 4 staple foods supply 60 to 80 percent of calories. While in theory it is possible that the other 20 to 40 percent of sources of calories might be rich in nutrients and ensure overall adequacy, in practice this is seldom the case. All too often these complementary energy sources are also low in nutrients, for example, sugar. It is for this reason that the nature of the staple foods usually determines the type and severity of malnutrition in a country; examples may be cited of regional differences in nutritional status of the population within a country attributable to differences in the staple foods. It cannot be overemphasized that when a very limited number of foods provides a very major proportion of the calories, the nature of these foods is of crucial importance and any policy on the staple foods must be watched not only with regard to the calorie value but also with regard to the overall nutritive value of the staples. This is of particular importance in countries where there is a need to increase the productivity of the labor force, which is in itself a high priority in most of the developing countries. The poorer the country, the greater the emphasis must be on an adequate food production. As Nicol has rightly stated, "The amount of food required to meet the energy and protein needs of individuals living in developing countries depends largely upon the nature of the staple food consumed, in particular the concentration of energy-producing sources and the quantity and quality of proteins." [35]

It is in setting priorities with regard to the qualitative aspects of food production that difficulties may arise since quantity (with its economic return) and quality (with its health return) do not necessarily go hand in hand. The protein content of foods may be cited as an example of the broad problem.

The report of the Advisory Committee on the Application of Science and Technology (ACAST) in 1968 on the International Action to Avert the Impending Protein Crisis [36] suggested 14 specific proposals to deal with the protein problem in the world, 8 of which relate to direct food intervention programs and 6 to training, research, and regulations. The above proposals were commented upon and enlarged by the FAO/WHO/UNICEF Protein Advisory Group (PAG) at its meeting held in Rome in February 1971, [37] the report of which was presented to the U.N. Expert Panel on Proteins in New York in June 1971. [38] Five additional specific proposals were added. These reports are basic documents for establishing priorities in food intervention programs on the international level as well as on the national level. The subject is too vast to be considered in this paper, but a few comments will illustrate the important role of agricultural and food sciences in nutrition intervention programs.

The PAG states that "it is a matter of serious concern that the per capita production of legumes . . . is actually decreasing in some countries as a result of the greater profitability of the new high-yielding cereals . . . and urges that legumes be given special emphasis in future efforts to improve plant production." However, the decrease in the per capita production of legumes was evident even before the introduction of the new high-yielding cereals. While the total production of legumes in developing countries increased 29 percent from 1950 to 1965, the population increased 43 percent [39]. In some countries there has been an absolute decrease in legume production in recent years leading to alarming per capita decreases. Moreover, very little attention has been given to the fact that many fewer varieties of legumes have been grown in the last thirty or forty years. Of the great number of varieties of legumes found years ago on the market in developing countries, it is at present difficult to see more than five or six.

In some countries policy decisions at the central level on the production of legumes have very little chance of success, because legumes are mostly grown in small areas around homesteads and are not part of agricultural planning. This is a serious difficulty for any guiding agricultural plan. Agricultural extension services are one answer to this problem. Price incentives may be another. The long-range solution, however, lies in research to develop higher yielding varieties of legumes that would be as profitable to grow as, and therefore can compete successfully with, the new cereal varieties.

Another reason for the decrease in legume production is the change in food habits resulting from the increasing purchasing power in some developing countries, which leads to increasing consumption of other foods. In view of the importance of the problem, revising the policy on legumes may need to be rated as a high priority measure in many developing countries.

As for production of animal protein sources, the main limitation is that the products are generally relatively highly priced and may, therefore, not be used sufficiently by the low-income groups, most of which are in need of better protein supplies. [37] It will be necessary, perhaps, to consider in the future official regulations allocating certain animal foods, particularly milk, on a priority basis to children and pregnant women, and prohibiting their use, for example, in the plastics industry or for feeding calves.

Similarly, oil-seed meals must be used to a much greater degree for direct human consumption rather than fed to animals or used as fertilizers. Linked with food production is the soil fertility problem. It is unfortunate that the costs of fertilizers are so high in developing countries, where the yields are lowest. It has been calculated that one kilogram of rice will buy 780 gm of ammonium sulphate in Japan, but only 240 gm in India. [40] A great deal of effort is therefore needed in the field of food production to combat primary causes of malnutrition, as discussed in detail elsewhere. [41,42]

There are many other possibilities for nutrition intervention programs involving foods at an intermediate level of prevention. Mention must be made of the need to reduce food waste, of the development of new sources of proteins through food technology, of the introduction of food fortification, and others. A major hope lies in the development and growth of genetically improved cereals of a higher nutritive value.

Nutrition Intervention Programs Acting on the Host
The action to be taken on human beings covers a broad range of activities which can be classified as follows: (1) Promotion of better food habits through education of the public. This includes, in addition to mass nutrition

education, school feeding programs, school gardens, and other related activities. They are oriented to primary prevention, aiming to raise the level of nutrition education in the population. (2) Specific protection of mothers and young children. This includes activities related to the promotion of breast-feeding, to maternal nutrition, to control of infections; family planning, periodic surveillance, provision of food supplements, and other related activities are included. (3) Treatment and nutritional rehabilitation. Activities framed under this heading include choosing the best and most economical ways to deal with the population already malnourished—hospital treatment, nutrition rehabilitation services, home management of malnourished children, and other related activities—which have been discussed elsewhere. [4,43]

This classification of activities is in some respects conventional; however, it also reflects clearly two different objectives. Programs under (1) are intended to improve the levels of general nutrition, while (2) and (3) are addressed directly to the reduction of mortality and morbidity from malnutrition.

The main question, in view of the limited resources available in developing countries, is whether to give greater priority to (1), (2), or (3). How should nutrition programs be started and what priorities should be established in a community where malnutrition in young children is highly prevalent? The answer will undoubtedly include activities to attain both objectives, but the balance will vary to correspond to each local problem. In a paper presented in 1965 to the First Western Hemisphere Nutrition Congress, [44] I stated that the relative priorities given to these objectives would depend upon the level of organization of the community and the resources available. The variation in local factors is so great that it may be impossible to standardize programs and approaches.

Three hypothetical stages of development can be considered. *First stage.* Those areas with very high prevalence of malnutrition and infectious disease in young children, very poor development of preventive health services, and very limited resources. In such areas efforts should be made *to establish or upgrade the local health services,* but in the meantime the best alternative will be to establish programs directed to the reduction of mortality and morbidity in young children (2) and (3), and progressively to introduce some activities of a promotional nature (1). *Second stage.* During the second stage, the community has a more reasonable network of basic health services, as well as other community services (such as education). At this stage a much better balance between (1), (2), and (3) may be established. *Third stage.* It is expected that in view of the action taken in the previous stages, the mortality rates and the prevalence of severe cases of malnutrition have been reduced to such a limited number that not many activities would be required in (3), while the educational programs (1) may be increased considerably in order to maintain or improve satisfactory levels of nutrition.

Figure 7 shows the trends of priorities on these main objectives at the three stages of development. The subject is of great practical importance since at present governments are spending large amounts for treatment of malnourished children in hospitals, while other less expensive alternatives are possible. [45] The subject of the cost of programs of treatment and nutritional rehabilitation has been dealt with recently by Cook. [46] Perhaps an urgent prerequisite, before embarking on promotional activities (1), may be to reduce the present economic burden of treatment of malnourished children in hospitals (3). This approach has the further advantage that it permits teaching through service and is more likely to be accepted by both the community and the professional than is a purely promotional educational program.

It is theoretically possible that once the present cost of dealing with malnourished children has been reduced to a reasonable level there would be more funds available for action on (1) and (2). To deal with (1), (2), and (3)

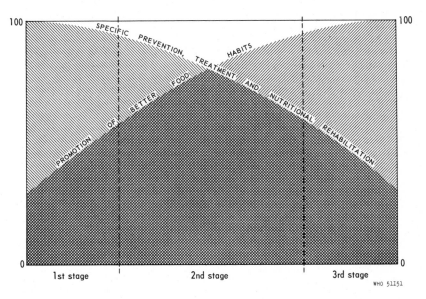

Figure 7. Desirable Trends in Activities in the Control of Malnutrition in Young Children

at the same time and with the same emphasis appears impossible in most developing countries.

In summary, although promotional activities represent the most logical and efficient approach to disease prevention, they can only become effective at a specific stage in community development. Existing demands must be met on a priority basis before the necessary level of satisfaction and trust is established that will motivate people to accept the relatively sophisticated concepts and long-range goals of health promotion. Furthermore, the very process of meeting demands for treatment and protection of the child provides the social contact and educational opportunity by which effective promotion may be achieved.

In practical terms, nutritional "first aid" is a cheap price to pay for community motivation and support, without which all other efforts are dissipated. In fact the best way to motivate the community is to demonstrate an ability to deal with people suffering now, not only with future generations. As Florio states, "The astute will give the therapy and exploit the opportunity to promote prevention." [47] At the community level I am in favor of more concentrated attacks on strategic needs and bottlenecks rather than attempting broad, indiscriminate, and dispersed coverage.

Priorities among Age Groups

Obviously the family is the target in any attempt to solve the nutritional problem in a given community. However, resolving the problem as a whole is not always sufficient to resolve its individual components. Within the family, some members are passing, nutritionally speaking, through a more critical period than others. The identification of such transitional points in the individual's life is essential in any nutrition intervention program. Fetal development is the first transitional stage in which good nutrition is a fundamental factor. The proportion of low birth weights is a good indicator of the nutritional situation in a community, which in turn may affect perinatal mortality. The second transitional stage of great risk is the weaning period. Early weaning may be acceptable when the standards of living attain a relatively high level, but this is not the case in developing countries. Breast-feeding needs to be supplemented after the fourth or fifth month. Perhaps the greatest period of risk is from the age of 4 to 5 months to 2 or 3 years. The mortality and morbidity from malnutrition—usually associated with infectious diseases—are extremely high in this age group in developing countries as compared with developed countries. As far as *nutritional rehabilitation* is concerned, children up to 7 years of age have to be considered. From the point of view of *nutri-*

tion education and the promotion of good feeding habits, schoolchildren and mothers of young children should have the highest priority.

Earlier in this paper, I asked if we are preventing death without improving life. The answer is almost certainly yes in the developing countries. I have tried to point out that this situation has arisen because in these countries we have been able to apply modern public health techniques to reduce mortality without waiting for the socioeconomic development that would of itself improve standards of living—the process that occurred in the already developed nations. We cannot be content with this situation. We must recognize a direct responsibility to the "survivors" to improve their health without waiting for major socioeconomic developments. We must recognize too that the current situation is notably without direct precedent in the history of the economic development of the already developed countries. These countries were not faced with a population of "survivors," a population which, with impaired abilities, may prove a hindrance to further socioeconomic development.

Clearly, we are confronted with a circular situation in terms of the interaction between improvement of health (rather than prevention of death) and socioeconomic development. There are points at which this cycle can be interrupted. Improvement of nutritional health is one of them. We must identify and implement those programs of direct intervention that will both improve the situation of the "survivors" and offer improved prospects for social development.

References

1. *Food and Nutrition Terminology. Definitions of Selected Terms and Expressions in Current Use.* FAO/WHO, in press.

2. American Public Health Association. *Control of Malnutrition in Man.* New York, 1960.

3. Bengoa, J. M. Priorities in public health nutrition problems. In *Proceedings of the Seventh International Congress of Nutrition, 1966,* Vol. 4. Hamburg: Wieweg, 1967, p. 811.

4. Joint FAO/WHO Expert Committee on Nutrition. *Eighth Report.* WHO Technical reprint Series No. A77, 1971.

5. Bengoa, J. M. Recent trends in public health nutrition; protein-calorie malnutrition. In *Proceedings of the Eighth International Congress on Nutrition, 1969.* Prague: Excerpta Medica International Congress Series, No. 213, 1970, p. 14.

6. Bengoa, J. M. Clinical and socio-economic aspects of PCM, presentation of the data on the prevalence of PCM. In *Protein-calorie Malnutrition*. A. von Muralt, ed. Berlin: Springer, 1969, p. 126.

7. Gomez, F., R. Ramos Galvan, S. Frank, J. C. Munoz, R. Chavez, and J. Vazquez. Mortality in second and third degree malnutrition. *J. Trop. Pediat.* 2:77, 1956.

8. Bengoa, J. M. Nutritional significance of mortality statistics. In *Proceedings of the Third Western Hemisphere Nutrition Congress,* August 30-September 2, 1971, Bal Harbour, Fla. New York: Futura, 1972, p. 270.

9. Facts on Health Progress. Scientific Publication 166. Washington, D.C.: Pan American Health Organization, 1968.

10. Gabaldon, A. Health services and socio-economic development in Latin America. *Lancet* 1:739, 1969.

11. Arriaga, E. E. and K. Davis. The pattern of mortality change in Latin America. *Demography* 6:223, 1969.

12. Bengoa, J. M. The surviving child. *Lancet,* Letter to the editor, 1:841, 1969.

13. Bengoa, J. M. Malnutrition and infectious diseases–the "surviving child." *Biotech. Bioeng. Symposium* 1:253.

14. Mata, L. J., J. J. Urrutia, and J. E. Gordon. Diarrhoeal disease in a cohort of Guatemalan village children observed from birth to age two years. *Trop. Geogr. Med.* 19:247, 1967.

15. Cravioto, J., E. R. De Licardie, and H. G. Birch. Nutrition, growth and neurointegrative development: An experimental and ecologic study. *Pediatrics,* 38, No. 2, Part II: 319, 1966.

16. Gillman, J. and T. Gillman. *Perspectives in Human Malnutrition.* New York: Grune and Stratton, 1951, p. 10.

17. Viniegra, A., R. Ramos Galvan, and C. Mariscal. Crecimiento fisico en un grupo de adolescentes del sexo femenino. *Bol. Méd. Hosp. Infantil* (Méx.) 21:105, 1964.

18. Jelliffe, D. B. The assessment of the nutritional status of the community. *WHO Monograph Series,* 53. Geneva, 1966.

19. Scroggie, A., O. Herrera, J. Santa Maria, R. Gantes, and G. Donoso. Caracteristicas del syndrome pluricarencial infantil in Chile. *Nutr. Bromatol. Toxicol.* 1:9, 1962.

20. Ronaghy, H. A., E. Kohout, and N. Hadidi. Body height and chronic malnutrition in schoolchildren in Iran. *Amer. J. Clin. Nutr.* 23:1080, 1970.

21. Cravioto, J., and E. R. De Licardie. The effect of malnutrition on the individual. This volume, pp. 3-21.

22. Villarejos, V. M., J. A. Osborne, F. J. Payne, and J. A. Arguedas. Heights and weights of children in urban and rural Costa Rica. *J. Trop. Pediat. Environ. Child Health* 17:31, 1971.

23. Nutrition in Japan. Tokyo: Ministry of Health and Welfare, 1964.

24. United Nations Research Institute for Social Development. Contents and measurement of socio-economic development: an empirical enquiry. Report No. 70.10. Geneva, 1970.

25. Bouchalova, M. and A. Gerylovova. The influence of some social and biological factors upon the growth of children from birth to five years in Brno. In *Compte rendu de la Xème réunion des équipes chargées des études sur la croissance et le développement de l'enfant normal,* 1970, Davos, Suisse. Paris: Centre International de l'Enfance, 1970.

26. Hundley, J. M., O. Mickelsen, N. Mantel, R. N. Weaver, and R. C. Taber. Height and weight of first-grade children as a potential index of nutritional status. *Amer. J. Publ. Health* 45:1454, 1955.

27. Bengoa, J. M., D. B. Jelliffe, and C. Perez. Some indicators for a broad assessment of the magnitude of protein-calorie malnutrition in young children in population groups. *Amer. J. Clin. Nutr.* 7:714, 1959.

28. Ohlin, G. An overall strategy of assistance in the field of nutrition. In *Proceedings of the 1971 Dag Hammarskjöld Seminar on Nutrition as a Priority in African Development,* July 1971. Uppsala, Sweden, in press.

29. Gordon, J. E. Ecologic interplay of man, environment and health. *Amer. J. Med. Sci.* 252:121, 1966.

30. Scrimshaw, N. S., and M. Béhar. Causes and prevention of malnutrition. In *Nutrition, a Comprehensive Treatise.* G. H. Beaton and E. W. McHenry, eds. New York: Academic Press, 1964.

31. Swedish Nutrition Foundation. *Famine: A Symposium Dealing with Nutrition and Relief Operations in Times of Disaster,* August 24-27, 1970, Saltsjöbaden, Sweden. Symposia of the Swedish Nutrition Foundation, IX. Stockholm: Almquist and Wiksell, 1971.

32. Early warning system for food shortages. Document ESCB, 1971/4. Rome: FAO, 1971.

33. Wisner, B. G. Personal communication to author.

34. Roubault, M. *Peut-on prévoir les catastrophes naturelles?* Paris: Presses Universitaires de France, 1970.

35. Nicol, B. M. Protein and calorie concentration. *Nutr. Rev.* 29:83, 1971.

36. United Nations. *International Action to Avert the Impending Protein Crisis.* Report of the Advisory Committee on the Application of Science and Technology to Development to the Economic and Social Council. New York, 1968.

37. FAO/WHO/UNICEF Protein Advisory Group. *Statements on the Nature and Magnitude of the Protein Problem and on the Specific Proposals Contained in ACAST Report* (see Ref. 36). New York: United Nations, 1971.

38. *Report of the Meeting of the Panel of Experts on the Protein Problem Confronting the Developing Countries,* May 3-7, 1971, New York. Annex to document E/5018. New York: United Nations 1971.

39. Food and Agriculture Organization of the United Nations. *Production Yearbook,* vol. 20. Rome, 1967.

40. Streeter, D. W. A geography lesson in food. *Nutr. Food Sci.,* No. 22, 1971.

41. Food and Agriculture Organization of the United Nations. *Report on World Food Congress, Washington, 1963.* Rome, 1963.

42. Food and Agriculture Organization of the United Nations. *Report on Second World Food Congress, the Hague, 1970.* Rome, 1971.

43. Bengoa, J. M. Nutritional rehabilitation programs. In *Proceedings of a Symposium on Young Child Nutrition Programs: Evaluation and Guidelines,* August 23-27, 1971, Zagreb. In press.

44. Bengoa, J. M. The prevention of malnutrition in young children. In *Proceedings of Western Hemisphere Nutrition Congress, 1965, Chicago.* Chicago: American Medical Association, 1966.

45. Bengoa, J. M. Nutrition rehabilitation centres. *J. Trop. Pediat.* 13: 169, 1967.

46. Cook, R. Is hospital the place for the treatment of malnourished children? *J. Trop. Pediat. Environ. Child Health* 17:15, 1971.

47. Florio, L. Health planning requirements in developing countries. *Publ. Health Rep.* (Wash.) 82:441, 1967.

13   The Economic Analysis of Malnutrition

Douglas Wilson
Senior Analyst
Evaluation Division
Office of Management and Budget
Washington, D.C.

Introduction

Malnutrition is recognized by many development specialists as a barrier to social and economic growth. The numerous studies that relate malnutrition to low labor productivity, increased morbidity and mortality, and poor achievement in school buttress this view. In brief, malnutrition contributes to a wasting of human resources. Reduction of this loss would increase the social effectiveness of the population and contribute to economic development. There may be a payoff, then, if nutrition is improved more rapidly than would occur through increases in earned per capita income. There is, however, considerable disagreement as to the amount of serious malnutrition, the means to combat it, and its importance relative to other development needs.

Analysis of these questions can assist the policy-maker in deciding where emphases on nutrition improvement are likely to have the biggest payoffs. The relative payoff from a particular target group such as children, mothers, or adult workers can be known only after judicious consideration of both benefits and costs. Since there are a number of target groups that can benefit substantially from nutrition improvement, the task is to determine the best approach for the public sector to take in improving nutrition. This paper explores ways to assess the magnitude of malnourishment as well as techniques to measure benefits and costs in selecting appropriate targets and remedies.

Counting the Malnourished

The number of people suffering from malnutrition may be summed in a variety of ways, including (1) those who exhibit clinical signs; (2) those who are biochemically at risk; (3) those who by some definition have "poor" diets; and (4) those who are unable to meet their food needs by spending only a certain portion of their income on food. Although these means of calculation are complementary, each measure will provide a different count of the number who are malnourished. The particular definition of malnutrition used affects the priority of the problem, the benefits expected from a program to combat it, and the means of alleviating it. For example, those who must

I have benefited greatly from the work of Mr. Dana Stevens and Mrs. Isabelle Sawhill, who studied this issue with me during the summers of 1969 and 1970. This paper does not purport to represent the views of OMB or any other government agency.

spend more than a certain portion of their income on food to gain an adequate diet form a group different from, though perhaps overlapping with, those who have clinical signs of malnutrition. The magnitude of these differences is illustrated with U.S. data in Table 1.

Attempts to relate measures of malnutrition to human performance require a number of caveats. Clinical findings provide reasonably clear-cut evidence of malnutrition, though diagnosis may be difficult and may vary with medical or nutritional training and opinion. Retarded physical growth illustrates well the problems of pinpointing malnutrition. Infection, as well as malnutrition, leads to the stunting of growth. There is some controversy about the role of genetic factors and appropriate standards of height and weight to use for each ethnic group. Also, growth retardation is usually an indicator of the incidence, not prevalence, of malnutrition and thus tells more about the past than the present. The chief disadvantage of the clinical approach is that it measures the top of the iceberg. A great deal of malnutrition is subclinical.

Biochemical findings indicate current or very recent nutritional status and may be affected by seasonal variation in available foods. These data, however, are preferable to other types of data in that they indicate what people have actually eaten rather than what is potentially available to them. Nevertheless, it is difficult to relate biochemical blood levels to levels of human performance.

Dietary information collected through surveys has the advantage of provid-

Table 1. Estimated Extent of Malnutrition in the U.S. Poverty Population, 1969

Indicator of malnutrition	Estimated % of poor persons affected	Number of persons (1969) (millions)[e]
Clinical signs[a]	Fewer than 4	Fewer than 1
Biochemically at risk[b]	38	9
With "poor" diets[c]	36	9
Unable to meet food needs without spending 50% or more of income on food[d]	44	11

a. Based on preliminary findings in the National Nutrition Survey in low-income populations of four states with respect to certain physical symptoms usually associated with primary or secondary malnutrition.
b. Based on preliminary data for the state of Texas. Indicates the number of poor with two or more biochemical values unacceptable. Texas results may not be representative of situation in other states.
c. U.S. Department of Agriculture data.
d. "Food needs" are defined as the cost of the "economy" food plan.
e. There were an estimated 24.3 million poor persons in 1969.

ing data on food sources and behavior of families with respect to the purchase, preparation, and consumption of foods; it has the shortcoming, however, of relying on recall. It also does not reveal the distribution of food within the family, and it is an imperfect indicator of nutrition, which depends upon individual needs. Also, many nutritionists feel that the failure to meet reference standards with regard to the level of food consumption is not tantamount to malnourishment. A diet can be considerably below a reference standard for one or more nutrients without necessarily indicating malnutrition for an individual or a small group. Conversely, an "adequate" diet can lead to malnutrition because not all the food available was consumed or because of the special needs of an individual.

Finally, malnutrition may be defined on the basis of the proportion of families who have to spend a certain portion of their income on food to gain an adequate diet. Such measures are purely descriptive and have no analytical meaning. This is clear insofar as the correlation between income and poor diet is far from perfect. A food balance sheet, an aggregate estimate of food availability, does not yield estimates of the number suffering from malnutrition. A positive food balance does not indicate an absence of malnutrition, although anything below a moderate surplus probably indicates that malnutrition is fairly common.

It is readily apparent to planners that none of these measures can easily be related to the number of people in a target group or to performance levels which nutritionists and physicians indicate are affected by malnutrition. Also, the descriptive data of dietary surveys, clinical examinations, and other such measures do not aid in determining what changes in human nutrition or performance will actually result from any initiation of the possible remedial programs.

Probably the primary use of such descriptive data is as a benchmark that can be compared to the administratively feasible target group. It is clearly a planning problem as to how the target group can be made coincident with the group described as suffering from malnutrition. Thus, to some degree, the nature of the remedial program is determined by the manner of estimating the number who are malnourished.

What's To Be Gained?
The investment benefits of health programs, including nutrition, flow from reductions in mortality and morbidity and a general enhancement of vitality. Low levels of health reduce the nation's effective labor supply. Premature

death and disabling diseases alter unfavorably the ratio of working population to dependents.[1] Chronic impairments due to parasites, fevers, and a lack of physical and mental vitality greatly increase the number of people needed to do a job. High mortality and morbidity rates require training men who are expected to be redundant. [1] In spite of education and on-the-job training, productivity per capita is low because of high absenteeism and short life.

Attention has been focused particularly on one effect of health programs: the unfortunate gains in population that follow a decline in mortality. It should be clear, however, that there is nothing incompatible between the goals of saving lives and reducing birth rates; the goals are at least complementary if not indeed inseparable. If births are to replace those lost by death, then conservation of the stock of lives reduces the need for additional births; thus improved health probably leads indirectly to a reduction in fertility. It is not clear to what degree better health contributes to a shortening of the lag between a fall in mortality and a fall in fertility. Lowering the death rate through health measures is generally not sufficient to generate population control. Population changes require supportive improvements in economic growth as well as improvements in health. There is little evidence that fertility rates can be reduced by direct measures in the absence of sustained economic changes. Even when there is economic growth and lower mortality, fertility rates may lag due to a failure of families to quickly adjust their behavior to changes in mortality. Harvey Leibenstein argues that although the pleasure gained from additional children falls, the increased income of the family means that more children can be afforded and the child's longer life expectancy increases his value to the family as a source of income and old age security. [2] Over time the advantages of an additional child decrease, and a decline in fertility occurs.

The specific benefits of nutrition programs include (1) a reduction in infant and child mortality; (2) an elimination of retardation due to protein malnutrition; and (3) improved learning behavior and productivity resulting from improved physical development, alertness, and reduced absenteeism due to illness. These benefits generally result from an improvement in protein and calorie intake as well as from a reduction of nutritional imbalances, such as severe deficiencies in vitamins A and B and in iron.

This description of nutrition benefits should be qualified in several ways. First, infant and child mortality is related to a number of other factors such

---

[1]The process of gaining a favorable rate is a long one, and the initial decline in mortality resulting from better health worsens the ratio.

as unsanitary water supplies, parasites, dietary mores, birth order of the child, and the age of the mother. [3] Thus, in discussing nutrition benefits, these significant interactions must be taken into account. [4]

The benefits of nutrition programs do not all occur at the same time. The social benefits of lower infant mortality come some years later: the decision to conceive fewer children, and the child's becoming employed. Other benefits are immediate, such as increases in adult labor productivity. Thus, the timing of benefits is a second factor that affects choices.

Decision-makers may be reluctant to consider differences in benefit timing when it results in a denial of resources to emaciated mothers and children. Either to entirely ignore the time at which benefits occur or to judge a health program entirely by the present value of benefits is incorrect. The present value of benefits relative to costs is by itself an incomplete criterion. The choice of a discount rate—5 percent or 15 percent—essentially implies a choice with regard to the distribution of resources between present and future generations. In a wealthy nation the use of a low discount rate implies a decision to redistribute resources toward future generations. Such decisions within a wealthy country are difficult to understand. There is no reason why the present generation should beggar itself for future generations which already promise to be richer than ourselves.

The usual economic conclusion is that, insofar as it is desirable to have more goods and services rather than less, it is difficult to justify allocating resources at a rate of return of 5 percent when projects with 15 percent return rates are available. The public role with regard to the discount rate, it is generally maintained, should be limited to meeting the demands of international trade, stabilization, and full employment. Such actions would affect the level of investment in both the public and private sectors. Externalities and complementarities accompanying investments should be accounted for in as rigorous a manner as possible and not be used as an excuse for lowering the discount rate. Lowering the discount rate for these purposes is simply arbitrary in the absence of direct measures of the value of such complementarities and externalities.

The concreteness of this counsel is deceptive. Economists are wont to put in what are essentially distributive criteria, either explicitly or implicitly. The issue in many countries, and especially less developed nations, is not only that the nation prefers more rather than less and thus should select projects favored by the opportunity cost of capital. It also concerns *what* a nation wishes to have more of in the future. This question becomes especially pertinent in developing nations, where markets are imperfect, the wealth of future generations is not at all assured, and the objective of government policy is to change the complexion of the society. I think it is highly probable that the economic dualism that characterizes developing nations will continue for several generations unless national governments adopt a conscious policy of eliminating it. The supply of capital in these countries is small relative to the number of opportunities at home and abroad for lucrative investment. Investments chosen for their lucrativeness alone generally deepen rather than broaden the capital stock. Under these circumstances, dualism can continue indefinitely.

There is then, clearly, a second criterion for investment decisions: What income classes are affected by the investment expenditure? Thus, the distribution of the benefits among income classes is generally held constant when investment decisions are based on the opportunity cost of capital. In the policy world, distributional considerations are never held constant. In fact, it is suggested here that the purpose of government intervention is to gain some degree of distributional justice.

The redistribution of income is a completely reasonable economic justification of public expenditures. Nutrition expenditures need not be rationalized solely as investments in human capital. Redistribution of income by redistributing cash, income-in-kind, or assets may be based on either the utility that the donors of transfers derive from the income of others or on their valuation of a particular income distribution in the society. An individual may desire particular levels of well-being for persons who are closely associated with him, and a particular distribution of income for society as a whole. Deriving utility from raising the income of other individuals and from the income distribution itself can lead to substantial income transfers. [5] The social question in redistribution is how should income be redistributed at minimum cost and by means deemed appropriate by the electorate. Redistribution may take the form of redistributing real assets such as land, or broadening human capital through improvements in health, literacy, and general education. Redistribution may also take the form of straight income transfers, in-kind transfers such as food donations, or reductions in the price of specified goods for beneficiaries such as health clinics, food stamps, or public housing, where the beneficiary pays only a portion of the cost.

It is clear that the investment returns to nutrition are only a partial criterion and must be considered jointly with the distributional impact of the proposed expenditure. The appropriate weighting of these criteria is a matter of judgment for policy-makers. The economist can, however, lay out the implications of the choices that confront policy people. Thus, an expenditure package may be rationally preferred that has investment benefits which occur later rather than sooner, and that is immediately redistributive toward very low income groups. A child-feeding program would be a case in point.

A third difficulty is the tendency to value all benefits in money terms. This practice is inappropriate insofar as it understates or neglects possible benefits. The contribution of women to society, for example, is difficult to assess. To rely upon some dollar value is at best arbitrary, especially given the crucial nurturing role of women in child-rearing. [6] Similarly, it is difficult to fully value the improvement in people's lives that a health program may make. The old saw about GNP falling because a man marries his housekeeper represents a very real type of bias when the decision-maker relies on the money value of benefits. Valuing all benefits in terms of existing relative prices implies an acceptance of the existing distribution of income and social institutions. Under different circumstances the relative value of benefits might be quite different and result in different public expenditure choices. For example, past levels of education, present discrimination, and a lack of mobility may adversely affect particular groups, with the result that their economic worth to society is not large. In the same situation there may be social groups which, because of the same institutional forces, are gaining significant economic rents. Thus, those benefits that are valued may be sensitive to assumptions about the reasonableness of the income distribution and social institutions. Consequently, estimates of the money value of benefits must be accepted with considerable reservation.

A caveat with regard to the effectiveness of nutrition programs is that even though severe malnutrition generally affects the poorest in any country, these people are poor for a number of reasons including lack of skills and opportunities, illiteracy, or outright discrimination. Thus, even if we can change an individual's nutrition levels, he will live in the same isolated village, indebted to the same people, with fears, beliefs, and attitudes essentially unchanged. Good nutrition will not initiate development.

Finally, benefit estimates must be based on rational models of beneficiary behavior, rather than on fulfillment of the value patterns of bureaucrats. There must be an understanding of the incentives and disincentives that a program alternative engenders. It is not sufficient to describe a nutrition need and a solution and be aware of neither the beneficiary behavior nor the supportive bureaucratic effort that the solution requires. Failure to assess either of these variables accurately can lead to gross misstatements of cost and benefits.[2]

Putting Some of the Pieces Together

A systematic framework can bring together some of the variables that are specifically needed to determine the level of benefits of nutrition programs, as distinguished from the above discussion about the occurrence of the benefits over time, the types of benefits such as reduction in mortality and morbidity, or the distribution of benefits among different income groups. A complete synthesis of these various benefit dimensions should be the final outcome, but this paper can claim only to provide a partial solution. [7]

The discussion will concentrate on a hypothetical estimation of the benefits of a nutrition program which has the objective of increasing output by augmenting the per capita productivity of the labor supply. Similar analyses could be undertaken for other classes of benefits. No claims of exclusiveness are made regarding the approach outlined here; however, it does possess the dubious strength of pointing out requirements for data and analyses which up to now have been generally neglected or overlooked in the nutrition literature.

Essential to this discussion of benefits is a means of connecting nutrition and other relevant inputs to economic outputs; that is, a production function. The purpose of a nutrition production function is to specify the relationship between the reduction of nutritional deficiencies and the enhancement of human performance and thus economic development. How is this helpful?

A production function approach takes into account three issues that the nutrition literature tends to skip over. First, it relates improvements in nutrition to improvements in human performance and output. A considerable body of literature indicates only the association between improvements in nutrition and the reduction in the level of deficiencies without indicating their social importance. Second, a production function can theoretically relate nutrition and other coincident inputs to levels of output. What difference does this make? Assume at the extreme that laborers are using extremely primitive methods of production. An improvement in nutrition would

---

[2]John E. Brandl, 1967, On budget allocations in government agencies, *Rev. of Social Economy* 25:29-46, argues another aspect of this view. He suggests that the failure to take account of the preferences of bureaucrats is a major source of misunderstanding by economists of public decision-making. What I am suggesting is that the incentive for bureaucrats is toward action and "doing good things," and that in this competition for short-term success the behavior requirements of the bureaucracy and the beneficiaries are unfortunately ignored.

increase output modestly and perhaps insignificantly, because the more energetic laborers were using very few tools.[3] On the other hand, if adequate equipment was available, an improvement in nutrition might lead to a rather significant increase in output through more dexterous and ingenious use of the equipment. Finally, the nutrition literature is generally silent about increases in output that result from increments in other variables which are coincident with nutrition levels in the output process. Improvements in the kinds of seeds farmers planted might lead to a greater increase in output than would an increase in diligence alone.

A production function, which highlights these problems and frames them in a rational manner, has among its desirable features the ability to indicate (1) equivalent increases in output among alternative combinations of inputs; and (2) the magnitude of marginal gains in output resulting from additional amounts of a resource.

The impact of nutrition on output is diagrammed in Figure 1. Algebraically it may be described as $Q = AL^l K^k$, where

Q = output

A = a conversion coefficient that relates labor-capital units to gross income

L = the amount of labor

K = the amount of capital

l = the percent increase in output per 1 percent increase in labor; the elasticity of output with regard to labor

k = the percentage increase in output per 1 percent increase in capital; the elasticity of output with regard to capital.

If there are constant returns to scale, l and k will sum to unity; increasing returns will sum to greater than unity; decreasing returns to less than unity.

At this stage the function can be used only for illustrative purposes. Assume the following specific function:

$$Q = (10) L^{0.5} K^{0.5}.$$

[3] A historical example may make this point clear. Henry Mayhew, in *London Labour and the London Poor,* published in 1861, sketched the working day of laborers on the London docks. Some of the workers turned cranks of winches, others pushed hand trucks back and forth, and still others spent an eight-hour shift in crews of a half dozen or so working an enormous casklike treadwheel that powered a cargo crane making 40 lifts an hour from the ship's hold. Stamping in time, and occasionally singing together as the day wore on, the men had delivered by the end of the day *less than the equivalent of one kilowatt-hour of mechanical energy apiece* (emphasis added); cited in Eugene S. Ferguson, The measurement of the "man-day," *Scientific American* (October 1971), p. 101.

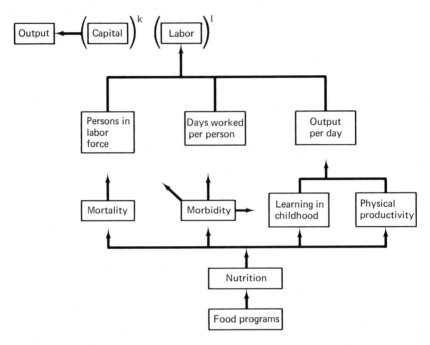

Figure 1. Schematic Representation of Food Program as an Investment in Human Capital

In the equation, assume that output is $40 billion gross value added,[4] the labor force is 200 million, and the capital stock is equal to $80 billion with an average capital-output ratio of 2.00, a not unusual ratio for developing countries. [8]

This discussion ignores the real-world problem of evaluating the increase in effective labor force resulting from budget expenditures on nutrition ($E \, dp'/dh$). The question is nevertheless real as to just how much nutrition can be expected to improve the productivity of the labor force. In the particular example, nutrition would have to increase the effective labor force by 2 percent to raise the gross value by 1 percent [(.02)(0.5) = (.01)] or $400 million ($Q$ = $40 billion). The importance of factor proportions can be seen in this

[4]The output to which improvements in nutrition are related should be appropriate ones, not necessarily increases in national income. Nutritional effects on education can be related to the number of graduates of a certain level, which in turn might be related through a second production function to improvements in national income. Nutritional effects on infant and child morbidity and mortality can be related to declines in future fertility. Also, the production function need not (and probably should not) be as aggregative.

example. If the elasticity coefficients were .67 and .33 for labor and capital, respectively, the increase in effective labor supply would have to be 1.5 percent rather than 2 percent. Clearly the impact of nutrition on output is affected by the elasticities of labor and capital employed in the economy.

The effectiveness of nutrition programs depends not only on the relationship of nutrition to improvements in physical productivity and reductions in absenteeism, but also to other behavioral values, such as the increased amount of food consumed out of additional income and the improvement in dietary quality resulting from an increase in consumption. These factors are, in addition to those already mentioned, the improvement in health (dp/dh), and the elasticity of output with regard to labor (l). Although it is not the purpose of this paper to examine nutrition alternatives per se, it is clear that the effectiveness of many of them can be examined by a single means.

In general the efficiency with which a given expenditure on food assistance is transformed into an improvement in dietary quality depends on the associated changes in four variables: (1) the number of low income individuals participating in the program; (2) the increase in real resources (food or income subsidy) available to each participant; (3) the increase in food consumption induced by these additional resources above the preprogram level; and (4) the improvement in dietary quality following an increase in food consumption. The failure of any one of these links in the chain to operate will reduce the effectiveness of a program.

More explicitly, consider the following identity:

$$N(df) = N(dy) \, (dc/dy) \, (dq/dc), \text{ where}$$

N = number of low income individuals at risk

q = the proportion of households with "poor" diets

y = family income

c = level of food consumption

dq = estimated percentage point change in the proportion of at risk individuals with "poor" diets

$N(df)$ = the expected number of low income individuals who move from a "poor" diet to a "fair" diet for any particular alternative[5]

dy = change in the real income of each participant

---

[5]"Poor" and "fair" diets are left undefined here, but nutritionists in different countries should have no particular trouble in putting together useful definitions, if they do not already exist.

dc = change in participant food consumption associated with the change in real income (measured in money value of food)

$(-)dq/dc$ = expected percentage point change in "poor" diets per dollar of additional consumption

This identity shows that food assistance programs can be studied as the interaction of several program variables. If the per capita subsidy value of the program is known, the consumption response can be predicted and related to an improvement in nutrition. By studying the expected value of each component variable for each food assistance program, differences in the effectiveness can be isolated.

Alternatives put forth to improve nutrition many times have the common characteristic of being equivalent to increases in real income. Alternatives generally considered for reducing malnutrition include (1) government sponsored or subsidized production and distribution of low-cost nutritious foods; (2) alteration of the price structure of foods in order to bring about an improvement in diet; (3) direct feeding programs in kindergartens, community health centers, and schools; and (4) nutritional fortification of staples, such as processed wheat and corn products.

Except for fortification, the above alternatives may substantially increase the income of the beneficiary.[6] How are nutrition improvement programs equivalent to an increase in real income? Assume that a family spends $200 per year on food, has an income of $300, and receives $50 per year in food supplements of some kind. Also assume that the family consumes $0.60 of each additional dollar of income as food. The food supplement allows the family, pressed on all sides to meet its needs, to substitute the $50 worth of food supplements for its own meager resources. In short, $50 of income is freed for redistribution toward other needs. The worth of food added to the family's diet as a result of the supplementation is not $50 but $30 ($50 X 0.6).

In addition to estimating the increased consumption induced by each food assistance program, it is necessary to determine the increase in dietary quality

[6]It should be noted that alternatives affecting relative prices of foods not only affect the level of income but tend to be poorly targeted, in that those who are less in need usually are the ones affected. For example, assume that a consumption tax is placed on polished rice. If the item is price elastic, then there will be less consumption. But if the main consumers of polished rice are those who consider themselves well enough off to consume polished rice, then they may well be better nourished than those with less income. That is, the amount of food eaten may compensate for the lack of nutrients in polished rice. Thus, programs of price discrimination are fairly inefficient in that they do not distinguish between benefits conferred on the rich and the poor.

associated with the consumption increase.[7] Household nutrition survey data may be used to estimate the elasticity of dietary quality with respect to the money value of food consumed. This elasticity measures the percentage change in the proportion of an income class with poor diets associated with the pecentage change in the dollar value of food consumed for a standardized household size and education level. The elasticity of dietary quality with respect to consumption quantity E_{qc} can be arithmetically rearranged to equal dq/dc, which equals the expected percentage point change in "poor" diets per dollar of additional consumption.[8] The precise level of dq/dc is a function of the behavior of beneficiaries and the alternative used to improve nutrition. A fortification program or low-cost nutritious food can be expected to increase dietary quality perhaps more rapidly than some other alternatives.

The nutritional effectiveness of a program may be determined by employing the identity described above, without an estimate of the economic impact of the improvement in nutrition. Practical application may require such a procedure. The following illustration, however, will use the hypothetical production function described earlier as well as the identity $[N(df) = N(dy) (dc/dy) (dq/dc)]$. Assume that the target group is 100 million members of the labor force, all of whom have "poor" diets; N = 100 million. A nutrition program is initiated that is equivalent to an increase in income of $5; dy = $5. The additional food consumed is equivalent to $3; dc/dy = 0.6. The percentage point decrease in "poor" diets per dollar increase in the value of food consumed is 2; dq/dc = 2. This means that if per capita food consumption were raised by $25.00, there would be a 50-percent point decline in "poor" diets. To put it another way, if a nutrition program induced increased food consumption of $25.00 there would be a 50-percent chance that the beneficiary would move from a "poor" diet to a "fair" diet. The exact value of dq/dc is a problem that nutrition planners must determine statistically. Those workers who move from a "poor" to a "fair" diet increase their output by 25 percent; dp/dh = 0.25. The actual increase in performance that can be expected from dietary improvement is largely unknown to nutritionists. The elasticity of output with regard to an increase in effective labor supply is 0.5, a quantity taken directly from the production function discussed earlier. The number of indi-

---

[7]A third effect which may be important in developing nations is the increasing proportion of food consumption dollars which go toward the cost of packaging and transportation as income increases and more food is purchased rather than produced at home.
[8]$E_{qc} = [dq/q \cdot dc/c]$; $dq/dc = [E_{qc} \cdot q/c]$

viduals who move from a poor diet to a fair diet is

(1) $N(dy) (dc/dy) (dq/dc) = N(df)$
(1a) 100 million ($5) (0.6) (2) = 6 million

The increase in effective labor is

(2) $N(df) (dp'/dh) = \Delta L$
(2a) 6 million (0.25) = 1.5 million

The increase in output is[9]

$$(3) \qquad Q \left[\frac{N(df) \dfrac{dp'}{dh}}{L} \right] l = dQ$$

$$(3a) \qquad 40 \left[\frac{(6 \text{ million}) (0.25)}{200 \text{ million}} \right] 0.5 = \$150 \text{ million}$$

Clearly the crucial estimates are the increase in effective labor supply resulting from the improvement in nutrition (dp'/dh), and dq/dc, the percentage
point decrease in poor diets per dollar of increase in consumption. The latter
is a function of technical possibilities and social organization.

The total effectiveness of the program should not be measured by a ratio of
benefits to costs. Distributive effects should also be assessed. In this case the
analysis should focus on choosing those programs which are most efficient in
reaching their target populations. If the decision-maker is most concerned
about relieving malnutrition for reasons of equity, then measures of the efficiency with which the target is reached become most important.[10]

[9]The change in output due to an increase in effective labor supply can also be estimated
in the following way:

$dQ = 2Q/2L \; \Delta L$

For the particular production function used here,

$2Q/2L = \beta A L^{\beta-1} K^{1-\beta}$ substituting: $dQ = (\beta A L^{\beta-1} K^{1-\beta}) \Delta L$.

The results from the differential and the elasticity are equivalent.
[10] It should be noted that an optimal nutrition plan may need to use more than a single
program or activity. This is particularly true in those cases where there are absolute con-

Looking Back
This paper has analyzed some of the data required to select targets for nutrition programs and to make decisions on their effectiveness. Nutrition survey data are required to determine the size of a potential target group as well as to facilitate an estimate of the change in the quality of diet that can be expected from increases in food consumption. Estimates of the additional food consumed out of additional income are necessary as well as estimates of the elasticity of output (national income, number of graduates, etc.) with regard to the input. Estimates are needed of the impact that improvements in nutrition have on the economic and social performance of the target population, dp'/dh.

The provision of these data will require generally more sophisticated research designs and social experiments than have been used previously.[11] The final choice among specific target groups and programs, however, is determined in part by benefit weights and the constraints under which the government is working, particularly resource limitations that determine shadow prices.

---

straints on the level of inputs. Such constraints are commonplace in developing countries. Among the constraints that a nutrition planner may face are budget constraints, limitations on fortification facilities, limitations on population that can be served by a particular program, regional concerns, capacity of local bureaucracies for administering the program, etc. More general constraints that can be binding are foreign exchange availability and balance of payments problems. In these cases a number of programs may need to be undertaken. The programs selected will depend on the relative shadow prices of the constrained inputs. Where there are multiple constraints the problem for the planner is to determine the shadow or accounting price for each constrained resource which equals the value of incrementally expanding the nutritional program or process. The shadow prices, then, may be used to determine the optimal level or mix of nutrition programs. The shadow prices will depend upon the ratios of the available resources. Generally speaking, where there are constant returns to scale, the number of programs required for the optimal nutrition program will not exceed the number of inputs in limited supply. To put it alternatively, if a health ministry is using 10 different nutrition programs and there are only 5 constraints, net benefits or effectiveness can be increased by reducing the number of programs to 5. Thus, the reader should be cautious about inferring that an optimal nutrition program can be derived by simply arranging available budgets to accommodate those programs with the maximum net benefits. For a discussion of this problem with regard to health programs see Martin Feldstein, Health planning in developing countries, *Economica* (1970), pp. 139-163. Further discussion of shadow prices is in I. M. D. Little and James Mirrees, *Manual of Industrial Project Analysis in Developing Countries, 2* (Paris: OECD, 1969), chap. 2. See also Robert Dorfman, Mathematical or "linear" programming, *Amer. Econ. Rev.* pp. 797-825, 1953.
[11] An advantage of a social experiment, beyond the fact that highly specific data can be collected, is that a great deal is learned about the administrative problems of delivering various nutrition program alternatives, as well as the biases of data routinely collected by statistical agencies.

References

1. For a discussion of this point see: Perlman, Mark. Some economic aspects of public health programs in underdeveloped areas. In *The Economics of Health and Medical Care.* Ann Arbor: University of Michigan Press, 1964, p. 295.

2. Leibenstein, Harvey, *Economic Backwardness and Economic Growth.* New York: Wiley, 1957, p. 161.

3. For a complete discussion of the role of nutrition in pregnancy see *Maternal Nutrition and the Course of Pregnancy* (National Academy of Sciences, Washington, D.C.: G.P.O., 1970). See also Jelliffe, D. B. *Infant Nutrition in the Subtropics.* Monograph Ser. No. 29. Geneva: World Health Organization, 1955.

4. For a discussion of the possible interactions see Scrimshaw, Nevin S. Ecologic factors determining nutritional state and food use. In *Alternatives for Balancing World Food Production and Needs.* Ames: Iowa State University Press, 1967. From a *realpolitik* view this is important in that joint ventures enable administrators to tap into other budget accounts and gain bureaucratic leverage.

5. For a discussion of these points see Thurow, Lester C. The income distribution as a pure public good. *Quart. J. Econ.* 85:327, 1971.

6. For a discussion of the importance of early childhood in societal development see Hagen, Everett E. *On the Theory of Social Change.* Homewood, Ill.: Dorsey, 1962.

7. For a discussion of a completely systematic examination of health sector planning see Feldstein, Martin S. Health sector planning in developing countries. *Economica* 37:139, 1970.

8. For a discussion of Cobb-Douglas production functions applied to India see Murti, V. M., and V. K. Sastry. Production functions for Indian industry. *Econometrica* 25:205, 1957. For an example of a Cobb-Douglas production function applied to agriculture data see Tintner, G., and O. H. Brownlee. Production functions derived from farm records. *J. Farm Econ.* 26:566, 1944. For an example of a production function approach to estimating the payoff from education see Niitamo, O. The development of productivity in Finnish industry, 1925-1952. *Productivity Measurement Rev.* No. 15:1-12, 1958.

14 The Importance of
Accurate Measures
of Malnutrition

Moisés Béhar
Director, Instituto de Nutrición de Centro
America y Panama, Guatemala City

Dr. Bengoa stressed in his paper—I believe very rightly so—the need of an
indicator that can be of practical value in assessing the extent of the problem
of protein-calorie malnutrition (PCM) in a community.

In the preindustrialized areas of the world, evidence obtained through dietary, biochemical, clinical, and anthropometrical studies, as well as from the
analysis of morbidity and mortality data, indicates that the prevalence of
PCM in all of its different forms and degrees is greater than would be suspected by nonspecialized persons on the basis of the occurrence of the severe
forms, kwashiorkor and marasmus. The above-mentioned studies are complicated, expensive, and time-consuming; furthermore, the information that
they provide is difficult for nonspecialists to interpret. Therefore, it would
be extremely useful to have indicators that are easily obtainable and that are
sufficiently specific and sensitive to be used in determining the magnitude of
the problem, both for diagnostic and for program evaluation purposes.

One of the reasons why malnutrition has not received sufficient attention by
policy-makers at a national level in many countries is that its real magnitude
is frequently unknown or underestimated. As of the last few years, great
efforts are being made in the planning of health programs, but even health
planners have been unable to give malnutrition its proper place among health
problems, partly because of the difficulties in estimating its real magnitude.

Only under situations of acute hunger, as have recently occurred in Biafra
and India, do health authorities and the entire society recognize malnutrition
as a problem. It would be extremely useful to demonstrate that under "normal" conditions of life more than half the population of a country has suffered or is suffering from some degree of malnutrition. [1] For this purpose,
indicators like the one suggested by Dr. Bengoa can be useful.

Responsible persons in underdeveloped countries, frequently even health
personnel, have accepted some characteristics of the population like small
body size, lack of initiative and ambition, and low work efficiency as genetic
characteristics, although available scientific information suggests that these
are more frequently the result of environmental factors, among which malnutrition is usually one of the most important. For this reason, it would also be
very useful to demonstrate a correlation between anthropometric indicators—like the one suggested by Dr. Bengoa—and functional parameters of
the subjects such as resistance to infection, psychological behavior, or learn-

ing capability, even if this correlation does not necessarily prove a direct causal relationship with malnutrition, but rather the influence of the total environment.

There are, of course, limitations in an indicator like body size, which were briefly analyzed by Dr. Wilson, but we should keep in mind that an indicator is not necessarily a direct measurement of the phenomenon but only a practical way of evaluating its magnitude.

In regard to the intervention programs for the control of PCM, we agree with the epidemiological approach recommended by Dr. Bengoa. Through this approach, it will also be possible to select population groups, either in terms of socioeconomic condition or in respect to age, which are more vulnerable and in greater need of attention. This is particularly true for the implementation of measures within the secondary or tertiary level of prevention, such as treatment, nutrition rehabilitation, supplementary feeding, or nutrition education.

In relation to the age groups that should receive greater attention, it is interesting to observe how the situation has changed as more and better information on the effects of malnutrition has been obtained. Until about twenty years ago, supplementary feeding and nutrition education programs were organized mainly for schoolchildren, probably because this group was easier to reach. However, experimental studies revealed that the small size of school-age children cannot be modified significantly by supplementary feeding. [2] Furthermore, the severe cases of protein-calorie malnutrition, mainly kwashiorkor, occurring predominantly between the second and fourth years of life, received great international attention. [3,4] On the basis of these and other related observations, emphasis was progressively and correctly moved from the school-age to the preschool-age child. It was also observed that in the more primitive communities where prolonged breast-feeding (usually over one year of age) is still a common practice, cases of severe PCM, particularly kwashiorkor, were seldom seen before the age of 1 year. For these reasons, the group of children from 1 to 4 years old was identified as the one at greater risk and was therefore granted the highest priority in applied programs. Later on, however, it was observed that even in those communities where prolonged breast-feeding is a common practice, the growth of children was not satisfactory as of the fourth to sixth month of age. Morbidity and mortality statistics also indicated a great risk for children during the second half of their first year of life and during their second year, decreasing rapidly thereafter. [5] In addition, because of its dramatic quality and probably also its exotic name, kwashiorkor initially received more attention, but later on the importance of marasmus and other severe types of PCM occurring before the first year of life was recognized in population groups undergoing cultural transition, where weaning takes place earlier, and often improperly. [6] It was then realized that all children under 5 years of age, including those under one year, would have to be considered.

More recently, interest has progressively been focused on the possibilities of permanent damage in young children's mental development caused by malnutrition both before and in the 6 months after birth. [7,8] So far, available evidence on the effect of the mother's nutrition on the newborn has been contradictory or inconclusive. [9] On a carefully controlled longitudinal study, now under way in Guatemala, information thus far obtained suggests a good association between caloric intake of mothers during pregnancy (estimated by dietary surveys) and the weight of their newborns. [10] Furthermore, preliminary data suggest that it is possible to correct the low birth weight, so frequent in these babies, by correcting the inadequate dietary intake of their mothers with supplementary feeding during pregnancy. [11] Babies with low birth weight are at a much greater risk of early death, as was recently confirmed by INCAP studies. [12]

All this information indicates the need for directing greater attention to pregnant and lactating mothers, and to children during their first months of life in any applied nutrition program. It seems, therefore, that high priority should be given to the development of a very strong program on maternal and child health within the health plans of the developing countries; not only family planning but also nutrition should be among its fundamental components.

Recent observations in Central America support Dr. Bengoa's contention that activities at the level of secondary and tertiary prevention, particularly those actions which are under the direct responsibility of health agencies, can reduce the incidence of severe and advanced cases without modifying substantially the prevalence of mild or moderate cases. These last forms, although clinically not very dramatic, can be of greater public health significance because they are more prevalent, and especially if their association with functional damage is further documented. The control of these forms requires a strong coordinated program at the level of primary prevention, which should correct the basic and interrelated problems of insufficient and inadequate supply of foods, low purchasing power, and low educational level. This can be done only through coordinated multisectoral programs, properly oriented by

a national food and nutrition policy and constituting an important component of the national development plan.

In order to convince the planners and the policy-makers of the need and
feasibility of this last approach, efforts are being made to sell the idea on an
economic basis, that is, to demonstrate that the expenses involved in measures of direct nutritional benefits are a good investment. Dr. Wilson indicated the complexity of this approach and the difficulty in obtaining the
basic information required. Still, I believe that it is possible to obtain a reasonably good estimate of the immediate economic losses due to malnutrition
in a given community by calculating, among other items, the expenses in-
curred in the treatment of cases, and the losses due to absenteeism of workers
because of diseases related to malnutrition, as well as those resulting from
reduced work performance. However, these immediate losses are probably
much lower than those stemming from early malnutrition. The effects of
malnutrition during the intrauterine period and in the course of the first few
years of life, in terms of lower learning capacity and inefficient integration of
the labor force in a technological society, are much more difficult to estimate
in economic terms; furthermore, they appear after a time lag of at least 10 to
20 years. This is, of course, a serious limitation to planners or to politicians
interested in investments with a more immediate return. Therefore, the improvement of these fundamental programs is postponed, and the gap between
the developed and the underdeveloped societies increases.

I agree that, for effectiveness, any intervention program to control malnutrition has to be an ambitious one, which may even require significant
changes in the socioeconomic and political structure of the country. Therefore, very careful planning is fundamental.

Some countries and international agencies interested in the field are already
working in this direction. In my opinion, the efforts for socioeconomic development in the last decade have demonstrated that greater attention to
human resources and improvement of the quality of life of the total population of the country is needed. This is not only the final objective of development but also a mechanism for achieving a real and harmonious socioeconomic development, not just economic growth.

I fully appreciate, therefore, the interest in and efforts toward utilizing a
more strict planning methodology, for which I am sure this conference will
be of great value. Still, I think that in planning the control of malnutrition we
should not completely forget the humanitarian aspects. Unfortunately for us
who are interested in nutrition, there is very little probability that a highly

influential or policy-making citizen will go to bed hungry or will have a child dying from kwashiorkor or marasmus, as is happening every day to thousands of people in large areas of the world. If that were the case I am sure that, in addition to the "rational" economic approach to the prevention of malnutrition, a higher social and humanitarian consciousness would be awakened.

References

1. Béhar, M. Prevalence of malnutrition among preschool children. In *Malnutrition, Learning, and Behavior*. N. S. Scrimshaw and J. E. Gordon, eds., Cambridge, Mass.: MIT Press, 168, p. 30.

2. Scrimshaw, N. S., and M. A. Guzmán. The effect of dietary supplementation and the administration of vitamin B_{12} and aureomycin on the growth of school children. In *Current Research on Vitamins in Trophology*. Nutrition Symposium Series No. 7. New York: National Vitamin Foundation, 1953, p. 101.

3. Brock, J. F., and M. Autret. *Kwashiorkor in Africa*. FAO Nutritional Studies No. 8. Rome: FAO, 1952.

4. Autret, M., and M. Béhar. *Síndrome Policarencial Infantil (Kwashiorkor) and its Prevention in Central America*. FAO Nutritional Studies No. 13. Rome: FAO, 1954.

5. Gordon, J. E., J. B. Wyon, and W. Ascoli. The second year death rate in less developed countries. *Amer. J. Med. Sci.* 254:357, 1967.

6. McLaren, D. S. A fresh look at protein-calorie malnutrition. *Lancet* 2:485, 1966.

7. Scrimshaw, N. S., and J. E. Gordon. *Malnutrition, Learning, and Behavior*. Cambridge, Mass: MIT Press, 1968.

8. Winick, M. Cellular growth in intrauterine malnutrition. *Ped. Clin. North America* 17:69, 1970.

9. Bergner, L. and M. W. Susser. Low birth weight and prenatal nutrition, An interpretative review. *Pediatrics* 46:946, 1970.

10. Lechtig, A., J. P. Habicht, E. de León, G. Guzmán, and M. Flores. Influencia de la nutrición materna sobre el crecimiento fetal en poblaciones rurales de Guatemala. I. Aspectos dietéticos. *Arch. Latinoamer. Nutr.* In press.

11. Lechtig, A., J. P. Habicht, E. de León, and G. Guzmán. Influencia de la nutrición materna sobre el crecimiento fetal en poblaciones rurales de Guatemala. II. Suplementación alimentaria. *Arch. Latioamer. Nutr.* 22:117, 1972.

12. Mata, L. J. *Nutrition and Infection*. Protein Advisory Group Bulletin No. 11. Geneva, 1971.

15 Nutrition and Agriculture

P. Mahadevan
Animal Production Service
FAO, Rome

Dr. Bengoa has approached the diagnosis of food and nutrition problems and the establishment of priorities from the viewpoint of a health-oriented nutritionist, while Dr. Wilson has viewed this topic as an economist interested in the effects of nutrition on human productivity. For my part, I would like to discuss the subject from the standpoint of an agriculturist concerned with nutrition.

The first question that comes to mind concerns the present balance sheet on the satisfaction of human food and nutritional needs. There is no doubt that man's food supply has expanded several hundredfold since the revolutionary change in his role from hunter and gatherer to tiller and herdsman. Technological advances in mechanization, irrigation, fertilization, and the chemical control of weeds, diseases, and insects have increased the earth's capacity for sustaining human populations. But, although the threat of famine has been more or less staved off for the time being, two-thirds of mankind are still hungry and malnourished. This means that food production is not improving at a fast enough rate, particularly in the developing countries, to offer an early solution to prevailing human nutrition problems.

The nutritionist viewing this situation has quite understandably drawn the conclusion that the stage has not yet been reached in food production that would permit establishing large-scale preventive programs directed against the major nutritional problems of the world. The result is that nutritional problems in the developing countries continue to be dealt with, for the most part, through treatment of malnutrition when it is diagnosed, through associated efforts at nutritional rehabilitation, and by concentration of effort on the child-mother complex.

This may be an oversimplification of the true situation, particularly in the light of Dr. Bengoa's reference to three possible types of intervention by the nutritionist in dealing with malnutrition: (1) action on the environment, both physical and social; (2) action aimed at improving the quantity and/or quality of food reaching the market; and (3) action aimed at promoting better food habits and providing specific protection for mothers and young children, as well as treatment and nutritional rehabilitation. It is principally the third type of intervention that has hitherto formed the basis on which governments have dealt with nutrition problems in most developing countries.

How can earlier interventions be encouraged? Securing up-to-date information on food availability, food consumption, and the nutritional status of different sectors of the population in each country would help, but this information will not in itself overcome the problem. The solution, as I see it, has to come primarily from the sector that formulates the development plans of each country. If nutritional considerations are to be an integral part of the food policy and planning process, then economic planners need to be persuaded, first and foremost, to accept the fact that increased food production programs without consideration of nutritional consequences are really of little value. The planning function requires the participation of specialists from a number of disciplines to ensure efficient utilization of all available resources. Only then can the necessary major changes be introduced that would permit the implementation of the first and second types of intervention referred to by Dr. Bengoa.

Let me offer an example to illustrate my point. If appropriate action is to be taken to improve not only the quantity but also the quality of food reaching the market, the available resources need to be reallocated. Today, research on high-yielding varieties of cereals has the lion's share of investments in agricultural research. By contrast, the only grain legume research that has received investments of any magnitude is that carried out in relation to the soyabean; and the soyabean has amply demonstrated the potential of a leguminous crop to respond to investments in breeding, selection, and management. Recent grain legume research at the University of the West Indies has shown that the pigeon pea, *Cajanus cajan,* can also be developed as a major source of protein for human consumption. What we did in the West Indies was to use photoperiod response to alter plant habits in such a way as to allow greatly increased plant population densities, a much reduced time before cropping, and the introduction of a new cropping system. The opportunity was thus provided for large-scale production—in place of backyard production—of an important tropical legume, the pigeon pea. Yet, despite such demonstrations of substantially increased productivity, investments in grain legume research in developing countries continue to be meager. The lack of liaison between economic planners and those concerned with food and nutrition thus becomes obvious. It is heartening, however, to note in this connection that the FAO/WHO/UNICEF Protein Advisory Group has recently urged that legumes be given special emphasis in future efforts to improve plant production: it is to be hoped that this will trickle down to the level of economic planners.

I have used relative investments in cereal and legume research only by way of example. The overall allocation of priorities would need to be made on the basis of balance, feasibility and constraints, and availability of resources. That a clear, universally accepted definition of priorities does not exist is therefore not surprising. Be that as it may, it is the duty of each country to set out priorities not only to match resources but also to achieve maximum impact in areas in which resources can be used most effectively. Dr. Wilson has drawn our attention to the Cobb-Douglas function and illustrated in Figure 1 of his paper (p. 138) the impact of nutrition on total economic output. That is one way of looking at the problem of priorities. Another way is to examine critically the food and agricultural situation and prospects for each country, with a view to identifying priorities for agricultural development, because it is here that the long-range solutions lie. By constructing quantitative economic models, it should be possible to establish the relative economic potential of alternative crop and animal enterprises to satisfy human food and nutritional needs within the framework of overall agricultural resource use. It may be noted here that there are vast areas of the world which man cannot harvest except through the intermediary of the grazing animal. Once relative economic potentials are determined, assistance can be given in defining more specific priorities relating to one or another of the chosen crop and/or livestock enterprises. It should also be possible to examine the response of the agricultural economy to price and other market factors. Such an approach would assist in identifying what needs to be done with regard to farm management problems, market prospects, agricultural policy, and technical (or scientific) research. I would, however, underline once again the multidisciplinary nature of the exercise that needs to be undertaken.

Finally, I would like to consider the question of priorities relating to nutritional intervention programs that are aimed at improving the social environment. Dr. Bengoa has drawn attention to the necessity, in many circumstances, of achieving profound changes in the behavior of society if nutritional problems are to be effectively resolved. Nutrition education programs have been introduced in many countries with this objective in mind. These have included mass nutrition education, school feeding programs, school gardens, and other related activities. Faculties of agriculture and other institutions have also been encouraged to incorporate nutrition and food economics into their curricula. Additionally, some effort is now being made to train high-level policy-making staff, and to a more limited extent professional level staff responsible for planning and supervision in ministries of agriculture and planning units, in the field of nutrition.

All of these activities are well worth undertaking, but the question that I would pose is where priority attention needs to be directed in nutrition education. If we employ as our criterion of priority what action occurs at the community level, there is little doubt that the more prestigious and more expensive formal education should receive a lower priority than nonformal education with its wider learning clienteles. Unfortunately, nonformal education has to assume so many forms and has to serve so many different clienteles that it almost defies definition, systematic planning, or integration into a total educational strategy. As Phillip Coombs said in another context, "little is really known about how to design or operate effective nonformal educational programs; its considerable body of experience, based largely on enthusiasm and dedication, has not been systematically examined by researchers." Yet, a massive effort in nonformal education must be made in this second development decade, else nutritional and agricultural development will suffer.

In the final analysis, the success of our efforts in alleviating human food and nutrition problems will depend on the focus and stimulus that can be provided for a fundamental reappraisal of existing agricultural and nutritional programs, and on a reallocation of resources on the basis of agreed priorities.

16 **Problems in Nutrition Diagnosis and Planning**   F. T. Sai
Director of Medical Services,
Accra, Ghana

The problems of nutrition are perhaps the most serious of the human problems facing the developing countries today. It is no exaggeration to say that there is no direct historical precedent for the complex issues raised. When the now more developed countries were at a comparable level of development, and their nutrition problems were serious, there were no powerful medicines to cut down infections and thereby help to maintain life, even at the cost of full development. Modern hospitals and therapeutic systems for treatment were not developed. Now we have what may be described as "primitive level" nutrition problems existing side by side with twentieth-century health practices which (apart from the humanitarian good they do) help to magnify and complicate the problem. By maintaining an "army" of mere survivors, the population growth rate is increased manyfold, and history has no lessons to teach as to how to cope.

Diagnosis of community food and nutrition problems can be undertaken in many ways, some of which have quite rightly been considered indirect. The food production and supply situation in a country can be a satisfactory indicator of its overall nutrition potential, but no more. When exports and imports are included, a more complete picture may emerge. Knowing that a country produces large amounts of oilseeds is useful only when the quantity used directly as human food within the country is also known. Of course, within-country distribution and transportation problems may make deductions from production quite invalid. However, production figures are invaluable in the planning of remedial measures, and efforts to get really adequate production statistics should be intensified.

Fluctuations in production and supply, especially if predictable, are valuable for making a timely attack on emergency situations such as famines following floods, rain failure, or locusts. Predictions of adverse climatic changes may be very useful in diagnosing nutrition catastrophes ahead of their actual occurrence, and thus help to mobilize resources on a national or international scale. Fortunately, throughout the world, famines are given the highest possible priority rating, but all too frequently action is unnecessarily delayed. Such catastrophes do deserve the priority accorded to them, both because of the suffering they produce and the opportunity they afford for better long-term nutrition planning.

With the increasing use of money, another indirect measure of the magnitude of the nutrition problem is the amount of money an individual family spends on food in relation to what is estimated to provide an adequate diet. In the fast-growing towns of the developing countries, the concept of the minimum adequate diet or the "Poverty Datum Line" is a good one, since it can be used to determine the percentage of families likely to be at risk in terms of nutrition. Such families can then be identified for special attention. It must be stressed that new townsmen and their families form a special risk group since they are unused to the harsh budgetary realities of town life and unaware of the services available.

As with all health problems, the more direct the diagnostic criteria, the better. However, making community surveys in an effort to appreciate the magnitude of nutritional problems is particularly difficult. First, the majority of the countries involved are not able to afford the manpower required for extensive surveys. Second, the funds, equipment, and transportation needed are short. Finally, and most important, there are still no universally acceptable diagnostic criteria for the major nutrition problems facing the developing countries—namely, protein-calorie malnutrition (PCM) and its complications.

It is right that PCM should be considered priority number one since it satisfies most of the criteria that a public health problem should to be accorded high priority in health planning. In numerical terms, it attacks more people than any other disease in most of the countries involved. Black Africa, with an estimated population of 250 million, has a 0-5 years population of 50 million (20 percent). At a conservative prevalence rate of 5 percent, 2.5 million children have various degrees of overt PCM at any given time. Given a very conservative death rate of 10 percent, this would amount to some 250,000 deaths from this one disease alone. Thus the load of morbidity and mortality that PCM throws on African countries is immense. Resources have to be spent on treating those that get to hospital, at most a very small fraction of the total. In Accra we have been treating about 500 per year in one hospital. Each child spent an average of three weeks in hospital at about $10 per day; a total of some $105,000. The amount spent on the 15 percent who died has to be considered as a waste. In assessing the financial cost of PCM, therefore, the national resources used up for the very inadequate treatment have to be considered in addition to the investment in lives that do not become fully productive.

Bengoa has quite rightly pointed out that the "mere survivors" need following up since they may be severely damaged. This cannot be ignored since there are more "mere survivors" than actual complete cures. However, while we have no easy diagnostic criteria for the disease itself, we are unlikely to have a good simple index for both biochemical and social cure. Height may be studied in relation to other human attainments, but international or even national general comparisons might run into serious difficulties. The people of southern Ghana are generally shorter than those of northern Ghana— though the coastal diets are on the whole better than the northern ones. Given equal heights of 7-year-olds from the two regions of Ghana, how do we interpret them? It is not my intention to draw the old argument about genetic growth potential into this discussion, but if sequelae such as height, brain damage, and vaguely understood "psychosocial" defects are to be used for allocating priority, then we have to be very careful of our grounds. Harassed political and financial decision-makers want very definite facts.

Apart from its mere extent, PCM affects an age group that is particularly vulnerable. Socially, the child is being weaned from one mother-child relationship to another; it is being weaned from one type of food to others; and finally it is being confronted with environmental hazards by way of exposure to disease that it did not face before. All of these interact with PCM to produce a complex health problem with far-reaching consequences. The very complexity of the problem makes the allocation of priority among the many possible approaches rather difficult, and often the most direct approaches turn out to be too simple and are effective only as short-term measures.

Probably the very first priority is the need to increase awareness and to translate that awareness into carefully planned action. One may consider this at the international, the "group country" or regional, the national, and finally the state or provincial levels. At the international level, the U.N. and its agencies have done a good deal of work in calling attention to the problem. The Advisory Committee on the Application of Science and Technology (ACAST) report of 1968, the Strategy Statement of 1971, and the 1971 Economic and Social Council (ECOSOC) response to these reports are all evidence of awareness. However, the handling of the problem is too diffused within the U.N. system at present, and the proposal of the Secretary-General's 1971 Panel to Formulate a Strategy Statement on the Protein Problem for a fund and policy body to handle this PCM problem should be heeded. The population problem and the food and nutrition problem are related and in many ways similar. The creation of a U.N. Population Fund is an outward sign of the central priority rating accorded to the population problem; a similar approach to PCM should be made quickly. This kind of complementary activity will silence the vocal critics of the present population activities, critics whose main argument is that instead of going for socioeconomic development of the developing countries, we are trying to decrease their numbers.

Regional or group country organizations are still not very strong in the scientific field in Africa. The Organization of African Unity (OAU), which is the major political organization, has a good potential in that it provides the forum for analyzing international issues in an African context and reacting in an organized way. All the members may be made aware of the PCM problem and what it requires. It may then be possible to provide the stimulus and leadership necessary for concerted action. Regional training and research programs may be sponsored more easily through existing WHO programs, universities, and other institutions than by the creation of new bodies. Regional groupings may also understand their role in liberalization of trade, which will make possible the easier importation and exportation of foods required for the treatment and prevention of PCM. An approach of this type must be vigorously pursued in Africa if the problem is to be tackled on a continental scale.

Not much can be done at either an international or regional level without strong national awareness and desire for action. Unfortunately, it is at the national level that the most reluctance, if not actual resistance to organized effort against PCM, exists. This resistance is only partly due to lack of awareness of the extent of the problem. It probably stems more from the complexity of the measures required and the inability to guarantee short-term results and rapid, obvious improvement. Efforts have been made to promote the idea of national nutrition councils and committees, and in the majority of instances (at least in Africa) these have quietly faded away. If such committees can really provide leadership, then there is a need to analyze their functions, tasks, and funding carefully, to enable them to deal on an equal footing with the planning departments which usually have so much power. The degree of international attention given to a problem may be viewed as a stimulus to national awareness and priority rating.

One of the questions posed by Dr. Bengoa needs to be discussed a little further, because in some ways it holds the key to the dilemma of specific as opposed to general intervention programs. He states: "Earlier in this paper, I asked if we are preventing death without improving life. The answer is almost certainly yes in the developing countries. I have tried to point out that this situation has arisen because in these countries we have been able to apply modern public health techniques to reduce mortality without waiting for the socioeconomic development that would of itself improve standards of living—the process that occurred in the already developed nations. We cannot be content with this situation. We must recognize a direct responsibility to the 'survivors' to improve their health without waiting for major socioeconomic developments."

This is precisely where nutrition and health planners generally confront and become involved in a circular argument with economic planners. In a situation where the growth rate of the population is 2.5 percent per annum, where there are not enough school places for all, where total numbers of available jobs are developing at a much slower rate than the increase in numbers of educated persons, and where the GNP is just about coping with the population growth, how does one make a meaningful case for a program that will merely save more people? Providing more good food to the "survivors" in itself is good. But good food is only one ingredient in the quality of life, and how it contributes to the other ingredients should be scientifically examined if we are to satisfy the economic planners. Statements about improvement in productivity should be backed up with careful studies. Food and nutrition must be viewed as part and parcel of general economic development and planned as such.

The problem of blindness was alluded to without being dwelt upon. Blindness due to poor nutrition, either by itself or in combination with infectious or parasitic agents, is a common scourge in the drier parts of the developing countries. As a human problem, no one questions the importance of this condition. It is also a serious economic problem. It seldom kills, so its negative effect on the home and nation is prolonged and severe. The blind adult is not productive, but consumes almost as much as a nonblind one, and in addition requires nonblind persons to help with his daily requirements. Next to PCM, it is therefore proper to consider nutritional blindness as a priority area for study and action.

The selection of priority programs cannot be generalized. As has already been pointed out so well, the socioeconomic and psychosocial environment might well be the major determinant of the type of action needed. The main criteria should be the relevance of the action, its cost-effectiveness—not only because of its direct beneficial effects on PCM but also because of its potential for contributing to the quality of life generally—its ease of application, and its acceptability. Finally, a concerted effort should be made to ensure success, since failure can set back many years any further attempts to allocate to nutrition a high priority.

17 General Discussion

Chairman: **Dr. D. M. Hegsted** (Harvard School of Public Health); **Dr. Olof Mellander** (University of Gothenberg, Sweden); **Mr. Paul Cifrino** (USAID, India); **Mr. Mogens Jul** (Danish Meat Products Laboratory, Copenhagen); **Dr. Victor E. Smith** (Michigan State University); **Dr. Gustavo Rojas** (Ford Foundation, Colombia); **Dr. Cato Aall** (Nutrition Council, Norway); **Dr. Vahlquist; Dr. deVries**

Mellander As a Swedish professor of biochemistry and as a worker in infant nutrition problems for about thirty years, I have for about ten years also been a member of a group working to include nutrition as a component in the Swedish Development Corporation system. My top priority is for encouraging breast-feeding and improved weaning nutrition, because of the increasing number of children ill and dying after too early weaning, and the lack of domestic weaning foods or misuse of imported weaning foods. In medical education public health, nutrition, and preventive maternal-child health care are too much neglected or misunderstood. There is need for improved teaching of simple standardized normal feeding procedures adapted to local situations, thereby improving the most effective channels, the mother-child health services.

Because today's average administrator usually has no technical or biological background, he has difficulty in identifying and understanding biological programs and he is forced to make difficult decisions at home and in U.N. policy discussions on the basis of consultations with experts which are difficult for him to follow and fully appreciate.

These limiting factors are the most difficult to deal with, and I can see only two possible remedies. One is to follow the U.N. recommendation of 1968 on incorporating nutrition experts in all government organizations dealing with nutrition problems; the second is to arrange courses and conferences like this one, but smaller.

Cifrino If you hypothesize a birth rate of forty per thousand, 1 percent of your population at any given point in time would be composed of pregnant women in the last trimester: that would mean for a country like India, right now, five and one-half million women in the last trimester of pregnancy. That is a much more manageable target than the eighty million children under 6 today in India. Five and one-half million is a huge number, but it is a much smaller number than eighty million; in any developing country this 1-percent figure generally would hold, meaning that the target—pregnant women at this most critical period—is perhaps one-tenth as great as the target group of preschool children, one-tenth or one-fifteenth as much.

If there were a delivery system able to reach the 1 percent of the population represented by pregnant women, 280,000 tons of food would provide a nutritional supplement of 200 grams a day for each one of these women; and with this food you would be reaching an entire generation at a period when the brain cells are being formed at the most rapid rate. The quantum of food just happens to be the amount that is used every year in India for the midday school feeding program; I think this would be a much more fruitful use for it.

The other thing that a program of reaching the pregnant woman in the last trimester would do is provide a delivery base for education and motivation of the key individual. If there is going to be an improvement in family planning or in child care and mothercraft, it will be through mothers, not through programs of feeding children. The mother is the key person.

Jul Professor Mellander introduced himself as a member of a group trying to introduce nutrition into Swedish bilateral aid. This is symptomatic. Fred Sai and other people here have been active in trying to get a protein fund established under the U.N. Development Program, to make certain that some of the development funds will be earmarked for nutrition purposes. But apparently some countries just aren't as convinced as we are that nutrition is a high priority subject.

We must have people in the field who can very intelligently advise countries of the need for projects in this field and help them design convincing projects. We are helpless until this is done, and I am suggesting that our colleagues in the United Nations take this plea and do their best to help develop feasible projects in this field for both bilateral and multilateral programs.

deVries I agree that every country should work out its own salvation in respect to nutrition. But I would like to support Dr. Sai in asking for international cooperation in this planning. I have specifically in mind a worldwide survey of exportable and importable proteins. I can mention three cases. One is the tremendous waste of fish protein on the west coast of South America: only a fraction is being used for human consumption, a great deal for fertilizer and for animal feed. I think that has to stop and it can be stopped.

The second is milk protein. Two years ago the European Common Market drowned in a milk ocean, then it completely dried up. But in the meantime, through UNICEF and other worldwide food programs, many developing countries were able to obtain additional milk protein. Now they are in trouble because they cannot pay world market prices for the milk. I think it is a shame that the Common Market could eliminate the surpluses without consultation with the rest of the world as to how the surpluses might be used and at what price level.

The third example is the tremendous waste of protein in the cakes of oil seeds and pulses that are now used sometimes as fertilizer and sometimes even as fuel, when they could be turned into human food. I hope that this conference requests the United Nations Protein Advisory Group to make an inventory and establish a sensible way of using proteins that are now wasted.

Smith I would like to support what Dr. Bengoa was saying about priorities and add a plea for the establishment on the part of nutritionists of some priorities among nutrient allowances.

The economist who is trying to see whether a country can produce the nutrients that it needs may well find that it cannot produce the whole set that he is told should be available. When that happens, his reaction is to say, all right, which are the important ones? Sometimes I find that if I can show a nutritionist that we can't do everything, he will tell me what is most important. We need that kind of information.

If you can, for instance, produce either enough calories or enough riboflavin, but not both, then make a choice that is important in terms of the present problem. The nutritionist should be able to inform us as to what that choice should be. Once you know what are the more important nutrients in terms of your country's production capacity, you can direct a plant breeding program to provide the kind of nutrient that is most difficult to produce locally or to obtain through international trade. You cannot choose only between breeding in the direction of more protein or more calories; you can choose which of the amino acids you want to breed for and direct efforts toward improving protein production as efficiently and as effectively as possible.

Rojas In the developing countries we are more or less used to the idea of the survival of the fittest. The question would be then, survival for what? When one looks at the panorama of the developing countries and their problems; when one also faces the fact of a declining mortality rate and an increasing birth rate and population explosion, what are the prospects for a well-nourished population, assuming that that is possible in the developing world?

Given scarce resources a planner may have to work with, and given the kind of investment needed for a growing economy and perhaps a growing standard of living, the question is how should we invest in human capital, of which we have plenty. The return on that investment is not altogether clear when we don't have sufficient employment and education and opportunities for more and more people to survive in the developing world.

I am not trying to build a case against nutrition; that would be a mistake. What I'm trying to point out is the fact that planners and economists in the developing world have to face this very serious problem of what is most desirable, and a trade somehow has to be made between population growth and economic development.

Aall   In an article in the *Journal of Tropical Pediatrics and Environmental Child Health,* Robert Cook questions the effectiveness of hospital treatment of malnutrition. I would go a bit further and put the question even more strongly. How much is hospital medicine hindering an adequate handling of this problem?

In Norway, the parliament is discussing what steps should be taken to improve nutrition policy. In that connection, a newspaper picture showed a group of people marching ahead on a road that ends with a cliff, and below an ambulance is waiting to pick up the people as they fall down. Is this a nutrition policy? Is the answer to get more ambulances, or is it to put up a fence or a sign to tell people where to go?

What I want to say is that, when planning for better nutrition, one ought to question the way the problem has been dealt with so far by the medical profession; perhaps our preconceptions and conventional assumptions need to be reassessed.

Part IV

Determinants of Malnutrition
and Alternative Nutrition
Intervention Programs

18 A Systematic Approach to Nutrition Intervention Programs

David L. Call
Professor of Food Economics
Graduate School of Nutrition
Cornell University, Ithaca, N. Y.

F. James Levinson
Department of Agricultural Economics
Cornell University, Ithaca, N.Y.

Introduction

Up to this point, this conference has focused primarily on the importance of nutrition to individual well-being and its role in improving national human resource potential for development purposes. There also has been discussion of the primary nutritional problems presently faced in low-income countries.

Where such problems exist and are recognized as obstacles to the development process, the problem for the planner becomes one of allocating or reallocating resources to most effectively combat these deficiencies in a manner consistent with the country's overall development strategy. Conceptually such decision-making might rest upon a process of investigation, discussed briefly here and in depth in the Berg and Muscat paper in Part V, which treats the same topic from a different point of view. The first level of such an investigation, already touched upon in the preceding papers, involves identification in a particular geographic area of the nutrition problem in terms of food availability and intake, and in terms of physical, clinical, and biochemical measurements. This first step in the analysis should also provide at least a general idea of the population target groups to be addressed.

All too often the process of investigation ends with this first step, after which project decisions are made according to the interests of existing administrative and technical entities. What is suggested here and in the Berg and Muscat presentation is the need for further levels of analysis to provide some basis for specific rational investment decisions. A second level of the investigation would identify the determinants or causal factors of specific nutritional deficiencies among a target group, while a third level would attempt, through cost-effectiveness analysis, to find the optimum means of positively affecting these determinants.

The second and third levels of the analysis not only require substantial amounts of area-specific data but depend upon the nature of the nutrition problem identified initially. The problem in a highly labor-intensive economy that is not labor surplus can be one of inadequate calories for the adult working populace. [1] Alternatively, in situations of food scarcity coupled with high fertility rates the primary problem might be maternal malnutrition, perhaps reflected in a high proportion of low birth-weight infants. In most low-income countries, however, the primary nutritional target appears to be the preschool-age child. For purposes of the following discussion we shall take the low-income preschool-age population as our target group.

Assuming then the existence of nutritional deficiencies and identification of the target group, we shall discuss what appear to be the primary determinants of this group's nutritional status and then systematically outline the types of interventions capable of affecting these determinants.

The Determinants

The determinants discussed in this section are limited to those which—unlike religion, caste, or genetic traits—lend themselves to intervention. These can be classified into what might be called direct and indirect factors. Basically the nutritional status of a child is determined by his food intake and his health, the direct determinants. These two, in turn, are functions of such factors as family purchasing power (involving income, commodity prices, and other demands on a family budget), the nutrition and health beliefs of the child's mother, the nutritional content of the foods consumed, the presence or absence of health care and nonfamily feeding programs, plus numerous environmental and social phenomena.[1] These determinants, presented diagrammatically in Figure 1, are considered separately below.

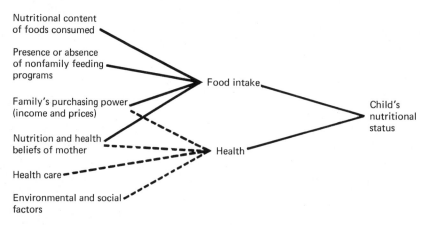

Figure 1. Determinants of a Child's Nutritional Status

[1] An attempt is currently under way in India to estimate the relative importance and the interdependence of these variables in northern India, using multiple regression analysis.

Family Purchasing Power

A family's purchasing power depends basically on (1) its wealth and income position, (2) the relative prices of food commodities it buys, and (3) the cost of other demands on its budget, particularly necessities that require cash. Thus, at least conceptually, increasing a family's purchasing power or real income for nutritional purposes can be accomplished by augmenting income flows to the family, by reducing the prices of food it consumes, or by subsidizing its other budgetary necessities, that is, housing, schooling, health, or clothing, thereby releasing additional funds for food purchase. The third approach suggests that existing government financing of education, health centers, and low-cost housing provides a secondary benefit to food consumption and hence nutrition.

Income and prices, the primary components of purchasing power, are discussed separately below and in the ensuing discussion.

Income. Probably no other single factor has so major an effect on the components of nutritional status in these countries as income. Examination of cross-section food consumption data [2] reveals highly significant differences in food consumption patterns along the income spectrum. Three trends appear to be almost universal, none of which is particularly surprising. The first, commonly referred to as Engel's law, finds that as income rises the percentage of that income allocated to food declines but that absolute expenditures rise.[2] A second trend is that the proportion of total calories supplied by carbohydrate staples (cereals and tubers) decreases and is replaced by more expensive animal or vegetable commodities as income increases. [3] A third trend is that within food groups there is a shift toward processed, more expensive items and varieties.

In nutritional terms the third trend, usually involving payment for various marketing services, may have a negative effect. The literature abounds with examples of shifts from brown rice to polished rice, high extraction to low extraction flour, and cane to refined sugar as income increases. [4] On balance, processed foods in general probably represent a nutritional minus where lost nutrients are not restored. In terms of overall nutritional effect, however, these negative effects of income are entirely outweighed by the positive effects of the first and second trends. While part of the increase in absolute

[2] The exception lies with the lowest income groups in most countries. Though the percentage of their incomes spent on food is quite high (60 to 80 percent) the absolute expenditures are still so low that the first income increments usually result in a still higher percentage spent on food.

expenditure suggested by the first trend results in the purchase of more expensive items, the increase will almost invariably result in the ingestion of more food, hence more calories, thereby overcoming a major, often limiting, nutritional obstacle. [5] In surveys that have examined caloric intake explicitly, a clearly positive linear relationship of calories with income emerges. [6]

While the amount of food consumed increases with income, so does the variety as suggested by the second trend. Diets based on cereals, plantains, roots, or tubers gradually become more diversified and legumes, fruits and vegetables, milk, and other sources of animal protein become more important in terms of total calories. With reference to some foods, notably legumes, consumption increases with the first income increments and then levels off. More often, however, consumption of nutritious foods increases more or less linearly along the income spectrum. Monthly family expenditures on milk, for example, increase fiftyfold from the lowest to the highest income groups in India (as compared with an eightfold increase in cereal expenditures). [7] These differences are best reflected in income elasticities of demand[3] for the commodities. In general the more nutritious items are those with the highest elasticities (although there is no evidence whatever that the relationship is causal). In Asia and the Far East (excluding Japan) the elasticities of vegetables, meat, and eggs are estimated at 0.9, 1.5, and 2.0, respectively, while the elasticity of cereals is 0.5. In the Near East, Africa, and Latin America the elasticities are somewhat lower but in almost the same proportions. [8] As a rule these elasticities decrease as income increases and tend to be higher in rural than in urban areas. [39]

Thus, for the population as a whole, increases in income almost automatically are translated into consumption of more nutritious foods, which in turn generally leads to improved nutritional status. Bringing about such increases for low-income population groups, however, is exceedingly difficult, as will be discussed below.

Commodity prices. Income is, of course, a relative concept, which takes on a specific meaning only in the context of its inherent purchasing power. This depends on food prices, which, together with income, clearly affect the consumer's purchases and hence the child's diet. While some might argue that availability should be included here along with price, availability is actually

---

[3] The percentage increase in consumption of a food as income increases by 1 percent. Thus consumption of a food with an income elasticity of demand of 0.6 will increase by 0.6 percent as income increases by 1 percent.

built into the price concept since any existing item becomes available at some price. In the case of "on the farm" consumption of goods that never reach the market, the "price" of the item becomes its imputed value or opportunity cost, in other words the amount of money the family "sacrifices" by not selling the item. Basically price is a function of the supply of and the demand for particular commodities and of their transfer costs. As will be seen in section 3 these become the points of possible intervention along with artificial manipulation of the price mechanism through price policy.

Rather than restricting this determinant to prices of "nutritious" or "protective" commodities, one should probably be all-inclusive since purchase of food is a function of relative as much as of absolute prices. In addition, certain groups with caloric shortages may have a primary need of the least expensive form of calories—the content of other nutrients being a secondary consideration. Still a nutrition intervention directed at price reduction would probably be concerned primarily with affecting the supply, demand, or transfer costs of "nutritious" commodities (including commercially processed products), thereby reducing their prices and, assuming a positive price elasticity of demand,[4] increasing their consumption.

Nutritional Content of Common Foods

A family's income and the prices of food commodities, to a significant extent, will dictate the amount of particular commodities purchased. The child's nutritional status then will depend in large part on the nutritional content of these commodities. Frequently the commodity itself implies a certain nutritional value, although differences within commodity groups or even among varieties of a given commodity can be significant. The food's nutritional content might also be affected by ecological factors or by processing between points of production and consumption.

Traditions and Beliefs

Almost regardless of the aforementioned factors, food consumption always has been based to an extent on preconceived beliefs relating to foods and their functions and on traditional preparation and consumption practices. In some cases these beliefs and processes have obvious validity relating to the health value of the item. In others the practice may support a basic cultural tenet of the population group and thus be equally valid. [9, 10] In still other cases, in both nonindustrialized and industrialized countries, where such

---

[4] The percentage increase in consumption of a food as its price falls by 1 percent. These elasticities generally correspond with the income elasticities discussed earlier.

validity cannot be ascertained, these practices have been, rightly or wrongly, attributed to ignorance.

Practices relating to the feeding of young children have been under particular surveillance in recent years. Two such practices emerge as being notably significant. The first involves the critical period of weaning where problems are numerous. In some cases breast-feeding continues well beyond 6 months but without supplementation. Elsewhere the milk is supplemented but with foods low in essential nutrients. Where more nutritious items are explicitly withheld, they sometimes reflect underlying association of these items with intestinal parasites or diarrhea. When weanling diarrhea does occur, any protein-rich foods that were consumed are often withheld or solid foods are withheld altogether, a practice that further exacerbates the problem.

To some these practices simply reflect ignorance. Probably more accurate is John Wyon's contention that behavior is based on empirical experience. In many cases a mother, recognizing the increased incidence of diarrheal infection when supplemental foods are given, and recognizing the incidence of mortality from the infection, makes a conscious, seemingly sensible decision to withhold such foods. What she will fail to recognize, largely because it is so undramatic, is the much higher mortality rate resulting from protein-calorie malnutrition and the child's inability to resist infection when supplemental foods are withheld. [11]

The preceding set of practices or malpractices is usually attributed to tradition. Yet tradition is not always the culprit. Frequently problems arise as a direct result of abandoning traditions, often as a result of direct exposure to more industrialized regions. The prime example is the cessation of breast-feeding in several parts of the low income world. Substituted is higher priced commercially bottled milk or powdered concentrate; all too often the higher price results in the use of inadequate quantities. Just as often the concentrate is reconstituted with unclean water. In either case the nutritional and health consequences are serious. [12, 13]

Health of the Child

Even if the right foods are available to the child, they may not have their full effect upon his nutritional status if he suffers from other health problems, particularly gastrointestinal infection. Such infection can lower nutritional status or precipitate malnutrition in several ways. It can reduce food intake through loss of appetite. It results in loss of nitrogen, hence requiring increased protein consumption thereafter. Where the infection is the result of intestinal parasites, such as hookworm, the blood loss from the intestinal tract frequently leads to anemia. Finally, where the infection causes diarrhea, absorption of nutrients in the intestine will be reduced. Where protein levels already are low, diarrheal infection can precipitate kwashiorkor. [14, 15] In addition, it has been well established that common childhood diseases like measles can have a drastic effect, either precipitating severe malnutrition or having a much higher degree of severity in the chronically underfed child.

The child also may be affected by the nutritional status of his mother during pregnancy and lactation, although findings here are less clear. [16] In general, the quality of breast milk, with the exception of its thiamine content, does not appear to be affected significantly by the mother's nutritional status. However, in times of severe food shortage the quantity of milk secreted might be reduced.

Nonfamily Feeding

In much of the world, the preceding four factors are the primary determinants of a target group's nutritional status. For increasing numbers of children in many countries, however, there is a fifth determinant in the form of food received outside the home. In most cases such feeding represents a government initiative, at times supported with international assistance. Such feeding may appear to be more an intervention than a determinant, but its widespread prevalence at present probably qualifies it for the latter category as well.

Intervention into the Determinants

To affect positively the nutritional status of the target group requires an intervention capable of affecting at least one of the five determinants described above in a desired direction while, theoretically at least, holding the others constant. The following sections reexamine each of the determinants in terms of possible interventions.

The interventions vary considerably in their nutritional effectiveness, cost, acceptability, and administrative viability. In addition they differ with respect to three other sets of criteria, which are considered in the discussions below. The first is the time frame, frequently the factor most overlooked in the selection of nutrition intervention programs. In industrialized countries the primary nutrition activity, except in wartime, traditionally has encompassed long-range education efforts, broad-scale enrichment and fortification, coupled with a reliance upon gradually rising incomes. In low-income countries the opportunity costs of relying solely on such long-run solutions may be exceedingly high in terms of the number of children missed in the interim.

Closely related to the time frame, and included with it in Table 1, is the degree of focus on the target group. Here again interventions vary widely, from those attempting to reach the selected group only, the so-called "targeted" approach, to those seeking to reach the selected group by improving the nutrition of the entire populace, the "blanket" approach. Child feeding programs would be an example of the former, while mandatory fortification efforts or agricultural production incentives are examples of the latter. Usually, but not always, the "targeted" approach is the shorter-run intervention.

A third factor is the presence or absence of economic or social multipliers affecting other development sectors. All too often interventions are evaluated solely on the basis of their effectiveness in achieving specific nutritional objectives while, in fact, they may be providing significant inputs to, say, the agricultural or education sectors.

The intent in the discussions that follow is the limited one of summarizing the interventions, highlighting their potential effectiveness and limitations, and presenting where possible considerations of particular interest to the economic planner. Where techniques are already well documented, particularly in the cases of indirect agricultural or health interventions, less attention will be given to the interventions themselves than to their linkages with the determinants.

Income

Traditionally, explicit nutrition improvement has not been a component of development theory or planning. Basically the key to development as postulated in most growth theory is growth of the capital stock, suggesting investment-oriented planning and capital goods production. According to this view, increased national income eventually will result in higher per capita incomes

Table 1. Long-run vs. Short-run Interventions; "Blanket" vs. "Targeted" Approaches

Long run	Short run
1. Increasing per capita income (blanket)	1. Government price intervention (blanket)
2. Commodity supply increases (blanket)	2. Rationing (blanket or targeted)
3. Plant breeding for nutritive quality (blanket)	3. Child feeding (targeted)
4. Nutrition education (blanket or targeted)	4. Food fortification (blanket)
5. Environmental sanitation (blanket)	5. Inoculations and mass anti-parasite programs (targeted)

with all the goods and services, presumably including better nutrition, that this suggests. Thus it is implied that money spent on nutrition programs, a consumption expenditure, will reduce the amount available for growth-promoting investment and hence delay the long-run provision of health and nutrition as viable services.

The problems with this position in practice are now reasonably clear. They relate essentially to weaknesses in the linkages between growth-promoting investment and improved nutritional status. First, the returns on capital investments in low-income countries have, as a rule, been lower than originally anticipated, resulting in relatively low rates of saving. [17] This is explained by numerous legitimate and often unavoidable factors, but remains true nonetheless. Second, to the extent a nation's capital stock does increase, it is divided among more persons than originally anticipated. Finally, and perhaps most important, income distribution even in periods of reasonably rapid growth has been far from optimal, given patterns of overall development that often exclude the bulk of the lower income populace from much of the development process. Recent breakthroughs in agricultural production in many of these countries have actually widened income differentials, resulting in at least relative reductions in real income by landless agricultural laborers and tenants. [18] With the nutrition problem concentrated in the lowest income segments, this lack of growth takes on increased importance.

Should per capita income of these disadvantaged groups actually increase, nutritional improvement would likely follow, as explained earlier. For the nutritional status of the preschool-age population to become adequate, however, would require very significant increases in income and a timetable well beyond what can be considered satisfactory. Aside from the difficulties described earlier, the preschooler's requirement for elusive and often relatively expensive nutrients, including protein, are proportionately far higher than for the rest of the population.

If for nutritional purposes the traditional "growth of the capital stock" approach in and of itself is inadequate, however, there may be other means of approaching income generation which more directly address these purposes. In many low-income countries today a factor critically inhibiting growth is productive employment. Until recently inadequate food supplies in these countries constituted a constraint against policies of rapidly increased employment, which under the circumstances would have put serious strain on existing food supplies. Had India, for example, expanded nonagricultural employment during the 1950s and 1960s at the otherwise feasible rate of 7 percent per year, agricultural prices would have been forced up by approximately 10 percent a year. [17] Today, with at least food grain production breakthroughs in many of these countries, such a policy becomes not only possible but clearly essential. Thus, the criterion for investment becomes not simply returns on capital but, perhaps more important, productive employment-generating potential.

Usually labor-intensive investment in low-income countries suggests public works or small-scale industry. As indicated by Mellor, however, there is potential for considerable employment-generating investment within the agricultural sector—investment directed, interestingly, at the increased production of nutritious commodites. [18] Such investment will be considered explicitly in the following section on price intervention.

Commodity Prices

As the relative price of a commodity falls, its consumption will increase if the price elasticity for the item is positive. As noted earlier, the income and price elasticities of demand for most nutritious food commodities are high. Where they are not, it becomes necessary not only to reduce the commodity's price but also to increase demand for the item through some type of consumer motivation. This will be discussed later. Another means of increasing demand is to increase income, as seen earlier. For present purposes, an assumption of constant elasticities and income will be made to facilitate the discussion. We can then assume that commodity prices are a function of supply, transfer costs, and government intervention.

At the outset two important caveats are in order. The first is the relationship of price to net returns for the producer in rural areas of most low-income countries. If lower prices lead to reduced net returns, two serious problems follow. First and probably most important, the lower returns provide a disincentive for future production of that commodity. Second, since the producer is also a primary consumer where the bulk of the population is in the agricultural sector, his lower income may adversely affect his own consumption and that of his family. Again the determining factor is the price elasticity of demand for the good. Where it is sufficiently high, the reduction in the commodity price (as long as it still covers the producer's variable costs) will be more than compensated for by his increased volume.

The second caveat relates to interpretation of income and price elasticities of demand for low-income populations. Where existing consumption of a more expensive food item is negligible to begin with, even a large *percentage* increase in its consumption as income rises or price falls will not significantly increase the consumption of that item in absolute terms. In India, for example, with price and income elasticities for milk of about 1.8, the economically average Indian earning roughly $5 a month purchases only 2 ounces of milk a day. To consume a pint of milk a day he would have to spend half of his disposable income. [19]

With these caveats in mind we now can examine means of increasing the supply or lowering the transfer costs of nutritious foods. The discussion will proceed in two parts, the first relating to the range of protective foods which will be considered as a group (pulses, oilseeds, livestock and dairy, fisheries, and fruit and vegetables), the second discussing commercially processed nutritious foods. At least the first group can be classified as a long-run, "blanket" approach. Where the prices of these protective foods exceed the purchasing power of low-income groups, they are unlikely to provide significant nutritional benefits to the low-income target group in the short run. At the same time, efforts to increase the supply of these foods may provide significant economic multipliers, particularly in terms of increased productive employment.

Attention is given to means of reducing losses of the particular commodity under discussion. Food losses in some low-income countries, however, are so vast that their reduction alone represents a primary governmental intervention. Where commodity losses in a country result from a few common problems such as moisture, insects, or rodents, explicit centralized storage or pest and rodent control programs cutting across the commodity groups may be necessary.

Protective foods. With the exception of fruits and vegetables, the so-called protective foods discussed here are considered primarily as sources of protein. Those with perhaps the highest likelihood of reaching the low-income target group are the pulses and oilseeds. Pulses with protein contents ranging from 18 to 35 percent are usually consumed as such while oilseeds such as ground nut, cottonseed, soya, and sesame are generally processed to extract the oil. The resulting meal, with protein contents of 40 to 60 percent, which is now used primarily as domestic or exported animal feed and to some extent fertilizer, can be processed into edible grade protein flours and concentrates for human consumption.

Both oilseeds and pulses, but particularly the latter, are hampered by serious supply problems, which have increased rather than diminished with the recent food-grain production breakthroughs. While acreage devoted to these crops on a worldwide basis is a third of that used for wheat and rice cultivation, the resulting production totals only one-sixth as much as these two cereals. [20] As cereal yields have increased, their production has become increasingly profitable relative to legumes, with the result that the latter are being increasingly replaced, particularly on more productive rain-fed or irrigated land. Per capita pulse consumption in India alone dropped 27 percent between 1964 and 1969.[5] [4]

The increases in cereal yields that have led to decreases in pulse production in parts of the world have increased interest in livestock, dairy, and poultry production. In some regions of Africa and Latin America where land is not in short supply there exists a potential for increased livestock production using resources with low opportunity costs. Frequently there is little likelihood of bringing these untilled areas under cultivation without large investments. Where the climate is conducive to year-round pasturage these areas can support considerably more livestock than they do and provide animal protein products to the populace at much lower prices than where production would compete for scarce resources. [13]

In most of the developing areas, however, where land is in short supply, regular milk and meat consumption is far beyond the purchasing power of low-income groups. Under these circumstances only an enormous supply increase and price reduction would have a noticeable effect on their diets. Short of this, increased investment in meat and milk production, representing far less efficient conversion of feed to edible protein, calories, and other nutrients, can actually have an adverse effect by transferring land and inputs away from food grain production and by directly competing for food grains with feed grains. This would have the effect of raising the prices of cereals, the staple of the less well-off, or of preventing cereal prices from falling. [1]

Within the agricultural sectors of both land-surplus and land-scarcity areas, however, there is probably no better means of improving the relative incomes of small cultivators and of creating additional rural employment than through labor-intensive livestock, poultry, and dairy production. [18] This then can become an important means of affecting income, our first determinant of nutritional status. In most cases this increased production would lead to direct increases in consumption by the producer's family since all of the increase will not normally enter commercial channels. In addition, increased livestock and dairy production will no doubt have positive benefits for certain middle-income population groups with suboptimal dietary intakes.

[5] The drought years 1966 and 1967 were excluded in this calculation.

As with dairy and commercial poultry production, fruit and vegetable cultivation presents a highly labor-intensive, employment-generating production
process within the agricultural sector. Also, as with dairy production, the end
products are frequently beyond the reach of the economically disadvantaged.

Interventions designed to increase the supply of these commodities in light
of the above considerations fall into several categories. One need common to
all these commodities is intensive, area-specific research. Increasing pulse,
fruit, and vegetable production requires research on breeding and disease control. Among the oilseeds the problem is toxic pigments or molds: aflatoxin in
peanuts and gossypol in cottonseed. In peanuts the incidence can be reduced
significantly by more careful harvesting and by drying prior to storage. In the
case of cottonseed, major promise lies in new glandless, gossypol-free varieties. Soybeans present a major problem of adaptation and cultivation in new
areas. Similarly, in the case of livestock, poultry, and dairy production, local-
ized research on productivity, breeding, and disease control is necessary to decrease risk and uncertainty and assure viability of the industry.

A second area of need is extension. Using existing knowledge, pulse production can be increased by including them (instead of fallows) in simple rota-
tion with cereal and cash crops, particularly in multiple-cropping situations
possible in irrigated or rain-fed areas. This has agronomic as well as nutritional
validity since pulse production does not deplete soil nitrogen. Second, production can be increased on existing legume acreage by improved crop management, that is, proper land preparation, weed and insect control, and
fertilizer application. [20] Extension is especially important in livestock and
fruit and vegetable production into which small cultivators are being encouraged to enter.

A third area is processing and marketing. In the case of oilseeds an important limiting factor will probably be the absence of adequate processing facilities. Where efforts are made to introduce new oilseed crops or to rapidly
expand existing ones, one frequently encounters a circular dilemma where
cultivators hesitate to produce without the necessary processing facilities,
while processors hesitate to erect facilities without assured production and
markets.

Marketing deserves highest priority in increasing livestock, poultry, and
dairy production. Bulky, perishable items such as meat and milk will continue
to be produced in small volume until inexpensive means are developed to increase the potential marketing area. Where these steps are not taken losses
will continue to be high, resulting in low net returns to the producer, a pro-

duction disincentive, and higher prices to the consumer, a consumption disincentive.

The same problem severely limits expansion of fruit and vegetable production. Much of this loss can be avoided by timely processing of the commodities or by temperature-controlled transportation. Where processing facilities can be established they also might permit the export of certain varieties with potentially large foreign exchange benefits. Finally, processing itself is usually labor-intensive and hence employment-generating.

A final need is the provision of adequate credit. Medium-term credit, primarily for the purchase of cows and buffalo, is a basic necessity if livestock and dairy production is to have the income distribution and employment features envisioned. Fruit and vegetables, considerably more costly to produce than food grains, require both short-term and medium-term credit.

Fisheries development represents a different case with a somewhat different set of needs and generally requires significant public investment for modernization throughout the industry. Traditional fishing vessels may need to be replaced by mechanized, better equipped craft capable of covering larger areas, fishing farther from shore, carrying larger loads, and staying out for longer periods. This in turn requires a progressive credit network coupled where possible with incentives for craft modernization. Improvement of shore facilities, particularly storage and refrigerated transport, are then necessary to minimize loss, thereby reducing consumer prices and increasing producer returns. [21]

Where a country's infrastructure does not lend itself to large-scale fish distribution or where fish are harvested but not sold directly for food, processing into fishmeal or animal feed or into fish protein concentrate for humans becomes at least theoretically possible. In the case of the latter, it may be many years before large-scale production in low-income countries becomes a reality. Large-scale usage of fish protein concentrates raises the same problem of delivery systems as various oilseed protein products. People do not eat protein powders, but they may eat traditional foods fortified with these protein ingredients. This implies a delivery system limited to those who buy and consume the products that can be so fortified. A modest, shorter term possibility in some countries is the shipping inland of dried fish where markets exist or can be easily developed.

Along with the above, there is considerable potential for inland fisheries—lakes, rivers, dams, and irrigation tanks. Still more effective in the long run may be pond culture, where fish are farmed rather than hunted. This requires fish stocking, fertilization, and supplemental feeding, species combination, and careful management. Yields are also dependent on adequate control of water pollution.

In summary, the increased production or reduction of transfer costs of particularly nutritious food commodities is a relatively long-term solution to a society's food needs. It can generate employment, important in and of itself, but seldom can it be considered a short-term solution to the nutritional needs of the low-income preschool child.

Commercially processed nutritious foods. A child's food consumption might be affected by lower prices (and hence increased availability) not only of the food commodities described above but also of any commercially processed nutritious foods produced in the country. During the past two decades, and beginning with dried skimmed milk, numerous such products have been developed and marketed with a view toward nutritional improvement: Vitasoy in Hong Kong, Pro-Nutro in South Africa, Incaparina in Central America, Faffa in Ethiopia, Laubina in Lebanon, Saci in Brazil, and many others. Other processed foods, particularly baby foods, have been promoted in these countries on nutritional grounds but make no pretext of aiming for other than the middle and upper income markets.

A wide range of problems has faced producers of such products, but one basic one has faced them all. This in simplest terms is the conflict between nutritional impact and profits. The fact that the two have been mutually exclusive in virtually all such efforts represents the basic dilemma facing this type of intervention. As suggested throughout, the disposable incomes of economically disadvantaged groups in these countries are often inadequate to afford even the regional food staple. In the production of a processed food, even with negligible margins, the cost of the raw materials represents no more than one-third to one-half, and usually much less, of the total product cost, which is dictated by costs of processing and packaging in these countries and by the normal marketing costs involved in any commercialization. This leaves the product well beyond the reach of most of those who need it.

The company faced with such a problem is left with three alternatives. It can produce the product anyway for those who can afford it, some of whom may need it, and hope to develop a profitable venture. Or it can seek some type of government subsidy (tax incentives, reduced transport rates, access to scarce materials, or outright grants) to permit lower consumer prices. Such subsidies have seldom been given either because of a basic mistrust of the private sector in many of these countries or because the government believes there are more effective and less costly means of reaching those in need. A third alternative is to attempt to develop a major public institutional market for the product, such as school lunch programs. This approach could insure sufficient volume to reduce fixed costs and hence make the product more viable in the commercial market Governments, however, are reluctant to help build the market for a branded product, in essence ensuring a monopoly. In addition, products such as corn soy milk (CSM) and nonfat dried milk contributed by aid donor countries frequently undercut the possibility of local product sales for these purposes.

While the effects of such commercial efforts on low-income groups may be limited, the chance to enlist the support of the private food industry for nutritional improvement in general should not be bypassed. It is clear that with urbanization and development a country's reliance on processed foods increases significantly. A country with a nutrition-conscious food industry working in company with rather than at odds with the government could well play a major role in long-term nutrition improvement.

Government price intervention. In addition to affecting price indirectly by changing supply functions or transfer costs, governments can intervene directly by the artificial manipulation of prices to achieve particular policy objectives. Intervention of this sort has been used frequently both in low-income and industrialized nations. During periods of scarcity or national emergency, price ceilings have been employed to keep prices from skyrocketing. Where the objective has been increased production, governments have established price supports or subsidies to provide incentives to cultivators. Where problems of inadequate production and high consumer prices exist side by side, as in England in the 1950s and 1960s, the government may resort to a discriminatory price system providing a high incentive price for producers and a lower one for consumers, the government picking up the difference. In countries where the problem has been one of excess supply, such as the United States, the government has sought to keep prices from falling by limiting supply through land retirement and other programs.

Price policies most widely employed in low-income countries during the past two decades have been producer-incentive oriented.[6] Such policies have several effects on an economy which relate to consumer prices and target group diets. First, positive price policies with no change in technology are more likely to shift existing acreage from one crop to another than to increase ag-

[6] Such policies have been pursued in India, Pakistan, Libya, Syria, Paraguay, Guatemala, Nicaragua, Peru, Senegal, Tanzania, the Philippines, and Indonesia. [22, 23]

gregate food production. If the country chooses to support food grain prices, which is usually the case, there may then be a concomitant decline in, say, production of pulses, which may be competing for the same land. This already has happened in several countries. Second, as is sometimes forgotten, while producer-incentive price policies provide higher returns to producers, they also result in higher prices to consumers. Often, of course, in low-income countries, the producer and the consumer are the same person. Where they are not, however, the consumer may be less well off than before.

Positive price policies in general have an income transfer effect from the consumer to the producer. The result is a welfare improvement in the agricultural sector at the expense of a decline in urban welfare. Within the urban sector increases in food prices will most seriously affect low-income groups, who spend a larger percentage of their incomes on food. Within the agricultural sector, since benefits of a positive price policy are in proportion to sales, they will accrue to the large producer who markets the bulk of his goods rather than to the small subsistence farmer who markets little or nothing. [24] Thus, while a positive price policy may increase production of desirable commodities and hence be a sensible course of action under certain conditions, it will not often, in and of itself, improve the nutritional well-being of urban and rural low-income groups in greatest need of assistance. On the contrary, it may well adversely affect their welfare.

If a positive price policy presents problems, a negative one, placing a ceiling on the commodity prices below the national market price, can be worse. The difficulty here lies in the nature of agricultural production. If production were in the hands of a few large producers, lowering the price of an item with a high price elasticity of demand might well prove economically advantageous. The lower price would stimulate increased demand and increased sales would more than compensate for the lower price per unit. Where production is in the hands of large numbers of smaller farmers, however, such an approach ceases to be possible. Unless farmers decide as a group to keep prices up, margins will remain low. Any farmer taking much of the profit on his goods is sure to be undercut by another producer. In economic terms a farmer's marginal revenue will not significantly exceed his marginal cost. Under these circumstances, fixing the price (the producer's marginal revenue) below the natural market price without concurrently lowering the cost of production will serve to decrease production and probably put many producers out of business in the process. As a result, while consumer demand for such goods as milk and vegetables would increase with the drop in prices, supply would decrease. What is produced would probably end up in the hands of the well-to-do, who are usually better able to procure scarce commodities, unless a rigid program of distribution to low-income groups were implemented. Low-income groups would probably be left with little more than frustrated expectations. Perhaps the classic failure of a negative price policy is that of Argentina between 1944 and 1955, where policies had the combined effect of lowering agricultural income and raising farmers' costs of operation through subsidization of the industrial sector. [25]

The one means by which low-income groups could be assisted by price intervention would be through some form of discriminatory prices. Under such a system producer prices would be unaffected or could be supported, if necessary, as a production incentive, but consumption would be subsidized for low-income groups. This could well take the form of special rationing, with the government purchasing a certain percentage of the supply of particular commodities at the market price and then making it available to the poor at a reduced price.

Another possibility is grading. Where commodities can be separated by qualitative indices other than nutritional value, "higher quality" varieties could be sold at the market price (or above, thus providing a form of disguised taxation) while the lower quality items could be subsidized. In some cases the market might tend toward such price levels without explicit government intervention once grading was introduced. Where consumption of these grades is primarily a function of income, and hence nutritional status, the "lower quality" products could be fortified with additives that might be too costly to supply to the entire populace. [26]

The problems with such price manipulating mechanisms are twofold. First is the cost, which might be prohibitive in a country with a large proportion of its populace below the selected "poverty line." Second, the logistics of operating such systems in a medium or large size country would be enormous and would call for considerable administrative time with particularly high opportunity costs. In fact the government might have to have monopoly control of distribution of the commodities involved. Still, in transitory periods of particular scarcity, such systems may be essential to prevent large-scale suffering.

Finally, consumer prices can be stabilized, rather than reduced, either indirectly through the use of buffer stocks (government purchase of commodities when price is low and release of commodities when price is high) or directly by retail sales of government stocks through fair price shops as is done in Burma and India. [27]

Nutritional Content of the Commodities

When for economic or social reasons diets themselves are difficult to change, the possibility arises of improving the nutritional value of the food currently consumed. In some cases, because of processing or canning or because of ecological factors in a region, a food's nutritional content may be lower than the same foods in other circumstances. In such cases the cause of the loss might be directly addressed. In general, however, the primary means of improving the nutritional content of foods are through genetic breeding of the item or by fortification. These are discussed separately below.

Plant breeding. Where feasible, the most effective means of improving the nutritional content of food commodities is through genetic manipulation of indigenous strains or introduction of new varieties. This assures that the entire supply of the commodity will be improved whether or not it receives centralized handling. Nutritional improvement is thus provided with no additional acreage requirements and generally no cost increment to the consumer. The target group is reached through a program with effects covering the entire populace—a classic example of the "blanket" approach to nutrition improvement.

Plant breeding for nutritional improvement, an approach of relatively recent vintage, has concentrated mainly on two objectives: improving the protein content of cereals and improving the quality of existing protein. There is at times lack of agreement among the breeders themselves as to which of these is of primary importance for individual crops.

Probably the most dramatic achievements in plant breeding for nutritional improvement have been the identification at Purdue University of opaque-2 and floury-2 mutant genes in corn, which double the lysine and tryptophan contents of that cereal. Opaque-2 has already been introduced into cultivation in parts of Latin America and is being introduced in commercial channels in processed products. In wheat, protein contents of 15 to 18 percent have been achieved at the University of Nebraska, in one case as high as 25 percent (as opposed to a content of 9 to 12 percent in most existing varieties). Lysine contents have been increased by 50 percent. Work at the International Rice Institute at Los Baños in the Philippines has more than doubled the protein content of rice and significantly increased lysine and threonine levels. Important work is in progress on sorghum and millets at Purdue University and at the Agricultural Research Institute in New Delhi, respectively. [28]

In some cases the protein content or quality of a grain has varied proportionately or inversely with its yield, but this relationship depends on numerous environmental factors, particularly soil fertility and water availability. Where conflicts do occur the priority for the present must go to higher yields. There also have been problems of consumer and producer acceptability with some strains, which limit their effectiveness regardless of chemical makeup.

As with the development of any new strain there is a considerable time lag between laboratory identification of a useful gene and large-scale usage of a new strain. The genes must be crossed and combined and several strains developed to form a ready backlog against disease or insect attack. Then, if the strains are sufficiently attractive to the cultivators, seed multiplication is necessary, itself a lengthy process. Thus the time element is an important factor that must be taken into account in the initial research investment decision-making. Another factor is technical feasibility. Where increasing the value of a particular nutrient is especially difficult, it may well be useful to proceed with alternative means of supplying that nutrient, at least on an interim basis.

Fortification. Where the breeding of essential nutrients into a food is unfeasible, too expensive, or antagonistic to higher yields, fortification of the harvested food item may be a useful alternative. In this case a more active recurring intervention becomes necessary and the choice of carriers is, by definition, more limited. Only foods that receive some centralized processing or handling can be considered candidates. In addition, to make practical economic sense, the fortification process should not negatively affect the characteristics of the carrier, should not significantly increase its price, and should reach a reasonable proportion of the low-income, vulnerable target group in greatest need of the nutrients being added. Where a fortification process meets these requirements, its effect on nutritional status can be significant.

Numerous fortification efforts have been undertaken in both low-income and industrialized nations, with varying results. Wheat flour has been enriched in many countries with vitamins and minerals and in some cases (Israel and India) with protein. This is usually done by preparation of a nutrient premix which is introduced in the stream of flour during milling through a calibrated feeder or by enrichment tablets or "wafers" introduced into the dough in a bakery. [29] Processes for adding nutrients to whole wheat kernels have been developed at the Western Utilization Research Laboratory of the U.S. Department of Agriculture but as yet have not been introduced commercially. Enrichment of corn flour with niacin and other nutrients has probably been responsible in part for control of pellagra in the southern United States. Limited enrichment of corn was also undertaken in Latin America and Egypt.

The technology is essentially the same as for wheat flour. In the case of corn grits, however, it becomes necessary to reintroduce a premix of corn and grits sprayed with water-soluble vitamins and minerals and appropriately coated. [30]

Rice enrichment was first attempted in the Philippines in 1948. Since then it has been introduced with varying effectiveness in parts of Japan, Thailand, Colombia, Venezuela, the Dominican Republic, Puerto Rico, and the United States. Rice also has been enriched for the armed forces in Formosa. Basically there are three techniques of rice enrichment. The rice as a whole can be coated with nutrients; a premix of fortified rice kernels can be reintroduced into the rice stream; or a premix of fortified, simulated rice kernels can be used. The technique to be followed depends in part on the cooking practices used by consumers. Where rice is cooked in a minimum of water any of the three processes will suffice. Where it is cooked in an excess of water which is then discarded (the practice in South Asia) none of the processes is entirely satisfactory. Where riboflavin has been added to the fortified or simulated premix, the added kernels take on a yellowish color which distinguishes them from the rest of the rice.

In practice, two sets of difficulties have inhibited large-scale effectiveness of cereal fortification. First, most milling is carried out in small village grinding units rather than by large centralized facilities. There are some 5,000 rice hullers in Thailand; 20,000 wheat "chukkis" in India. The difficulties of installing necessary equipment, providing the additives, and then inspecting each of these units presents a logistical chore of huge proportions, generally at a high opportunity cost. Second, consumption of cereals, as of all foods, is largely a function of income. In most nonindustrialized countries, those groups at the lowest end of the income spectrum may consume relatively little of the primary cereal staple, subsisting instead on roots, tubers, or coarser grains such as millets. As a rule the logistics of fortifying these items are even more difficult than reaching the primary staples.

Enrichment and fortification have not been limited to cereals. Margarine is fortified with vitamins A and D not only in industrialized nations but also in Brazil, Colombia, Costa Rica, Chile, Peru, Venezuela, and Turkey. Similarly, milk in the United States and Europe used for domestic consumption and for food aid to low-income countries is generally fortified with vitamins A and D. In general, of course, the fortification of these animal protein products is beneficial only where those segments of the populace in need can afford them.

Still other carriers consumed by most population groups but centrally processed have important fortification potential in low-income countries. These include such items as salt, sugar, tea, flavoring agents, and cooking oil. To some extent these have been used as carriers in the past. Salt is iodized in many countries to combat goiter; it also has been used as a carrier of chloroquine, an antimalarial drug, and of fluoride. Vegetable oil is enriched with vitamins A and D in several countries in spite of major losses during cooking. Monosodium glutamate, a flavoring agent used with remarkable regularity in the Orient, has been fortified with amino acids on a small scale. Tea has never been fortified outside the laboratory, but as far back as the 1930s the eminent nutrition pioneer R. R. Williams recommended its fortification with vitamin A.

In general, prospects for effective fortification programs in low-income countries increase over time as production of the nutritional additives improves and its relative cost decreases. Costs of vitamin and mineral supplementation in industrialized nations are often negligible, although the costs of producing vitamins and other additives in less industrialized countries are still significant. Considerable work has been done over the past two decades on the development of edible grade flours, concentrates, and protein isolates from ground nut, cottonseed, and soy, and efforts continue to produce on a large-scale acceptable protein concentrates from fish, leaves, and single-cell organisms. Perhaps the most significant technological strides in recent years have been in the production of synthetic amino acids at continually decreasing cost. [31, 32] At present, however, protein fortification is a relatively high cost intervention when considered on a per capita beneficiary basis, since this blanket approach is likely to benefit only a small proportion of the total population. [33]

Recognizing the potential effectiveness of food fortification, several governments have passed legislation permitting or requiring fortification of particular commodities. In addition to many industrialized countries, compulsory flour enrichment legislation has been passed, although to date not enforced, in Chile; São Paulo, Brazil; and Peru. In India legislation requires the addition of vitamin A to all commercially produced cooking oil.

Traditions and Beliefs

As described earlier, there are ways in which changes in traditional beliefs and practices can lead to nutritional improvement of the target population. First, where nutritionally valuable foods such as pulses have low-income and price elasticities of demand, increasing their supply and lowering their cost or increasing family income will have little effect on the item's consumption in any kind of a market economy. What is called for are concurrent efforts to raise these elasticities by changing consumer conceptions of the product. Second, there are the broader sets of beliefs and practices, outlined earlier, that relate to the feeding of young children. Almost regardless of the other interventions described here, adherence to these practices where they exist will make significant nutritional improvement virtually impossible.

Before discussing specific interventions per se, a few general comments should be offered. First, as suggested earlier, traditional beliefs are often highly complex patterns, frequently with considerable logic or with important cultural linkages to structural elements of that society. Seldom can this logic or these linkages be observed on the surface of everyday behavior patterns. Yet any attempts to intervene in these patterns without a thorough understanding of their underlying base not only has a reduced chance of success but also suggests a kind of cultural imperialism which in and of itself is wrong.

Where an effort has been made to determine the underlying base of particular behavioral patterns, several further determinations should be made. First, what is the nutritional effect of the existing practice? Where the practice is nutritionally beneficial or neutral, clearly no intervention is called for. Where the practice is nutritionally harmful it is necessary to determine the extent to which the practice is ingrained and hence the degree of resistance that might be anticipated. A proposed intervention then can be evaluated by comparing the resistance with the resources and time period available to overcome it.

Basically, intervention into traditional beliefs and practices can take one of two broad forms: person-to-person or mass media. The former is an example of the targeted approach, while the latter attempts to affect the target group by reaching the larger population. Each is discussed briefly below.

Person-to-person nutrition information dissemination has been undertaken as part of U.N.-assisted Applied Nutrition Programs, as part of nutrition rehabilitation centers, and by government extension agents, health clinics, and voluntary agencies. In some cases it is incorporated into the formal education curriculum. These efforts have varied considerably in three basic respects: (a) the skill and training of the disseminators; [25] (b) the content of the messages being disseminated; and (c) the means by which these messages are communicated. Where programs are weak in these respects they might be boosted by more careful study of existing practices and attitudes, knowledge of the initiators of change in the particular social system, development of means to more fully enlist the active cooperation of that social system, greater use of professional communicators and communication skills, [13] and careful pretesting of techniques. [34] In general the effectiveness of a particular dissemination will be in direct proportion to its specificity and its simplicity. Much of the above occurs more or less automatically when the dissemination is carried out by local individuals. [10, 12]

The critical questions to be answered in the case of person-to-person information dissemination are two in number. First, what are the cost and time period necessary to reach the bulk of the population in a medium or large size low-income country? While nutrition rehabilitation centers have had considerable success in Haiti, the cost of similarly reaching the preschool-age group of India, for example, would exceed $1.5 billion.

The second question is the effectiveness of such intervention as measured by the ultimate criterion of improved nutritional status. Equally important are the carryover effects over time and space. Does the mother who has received such education continue to observe the recommended practices a year later? Does she observe them with her subsequent children? Does she effectively pass the knowledge to her neighbor or must the neighbor also be reached directly? Unfortunately few nutrition education programs gather such information, which would be of considerable value in refining existing programs and designing new ones.

Mass media efforts are carried out through newspapers and magazines, cinema, billboards, radio, television, and through messages on everything from buses and rickshaws to calendars and yo-yos. Operating on a "mass" basis they circumvent the basic problems of cost and time cited above in relation to person-to-person efforts. While many mass media initiatives may lack the human, personal approach of more traditional nutrition education, others may provide it more effectively through the broadcast speech of a prime minister or important religious figure. Furthermore mass media efforts are usually undertaken by groups better capable of communicating than traditional nutrition educators. They must of course be provided with the right messages—as they sometimes have not been—if this communication is to have the desired effect.

The primary questions to be answered by advocates of increased investment in the mass media approach would be the following:

1. How much does the approach depend on the skills or sophistication of the lowest income groups in need of the assistance? Where literacy is required these groups automatically may be eliminated in many countries. Similarly,

westernized techniques of selling a product or concept, which might have considerable appeal to the communicators and to the well-educated segments of the population, might bypass most of the lower income group for whom the communication was intended. [12, 35]

2. What is the cost of introducing large-scale but decentralized broadcasting or television capable of reaching the bulk of the populace, rural as well as urban, but still keeping the messages relevant and in the right language or dialect?

3. While presumably capable of successful motivation if handled intelligently, how effective are the media (television aside) in disseminating the techniques of new practices to an illiterate populace?

4. Can low-income groups translate the messages into improved practice and well-being without income increments, or will they merely widen their expectations gap with possible social and political consequences? [36]

Most of these questions cannot easily be answered, partly because experience with mass media utilization for nutrition purposes in low-income countries has been limited, and partly because, as with nutrition education, there has been little evaluation. While evaluation of mass media efforts is considerably more difficult it is undertaken regularly in industrialized countries, and measurement techniques exist that could be usefully employed.

Although new foods are not intended primarily as vehicles of information dissemination, food consumption patterns in some countries have changed with their introduction. This occurred in West Africa, for example, with the European introduction of corn. It took place in Japan with the introduction of milk in school lunch programs during the American occupation.

Health of the Child

Malnutrition seldom occurs as an isolated phenomenon. Generally it is accompanied by more general health problems including gastrointestinal infection, which, as described earlier, exacerbates the nutritional problems and in turn is adversely affected by them. In some cases the limiting factors are clear and require direct and immediate action if the child's well-being is to be restored. Frequently, however, there are possibilities for trade-offs. In such cases intervention directed either at improving the food intake or at eliminating the infection will, if effective, serve to improve both conditions. When this situation exists the choice of direction will depend on relative costs and feasibility as well as relative effectiveness. A recent example would be the widespread use of measles vaccine, which can dramatically reduce the incidence of kwashiorkor that may follow this disease.

Costs and feasibility of nutrition-related health interventions vary as widely as nutrition intervention. As with information dissemination, a "personalization" spectrum might usefully be constructed with person-to-person attention at one end and mass programs at the other. In general, costs will decrease and feasibility increase as one moves toward the mass end of the spectrum. At the same time effectiveness at the level of the individual patient might decrease.

On one end of the spectrum lies the traditional western doctor-patient concept. One notch over is the hospital or health center. Such personalized service for an entire populace, often taken for granted in industrialized nations, is a luxury that seldom can be afforded in the low-income countries, which might claim only one doctor for tens of thousands of persons. One answer to this problem is greatly increased training and utilization of paraprofessionals capable of treating uncomplicated health problems. Such paraprofessionals can give the routine case the special attention it would not otherwise receive, and at the same time considerably relieve the strain on doctors. [23]

Further along the spectrum are the nutrition rehabilitation center and the under-five clinic. Both are multipurpose institutions but with major health components. Both have made important contributions in practice although, as noted earlier, these have been primarily in smaller countries. The nutrition rehabilitation center is essentially a day-care center where children are selected on the basis of nutritional and health status. Usually these are moderate cases not requiring hospitalization but needing more assistance than might be provided through outpatient services. The centers, staffed with trained but nonprofessional local women, might handle 30 children from the age of 3 months (8 to 10 hours a day), providing nutrition and health rehabilitation and making a special effort to educate their mothers. The centers are also designed to provide some demonstration effect to the community so that every child need not go through the program. [37]

For still less serious cases, outpatient services of an under-five clinic may be adequate. Such clinics provide inoculations, distribute supplements, and carry

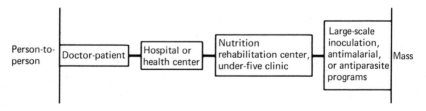

Figure 2. Health Intervention Spectrum

out height and weight measurements. In some cases mothers are given height-weight charts for their children, which provide useful health indices and detect children at high risk of developing clinically observable malnutrition.

In large, overpopulated countries, even these more modest types of health intervention may require greater financial and administrative resources than are available. In these cases it becomes necessary to move even further out along the spectrum. Some nutrition-related mass health solutions have been undertaken with considerable success, notably the antimalarial campaigns and mass immunization programs. The nutritional impact of such programs has never been estimated, but they probably achieve more than most direct nutrition interventions that have been attempted in low-income countries. The effectiveness of these programs raises the question of similar mass intervention designed to deal with other nutrition-related health problems, notably gastrointestinal infection and parasites. There is sometimes reluctance among medical personnel to consider such mass solutions, because of the possibility of negative reactions by a few although the overall benefits may be overwhelmingly positive. Clearly, further research in and creative thinking about mass, nutrition-related health intervention are called for if these solutions are to become viable and reach those in greatest need.

Nonfamily Feeding

Over the past twenty years numerous efforts have been made to carry out special feeding programs for children. In many cases these programs have been actively supported with international commodity and financial assistance. Overall, no single direct nutrition intervention effort has received anywhere near the magnitude of resources that have gone into child feeding. Basically, child feeding programs can improve well-being in three ways: first, by directly improving the nutritional status of the child; second, by increasing the real income of his family enough to release a portion of it for other uses; third, by strengthening institutions that serve as distribution outlets for the food. Where feeding is carried out through the schools it may boost registration, decrease absenteeism, and improve performance. Where food is distributed through a family planning clinic it may well increase the clinic's effectiveness. [1,38] The second and third roles represent economic and social multipliers and clearly should be taken into account in any effort to evaluate the effectiveness of feeding programs.

As with other intervention programs, child feeding must be examined in the context of broader economic and political realities. If child feeding represents nothing more than a palliative in the midst of a pattern of development that essentially excludes the low-income populace, it would be a questionable pursuit—one that probably would have the effect of delaying the day of reckoning on the larger issue. If, however, one is satisfied that this is not the case, and if other longer term, more viable efforts are under way to improve nutritional status, the case for such immediate efforts to reach vulnerable groups can be convincing.

Intervention in existing child feeding programs might profitably proceed in three directions. The first would be aimed at institutionalizing the feeding in the domestic food distribution system where this has not yet been done. Unless it is done, low-income countries will remain dangerously dependent on international assistance, which in and of itself is problematic. Mechanisms to accomplish this goal usually need not be developed from scratch. Where governments are actively engaged in the buying and selling of food commodities, particularly as the supply of these commodities begins to exceed effective demand, portions of government stocks might automatically be earmarked for child feeding. Beyond this, an agricultural planning body projecting supply requirements to meet domestic demand, buffer stock, and export needs could without major complication add a fourth category, namely child feeding requirements.

A second type of intervention would be directed at a change in the age of the recipients. At present, probably 90 percent or more of the commodities available for child feeding in low-income countries are distributed through school feeding programs. The reason for this is clear and understandable. The schools not only represent the easiest and least expensive distribution outlet; they represent, in many countries, the only official, nationwide center capable of reaching such large numbers of children. Nevertheless in nutritional terms and probably in overall economic terms, the impact on schoolchildren may be considerably less than on younger children. Thus, it may be necessary to restructure existing feeding to reach the preschool-age child through some combination of noneducational outlets (primary health centers, local clinics, nurseries, rural mothers' organizations, nutrition rehabilitation centers, and maternal-child health centers) and the existing school distribution system reinforced for after-school feeding. [39]

Where the second type of intervention involves the recipients, the third involves the food used in such programs. At present, food commodities are usually delivered to the school, where they are prepared on the site. This method presents two problems. First, the schools are seldom equipped for efficient and sanitary preparation of food. This can be particularly counterproductive when unclean water is used, thereby adding to gastrointestinal infection. Second, the on-site preparation of food requires considerably more time and effort than most schools have available. The solutions to these problems would seem to lie in the use of foods requiring no on-site preparation. One possibility is the model of "central kitchens" developed in the South Indian state of Tamil Nadu. These central processing and cooking facilities prepare the food, which is then systematically transported to all distribution outlets within, say, a 20- or 30-mile radius. Such a network would permit use of virtually any distribution outlet regardless of how inadequately staffed or equipped. The food might be normally cooked commodities transported to the outlets in large vacuum vessels. Or it might utilize ready-to-eat extruded products where such equipment can be provided. Finally, if the clientele were limited to preschoolers and their mothers, an effective mechanism might be the distribution of processed weaning foods for home preparation. [39]

Conclusion

The above categories of interventions constitute the major alternatives, and in some cases complementary nutrition-related investments, which can be considered by the planner. Their relative attractiveness, of course, varies considerably from region to region depending not only upon the nature of the problem identified, but also on the relative importance of such criteria as costs, political viability, and speed of implementation used in selecting among them.

The remarkably broad range of possible interventions underlines the contention made throughout that nutrition programs can and must be designed in a manner which reinforces, and is fully consistent with, desirable patterns of economic growth.

References

1. Levinson, F. James and David L. Call. *Nutrition Intervention in Low Income Countries: A Planning Model and Case Study.* Department of Agricultural Economics and Graduate School of Nutrition, Cornell International Agricultural Development Monograph 34.

2. Food and Agriculture Organization of the United Nations. *Consumer Survey Listing.*

3. Bennett, M. K. *The World's Food.* New York: Harper, 1954.

4. Berg, Alan D. Increased income and improved nutrition: a shibboleth examined. *Internat. Develop. Rev.* 12:3, 1970.

5. Food and Agriculture Organization of the United Nations. *State of Food and Agriculture.* Rome, 1957.

6. Operations Research Group. *Food Habits Survey–Gujarat and Maharashtra.* Conducted for the Protein Food Association of India, 1969.

7. India, Directorate of National Sample Surveys. *National Sample Survey, 1952.*

8. Food and Agriculture Organization of the United Nations. *Agricultural Commodities– Projections for 1970.* Rome, 1962.

9. Cassel, J. The social and cultural implications of food and food habits. *Amer. J. Pub. Health* 47:732, 1957.

10. Mead, Margaret. *Cultural Patterns and Technical Change.* Paris: UNESCO, 1953.

11. Wyon, John B. and John E. Gordon. *The Khanna Study: Population Problems in the Rural Punjab.* Cambridge: Harvard University Press, 1971.

12. Jelliffe, D. B. *Infant Nutrition in the Subtropics and Tropics.* World Health Organization Monograph Series, No. 29, 1955.

13. Latham, Michael C. Increasing production and consumption of dairy products and eggs in developing countries. In *Proceedings of the Seventh International Congress of Nutrition,* Hamburg. Vol. 3, p. 61, 1966.

14. Latham, Michael C. Diet and infection in relation to malnutrition in the United States. *New York J. Med.* 70:558, 1970.

15. Scrimshaw, N. S. *The Effect of the Interactions of Nutrition and Infection in Pre-School Child Malnutrition.* Washington, D.C.: National Academy of Sciences/National Research Council, 1966.

16. Hegsted, D. M. Amino acid fortification and the protein problem. *Amer. J. Clin. Nutr.* 21:688, 1968.

17. Lele, Uma J. and John W. Mellor. *The Political Economy of Employment Oriented Development.* Occasional Paper No. 42. Cornell University, Department of Agricultural Economics, USAID Employment and Income Distribution Project, June 1971.

18. Mellor, John W. *Technological Advance in Indian Agriculture as It Relates to the Distribution of Income.* Report prepared for the International Bank for Reconstruction and Development, December 1969.

19. Abbott, John C. Economic factors affecting the distribution of world food protein resources. In *Protein Enriched Cereal Foods for World Needs.* Max Milner, ed. American Association of Cereal Chemists, 1969, p. 13.

20. van Schaik, F. H. Pulse production: status and potential. Paper delivered at AID Conference on Nutrition and Plant Breeding, 1970.

21. Food and Agriculture Organization of the United Nations. *Provisional Indicative World Plan for Agricultural Development.* Rome, 1970.

22. DeMuelenacre, H. J. H. Development, production and marketing of high protein foods. In *Protein Enriched Cereal Foods for World Needs.* Max Milner, ed. American Association of Cereal Chemists, 1969, p. 266.

23. King, Maurice, ed. *Medical Care in Developing Countries.* Oxford: Oxford University Press, 1966.

24. Mellor, John W. The functions of agricultural prices in economic development. *Indian J. Agric. Econ.* 23:23, 1968.

25. Griffiths, W. The educational approach to health work. *Health Educ. J.* 15:1, 1957.

26. Dalrymple, Dana G. *Economic Aspects of Nutrition Improvement in Tunisia.* Washington, D.C.: U.S. Department of Agriculture, 1970.

27. Food and Agriculture Organization of the United Nations. *Food and Agricultural Price Policies in Asia and the Far East.* Bangkok, 1958.

28. Mattern, Paul J. New approaches to amino acid and vitamin improvement of cereal products: Protein improvement by breeding. In *Protein Enriched Cereal Foods for World Needs.* Max Milner, ed. American Association of Cereal Chemists, 1969, p. 234.

29. Brooke, C. L. Enrichment and fortification of cereals and cereal products with vitamins and minerals. *J. Agric. Food Chem.* 16:163, 1968.

30. Menden, E. and H. D. Cremer. The problem of improving nutritive value. *Food Manufacture,* July-November 1958: pp. 293, 330, 379, 417, 463. February-March 1959: pp. 65, 121.

31. Altschul, Aaron M. The agricultural, scientific and economic basis for low-cost protein foods. Paper presented at the International Conference on Single-Cell Protein, Cambridge, Mass., October 9, 1969.

32. Altschul, Aaron M. The world food problem: Food proteins for humans. *Chem. Eng. News* 47:68, 1969.

33. Call, David L. Some notes on evaluation of amino acid fortification. Paper presented to FAO/WHO/UNICEF Protein Advisory Group, 1969.

34. Knutson, A. L. Pretesting health education materials. *Amer. J. Pub. Health* 43:193, 1953.

35. Foster, G. M., ed. *A Cross Cultural Analysis of a Technical Aid Program.* Washington: Smithsonian Institution, 1951.

36. Freedman, M. A report on some aspects of food, health and society in Indonesia. Mimeo. Geneva: WHO, 1955.

37. *A Practical Guide to Combating Malnutrition in the Preschool Child: Nutrition Rehabilitation Through Maternal Education.* Report of a Working Conference on Nutritional Rehabilitation or Mothercraft Centers. Bogotá, 1969.

38. Berg, Alan D. Toward survival: Nutrition and the population dilemma. *Interplay* 3:24, 1970.

39. Levinson, F. James. Our child feeding overseas: a development resource for the seventies. *J. Amer. Dietetic Assoc.* 59:503, 1970.

Additional References

Adams, R. N. An analysis of medical beliefs and practices in a Guatemalan Indian town. Mimeo. 1951.

Bacigalupo, Antonio. Protein-rich cereal foods in Peru. In *Protein Enriched Cereal Foods for World Needs.* Max Milner, ed. American Association of Cereal Chemists, 1969, p. 288.

Berg, Alan D. Priority of nutrition in national development. *Nutr. Rev.* 28:1, 1970.

Burgess, Ann. Nutrition education in public health programs—what have we learned? *Amer. J. Pub. Health* 51:1715, 1961.

Call, David L. Alternative approaches in combating the protein problem. Paper presented to the Conference on Amino Acid Fortification of Protein Foods, Cambridge, Mass., 1969.

Dalrymple, Dana G. *The Diversification of Agricultural Production in Less Developed Nations.* Washington, D.C.: U.S. Dept of Agriculture, 1968.

Davies, T. A. Lloyd. *Nutrition in Industry.* Proceedings of the Sixth International Congress of Nutrition, 1964, p. 24.

Food and Agriculture Organization of the United Nations. *Possibilities of Increasing World Food Production.* Freedom from Hunger Basic Study No. 10. Rome, 1963.

Howe, E. E., G. R. Jansen, and M. L. Anson. An approach toward the solution of the world food problem with special emphasis on protein supply. *Amer. J. Clin. Nutr.* 20:1134, 1967.

Inter-American Committee for Agricultural Development. *Inventory of Information Basic to the Planning of Agricultural Development in Latin America.* Pan American Union, 1963-64.

Kracht, U. Economic aspects of the supplementation of cereals with lysine. Ad Hoc Group on Amino Acid Fortification, FAO, May, 1969.

Krishna, Raj. Agricultural price policy and economic development. In *Agricultural Development and Economic Growth.* H. M. Southworth and B. F. Johnston, eds. Ithaca: Cornell University Press, 1967.

Krishnaswamy, P. R. *The Protein Foods Association of India.* FAO/WHO Protein Advisory Group Document 8. Rome, 1969, p. 47.

Latham, Michael C. Some observations relating to applied nutrition programs supported by the UN agencies. *Nutr. Rev.* 25:193, 1967.

Levinson, F. James, and Alan D. Berg. With a grain of fortified salt. *Food Technology* 23:70, 1969.

Mellor, John W. *The Economics of Agricultural Development.* Ithaca: Cornell University Press, 1966.

Parman, G. K. Fortification of cereals and cereal products with proteins and amino acids. *J. Agric. Food Chem.* 16:168, 1968.

Patankar, V. N. *Protein Foods Marked Development Program in India.* FAO/WHO/ UNICEF Protein Advisory Group Document 8. Rome, 1969, p. 17.

Senti, F. R. The case for plant proteins. Paper presented to the American Society of Animal Science Meeting, Cornell University, 1967.

Shaw, Richard L. Incaparina in Central America. In *Protein Enriched Cereal Foods for World Needs.* Max Milner, ed. American Association of Cereal Chemists, 1969, p. 320.

19   Nutrition Intervention
Programs: Identification
and Selection

Leonard Joy
Fellow, Institute of Development Studies,
University of Sussex, United Kingdom

A paper offering a systematic approach to food and nutrition intervention
programs is very welcome, especially when it sets out to challenge such system as there is in current approaches. The major points of this paper are so
fundamental and, incredibly, so radical that comment must start by firmly
endorsing them. The most important points made by Call and Levinson are
surely that planning must work from demand to supply and not vice versa;
that where poverty is the principal cause of inadequate nutrition, intervention
programs must seek lowest-cost diet supplementation; and a related issue—
that where protein-calorie malnutrition can be traced to total calorie deficits
we are foolish to provide the needed calories in expensive protein forms.

But the paper has said more than this, for it demonstrates also a systematic
approach to the review of policy instruments and the assessment of their
relevance, judged in relation to the analysis of the causes of particular categories of poor nutrition. Rather than recite a list of minor qualifications that
might be made with regard to the detailed observations contained in the
paper, I propose to attempt to place the discussion in the wider context of
the planning process as a whole and to make explicit other important implications of the Call-Levinson paper.

The identification of relevant policy instruments for the improvement of the
nutrition of specified, or target, groups is seen by Call and Levinson as the
basis of an approach to the preparation of a national policy/program package
of appropriate size and pattern consistent with overall development aims.
Certainly one can agree that the identification of relevant policy instruments
is a key stage in the food and nutrition planning process, but more guidance is
needed if policy instrument identification and choice are to proceed effectively and to culminate in a comprehensive food and nutrition plan well integrated with other national development plans.

As the paper has stressed, the identification of nutrition intervention programs must stem from a first stage investigation to provide at least a general
idea of the alternative population target groups where nutrition problems
exist. However, it would seem that the more general and the less specific this
idea is, the less effective is likely to be the subsequent identification of instruments and their relevance to solving target group problems. This is well illustrated by the paper itself, which uses as its example of a target "preschool
children." In most countries it would be desirable to subdivide this category.
One would certainly wish to distinguish urban from rural groups, and each of

these sets would need to be subdivided. For example, rural might need to be subdivided not simply into broad regional or ecological zones but perhaps more finely, viz. pastoral/dry arable/irrigated farming areas; by degrees of accessibility; by the nature of domestic water supplies; by the nature of public health services. Possibly tribe, religion, period of settlement, and socioeconomic categories also would need to be considered—migrant, landless, part-employed, and so on. Clearly the precise enumeration of the poorly nourished into such refined categories is not immediately possible in most countries and the absence of so detailed a functional classification cannot be an excuse for not tackling the problems that can be clearly defined—if not fully enumerated.

However, it is also clear that failure to differentiate classes of the problem will mean a failure to be able to estimate the scope and relevance of different policy instruments. Failure to specify most explicitly the groups that can feasibly be the targets of any instrument will lead to its misguided application. While Call and Levinson emphasize the need for causal understanding they do not sufficiently emphasize the need for causal discrimination. In practical terms, we are arguing that when government planning bodies seek assessments from ministries, agencies, and others of the potential relevance of particular instruments, they must pose their queries in relation to target categories considerably finer than "preschool children." Not only might different instruments be more or less relevant to different subgroups (for example, high protein infant foods for remote subsistence farming communities without clean domestic water, or price policies as they are relevant to food "surplus" or "deficit" farmers) but they may be more or less costly also, and cost estimates must be related to specific programs.

No doubt the evolution of a good functional classification of various categories of poorly nourished is something that will itself be stimulated by its application to policy instrument assessment, but it is essential to attempt an explicit—and fairly fine—classification to which the assessment can be applied from the start.

Call and Levinson assume that instrument assessment will be preceded by a definition of regional nutrition problems "in terms of food intake and availability." This seems to need spelling out and, perhaps, querying. What is wanted initially is an identification of *nutrient* deficiencies (including calories) and their nature and extent within different categories of the functional classification. Nutrition policy will aim to make good these nutrient deficiencies. In doing so, it has not only a choice of instruments but also a choice of foods or other sources of the required nutrient intake supplementation. Choice of instrument is also, in part, choice of form of supplementation. The question of which food is appropriate for diet supplementation must not be prejudged. Since much of the nutrition problem is a poverty problem, whether we are concerned about the cost to the individual whose diet we are trying to improve or the cost to those who are bearing the burden of income redistribution, we must seek least-cost methods of diet supplementation. Apart from anything else, methods with high per capita costs will, in practice, mean that fewer will benefit than would be the case were per capita costs lower. Thus, least-cost diet studies, combined in some cases with studies of food habits in relation to the possibilities of diet modification, are an important step in the tentative expression of nutrient deficits as food deficits.

Once we have defined likely targets, the problem is then how to achieve them. We are seeking to increase, or modify, food intakes of a section of the population which is poorly nourished. This must mean that if we succeed we shall augment the total demand for food in a country. We shall also, no doubt, augment the total demand for administrative and other services. Our planning problem is to choose the most desirable size and pattern of nutrition program. The paper under review has said nothing about size, yet it is a major issue in comprehensive planning. Let us assume that some preliminary assessment of the relevance, scope, and cost effectiveness of different policy instruments has been made, and that we can now examine the implications of a given scale of program. We should be able to assess by how much a successful program of the pattern and size tentatively under consideration would increase the total demand for food. From this point we can attempt to assess the general equilibrium effects on demand, supplies, and prices of foods and of these in turn upon the economy as a whole. If demand is increased above expected trend values, as it must be if the nutrition policy is successful, then prices will be higher than they would otherwise have been. How far supplies will respond, what the total impact of food prices, wages, growth, employment, and migration will be, and what the pressures for food importation will be are likely to be among the questions posed to economists and econometricians. In turn, the answers to such questions will relate to the assessment of the net impact on the nation's nutrition problem.

A further, related question is the order of magnitude of income redistribution implied by the size of the proposed program, measured by the transfer element in the increment of demand, and the way in which, directly by the nature of the policy instruments to be used and indirectly by their repercussions on the economy as a whole, these are borne. Indirect income redistribution effects will arise, for example, from shifts in the relative prices of farm products or from the relative movements of wages, profits, and rents. Direct effects will be represented, for example, by taxation imposed in order to finance subsidized feeding programs or fair-price/ration schemes.

It is widely observed that, for the most part, poor nutrition stems from poverty. The alleviation of this poverty can be achieved either by measures to engage the poor in more productive and rewarding employment or by measures to transfer incomes in favor of the poor. Call and Levinson would seem, generally, to pass too pessimistic a judgment on the immediate value of policies to improve the employment and earnings opportunities of the poor. (If this is not what they intend, then it seems that they bracket them too sweepingly with policies to raise the general level of income.) It is clear, however, that, where the poverty problem is too vast to be tackled readily by improving employment and productivity, the problem posed by the extent of income transfer required to alleviate poor nutrition in the short run will also be great.

Certainly, the limitations on the possibilities of overcoming poor nutrition are likely to be imposed primarily by the extent to which employment or productivity can be improved and by the size of the income transfer that is feasible. Conceivably, food supplies might not respond to increased demand, nor might it be feasible or acceptable to augment them indefinitely through imports, so that nutrition improvement becomes constrained by supply rather than by demand. Thus, preliminary assessment of the feasible scale of nutrition improvement targets must revolve around an estimation of these constraints.

Call and Levinson emphasize the need to appraise systematically the relevance and effectiveness of policy instruments designed to improve nutrition. I would emphasize the desirability of appraising policies whose objectives are not primarily nutritional for their indirect effects on nutrition. Agricultural ministries need to be sensitized to consider the employment and income distribution effects of their various development programs and to estimate the extent to which those around the margin of adequate subsistence are pulled above or pushed below the threshold of adequacy. Moreover, while it is essential to build up a detailed picture of the extent and nature of malnutrition in relation to a functional classification of the various categories of the problem, it is also important that the dynamics of the problem should be monitored and that attempts should be made to forecast changes in the numbers of poorly nourished in the various categories and the extent to which these result from program and policy measures, including those not primarily pursued for nutrition objectives.

Insofar as effective demand for food can be increased by a successful nutrition policy, programs to match supply increases to demand increases become vital. It is to be noted, however, that supply increases alone may have little impact on the nutrition problem; insofar as they result in falling food prices, supply may cease to grow long before desirable supply targets are met. Call and Levinson rightly distinguish the effect of changes in relative prices in changing the *pattern* of supply from the impact of changes in the *general level* of agricultural prices on the general level of farm supplies. They fail to emphasize, however, the significance of the pattern of supplies in relation to nutrition problems. Not only must we note the food-nonfood balance of farm output, we must also note the cheap food-dear food balance of farm output. In particular, we must be concerned that efforts to promote "improved" diets through increased production and consumption of animal products may be costly in terms of the displacement of resources from the production of cheaper foods. "Improvement" in already "adequate" diets may mean increases in health and performance which are small compared with the cost of the loss of health or performance resulting from deterioration of, or failure to improve, low-income diets.

In addition to the need to improve procedures for the identification of relevant intervention programs, another, most serious, gap still to be filled in the systematization of the planning process relates to the elaboration of procedures for the selection of nutrition programs. It is clear that cost-benefit analysis, as conventionally applied, is inadequate as a final arbiter of choice. With nutrition measures we are very evidently concerned not simply for the value of total food production, or even for the value of the incremental increase in production of all outputs stemming from a nutrition measure; we are concerned with the level and nature of consumption and its pattern between people and over time. We should count it a gain if people were to be saved from blindness even if this result were not reflected in an increase of other, marketable, outputs. Thus if we are to use cost-benefit calculations to assist in resource allocation for nutrition intervention programs, we must be prepared in some way to include nonmarketable benefits and to become involved in interpersonal comparisons of utility, valuing differently the increment of consumption of an underfed man from the increment of consumption of a well-fed man.

Certainly, in some way or another, we need to measure the cost of improving nutrition and to compare the costs of alternative intervention measures. Hard decisions have also to be made about how much can be afforded for the improvement of nutrition and who is to benefit. Since the cost is the reduction of somebody's present or future consumption, the questions of who pays and when are also important. These are questions not explicitly faced by conventional cost-benefit analysis.

The flow chart of nutrition policy decision-making (Figure 1) may help in retracing this discussion and in setting the Call-Levinson procedures in a wider context. The Call-Levinson paper centers around the use of causal analysis as a basis for the systematic identification of relevant intervention programs. Examination of the flow chart shows that causal analysis (1) assumes a previous assessment of who is short of what nutrients and calories (the "data analysis" and "functional classification" stages). The use of "typical profiles" of the situations of the poorly nourished, as suggested by Berg and Muscat, would be a valuable adjunct of a "functional classification." The flow chart also implies the appraisal of alternative intervention programs and the elimination of ineffective or overcostly options. Thereafter, the flow shows (2) the total impact of preliminary intervention proposals that needs to be assessed in terms of general equilibrium effects (3), and the impact on the magnitude of the nutrition problem and its trends (4) as discussed above. The impact of development policies and projects—in, say, transport, rural and urban development strategies, population, employment, and wage policies—upon trends in the nature and extent of poor nutrition should also be explicitly considered (5). Decisions need to be made with regard to the overall magnitude and composition of nutrition intervention programs (6) that are not otherwise specifically nutrition oriented (7). Following broad strategic decisions on the size and pattern of programs which in turn depend, as we have said, on the feasibility of targeted income generation and/or income transfer as well as, maybe, on the feasibility of stimulating food supply responses, agencies need to be briefed to present detailed policy and program designs within budgetary and manpower limits defined for them (8). Thus the detailed programs of diverse agencies may be made to cohere into a total nutrition plan which relates nutrition and food policies and which also relates separate agency programs within a macroeconomic framework.

What the flow chart implies, but does not make explicit, is that different agencies and ministries need to be directed with regard to the information that they provide and the planning and appraisal procedures that they employ. It also implies roles for each of the contributing analysts and agen-

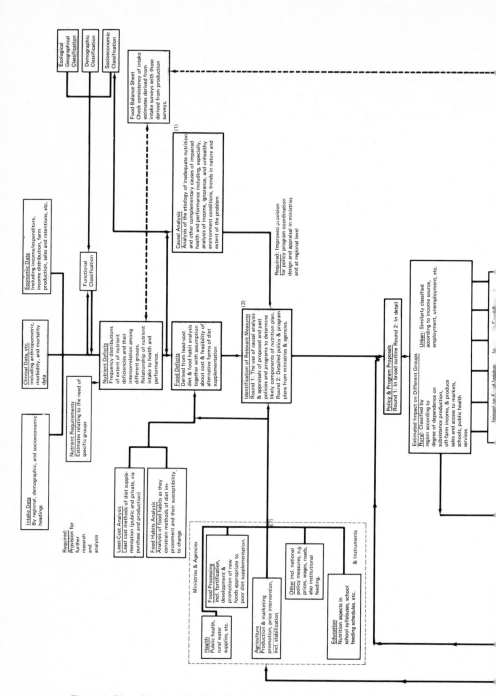

Figure 1. Flow Chart of Nutrition Policy Decision-Making

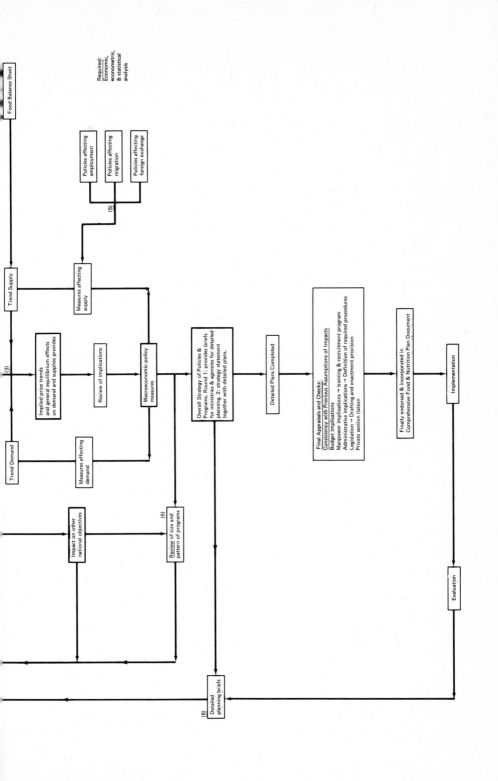

Food Balance Sheet

Required:
Economic,
econometric,
& statistical
analysis

Trend Supply

Policies affecting
employment

Policies affecting
migration

Policies affecting
foreign exchange

(5)

Measures affecting
supply

(3)

Implied price trends
and general equilibrium effects
on demand and supplies provides

Review of implications

Macroeconomic policy
measures

Overall Strategy of Policies &
Programs. Round 1: provides briefs
for ministries & agencies for detailed
planning. 2: strategy statement
together with detailed plans.

Detailed Plans Completed

Final Appraisals and Checks:
Consistency with Previous Assumptions of Impacts
Budget implications
Manpower implications → training & recruitment program
Administrative implications → Definition of required procedures
Legislation → Drafting and enactment provision
Private section liaison

Finally endorsed & incorporated in
Comprehensive Food & Nutrition Plan Document

Implementation

Trend Demand

Measures affecting
demand

Impact on other
national objectives

(6)

Review of size and
pattern of programs

Evaluation

(8)

Detailed
planning briefs

cies, especially for nutritionists, statisticians, economists, econometricians, sociologists, agronomists, food technologists, and public health experts. It is clear, too, that the chart, while helping conceptually to relate the various stages and components of the total planning process, needs translating into a structure of administrative bodies and communications flows. This would need to be done in relation to particular countries to suit existing administrative and planning structures. Required communication networks might in fact be rather more complex than is suggested by the chart. It is appreciated that neither the creation of the required administrative and decision-making structure nor the execution of data collection and analysis such as may ultimately seem desirable are likely to be achieved other than over a period of several years. However, steps toward the suggested pattern of decision-making would be immediately rewarding for any country and would be likely to improve current food and nutrition planning. This, in the author's view, and contrary to a much expressed belief, is generally limited in its efficacy because of failure to correctly conceptualize the nutrition problem or to adopt a relevant systematic approach to its solution rather than because of limitations in data. Call and Levinson have rightly drawn attention to one major respect in which conceptualization is weak and in which nutrition planning might be readily improved.

20 Possible Modifications in Development Aid Policy

Saburo Okita
President
Japan Economic Research Center, Tokyo

The keynote paper gives a clear and realistic picture of the alternative policies for improving nutritional standards in low-income countries, focusing attention specifically on low-income groups in such countries and on preschool-age children. The content of this paper and the discussions on other topics of this conference indicate the necessity of seeking for a new approach to development policy and planning on a global scale. As already pointed out by some of the participants of this conference, nutrition problems will have to be treated as a part of the global strategy covering both developed and developing countries. Internal policies at micro and national levels should perhaps be reinforced by an international policy geared to the solution of widespread malnutrition in developing countries at the same time that food surpluses exist in developed countries.

Two years ago the Pearson Commission Report on aid strategy was published at the World Bank annual meeting; I was involved in the preparation of this report as a member of the commission. It stressed, among other things, the importance of the "efficiency principle" in development aid. It expressed an expectation that the developing countries would "graduate" one by one from the status of aid recipient by effectively mobilizing their domestic resources, by promoting export trade, and by utilizing efficiently the foreign resources supplied to them. If we consider nutrition problems seriously, however, we may have to introduce a new objective for development aid policy. More emphasis may have to be given to the elimination or reduction of malnutrition on a global basis. Ideas about the geographical distribution, volume, and terms of aid will have to undergo a substantial modification. If the emphasis of development strategy is to be geared to breaking up a vicious circle of malnutrition and low productivity, concentration of development aid to lower income groups of low-income countries will become necessary, and this will imply a substantial departure from the efficiency principle mentioned earlier. It should not be overlooked, however, that improvement in the nutrition level will take place more or less in parallel with income rise, and the overall strategy for accelerating economic growth, particularly of countries in the lowest income group, should play a crucial role.

Another important consideration is the possibility of a sharp drop in the birth rate if the per capita income rises above a certain critical level. Both the time series data of Japan and the cross-section data of other Asian countries show a close relationship between income level and the rate of population increase. Development aid also may have to be geared to the shortening of the transition period from the stage of a high birth rate and a low death rate to that of a low birth rate and a low death rate, by pushing up the rate of economic growth in countries with income levels lower than the above-mentioned critical level.

One of the interesting observations in the Call-Levinson paper is on the importance of pulses as a cheap source of protein. In prewar Japan the soya bean composed an important part of the diet and was one of the major sources of protein intake. Japonica type rice is also relatively rich in protein. For poorer nations, an increasing supply of pulses and protein-rich staple grains would be desirable. The fact that the production of pulses in India declined substantially in recent years as a result of the introduction of high-yielding varieties of staple crops is disconcerting. High production will have to be restored and, in this connection, food aid in the form of soya beans or other pulses may deserve attention.

Concerning the experience of a rapid improvement in the nutritional level of Japan, I will not dwell on details for Dr. Oiso and Mr. Orita are covering that. However, as I was directly in charge of preparing government economic plans, including the National Income Doubling Plan of 1960, I may be able to contribute a few points.

The remarkable improvement of nutritional level realized in the postwar years in Japan was brought about by the combination of nutrition policies (as illustrated in Dr. Oiso's paper) and a rapid increase in income. Per capita national income, which was U.S.$160 in 1952 rose to $380 in 1960 and further to $1,515 in 1970. During this period Japan moved from an under-nourished low-income society to a reasonably well-nourished and relatively high-income one. Per capita calorie intake rose by about 10 percent, and animal protein intake was about doubled. Fat consumption was also more than doubled during the same period.

One of the interesting aspects of Japan's experience in the postwar years may be the compression of growth and resultant changes in social, economic, and nutritional conditions in a relatively short span of time. This compression may provide a useful model for analysis of the interrelationship between economic growth and the various aspects of social development.

It is rather unlikely that the extraordinarily high rate of economic growth in Japan will continue into the future in view of the various factors working against rapid growth. A growing labor shortage, increasing need for directing resources to housing, urban, environmental, and other infrastructures, and the inability of the world market to absorb ever growing exports from Japan are among those factors. Social and economic problems in Japan, including nutrition problems, are likely to become more similar to those of the present western society.

At the same time, there will be an increasing realization of the necessity of gradually decelerating economic growth, particularly growth in physical output, in the highly industrialized countries as a whole while accelerating the growth of the developing countries. Population growth of both the developed and developing countries will also have to be slowed down until it reaches a stable level. Both trends seem desirable in view of the finite nature of the life-supporting system of the globe and the natural resources supply of the world. Moreover, the marginal utility of incremental material production is tending to decline in a rich society, while it will stay very high in a poor society. Approaches to nutrition intervention programs will have to be based on a global strategy for the entire human society.

21 Importance of Project
Preparation and Evaluation

Mogens Jul
Director
Danish Meat Products Laboratory,
Copenhagen
Protein Advisory Group, U.N.

Several years ago the U.N. Advisory Committee on the Application of Science
and Technology to Development proposed that systems analysis should be
used in considering plans for overcoming world protein problems. The proposal was discussed in the Protein Advisory Group (PAG) on the basis of an
earlier paper by Levinson and Call (1969). This resulted in PAG statement
No. 10, drawing attention to the fact that the available data are as yet inadequate for the quantitative application of sophisticated models, and stating
that attempts to build models with inadequate data may yield seriously misleading results.

In the present paper, Call and Levinson have thrown further light on this
subject. They discuss in detail how a great many different factors determine
the nutritional status of a population. Indirectly this suggests that the previous discussion as to whether or not income determines nutritional status is
somewhat academic. It is undoubtedly true that income has some influence
on nutritional status and it is definitely true that income is not the only factor or even the major one.

Six determinants for a population's nutritional status are identified by Call
and Levinson. Further, they give an estimated 26 examples of different classes
of interventions that could be used, and they suggest 7 different criteria
according to which each type of intervention should be evaluated. To these
criteria may be added that of technical feasibility. Including this, the criteria
suggested are listed in Table 1.

Considering that we here have a system with 6 determinants, 26 different
classes of interventions, and 8 different criteria, it is obvious that we face
such a complicated grid of interrelationships that a true systems analysis is
indeed called for. However, as the discussion by Call and Levinson also clearly
indicates, we do not have the quantitative data on which to base such a
sophisticated system. The value of the paper lies in the authors' contention
that a systematic approach should be used in planning nutrition programs and

Table 1. Criteria for Each Type of Intervention

1. Nutritional effectiveness	5. Time frame
2. Cost	6. Focus
3. Acceptability	7. Multipliers
4. Administrative viability	(8. Technical feasibility)

interventions, and the paper provides an excellent outline to use in evaluating proposed steps in this field.

The usefulness of this approach is brought out if one tries to apply it to some already existing projects, for instance, that of producing high-yielding, high-protein cereal varieties and protein-rich foods for infants and young children. Using it in this manner one arrives at the conclusion that these projects would indeed have withstood the acid test of such preevaluation. As experience has shown, they have been reasonably successful. Using the same test for some other projects, we must conclude that these would not have met the criteria suggested by Call and Levinson, and some would not have been launched had such pre-project evaluation been used. Again, we must concede that some such projects in the edible protein field have not been as well planned as should have been the case. In general, when evaluating aid activities—whether these be carried out by the United Nations or by bilateral agencies—it does seem that most projects have not been as well prepared as is required for successful results. In comparing our aid efforts with, for instance, development efforts within the industrial sectors of society, it becomes clear that aid projects generally are not prepared with nearly the amount of care used in industrial development work.

This opinion may sound strange, in light of the contention by Berg and Muscat that we are inclined to devote more time to precise analyses of the problem than to its solution. Yet, these statements are in agreement. It is customary in aid work to analyze in great detail, but such analyses are in themselves projects and as such they are often not well enough prepared. Then again, when such analyses eventually lead to a project, the contention often is that the project has not been prepared in sufficient detail. What are the causes for this? Those responsible for the projects are usually highly qualified and devoted individuals, but the system seems somewhat ill-designed. One objection constantly heard in all international work is that too much expense or time is devoted to "overhead," "administration," or whatever it may be called. Consequently, expenses for this part of a project are kept extremely low. In comparison with industrial development work, they are much too low. If one observes the pattern of work in the various organizations responsible for these projects, it is apparent that the staff professionals are really overworked. They just do not have time for proper project preparation.

Much has been said about explaining to the planners the problems of world protein nutrition. We probably have to admit that planners really do not decide in these matters. Decisions, both with regard to priorities and projects, are made by politicians, admittedly on the advice of planners and sometimes nutritionists. However, politicians abhor anything that looks like an adminis-trative expense. They consider this sheer waste, building up of bureaucracies, and so on. This is a most unfortunate situation because it prevents us from doing that careful project preparation, using a systematic analysis of what we propose to do, which could so well be carried out following the suggestions by Call and Levinson and which is absolutely essential to the success of the project. Therefore, the real problem may be whether we can convince politi-cians that more effort must go into project preparation and more funds must be allocated for this activity. However, one may have great doubts as to our capability of convincing politicians of the need for such expenditure. There-fore, it might be prudent to suggest doing what again is commonplace in industrial research and development, namely, adopting a policy of continu-ously monitoring results, carrying on post-project auditing, post-project calcu-lation of cost/effectiveness, and so on.

In international development work such post-project evaluation is not very common. There are some psychological reactions against it; it seems that the person responsible for a project feels that this procedure may imply criticism of his original plan. In reality this procedure implies no more criticism than does that of a scientist carrying out control experiments to check on his own findings, or a company doing detailed bookkeeping to ascertain to what extent each of its products is or is not profitable in the marketplace.

It is also difficult to sell post-project evaluation to politicians because they sometimes feel that even the suggestion that a project should be evaluated implies that it may not have been successful. This may be politically unpalat-able, especially if the project has indeed failed. However, serious efforts must be made to adopt post-project evaluation as standard practice. We must see which projects have been successful and which have failed; this would be useful in subsequent preparation of new projects, and it would indicate prob-lems that could not have been foreseen. Also, it would force us to use the systematic approach in project formulation for which the paper by Call and Levinson gives such valuable guidelines. Certainly some excellent post-project evaluations have been carried out, notably by UNICEF and the Danish Inter-national Development Agency (DANIDA). The contention is that these should be standard procedures.

22 Marketing Unconventional Protein-Rich Foods—One Form of Nutrition Intervention

Uwe Kracht
Marketing Research Manager, International
The Quaker Oats Company, Chicago

The objective of this session is to evaluate the major alternative or complementary nutrition intervention categories outlined in the keynote paper. At the outset, let me comment on one particular form of nutrition intervention: the commercial marketing of unconventional protein-rich foods.

Despite considerable effort in this field during the past decade, it now becomes evident that the contribution of this intervention approach has so far been low. In the case of Incaparina in Guatemala and Colombia,[1] less than 5 percent of the target groups consumed this product regularly in significant quantities, as shown by consumer surveys performed in 1969 for the Technical University of Berlin. [2] And among the total product group of unconventional products in developing countries, Incaparina so far shows one of the best marketing performances. Probably only Pro-Nutro in South Africa surpasses Incaparina in terms of sales; however, apparently most of the Pro-Nutro consumption does not occur in the target groups.

What are the reasons for the insignificant contribution of commercially distributed unconventional protein-rich foods? The keynote paper mentions the price premium of these products over the price of staple foods as the crucial factor, which leaves the commercial product "well beyond the reach of most of those who need it." [3] This statement needs some clarification. In Colombia, the corn-based Incaparina costs U.S. $0.21 per kilogram at the retail level; as compared to the staple food, corn, this represents a price premium of 50 to 60 percent. However, Incaparina's price amounts to only half of the average retail price for beans, another staple in the diet of low-income groups. In the case of the recently introduced rice-based Incaparina, a comparison shows approximately equal prices for the commercial high protein product and the highest quality grade of the staple food. Hence, in Colombia, the price of the commercial, unconventional food product is well within the range of staple food prices.

In Guatemala, the situation is different. Here, the Incaparina price is 350 to 400 percent of the price for corn (U.S. $0.40-0.44 per kilogram of Incaparina). In the above-mentioned survey, price was found to be an important

The views expressed in this paper represent the author's personal opinion and do not necessarily coincide with the position held by The Quaker Oats Company.
1 Incaparina was introduced in two different formulas: in Guatemala, formula 9A, with 58% corn and 38% cottonseed flour; in Colombia, formula 15, with 58% corn, 19% cottonseed flour, 19% defatted soy flour. Protein content, 27%. [1]

variable for Incaparina demand—yet it became evident that economic factors were not the only determinants. Economic factors are sometimes much less important in consumer behavior than generally assumed; this also holds true for low-income groups in developing countries. Consumers with budgets that can hardly meet expenses for staple foods sometimes spend a considerable share of their incomes for processed foods with high prices: a study in West Bengal reports exorbitant purchases of processed baby foods at much higher prices than that of cow's milk. [4] Similar situations exist in several African countries. Soft drink consumption by low-income groups—another example of "anti-economical" consumer behavior—is a worldwide phenomenon. [5] These few examples demonstrate that price, however important it may be, is far from the only factor responsible for the so far low success of commercial marketing programs.

One extremely important factor is the product and marketing concept, as explained below.

1. As a basis for successful marketing, a product should have a perceivable "point of difference" from other products. [6] Incaparina's organoleptic and functional properties resemble those of corn flour; its important "point of difference"—added nutrition—can hardly be perceived by the consumer, who therefore sees no reason to pay a premium price of 350-400 percent. This is a general problem with vegetable mixtures and fortified staple foods.

2. In Colombia, where a premium price does not represent a major problem, organoleptic properties of Incaparina become an important factor. The new rice-based Incaparina formula represents a remarkable organoleptic improvement. This has diminished or eliminated the observed negative point of difference and has increased demand. However, mere organoleptic improvement does not by itself create a new product concept with the strong point of difference necessary for stimulating continuous—as opposed to temporary—demand.

3. If the marketing concept calls for product promotion as "food for the whole family," it should be no surprise that the generally low household consumption is spread over all family members rather than concentrated in the target group within the family—an observation made for Incaparina in both countries. This is the cost of the "blanket" approach as opposed to the "target" approach. [3]

The basic reason for the unsatisfactory contribution of commercially marketed unconventional foods is the product—and in part the marketing—concept. The concept factor is, on the basis of experience in Colombia, still stronger than the price variable. What we need are more attractive product concepts. And here lies the dilemma: more sophisticated, more attractive product concepts increase product cost, and thus increase the stress on the tight family budget.

There is another aspect to be kept in mind with regard to product concept and consumer behavior. Even if we come up with a product that has a basically attractive concept, let us not expect that this one product alone will—in the long run—significantly improve the nutritional situation in a given country. Experience in consumer behavior shows that consumers do not adopt brand products on a continuous basis. [6] The dynamics of product adoption and disadoption lead to the well-known product life cycles, [7] and the less attractive the product concept, the shorter is the product life cycle. In order to counteract these life cycles of individual products, we need a number of products, both varieties of one brand and various brands.

Finally, marketing experience shows the enormous difficulties in reaching rural populations, in terms of stimulating continuous demand at significant quantity levels. With a number of good product concepts, combined with ingenious marketing concepts, we may be able to reach urban and semirural target groups. However, nutritional improvements among the rural target groups call for an approach that goes beyond traditional marketing. We have to search for unconventional marketing approaches, which will involve some form of government-business cooperation. Some alternative or complementary approaches were recently indicated by Alan Berg; [8] however, this extremely sensitive area should be the object of further, top-priority study.

References

1. Shaw, R. L. *Incaparina, Low-Cost Protein-Rich Food.* Nutrition Document R. 10/Add. 92. Geneva, 1966, p.2.

2. Kracht, U. The economics and marketing of protein-rich food products; Status report: Incaparina and competitors. Paper presented at the Western Hemisphere Nutrition Congress III, Bal Harbour, Fla., 1971.

3. Call, D. L., and F. J. Levinson. A systematic approach to nutrition intervention programs. This volume, pp. 165-197.

4. Roy, J. K. A social custom associated with the feeding practice profoundly affecting the protein intake. *Proceedings of the Nutrition Society of India,* No. 6, 1968.

5. Burgess, A., and R. F. A. Dean, eds. *Malnutrition and Food Habits.* New York: Macmillan, 1962, p. 39.

216   Uwe Kracht

6. Angelus, T. L. Why do most new products fail? *Advertising Age.* Chicago, Grain Communications, March 24, 1969, p. 85.

7. Levitt, I. Exploit the product life cycle. In *Managerial Marketing, Perspectives and Viewpoints.* E. J. Kelley and W. Lazer, eds. Homewood, Ill.: Dorsey, 1967, p. 427.

8. Berg, A. Harnessing industry for better nutrition: A look at the problems and the prospects. *Harvard Business Review,* in press.

23 The Mass Media Contribution to Intervention Programs

Richard K. Manoff
Chairman, Richard K. Manoff Inc.
New York

Not long ago, such a catalogue of nutrition interventions as we have heard presented here this morning would not have included either the system of food marketing or the use of mass media. Their inclusion is both a belated acknowledgment of their importance and a tribute to the professional perception and social sensitivity of Professors Call and Levinson. But that by no account means that I am at all satisfied. "Criticism," an astute social critic once wisely declared, "has a ritual quality. It doesn't have to be entirely true to be valid." Robert Browning said it another way:

A man's reach should exceed his grasp.
Or what's a heaven for?

I extend the reach of my criticism beyond truthful limits, only to grasp even more prominence for mass media, particularly the electronic, nonliterary media—television, radio, and the cinema.

The authors suggest a three-level process of investigation: (1) identifying the nutritional problem; (2) determining the causal factors; and (3) ascertaining through cost-effectiveness analysis optimum intervention means. I urge a fourth level of investigation into the media life of the community and its inhabitants. What is the penetration of radio and television—that is, how many radio and television sets are in operation in homes or in communal situations? How many cinema theaters? What percentage of the people, by geographic area, makes up the audience of these media? With what frequency? What are their viewing or listening habits? In short, to the demographic and the psychographic data of our target groups I urge the addition, if you will permit me a word of somewhat questionable coinage, of *communigraphic* information—the communications profile of the area and its people. It will prove to be essential to success in more than one nutrition intervention opportunity: (1) the marketing of new food formulations; (2) encouragement to eat new food combinations; and (3) the propagation of nutrition concepts and better nutrition practices.

Mass media influence, though widely acknowledged, is still not fully appreciated. Let me cite an example from one specific reference made by our speakers. They report that "within food groups there is a shift toward processed, more expensive items and varieties" as income rises. I have misgivings about such a strictly linear correlation. In complex social situations such simplistic one-way correlations can obscure other correlations of possibly greater significance. How can we be sure that the relationship to income is direct? Or is the relationship more accurately traceable to some new and special factor that usually accompanies rising income? A radio set? A television set? Or more frequent visits to the cinema? (Or newspapers and books for that matter, among the functionally literate?)

In the United States the marketing of foods has been utterly dependent on the development of our mass media capability. Without a highly developed television and radio connection to the American people, the mass marketing of processed foods would have been impossible. We know that people do not make a mass market. The mass media do. We know that the grocery store is not the marketplace. Radio is. Television is. The store is a distribution point. It is a display area. But the marketing of foods is done on the air waves. Neither the people nor the stores are the market. *The medium is the market.* The *mass* medium is the *mass* market. This explains the astronomical advertising expenditures of food companies in television and radio, particularly, as shown in Table 1. The result is that the average American supermarket now stocks between six and eight thousand food items, most of them not even in existence twenty years ago.

This great outpouring of processed foods—both good and bad—since World War II in the United States can certainly be meaningfully correlated with income. But it is more meaningfully correlated with the introduction of television and its widespread development since 1949. Rising income increases the opportunity for consumer discretion, but it is the mass media—the new

Table 1. 1970 Food Products Advertising Expenditures as Percentage of Total Advertising Expenditures

	Total national adv. expenditures ($ millions)	Food products adv. expenditures ($ millions)	% total
Spot television	1,477.6	356.9	24
Network television	1,732.1	303.5	18
Radio (network & spot)	413.0	47.0	11
Magazines	1,192.8	90.2	8
Newspapers	948.4	101.1	11
Outdoor	115.0	9.5	8
Total	5,878.9	908.2	15% of total

Source: Grocery Manufacturer, August 1971, pp. 5-7.

marketplace for food—that exercise the decisive influence on the discretionary food decisions. Today, in almost any country, this is tantamount to a decision in favor of commercially processed foods and, therefore, a continuing commitment to nutritional indifference.

Today's commercial food processor has no obligation, no mandate, to satisfy the nutritional priorities of his market even if he were aware of them. His obligation is to market foods he can persuade people to buy for the purpose of returning a profit on his investment. He is not to be blamed for preferring "fun-in-food" over nutritional value as a buying incentive. It is an easier, less complicated selling proposition. Why should we expect the commercial processor to assume a responsibility that neither the government nor its food officials have clearly defined? Not even the farmer has had such a policy spelled out for him so that agriculture might be more responsive to nutritional needs. In the absence of such policy, marketing dynamics prevail. The farmer grows what the market will absorb. The processor produces what he can most profitably sell. And he has monopolized the marketplace. Is it any wonder that the housewife whose rising fortunes have now made radio or television possible in her home must inevitably become his customer? This imposes on the nutrition advocate the obligations of the marketing man. He can no longer ignore the marketplace as the major arena for his activity. This means he must not disregard the central importance of the mass media in all his plans.

Now, it is erroneous to think of the mass media as essentially *commercial* media and of the advertising technique as exclusively a *commercial* methodology. The advertising technique is an ingenious employment of the principles of "reach-and-frequency" in mass media communication: to reach the broadest possible target audience with a desired message and to deliver that message as frequently as possible. Its key element is the *brief* message—a minute, 30 seconds, or even less—carefully designed to register a single idea memorably and to initiate the desired action. It seeks out its target audience among those programs where available audience data inform us that it can be found. It interrupts those programs briefly and, because briefly, it can do so repetitively over time—accumulating greater audience awareness and, almost always, increasing acceptance for and practice of its central idea. Clearly such a technique is not a mystique of commerce. It can be used for nutrition ideas. Other uses of the mass media, one-time programs, speeches, and the like, have their value but do not have the reach to *masses* of people, the potential to emphasize key ideas, the opportunity for repetition, for frequency.

The speakers here have correctly said that, in nutritional terms, the trend to processed foods "may have a negative effect—shifts from brown rice to polished rice, high extraction to low extraction flour, and cane to refined sugar as income increases. On balance, processed foods, in general, probably represent a nutritional minus when lost nutrients are not restored. On the other hand, certain types of marketing service can contribute importantly to nutrition."

A Kellogg's cereal need not be better known than protein, and the ordinary unbranded commodity foods which it enriches. A Campbell canned soup need not be better known than vitamin A and the unbranded food commodities that effectively deliver it. Coca-Cola should not be better known than iron and its ordinary food vehicles. Nor should Lipton's tea be better known than vitamin C and the ordinary foods in which we find it. Nutrients and the foods in which they are to be found make just as effective advertising messages as the brand names of manufacturers and the foods they process. We may have difficulty in visualizing this possibility because we are creatures of the custom of commerce. But the technique of mass media reach-and-frequency communication can be a helpful handmaiden to those with the wisdom to woo her and not merely to those who have quietly and passionately possessed her for their very own.

Moreover, time pressures make this procedure imperative. Radio and television are *time telescopes*. Whatever is bound to happen is made to happen faster by radio, television, and the cinema. The speakers tell us that intervention into traditional beliefs and practices can take one of two broad forms: the person-to-person approach or the mass media approach, and they correctly take the U.N.-assisted Applied Nutrition Programs (ANP) and Nutrition Rehabilitation or Mothercraft Centers as examples of the person-to-person pattern. Person-to-person efforts are indispensable but suffer from inadequacies of time and target audience reach. In India in 1970 I was informed that ANP had expanded its reach in 10 years to 900 of the 5,000 development blocks into which all Indian villages are grouped. In other words, ANP had in 10 years covered 18 percent of the villages. This is a remarkable logistical achievement, quite apart from considerations of program performance. Yet the number of people covered was less than the total added to India's population in the same time. Needed: a *time telescope*.

Similarly, because of staff and facility limitations, the excellent Mothercraft Centers of Haiti were forced to offer their services exclusively on the basis of malnutrition severity according to the Gomez classification. Furthermore, as a rehabilitative facility, such a program concentrates on only a small segment of the target population, is forced to be therapeutic rather than preventive, corrective rather than educational, at the risk of being temporary rather than permanent in its benefits.

Assuming appropriate messages, the mass media can reach out to all the target audience on a preventive basis, with nutrition education and motivation in a continuing program, limited in its content but total in its impact.

There is the problem of money. The commercial product pays for its own message. Who shall pay for the message about protein or for the message about legumes or pulses or dark green vegetables or any of the nutritious commodity foods from which all the people in general, but no one in particular, can profit? Who shall pay for this, if not the people through their government? But how? If radio and television are operated by the government, then the kind of nutrition education campaign we have been describing should be given its share of air time—inserting its brief reach-and-frequency messages into, before, and after regular programs. Where the media are licensed to the private sector, a public service obligation is almost always written into the charter. However, without direct governmental intervention, a time allocation is not always a certainty. It is unthinkable and, in my opinion, contrary to public policy to compel a nutrition education program to pay for a facility that is held in trust from the people and operated in its behalf.

I have felt for some time that a far more practical system is to withhold a fixed percentage of all time periods on radio and television, to be administered by a public corporation in behalf of all nation-building programs. A 10 percent reserve was recommended for the United States at the 1969 White House Conference on Food, Nutrition, and Health. It has not yet been acted on. Mexico adopted a 12.5 percent public service media time reservation in early 1970. This proposal does not suggest a displacement of commercial food promotion. It merely acknowledges that the food marketplace must no longer be the exclusive province of haphazard food promotion fashioned mainly by profit incentives. It reestablishes the fundamental philosophy that food is a vehicle for nutrition, and that nutrition is not merely the responsibility of the school, the health clinic, or the professional facility. Against the power of the mass media to fashion food habits, nutrition education, confined to these traditional channels, does not stand a chance. All foods— branded and unbranded alike—are entitled to equal use of the mass media or any future forms in which the marketplace may reconstitute itself.

This government-assisted promotion of nutrition and high-nutrient foods need not compete unfavorably with the private sector. It merely brings to the marketplace a food dynamic that belonged there in the first place. It stimulates interest in nutrition and thereby actually creates new opportunities for the commercial marketing of nutrition-intensive food products. Show a food processor a new market that will yield a profit, and he will leap into it. Government incentives to inspire such commercial activity would be consistent with government incentives for national development in general. Since marketing costs are generally second only to the cost of raw materials themselves, free mass media time for advertising, normally a sizable expenditure, would be a major marketing incentive. There is warrant for such a policy in the established pattern of incentives for industry in the form of tax abatement, investment credits, financing, and the like. Why not the extension of government assistance policy to food promotion in behalf of nutritional priorities? It would require no additional capital. What is involved is merely the reallocation of time on radio and television to the promotion of an approved product classified as essential to the nation's health.

This is not philosophically different from government assistance to education, agriculture, national defense, or priority industrial development. The form is radically different. It consists of air—air-time to be exact. It is a non-capital asset of tremendous capital significance to marketing enterprise. The concept of air-time as a major capital asset is new and elusive. Government planners may have trouble capitalizing it because it has no intrinsic value. But that is because mass marketing is a new and elusive enterprise mainly made possible by two other elusive abstractions—radio and television—that have extended the powers of man, the communicator and the market maker, far beyond anything he could have dreamed possible two or three generations ago.

24   Suggested Components of
Intervention Programs

Amorn Nondasuta
Principal Medical Officer
Department of Health, Bangkok

The Call and Levinson paper offers a rare opportunity to look at the problem of nutrition in a systematic way. The discussion of the intervention methodology gives the reader an insight that should certainly be of great help in the development of nutrition programs. Thailand has had nutrition programs similar to Applied Nutrition operating for the past decade, while new modifications of the old programs and newer approaches to the problem have been initiated within the last two or three years. Following are some salient points brought out by experience in the conduct of our program.

Protein Food Promotion

Local Production
In a traditional society where people produce nearly all the foods for their own consumption, a plan to promote agricultural output is necessary. The agricultural sector usually assumes the responsibility of developing such a plan. In this connection, it should be noted that there may be a clash in policy objectives: the agricultural plan would normally give high priority to cash crop production for export purposes; the health plan, on the contrary, would call for the production of nutritious food crops for local consumption. Obviously, a balance between the two extremes must be sought and spelled out somewhere in the agricultural plan. If this is not done, difficulties in coordinating food production and nutrition activities at the field level may be expected.

In making a plan to promote food crops at the local level, the decision on the type and quantity of crops would depend largely on the ecology characteristics of the particular locality, the amount expected to be consumed by the target groups, customs and beliefs pertaining to the use of the food, and other relevant considerations. To provide an incentive, an extra amount should also be raised and sold as a source of income for the family. The plan should also be tied in closely with the service program of the target group in order to give it a more meaningful purpose in the eyes of the participating community.

Commercial Protein Food
Another avenue which should be carefully explored is the development of cheap protein foods for commercialization, with the aim of covering a wider

proportion of target groups in a society with a market or transitional economy in a short period of time. Cheap sources of protein are mostly vegetable and some forms of marine products. Utilization of such protein would help alleviate the need for higher production of animal protein to satisfy the demands of increasing population. For this type of program to last, the sources of protein to be used will have to be produced in adequate quantity and with a relatively stable price. The development of protein foods also aims at producing formulas that are locally acceptable, with the highest protein quality technically and economically feasible.

In some areas of the world, where a high-quality vegetable protein source such as soyabean is not traditionally included in the local diet, introduction of such an alien product in a raw state may encounter resistance. Utilization of such a source should involve food processing techniques that give the products a form and character acceptable to the general public. In addition, a corps of food technologists should be developed and their work coordinated with nutritionists under an integral food and nutrition plan.

An important consideration in the success of a protein food development program is the plan for marketing and distribution of the finished products. In this connection, food industries should play an important role in the takeover of production and commercialization. In an agricultural country where food industries have not been fully developed, incentives are needed such as promotional privileges offered to the protein food industries as part of and in conformity with the overall strategy of agroindustrial development. On the other hand, development of community organized programs with a feeding component, such as school lunches or a day care center network, with or without government subsidy, may represent a fixed portion of the market for the protein foods and act as another incentive for the food industries.

Improving Protein Quality

Rice Research
Research on the genetics and ecology of plants has recently produced significantly high-yielding rice varieties. This discovery should solve the problem of calorie deficiency at least for the time being. However, high-yielding rice does not serve to alleviate protein deficiency in the population unless the protein content of such rice can be improved; it may be noted that these two properties do not generally go together. But experiments in Japan have shown that they *can* go together. The development of high-protein, high-yielding varieties should be one of the major objectives of rice research.

Fortification

In certain developing countries, fortification programs currently under way at different stages include salt iodization, rice enrichment with vitamin and mineral premix, rice fortification with amino acids, vitamins, and mineral granules. In developing new fortification programs certain criteria should be considered, including:

1. Degree of causal relationship. How direct is the causal relationship of the nutrients to be fortified and the occurrence of the deficiency state to be corrected? If the cause of the deficiency is multiple, or if there are other predisposing factors (such as environmental) involved, the influence of these factors will have to be determined. For example, the effect of amino acid fortification on a community where sanitary conditions are poor will have to be determined. Field trials in well-controlled feeding programs in orphanages may not give answers applicable to the wider field situation.

2. Level of fortification. It should not be so high as to produce an adverse effect on the quality and appearance of the carrier.

3. Requirement level. It varies according to age, sex, and physiological state. If this variation is wide, fortification at a single level cannot satisfy the needs of all target groups. If the level is set high the cost of production will be higher, and undesirable or unacceptable products may be produced. There will also be high wastage. If the level is set low, the priority group may not benefit totally from it. Fortification at a low level may also be ineffective in inducing change in the prevalence of the deficiency state of the target group or groups.

4. Administrative feasibility. Fortified foods imply technical control in production, at least to a certain degree. The control problem may become enormous if the points of production are many and varied. The fortification program will succeed better if these points are kept at a minimum. The use of entirely new methods of fortification should be considered against the backdrop of the production situation of the carrier (be it rice or salt or others) and the distribution facility. The use of imported raw materials in large amounts is hardly justifiable unless it can be shown that the value derived from the program is decidedly higher than expenditure on it.

Preschool Child Program

Before going on to discuss the development of the preschool child program, a few principles deserve consideration at this point.

First, it is generally accepted that malnutrition seldom occurs as an isolated phenomenon, but is generally interwoven with other health problems of the child. Prominent among the latter in developing countries are the infections of the gastrointestinal and respiratory tracts. Hence, service programs for the preschool child must necessarily provide for effective control and early detection of such diseases and the control of environmental factors. Furthermore, if the importance of the preschool-age group is considered in a wider context, the program activity should endeavor to encompass developmental aspects such as educational and social training and the promotion of intellectual growth and mental well-being.

Second, supplementary feeding program effectiveness has recently become a center of controversy. It is believed that supplementary feeding of the target group is useful and justifiable only when adequate health care can be provided simultaneously. In the case of the preschool child, the objective of the program is, obviously, to supplement but not provide all of the child's daily protein intake. This implies that the daily diet at home has already supplied adequate calories and that no reduction of the home diet is made while supplementation is under way. In practice, it has been found that this is not usually the case. Hence, the supplementation program has to be developed concurrently with nutrition education and food production plans. As such, the program may be considered an educational instrument to effect changes in child feeding practices.

Organizing a Service Program

In Thailand, a system has been organized recently to collect selected preschool children of a community in one place during the day. Referred to as a "Child Nutrition Center," this is in essence a day care center with special emphasis given to nutrition.[1] The primary objective is to effectively and continuously supplement the child's daily diet with a sufficient amount of protein-rich foods. Other objectives include more effective control of childhood diseases and promoting mental and intellectual development.

The care of children in the center encompasses several aspects, but emphasis is placed on supplementary feeding. Parents are asked to contribute by supplying foods that are usually available at home, such as rice and vegetables. In many cases, they are also enlisted to participate in the home food production program, with a portion of the produce being donated as supplementary foods for the center. Processed protein foods and milk, when available from external and other sources, are also used.

Responsibilities for protecting the general health of the child include immunizations and periodical physical examinations. Routine activities while

[1] These are similar in principle to the Nutritional Rehabilitation Centers or Mothercraft Centers of a number of countries in the Western Hemisphere.

attending the center include oral reading, group play and other games, and the practice of personal hygiene and good manners. Ample time is allowed for rest and sleep.

The "day care center effect" upon the child's growth and development is striking in most cases. Aside from the benefits derived from the way the system is organized, it is found that the center indirectly influences a redistribution of the protein foods in the diet of the family in favor of the preschool child.

Parents' Benefits
The child nutrition center is also used as a springboard to provide education on food and nutrition and child-rearing practices to the mothers. Convenience to the mother cannot be overlooked; by sending her child to the center she is free to go about her work outside the house. Regular contact between the mother and the center staff also promotes interchange of ideas and better understanding. This is expected to lead eventually to a change in the mother's attitude and practice in the care and feeding of her child, which is the long-range objective of the program.

Administrative Considerations

Coordination
The use of a targeted approach in problem-solving may be considered more specific, controllable, and appropriate when resources are limited, but it is not without its own problems, one of which is coordination. Since corrective measures in nutrition, when directed at the target group, will in most cases involve concerted effort of more than one discipline, a mechanism is required by which coordination may be achieved. To create such a mechanism, at least the following actions may be needed:

1. Setting up at the national level a coordinating body, whose members represent the various disciplines involved, and which has its own secretariat.

2. The creation of a master plan at the national level, in which important guidelines to the development of a coordinated program by each agency concerned are outlined. The master plan may be considered the instrument by which the coordinating body executes its functions, and the two elements together form an axis around which all food and nutrition activities revolve.

Infrastructure
Only through adequate infrastructure can a successful program be implemented. This involves creating new or reorienting traditional roles and functions of existing personnel at the village level, usually the nurse or midwife

who mans the health center, who should function at the village level in such a way that continuous contact with the people is possible. This goal is not always easy to accomplish when the ratio of technical personnel to population may run as high as one in several thousand. Hence, it is important that a pyramid of local helpers be organized and trained to help in delivering service to the target group.

Local Resources

Whenever possible, a plan to utilize nongovernmental resources should be included as a component of the intervention program. The tapping of external resources at both local and national levels helps to alleviate the extra strain that is bound to be placed on government budget and manpower and, in many cases, is crucial to the success of the program. Foreign sources of help may be sought but their role should be considered catalytic and temporary. Nongovernmental resources may include local manpower or contributions in money and materials from the community, private enterprises, social clubs, voluntary agencies, and international organizations.

25 General Discussion

Chairman: Dr. F. A. Bacigalupo (Agricultural University, Peru); Mr. Jul; Dr. Joy; Mr. Levinson; Mr. S. Venkitaramanan (Finance Secretary, Tamil Nadu State, India); Dr. Nondasuta; Mr. Manoff; Dr. Latham; Dr. Call; Mr. Robert Choate (Washington); Dr. Jelliffe; Dr. Béhar; Dr. Paez-Franco; Dr. De Sweemer; Dr. Edwin Mertz (Purdue University); Dr. Joshi; Dr. Tadataka Fukui

Bacigalupo Mr. Jul mentioned that the planners are not making the decisions. Who should be involved in making the decisions in this whole process of finding a systematic approach to the solution of nutritional problems?

Jul We know that it's the policymakers, the politicians, who are making the final decisions, and we also know that they have to be aided by someone; as Dr. Joy pointed out, planners have to show them the consequences of their choices and, in fact, often indicate what choices are open to them.

Joy I think that's right. The important thing is we shouldn't let the economists make the decisions, absentmindedly and apparently objectively, by putting cost-benefit ratios with all sorts of implicit value assumptions into the planning process and making this the final arbiter of choice. What tends to happen then is that either the policy is accepted as being apparently objectively justified by this type of analysis—which, of course, is not objective at all—or alternatively it is rejected on the grounds that while it may be a sound economic analysis, it doesn't take account of political or social considerations.

Either way the economist is prostituting himself in this situation. What he needs to do is to really identify choices, predict consequences, and raise the key, unpleasant issues of whether we want children to go blind or to die and whether we are prepared to pay for preventing that by taking income away from some people for some period.

Levinson Dr. Amorn Nondasuta raised an interesting related question, the question of coordination. Given the broad range of disciplines involved in the choice, given the wide range of ministerial responsibility in most countries, which kind of a group makes nutrition policy? Is there a coordinating body in a directive capacity, or are the ministries left to make decisions?

Nondasuta We have been having difficulties in coordinating the applied nutrition program in Thailand, and recently we came to the conclusion that in order to successfully organize this program we needed coordination at the central level.

When we tried this previously with a national coordinating committee, it didn't work well. Why? Because everybody on that committee was high-level, had lots of things to do, and couldn't take time to explore the problem of nutrition deeply.

The solution that we thought would be appropriate was to create a secretariat in the form of an institute, the Institute of Food and Nutrition, which would carry out plan analysis and program evaluation and also coordinate activities among various disciplines. This body, we hope, will solve at least part of the coordination problem at the national level.

We cannot start coordination at the local level first because, although workers in the field from various disciplines may get along well together, all of them will have to obey orders from their own departments or ministries. And if there is no coordination at the top level there may be a clash of objectives, posing serious difficulties in coordination in the field.

Venkitaramanan   In the state from which I come we have had the experience of organizing nutrition for about 2,000,000 schoolchildren a day, and below that we have the preschool feeding program for nearly 900,000. This program does involve problems of organization. The crucial question is whether a separate nutrition body at the state level, the national level, a coordinating body of the kind Dr. Nondasuta suggested—whether that will really help. I do not know, because ultimately the person who delivers nutrition is either someone in the preschool child feeding center or the teacher himself. So, while in terms of policymaking it may be useful to bring the disciplines together at the national level or at the regional level, for implementation we have to give an incentive to the person who actually has to see that the food reaches the target individual or group.

We have tried a number of experiments, including the central kitchen idea, which has spread in South Asia for the school feeding program, but we immediately encounter problems of transport. There are also local problems of coordination. For instance, food has to be hot, and hot food doesn't keep in tropical climates. There is a problem in getting it to the child in an edible state. Perhaps we have to tackle it through a new technology; traditional methods of cooking may not be the answer; perhaps extruded foods should be explored. But to win acceptance for extruded foods we come again to the need for communication and coordination.

Implementation has thrown up a number of new policy issues which impinge on the whole spectrum of the economic system. Pricing policy, for instance, has been a problem. We started last year a very large pulse production program because, as a result of the development of high-yielding cereal varieties and the price incentive there, the production of pulses was going down. We decided to offer a specific price incentive for pulses within the state, and we found that pulse production does grow if incentives are offered either in the form of price or of preferential allocation of scarce goods like fertilizers and credit.

There is really no need to justify an issue like feeding hungry people, as Dr. Joy pointed out; the politician is already for it and would like very much to go ahead. It is we, the planners, who tell him the cost is too high.

Now we are finding that if you take the system as an integrated whole— education and nutrition together, for instance—the investments made on education will become much more meaningful. In a society that spends nearly one-fourth of its budget on education, if 10 percent of that allocation is not utilized properly because the children are undernourished and cannot concentrate, we can certainly justify expenditures on nutrition. It is the planner who needs to be convinced; the politician is willing to accept the hard decisions involved.

Manoff All the politicians I have ever known were highly interested in doing something, if only to retain a political power base. What they are looking for are specific programs of action; and most often what they get is study and consideration and analyses of problems on which action is hardly ever possible.

Most of the problems are approached as subjects for action with traditional methods and techniques. The applied nutrition program is a good example of an excellently motivated program which depends on traditional techniques at a time when we need techniques that will telescope time far more rapidly than is possible in a person-to-person information delivery system.

When I was in India about three years ago, on an AID project on nutrition education, I learned that the Applied Nutrition Program had been in operation for 10 years. In that period it had covered some 900 blocks of the 5,000 development blocks into which Indian villages are grouped; that is about 18 percent of all the development blocks of the country, and the population of that 18 percent comes to less than the total number of people added to the population of India during that same period. So obviously, while it is a valuable technique, it simply cannot meet the needs that have been multiplied by the intensity of the problem.

The lack of coordination in the Thai program, referred to earlier, essentially is a reflection of the fact that a program of that kind is hampered to begin

with as an information delivery system; information about agricultural inputs
and priorities and information on nutrition education cannot depend exclusively on person-to-person delivery. The most unreliable system for the
delivery of information is from person to person. I am obviously again advocating the use of mass media and underlining the absolutely essential role that
the mass media must play.

Another example is the Mothercraft Centers operated with such effectiveness in Haiti. Because they could handle only 35 children at a time, they
were forced to accept children on the basis of malnutrition severity according
to the Gomez classification. This technique, again, though essential, cannot
be a major cornerstone of a nutrition project; if you examine it philosophically, it is therapeutic rather than preventive; it is corrective rather than
educational, and it must to a large extent be temporary rather than permanent in its benefits, because after the children have been discharged no
other system takes up where the centers leave off.

Levinson   Is there some reaction to Mr. Manoff's doubts about the effectiveness of the person-to-person approach in applied nutrition programs and
Mothercraft Centers?

Venkitaramanan   The applied nutrition program is a special problem in itself
because it is disoriented or disorganized insofar as target groups are concerned. The applied nutrition program is very much a production program
with little relationship to the market. I think this is the real problem in
applied nutrition and it deserves a separate discussion. It asks the people to
concentrate on producing more poultry, more milk, but there is no relationship that they can see between that production and what is being eaten in
the village itself. That is why the applied nutrition programs of UNICEF and
FAO-WHO have not made the expected impact.

Latham   With regard to applied nutrition programs nearly everywhere, one of
the important omissions has been a good evaluation. Because of this it is very
difficult to say which nutrition programs have been successful, which have
failed, and which have been partially successful. I have been particularly interested to see clear objectives included in plans for applied nutrition programs
and evaluation built in as part of the programs.

Until we do this, or by other means really look at how effective or ineffective are various programs such as Mothercraft Centers or under-five clinics
in different parts of the world, we will not know whether we are spending
money wisely or not. We need to determine the relative effectiveness of alternate strategies and to add some cost-effectiveness figures.

We have been skirting the issue of politics in regard to nutrition. It has been brought up a number of times, but the issue has not been squarely faced; and both in strategy and in priorities politics is absolutely essential. We keep talking about the lower 20 or 30 percent of the population as being our target group. But nutritionists I think have failed to be spokesmen, lobbyists, for this 20 or 30 percent. I would like the panel to say whether they think that nutritionists should be more involved in political action and lobbying. When one sees that the United States itself, this very wealthy country, has not been able to meet all the needs, and when one looks at some of the priorities put forward, it is clear that they are establishment priorities and not minority priorities. Lead poisoning, for example, is a disease, an important disease of ghetto children who live with peeling paint walls, but very little attention or money is given that; a great amount of money was devoted to, say, polio-myelitis, which had afflicted a former president of the United States, but the sons of presidents of the United States do not get lead poisoning.

Similarly one could look at sickle cell anemia, which is a disease of the nonwhite people in the United States. Very little attention goes to it, whereas something like PKU or cystic fibrosis receives a great deal of attention because these maladies affect the establishment and nonestablishment families equally.

A second topic that I don't think has been addressed adequately here in regard to the politics of nutrition is variation in economic systems and the ways other systems have tackled food and nutrition problems. This is an international conference, but we haven't heard any representatives from Cuba, from the Soviet Union, or from the People's Republic of China; it would be interesting to make some nutritional comparisons between, for example, Cuba and the rest of Latin America; between China and India; perhaps between socialist Tanzania and some of the nonsocialist countries in Africa.

I would like to hear more discussion of the politics of nutrition, to hear what the panelists feel could be the role of both planners and nutritionists in trying to get these political decisions made. In the United States, for example, we have failed to get national fluoridation. In South Africa millions of dollars are spent on heart transplants when the same amount of money could almost eradicate measles in the whole country. The allocation of money, in my opinion, has often been wrong.

Manoff I wish you hadn't used as your prime situation the United States because it is the most developed and the wealthiest. It is perhaps the most difficult place to solve the politics of nutrition because the patterns and the interests are so set and the structure is so committed. I don't mean to suggest that the effort shouldn't be made, and the effort is being made, but we are talking essentially about planning activities in developing countries, where there is an opportunity to review the mistakes made by the highly industrialized societies and to plan to do things differently.

For example, the incentives for the manufacturer of processed foods in the United States to switch to a more highly nutritious selection of foods, either fortified or at least not reduced in nutrients, simply don't exist as yet. A developing country, it seems to me, is in a position to provide such incentives and to establish new patterns of manufacturing processed foods. This is not inconsistent with the philosophy of incentives applied in other areas of national development, such as health or education.

One of the delicious ironies of that situation, it seems to me as a communications person, is that one of the assets available for educational purposes in a developing country is a noncapital asset that can be capitalized to a fantastic extent. What I'm talking about again is air time—radio time, and television time where it exists. Radio is practically a universal medium throughout the developing world, in some villages less than others but present in practically all.

In distributing foods, marketing costs are second only to the cost of the raw material itself, and of those marketing costs one of the biggest portions is the communications cost.

Air time is now often being used frivolously in developing countries; when I was in Iran in January, the number one television program (about 40 percent of the homes have television) was "Peyton Place." Although it is amusing at this distance, I was appalled by it. Why that air time should not be capitalized for purposes of education in consonance with national priorities and national development—particularly nutrition—escapes me. Why hasn't it become apparent that this asset, rather than being used for rambling ministerial speeches, can be the medium for short, focused messages on nutrition? This requires no capital investment. It simply requires a reallocation of time from frivolous entertainment to a meaningful use of radio and television for educational purposes.

Call When you get the government convinced they ought to allocate time and then you turn to the nutritionists and say, what message should we broadcast, there's going to be a long argument with substantial disagreement: shall we talk about calories, or protein, or vitamin A, or some other nutrient. There is a complete lack of scientific consensus among the nutritionists in many, many countries and that in and of itself is a major obstacle to progress.

One of the problems in talking to the politicians is that we cannot reach a consensus. The politician can find a nutritionist in the United States, for example, to support just about any position he wants to take.

Choate I think the keynote paper was excellent, though I wish it had stressed even more the prudent selection of foods that are available. Mr Manoff did reveal that there is a food industry, and after a day and a half of talking this is a very interesting fact to introduce at a nutrition conference. The food industry and mass media in the United States are one and the same. Over 50 percent of television's revenue comes from the grocery industry. The child who watches a moderate amount of television in the United States today has seen 80,000 food commercials by the time he is 16. Mother and grandmother can't compete with that kind of brainwashing.

The generation gap is nowhere so evident as in the kitchens of the United States. The teacher in the classroom cannot possibly compete with the Madison Avenue cartoons, songs, and jingles. Eighty thousand food commercials by the time you are 16 years old pretty well sets your food patterns and attitudes for the rest of your life. Fraud, fun, and fantasy are selling far too many of today's foods in America. Over half of the foods that we consume, whether it's at home or in a restaurant or in an airplane, are prepared or partially prepared on other premises than where we eat them. These same advertisements could be urging, both in this country and other countries, more prudent food habits. Ads can educate if nutritional worth is made a selling point. Public service ads alone will never have the impact of commercial ads.

We can change the soap operas that we export to Iran so that they also advocate prudent food habits, even as they emote. We can change the ads in this country so that they educate in a positive direction—about foods, about nutrition policies and nutritional development. If we had used advertisements to awaken Americans to the problems connected with nutrition, perhaps it would not have been so difficult politically to get sufficient money spent on the school lunch program. One has only to look at the Department of Agriculture to realize we do not have any nutritional policy here; we are still reimbursing farmers for tons and bushels and not for protein tons or vitamin bushels.

I don't think Mr. Manoff was advocating that commercial food ads be drastically changed; he, and I, would prefer they be done by private enterprise and not by government, but certainly if they are not corrected and improved soon by private enterprise they will have to be corrected by government. Today we are practicing malnutrition over television.

Jelliffe I would like to take up Mr. Choate's argument and put it in a global perspective. What is the effect of the type of advertising he has referred to when it is exported widely all over the world? I have not the slightest doubt that at present a great deal of unnecessary malnutrition in developing countries is related to the deployment of unnecessary, and economically and hygienically inappropriate, foods into countries of the Third World.

What can we do about this? I believe that first of all we can take cognizance of the fact. We talk naively about the mass media and what the mass media should do. We should rather ask what the mass media are doing at the present moment. I have no doubt whatsoever that at the moment the mass media in developing countries, taken on balance, are a minus force, and that there is such a thing as what we may call commerciogenic malnutrition. I realize that malnutrition has many causes and one is the export of ideas by pediatricians, such as myself, from developed countries to the Third World. Some is iatrogenic, in other words, but some is commerciogenic.

One of the things that we have to do in choosing alternative strategies in nutrition intervention programs is to consider the current impact of totally inappropriate and harmful commercially processed foods on feeding patterns—the breast-feeding patterns, the weaning patterns, and so on—of developing countries.

The situation is not totally gloomy, because in the last eighteen months there have been some possible signs of an accommodation. There is an effort to persuade commercial concerns that their advertising is totally inappropriate and is pushing mothers to feed their children in a way that is harmful.

At the same time there has been a move to open some sort of dialogue between pediatric nutritionists experienced in developing countries and processed food manufacturers; and I'm happy to say that a committee of the Protein Advisory Group, under the chairmanship of Professor Vahlquist, has been encouraging this type of dialogue.

Surely we have to move toward a more responsible attitude. Surely we have to realize from our point of view as nutritionists that the commercial concerns are in business for profit. Let us try to see whether it is possible to use their expertise in marketing and in salesmanship, their funds, to convey a nutritional message. The equation that should satisfy both them and us is nutritional relevance times modest profit times mass market.

Jul I come from a country that is apparently not covered in this discussion. We have no radio or television advertising, but still we do buy food; so the air is not the only marketplace. Perhaps this aspect has been a bit overdone, but I feel very encouraged by it, because food technologists have tended to say that food habits cannot be changed. And now we hear that television makes an enormous impression on the American public and can change their food habits.

There are also nutritionists who say that people don't buy nutrition, they buy food; I think that is incorrect. People rush to health stores to buy all sorts of expensive things but I think most nutritionists are very skeptical about the results. We also know that in developing countries people have peculiar habits of using all sorts of herbs and spices that they think have a beneficial effect on their health. My conclusion, therefore, is that food habits can be changed and that people will listen to a nutrition message. Then the question is, have we prepared that message? Mr. Manoff and others certainly have the technique of distributing these messages very efficiently over the air. So the comparatively easy job for nutritionists is to design the messages, simple and with public appeal; that's what we should be doing now.

Joy   While undoubtedly education is a problem that we have to turn our minds to, education isn't the only problem. A necessary precondition of successful education by whatever media is the means to acquire the food for adequate nutrition; that brings us back to income problems and to politicians. Quite apart from my having sympathy with the ministers who don't wish to get involved in giving radio or television messages about how to cope with low-income feeding situations, I feel that there is a really big political problem. I think one must first of all say it is a tremendous step forward that we have actually recognized that the problem is a political problem; that is, it is a question of who gets what, and that is politics. Let us remind ourselves that politicians will want costless solutions if they can get them. They would really very much like to be able to solve all our problems with processed foods, with fortification programs and other things which would meet both markets—political markets and mass markets, low-income groups and also commercial interests.

Maybe there are some solutions to be found there. If there are, splendid, but let's not be sold them because politicians would prefer those solutions. Let's find the solutions that really are relevant, and let us look particularly at the problems of income redistribution.

Paez-Franco   In a recent meeting of the Latin American Society of Nutrition held in Peru, we discussed the development of integrated nutritional policies and came to the conclusion that the process of decision-making should involve all participants, not only the politicians and technologists in different fields related to nutrition, but also the public, the object and subject of our concern. What is the opinion of the members of this panel about participation of the consumers, often undernourished consumers?

Manoff   There's no question that the consumer should participate, but before the consumer can become an effective participant, he has to have some knowledge of the subject. Consumers all over the world are nutritional illiterates. In the most sophisticated country of the world, the most highly literate country in the world, the United States, the consumer is a nutritional illiterate, and we have managed to keep him that way.

Now, the consumer has a right to know and he should be in a position to make correct nutritional decisions. There is no possible way for intelligent participation by any constituent group in the nutrition problem, unless its members understand the issues and can make intelligent decisions on that basis. The consumer must have this knowledge before he can make demands for nutritional inputs or make consumption and purchase decisions. We need the shortest and most effective way of reaching the consumer with this information.

It is a mistake for us to say that certain solutions are simplistic, that there are more basic solutions to be found. For example, virtually all of us would agree that income redistribution is the basic solution to the problem. But it is also the most political aspect. That doesn't mean it should not be dealt with, but should we wait until that problem is solved before we take other incremental improvement steps like education? Shall we refuse to make a 10 percent improvement because there is some long-range solution that will give us 90 percent? Shall we refuse to take those planning decisions today that can produce results and give a 6-year-old normal mental growth; that can lower from 40 percent the mortality of children under 6 in developing countries; that can reduce the brain damage that has already taken place at the age of 2? Shall we refuse to take those incremental decisions when we all know that progress of any kind consists of a series of incremental decisions and improvements?

Call   In the United States we learned that when we involved the recipient in the planning of commodity distribution programs, food stamp programs, school lunch programs, and so on, we got more effective programs. But it took a lot of grief and strife to formally establish the role of these recipient groups; it took a lobbying organization like the National Welfare Rights Organization.

The second problem is, who speaks for the consumer? Who is the representative of the consumer when you want advice? I'll draw an analogy from the farm situation in the United States. If you ask today who speaks for the farmer in the United States, six or seven groups will come forward, all of them claiming to speak for the farmer. The politician of course can pick whichever one he wants—the right, the left, the middle.

Joy I want to respond to something that has come up two or three times in the overall conference, and that is the implication that income redistribution or income-raising measures must necessarily be long-term and must contrast, therefore, with these other marginal intervention areas. By all means we need the marginal intervention measures, but there's no reason to suppose that income distribution and income-raising measures need be long-term.

There can be immediate measures, discriminatory measures to identify poor farmers and to raise their incomes, perhaps by credit schemes, rather than by mechanization programs to increase total agricultural output. There can be immediate rationing and fair price subsidies to redistribute income, and there are various other discriminatory schemes that do focus upon those people who are short of income and do transfer income to them or allow them to augment their own income. These needn't be long-term schemes at all.

Mertz I would like to point out that in spite of all the discussion on income distribution over many years, and with much research and education in this country, we have not achieved very much in terms of income distribution with our own farmers.

Approximately half of our farmers probably sell less than $5,000 worth of product and get less than $1,500 a year income from doing so; and incidentally, in Indiana, where I come from, the smallest farmers get half the corn yield per acre that the largest farmers get in terms of averages for the group. So this problem of income distribution is a pretty durable one among farmers.

De Sweemer A few days ago I attended Yom Kippur services and I'm strangely reminded of it because Mr. Manoff sounded to me like the rabbi leading us in the confession of societal guilt. There are two ways of feeling guilty: one is becoming very humble, and the other is being terribly proud that one can be so guilty. I fear a little that we have taken the second alternative.

Having worked in Punjab, I can testify that the farmer does not get any meaningful nutritional advice through the mass media. He has a radio, but it's government controlled and the nutritional advice is of the orange-juice-and-toast-to-children-of-6-months type and it just passes in one ear and out the other.

The power of mass media in India is very beautifully shown in the study we did of family planning. Although there was definitely a great effort to publicize family planning, only 2 percent of the villagers even knew the term or any of its vernacular equivalents used in the official propaganda.

I think we should follow Mr. Manoff's advice and look at the real communications system in a village, which is from person to person. The real market is the shopkeeper, and the shopkeeper is largely influenced by urban value systems and by what he visualizes to be western food norms. That's how biscuits get to the children.

Another reason that we can discount mass media effectiveness for rural areas is that though the farmer is nutritionally illiterate he is very astute. He is not going to believe what we say unless we can prove it; the only proof is pragmatic. You have to be able to show that nutrition makes a difference.

Another mistake we make is to assume that Indian farmers, and we, have the same conceptions about nutrition. We don't. We have first of all to structure the framework within which we are going to communicate. The farmer's framework is hot and cold food, and his belief about marasmus is that it is a shadow (*parchawan*) or an evil eye (*nasar lagna*). We can construct the framework only through action programs right in the village that show we know what we are talking about.

Joshi I was somewhat disappointed to see the experiences of highly developed countries being applied to the developing nations in the solution of nutritional problems. But the keynote paper presented this afternoon was very illuminating as to the place of income distribution and average per capita productivity increase in solving the overall nutrition problem. In a country like mine, where two-thirds of the population always have been underfed while one-third exports surplus products, there cannot possibly be an even distribution of income. So alternative intervention programs definitely have to be devised to solve the existing problems in these countries.

To return to specific package programs, such as high-protein supplementary food products, I think this sort of thing should be feasible. In my country we do produce corn, we do produce soyabean and some of the legumes, but we do not know their proper use. By proper manufacture and distribution of products, I am sure that most of this protein deficiency can be overcome even in the low-income groups. But in many developing countries the highly developed industrial research and systematic analysis necessary for nutrition programs involving processed foods may not be in existence.

Fukui There are two points I would like to make about nutrition programs. First, the improvement program should be undertaken by the affected nation itself insofar as possible. Second, once malnutrition has been alleviated and the physical condition of the population improved, leading to increased labor output, food and nutrition requirements will rise. It is important that program planning take this into account; otherwise an even more severe malnutrition could follow the initial improvement.

As other speakers have noted, adequate nutrition is especially urgent for infants and young children. The most desirable calorie sources in their diets are wheat and rice, fortified with vitamin B_1 and the limiting amino acids, lysine and threonine. Development of a protein-rich rice is thus particularly important to Asian nations. The best protein source is milk. Research studies have shown that better growth in children results from diets supplemented with the amino acids mentioned (see T. Fukui et al., Effect of amino acid supplementation on growth of school children, *Tokushima J. Experimental Medicine* 16:71-83, 1969). In the first experiment described, the subjects were 160 elementary school children; 862 children in other schools of the same district constituted the control groups. The second experiment divided 310 children into three groups: the first received lysine-supplemented bread; the second was given tablets of threonine, tryptophan, and methionine, in addition to the bread; the third was a control group. In both experiments there was a clear increase in weight and height of the children receiving the amino acid supplements as compared with the development of children in the control groups.

Béhar   From some of the information presented earlier by Mr. Kracht, it could be interpreted that Incaparina has been a failure. I would like to indicate that, in my opinion, this is not the case, at least in Guatemala.

Mr. Kracht mentioned that in Guatemala only 5 percent of the target population were regular consumers of Incaparina. Since he made his study in 1968 the sales of Incaparina have almost doubled; if we assume a similar pattern of consumption, about 10 percent of the target population are regular consumers. This is not a negligible figure. It is, in fact, larger than most programs of free distribution of food are achieving, which is not bad for a product that consumers have to buy. Furthermore, sales are still increasing (Figure 1).

Before Incaparina was available, I worked in outpatient pediatric services and suffered the frustration of seeing malnourished children who I knew were in need of milk or meat or eggs; but I knew their mothers could not afford to buy those foods, which frequently were not even available in the villages where they lived. Now the physician or nurse confronting similar cases can use Incaparina as it is commercially available throughout the country and at a price most families can afford.

INCAPARINA SALES IN CENTRAL AMERICA & PANAMA
1961 — 1971

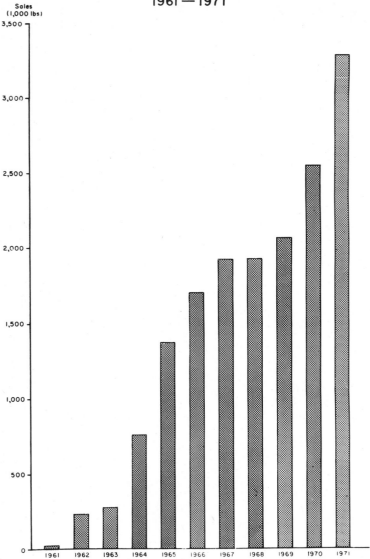

Figure 1. Incaparina Sales in Central America and Panama, 1961-1971

Finally, I would like to stress that we have never pretended that Incaparina was going to be *the* solution to the problem of protein-calorie malnutrition. There is no one solution to this complex problem, and the availability of protein-rich foods at a low price can only be considered as a contribution, in some instances a transitory one. Many other actions are needed to correct the basic socioecomic, agricultural, and health deficiencies. INCAP is recommending them in Central America, but they are long-term propositions. In the meantime, some immediate measures must be taken utilizing available knowledge and technology, and the production of vegetable mixtures like Incaparina is one of them.

Bacigalupo We have perhaps more questions than answers, but the important thing is that we are trying. We are trying honestly and candidly to deal with a new and puzzling field: how to relate the scientist, the sociologist, the economist, the planner, the politician. I don't know whether there is an easy answer for this complex interaction, but I'm sure that we are not bringing merely the same kind of answer for this old and stubborn problem of malnutrition—which comes first, the chicken or the egg.

Part V   A Conceptual Approach
                                to National Nutrition
                                Program Planning

26 Nutrition Program Planning: An Approach

Alan Berg
Senior Fellow, The Brookings
Institution, Washington, D.C.
Belding Scholar, Association for the
Aid of Crippled Children, New York
Visiting Professor, M.I.T.

Robert Muscat
Chief
Near East-South Asia Planning Division
Agency for International Development
Washington, D.C.

Traditionally development planners have directed little attention to the problem of malnutrition, largely because they have viewed it as a welfare problem and have budgeted accordingly. Only recently have planners begun to recognize that malnutrition may have significant developmental implications—that it may be a basic impediment to national growth. [1,2]

In discussing malnutrition with planners newly concerned with this problem, we have observed two common reactions. First, they frequently suggest that better nutrition is an automatic outgrowth of economic development, and that total energies should therefore be devoted to increasing per capita income. Although income and diet clearly are related, we now recognize there are several reasons that make complete dependence on the general rise of incomes an incomplete answer to malnutrition. For example, there is the time factor. A good portion of today's malnourished people cannot increase their incomes sufficiently in their lifetime to meet even minimum nutrition requirements. [3] There is the increased understanding that more income per se does not assure better nutrition, especially for those at the lower end of the income scale. [4] There is also an emerging appreciation that malnutrition is not only a consequence of underdevelopment but a contributing factor; malnutrition is a drag on the income potential from which better nutrition could presumably be provided. [5] Although in many countries mass poverty is the underlying cause of malnutrition, it does not necessarily follow that, by itself, an attack on general poverty is an adequate means of getting at malnutrition.

Second, planners point to the emphasis already being given to increasing food production in their countries. Agriculture typically accounts for a large fraction of the gross national product in developing countries and for more than half of the labor force. Clearly, one of the most pronounced characteristics of recent development programs in low-income countries has been the attention to agricultural production. However, this emphasis has resulted

The interpretations and conclusions are those of the authors and do not necessarily reflect the views of the organizations with which they are affiliated.

not from a specifically stated and analyzed nutrition objective but rather
from a broad interest in growth of national output. Agricultural production is
shaped to meet such economic objectives as reducing dependence on foreign
supply for major staples, expanding exports, producing nonfood agricultural
raw materials to feed industry, and providing consumers with adequate food
supplies to maintain stable prices and avoid pressures on industrial wages and
prices. The supply of nutrients produced in pursuit of such economic goals—
not deliberately shaped by nutritional considerations—can affect the nutritional status of the needy in a variety of ways, from beneficial to perverse.
[6] Serious problems of undernutrition and malnutrition remain in much
of the developing world, even in countries boasting rapid agricultural modernization. Mexico, for example, world-famed as the source and a large
producer of the new miracle wheat and corn varieties, continues to be
plagued by malnutrition in its low-income regions, even though it is now an
exporter of cereals.

  Most governments have also had small programs in nutrition per se, such as
nutrition education, nutrition components in the curative health delivery
system, institutional child feeding programs, and perhaps even some medical
or technical research and status surveys on nutrition. These are the province
of the professional nutritionist, but the limited scope of programming usually
envisioned for his domain has not permitted a significant impact on the problem. In fact, if one looked for those elements of public policy that have had
a major impact on a nation's nutritional status, one would omit nutrition
with a capital "N."

  Therefore, as things now stand, some of the major factors and policies influencing nutritional status—agriculture, income redistribution, transport, and so
on—are outside the interest and reach of those who are supposed to be looking after their country's nutrition, and those who do formulate such policies
do not specifically include nutrition needs as part of their planning equation.
This is the crux of the nutrition planning dilemma.

  This situation is unlikely to change without a broader and more systematic
approach to understanding malnutrition and planning for its alleviation. The
purpose here is to try to lay out such an approach, to propose a framework to
analyze nutrition needs, and to identify the most appropriate methods to
fulfill them. Essentially this is an adaptation for nutrition of established planning techniques.[1] The paper assumes that the decision-maker recognizes the
problem, is aware of its relationship to broad national objectives, accepts the

[1] With the dual nature of the conference audience in mind, an attempt has been made
here both to familiarize the nutritionist with some of the fundamentals of the plan-

notion that good nutrition is an investment in human capital analogous to
education, and has decided to give increased attention to the nutrition sector.
It starts with the premise that malnutrition will not be alleviated sufficiently
or quickly enough under current development policies and trends, that important shifts in policies and practices may be required to effect changes, and
that the scope of such shifts may involve many people and entities not now
regarded as part of the nutrition universe.[2]

The Nutrition Planning Sequence
The nutrition planning sequence starts with a definition of the nature, scope,
and trends of the nutrition problem, leading to a preliminary statement of
broad objectives. It then moves through a description of the system in which
the nutritional condition arises. In the process of tracing causes, the planner
begins to sense which programs and policies are relevant to the objectives.
Next comes a comparison of the alternatives, which in turn leads to constructing an interrelated nutrition program. Final selection of objectives,
programs, and projects emerges after a budgetary and political process in
which programs to attack malnutrition are pitted against other competing
claims on resources and, if necessary, redesigned within actual budget allocations. The last step is evaluation of the actions put forth, feeding the conclusions back into subsequent rounds of the planning sequence. (There is
nothing sacrosanct about the approach described here. There are many variations—some have 5 steps, some have 10—but all are similar in that they begin
with problem identification and end with evaluation.)

In practice, planning does not simply follow a series of textbook steps, but
is rather an iterative process that resembles more the tango—four steps forward, three steps back, with an occasional turnaround. Objectives, for example, are not settled on early in the game. Sifting through the various pro-

---

ning process and to acquaint the planner with some of the basic nutritional implications
as they relate to his functions. In the process of preparing this paper, the editorial engineering complexities of our assignment to build such a two-way bridge soon become
apparent. Our dilemma was that any effort to lay out the unfamiliar basics for one of the
two groups threatened to be overly fundamental to the other. If there is some magic
editorial formula allowing for a common level of depth and abstraction under such circumstances, we have not stumbled upon it. We therefore ask the reader's patience
through those portions of the paper which to him may seem elementary.
[2] Since the developmental importance of malnutrition has not been recognized until
recently and nutrition priority accordingly has been low, it may appear as if advocates—
including the authors—are overstating their case in an effort to get a hearing. Although
zealousness may show through from time to time, we do recognize that nutrition is but
one of several contributors to human capital and well-being, and in the final analysis will
need to be judged in that light.

posals, the planner judges the worth of one objective against the worth of another. Having modified his objectives, he reexamines program proposals in a continual process of testing the desirable against the practical. In short, there is no simple formula, but a planning process does provide a framework that can help force clarification of nutritional objectives and identification of the better alternatives to achieve them.

Identifying the Problem

Step one in the planning process is problem description. What are the specific nutritional deficiencies? How severe? Who is affected? Where are they? What are the trends? Such problem identification poses no particular conceptual problems. For the most part, this step consists of a straightforward collection of already available or easily obtainable hard data through a variety of established techniques. Methods for measuring the nature and extent of malnutrition fall into four standard categories: food balance sheets, consumer expenditure surveys, food consumption surveys, and direct medical nutrition surveys.

Food Balance Sheets

A measurement technique developed in great statistical detail by the Food and Agriculture Organization is the food balance sheet. Estimated supplies of different foods within a country (or region) are translated into calories and nutrients to compute the per capita amounts available for human consumption, after taking account of losses and other uses. Availabilities can be compared with recommended standards for that country, to arrive at an estimate of the aggregate nutritional gap. Possible changes in this gap can be projected forward, based on assumptions of future changes in population, food output, and other variables. One problem associated with this method is that aggregate measures conceal individual features of the complex reality they describe. The approach does not take into account the dispersion of the income distribution within the population, regional variations, intrafamily food distribution mores, or seasonal hunger. It does not yield an estimate of how many actually are suffering from malnutrition nor give a profile of who they are. To strike an average as a means of ascertaining collective need for additional nutrients may be worse than meaningless; it can be dangerously misleading.[3]

---

[3] A positive food balance does not indicate absence of a problem where an aggregate surplus exists, as best seen in countries showing large surpluses of nutrients on the food balance sheets but still facing malnutrition. When a country has anything less than a moderate surplus, it is almost certain that a serious problem exists within individual regions or social classes.

Consumer Expenditure Survey

A second measurement technique uses a combination of income distribution data and consumer expenditure surveys. The latter often reveal how much and what kind of food is purchased, at specified levels of income or expenditure. This information can be paired with income distribution data to derive estimates of the numbers of people consuming different levels of calories and nutrients, and this information can then be compared to minimum nutritional requirements. Depending on the reliability and detail of the data, such surveys can give a good picture of the overall magnitude of nutritional deficits, the distribution of the deficits among areas and groups of the population defined according to various characteristics, and the apparent consumption levels of different nutrients. Although this technique provides a closer look than the balance sheet approach, it still omits important factors affecting nutrition such as the impact of cooking methods on the nutrient content of food, intrafamily distribution habits, and the incidence of parasites or other health problems that reduce food utilization.

Food Consumption Survey

The third method of assessing nutritional deficiencies is the food consumption survey. Data are gathered on the kinds and quantities of food consumed in selected households which represent the sociological, demographic, and economic patterns of the general population. By calculating the nutritive value of diets and comparing the value with nutritional requirements, deficiencies can be estimated. This method is not without problems. Precision is required to determine the actual quantity and quality of food eaten by the various members of the household. Answers given may reflect errors in judgment as well as a manipulation of the facts to present a favorable image of the family being questioned. Special influences on dietary patterns—such as season of the year, periods of the month and week, paydays and holidays—must be accounted for. Food reported as "consumed" may in fact have been wasted in cooking or left on the plate. Nutrients may have been lost because of malabsorption.

Medical Nutrition Survey

A fourth technique is the direct nutrition survey, involving a field examination of the nutritional status of a sample of the population. For the specific group studied, this is the most accurate of the four measures but also the most costly, the most time-consuming, and the most difficult. By necessity, the samples are small, thus raising the question of how representative they are of the whole population. In comparing various surveys to project a broader picture, one often runs into a lack of standardization of clinical definitions, uneven representativeness of the materials, and methodological problems such as failure to make allowances for seasonal variations.

Each of the above methods has shortcomings, but together they are capable of presenting a reasonably reliable picture. All four techniques would benefit measurably from greater policy issue orientation in the survey designs. What appears on the surface as a potentially rich mine of data is often of limited usefulness to the planner; usually the survey is designed without regard to unanswered (and generally unstated) policy questions and without regard to how the data would eventually be used.

Second-Source Survey

In addition to the approaches already described, there is a less formal, less imposing technique, capable of providing quick, generalized conclusions if the above studies are not available—and a technique that adds a helpful dimension even if they are. This is the second-source survey based on (1) collective impressions from interviews with nutrition experts as well as with an appropriate sampling of local public health officials and others on the local scene likely to have insights from constant exposure to the problem; and (2) a compilation and analysis of all relevant earlier studies—including village work of cultural anthropologists and medical surveys conducted for other purposes —which, when patched together, may begin to present the outlines of a distinctive pattern. The second-source survey technique lacks the desired precision for later detailed quantification and therefore should not be considered a substitute for the more comprehensive approaches mentioned above. In most countries, however, the second-source survey can, for planning purposes, offer prompt information which helps in gaining a useful first perspective of the problem.[4] For many planning situations, a 75 percent answer today is worth a great deal more than a 90 percent answer three years from now.

In the process of problem identification, the planner pinpoints the need. He now recognizes the specific nutritional maladies—for example, protein-calorie malnutrition, iron-deficiency anemias, vitamin A deficiency—and he is able to quantify the extent of the problem (for example, a 25 percent consumption shortfall in meeting minimum protein or vitamin A requirements). This may then be translated into specific nutrient requirements.[5]

[4] For an example of this interview-cum-survey technique designed for a quick overview of the Indian nutrition scene, see [7].

[5] In estimating quantities of gross requirements, allowance needs to be made for nutrient losses that can be anticipated from such causes as vomiting, diarrhea, and administrative mishaps.

Nutrition Objectives
With an adequate description in hand of the scope, nature, and victims of a
country's nutritional problems, the next step is to begin identification of
possible objectives. Lack of attention to this seemingly most obvious step in
the planning process has caused many nutrition programs to flounder. Government officials, often incorrectly assuming that the objectives are understood, give little if any time to formulating them. In neglecting this step they
risk setting forth a program of little consequence.

The first look at objectives is a general one, emerging from some kind of
interaction between the decision-maker and the planner. The nature of the
interaction will vary. In some countries there may be an explicit dialogue.
In others, the communication will be much less direct. (The distinction
between decision-maker and planner should be clear. The planner may be in
a position to advise, but not to establish objectives. No amount of planning
analysis substitutes for the kind of moral and political value judgments that
enter into policy decisions.) The early discussions block out the desired aims,
such as preservation of life, reduction of deficiency diseases, freedom from
infection, and development to full genetic potential. Also, they raise such
concerns as whether the program is developmental or humanitarian; whether
it is looking for immediate results or concentrating on long-term improvements; and whether it should aim to appease hunger or raise nutritional
standards.

One of the planner's early analytic strategy concerns is the determination of
proper scope for analysis. He wants to reach as far as possible while still
keeping his feet on the ground of realistic attainment. He recognizes that the
narrowness of nutrition activities to date may in part reflect the limitations
imposed by the nutrition advocate because of his assumption that only token
resources would be available. This has resulted in a "pilot project here, research activity there" characterization of the nutrition field, which often
misses the real determinants of nutrition status. So the first look at alternate objectives should be ambitious. Adjustments can be made later as
the planner begins to match need against resources, but at the outset he
should not restrict thinking by automatically closing off imaginative avenues of intervention. Even if certain programs emerging from this type
of thinking later prove beyond the reach of limited resources, the exploration of such avenues may yield insights leading to otherwise un-
identified possibilities.

An important element in objective-making is selection of targets based on
findings of the earlier problem identification. [8] Should the program be

directed to the infant? The preschool child?[6] The school child? The pregnant woman? The nursing mother? The breadwinner? Or what combinations of these groups? The sick or the well? A hospital bed for a severely malnourished youngster may cost as much as food supplements for thirty other needy children, who without supplements may themselves soon fall into the queues for hospitalization. The pros and cons of various targets and the techniques to weigh the alternatives, including relative growth dividends, have been discussed by Doctors Bengoa and Wilson and will not be reiterated here. [9]

The responsible officers might begin formulating tentative but specific nutrition objectives; for example, by 1978 to achieve in country X the provision of adequate protective foods and services in types and quantities required to reduce from 30 to 10 percent the number of 6-month to 24-month-old children suffering third-degree and second-degree[7] protein-calorie malnutrition.

At this point we will note briefly three aspects of our illustrative target that should be characteristic of any meaningful, "plannable" nutrition objective, and that will affect the planning and budgeting process at different points as it progresses. First, compared with broad national goals like "eradication of malnutrition" or "improvement in the quality of life," the objective cites a specific deficiency and a numerical target, or final output, which provides a concrete benchmark for estimating the needed resource inputs.

It is important to stress that at this stage the objective is still illustrative. Its formulation helps point the way for the kinds of analyses needed, but without the attendant data on costs (specifically the relation between increasing inputs and higher levels of benefits) one does not know how much any proposed target would cost or whether having achieved (say) the reduction to 10 percent, it would take a great deal more money, or perhaps only a very small increment, to reach 5 percent or virtually zero.

Second, the objective has a time frame that requires a definite sequence of action for attaining the objective by a given date, and the specification of resources to be allocated at each step in that sequence to achieve the objective of defined magnitude.

Third, there is need to know what resources the program will require. An-

---

[6] The term "preschool," commonly used in nutrition parlance, is not a totally satisfactory description. In part this is because the term means different time periods in different settings (in some countries preschool means 0-5 years of age, in others 1-4, and all permutations thereof). It is also misleading in that among the nutritionally most needy there is often no school to be "pre" to.

[7] Third degree is below 60% of standard body weight per age; second degree is between 60 and 75% of norm.

swers to this question will become subobjectives, marking paths of the programs and specifying conditions that will have to be created along the way toward the specific target. Examples might be increased production capacity for certain foods or food products, or reduction of associated health and environmental problems. Or it may be recognized that a precondition to acceptance for some program is an understanding by legislators or other policy-makers of its significance. Thus, a subobjective may be to create sufficient awareness of the implications of the problem, with an eye toward providing the necessary receptive climate for required legislation and appropriation. Subobjectives also should be translated into a program quantified and positioned in a time frame. In short, as objectives are stated with increasing precision, one becomes increasingly able (and aware of the need) to develop a systematic program of inquiry and action.

Anatomy of the Problem
Most nutrition study has concentrated on identification of the nature and scope of the problem. Less attention has been directed to the root causes, often perhaps because the causes seem too obvious to merit serious attention. Surface conclusions on causes, however, can be misleading, and the lack of better analysis may lead nutrition advocates astray in the quest for solutions.

One can distinguish three strata of causes of malnutrition. The first or most proximate causes, from the medical point of view, are insufficient nutrient intake, poor utilization of nutrients from the food ingested, and the heightened nutritional needs caused by bouts of nutrition-related illnesses. At the other end of the spectrum are such factors as general inadequacy of national resources, rapid population growth, and the whole constellation of causes that together constitute underdevelopment. In between, constituting the area on which the following discussion will concentrate, are those socioeconomic factors directly influencing diet and utilization that can possibly be manipulated to improve nutritional status. Here belong such causes as low family income, local ecological deficiencies, distribution shortcomings, price relationships, food waste, and errors of consumer behavior. The understanding of such causal factors lags far behind the medical nutritionist's knowledge of physiological causal connections.

A Systems Approach
There recently has been growing recognition that, because malnutrition is a problem deeply imbedded in the surrounding socioeconomic environment, a

more comprehensive and systematic or "systems" approach could provide a powerful analytic and programming tool. Early attention was directed to the broad interactions of nutrition and the socioeconomic setting, going beyond the proximate causes or first stratum referred to above, by Cicely Williams [10] and Joaquin Cravioto, [11] both of whom called for development of appropriate analytic techniques to sort out these interactions. Recent first attempts to apply standard systems techniques to the nutrition problem have mapped out the ground but have produced results too broad for practical usefulness. Systems practitioners tend to produce flow charts reflecting the relationships of everything to everything, the result being something more akin to a Jackson Pollock canvas than to a useful planning chart. Comprehensiveness is desirable, but it becomes counterproductive if it focuses time and attention on tertiary variables or strives for precision that may be spurious because of limited and inaccurate data.

A practical application of a systems approach in the field of nutrition will probably be one that (1) can yield guidance for the decision-makers within a reasonable time period, (2) would identify and analyze not the entire complex of causes but those major determinants of nutritional status in particular malnourished populations, and (3) is subject to policy levers. Exposing this system, even in a limited form, should have more than explanatory value. It should show which of the many causes are the major factors and how they operate. It should reveal, thereby, points where interventions might effect desirable changes and result in improvements in nutritional status.

There is a basic difference between the systems approach and the conventional means of nutrition planning. In the latter, the analysis and solutions focus on the most immediate determinants of the problem. Generally the identification of a nutrition deficiency prompts reflex responses such as proposals for new formulated foods or for health center activities. A systems approach, instead of jumping forward from problem to solution, moves backward to a study of the system or environment within which the problem arises and within which one finds complex, interacting forces.

It may be useful at this point to outline an example of the kind of perspective a systems description would give the planner on a specific malnutrition problem. Let us take protein deficiencies among children under 2 years of age. One would first separate for individual treatment the two prime (and related) determinants—their food intake and their health. Food intake is further subdivided by asking "What affects it?" Here the analyst is able to suggest a number of possible answers: (1) family food purchases, (2) family food production, (3) family food habits, (4) food provided through institutional feeding programs, and (5) food provided from the mother's breast. Each of these, in turn, can be further subdivided, with planner attention being directed at each stage to the most important or potentially important influences. Quantification should be made whenever possible.

Take, for instance, the problem of the decline in breast-feeding, which may turn up as an important factor in the analysis. Breast milk is capable of providing all the protein needs of the 0-to-6-month-old and 75 percent of the needs of the 6-to-12-month-old, but because mothers are breast-feeding fewer months or not at all, this milk may be providing only 30 percent of the need. Factors determining this decline might include (1) lack of opportunity because of work requirements; (2) social attitudes, such as esthetic considerations connected with the breast as a sex symbol or the attitude that breast-feeding is an old-fashioned peasant practice; (3) repeated pregnancy; or (4) physiological problems (such as breast abcesses or inverted nipples) or individual psychological problems.

Analysis may lead in later steps to the conclusion that the breast-feeding trend in urban areas of nation X could be reversed if conditions of female employment were altered in ways to enable mothers to feed their children. A possible intervention would be provision for nursing leave, compensated by the government, with additional assurance of job placement upon return. (This technique is already in use in Switzerland, the Soviet Union, and Israel.) Costs and implications can be quantified in ways to be pointed out shortly. Also, alterations can be made in conditions of employment, for example, the establishment of facilities at a factory where mothers might house their children during work hours and nurse them during allowed feeding breaks. Again, the cost of the extra room, infant care, and time lost from work are easily measurable for purposes of later comparison.

Alternatively, the attitudinal constraints to breast-feeding may be a major factor. These are influenced by custom and education, both from formal schooling and information less formally communicated from mass media and local figures of influence. Here, too, quantifiable interventions for change come to mind: stress in the school curriculum on the importance of breast-feeding; a mass media campaign extolling the virtues of nursing; special education for medical students and doctors to encourage greater attention to the problem. The planner goes through a similar sequence of questioning for each of the other subgroups of food intake and follows the same procedure in studying health.

Working through such a simple schematic process is a first step to under-standing the causes of and potential solutions to the problem. Even if no fur-ther analysis were undertaken, this would represent an improvement over the impressionistic or unstructured nutrition planning one often finds today. However, for appreciation of the total system, more data often will be re-quired, as will a clearer understanding of the interrelationships of the many factors in the system. To simplify measurement and description of such inter-relationships, it may be convenient to divide the total system into three sub-systems that are sufficiently distinct to form somewhat separate analytic wholes. These would be (a) food production, (b) food processing and distri-bution, and (c) the consumer or family group with its food acquisition and utilization capabilities and behavior.

By specifying the factors that relate the nutritive intake of the family sub-system to the distribution subsystem (for example, the extent to which the family derives food from central processing or commercial sources) and re-lating the distribution subsystem to the food production subsystem behind it, the planner should be able to foresee, or at least hypothesize more intel-ligently, (a) how an intervention in one of the systems is likely to work its way through to final effect on the consumer, (b) the relative costs and the limitations of specific interventions, and (c) how sets of interventions might relate, thereby reinforcing each other and producing a more powerful impact on ultimate nutritional status. Where sufficient data exist or can reasonably be generated, it is conceivable that in some circumstances simulation models of these interrelated systems might be constructed to test the poten-tial impact of different interventions, thereby increasing the likelihood of selecting the most effective ones. For most countries, the planning apparatus, to be workable, must be more modest. Generally the funds, data, trained planners, and administrative talent are so limited that a complex nutrition planning undertaking could be counterproductive. Obviously the degree of complexity of any planning effort needs to be scaled to existing capabilities. The point is that nutrition planning need not be—and in most cases should not be—regarded as a highly sophisticated, computerized model requiring extensive investment of time, talent, and money. Rather, it should be re-garded as a conceptual approach, a systematic way of looking at a problem to sharpen decision making.[8]

By casting a wide enough net, this approach should make it possible to catch

[8] It should be emphasized that complex techniques are not a prerequisite to good planning. Charles Hitch, one of the pioneers of systems planning, has written that in his

those useful points of intervention in the food/health complex that give promise of providing a handle that can be cranked a couple of degrees to produce favorable results. What has been described in some places as a nutrition problem may from this view be identified as a transportation problem. Thus, a powerful factor for better nutrition might be the improvement of an interregional transport or storage system enabling needed foods to move more easily or at a lower cost from surplus to deficit areas. For example,

1. It has been observed that probably the major contribution to the solution of the regional famines in India was the construction of the railroad. The project was not undertaken with this in mind, but one might ask whether, if a nutrition planning exercise had been undertaken in India a hundred years ago, it would have recognized that an improvement in the transportation system, that would enable surplus areas to feed deficit areas, would in fact make the most substantial contribution in alleviating the mortality and morbidity from malnourishment in India.

2. Peru has the largest per-capita fish catch in the world, but it rarely is consumed much beyond the immediate fish-catching region. This suggests that provision of appropriate transport facilities to move the fish inland may be a worthy nutrition investment.

3. Another example is in Korea, where there is a common seasonal shortage of certain nutrients in the diet. This has been traced to the lack of adequate storage facilities that can store the kinds of foods that carry these nutrients. [13]

Price incentives, which have proved effective for changing production patterns of masses of farmers, may turn out to be a critical lever. It is conceivable that a shift in price policies on legumes can do more for the nutritional status of large numbers of children by 1978 than the many current efforts to produce and distribute formulated foods; yet price incentives have seldom, if ever, been explored in relation to nutrition objectives beyond sheer increase in grain supply. Because of the relationship between malnutrition and parasitic and infectious diseases,[14,15] under some circumstances a mass immunization program or improvement in water supply may do more for nutri-

experience the hardest problems "are not those of analytic techniques. In fact, the techniques we use are usually rather simple and old-fashioned. What distinguishes the useful and productive analyst is his ability to formulate (or design) the problem; to choose appropriate objectives; to define the relevant, important environments or situations in which to test the alternatives; to judge the reliability of his cost and other data; and finally, and not least, his ingenuity in inventing new systems or alternatives to evaluate." [12]

tion than a food supply approach, or perhaps needs to be combined with food for most effective results. In some situations, the maintenance of a father's good health and productivity may be the best means of assuring nutritional adequacy among his young. A description of the child's diet and the influences at work in that diet may suggest new foods, potential carriers for fortification, or potential mass media presentations designed to change food habits. The validity and relative usefulness of any of these approaches depend on the conditions and relationships laid out in the systems description.

A prototype activity, currently under way in the Indian state of Tamil Nadu (formerly Madras), gives some insight into how such a project might be approached. The Indian government is attempting to develop an analysis that reviews the nutritional status of target groups and describes the factors and relationships affecting this status. A model is being developed against which a variety of nutrition interventions can be tested. [16] (Mr. Venkitaramanan describes the project in this volume in the General Discussion at the end of this section.)

Identification and Comparison of Alternative Interventions
Once the above factors and their relative importance are identified, the nutrition planner has a basis for (a) judging the relevance and relative effectiveness of the kinds of interventions the nutritionist often recommends—nutrition education, fortification, maternal child-health facilities, blended foods, and so on—and (b) developing new or particular interventions suggested by the particular anatomy of that country's nutrition problems—for example, interventions relevant to local ecology, regional storage and distribution, opportunities for income supplements, or price policies.

Econutrition Profiles
The attractiveness of any intervention will depend on the nutritional problem at issue, the particular population group comprising the target, the factors that determine the nutritional status of that group, and the intrinsic characteristics of the intervention. For any one population group, the systems description would provide information translatable into what might be called an economic or econutritional profile, which would characterize the group by the important variables defining and determining its nutritional status. Such a profile would serve as a kind of litmus paper against which any of the standard nutrition intervention programs can be tested.

Typical profiles to be found in many parts of the world can be briefly sketched as follows.

1. **Nonmonetized subsistence.** Very low real income. Regional or local ecologically determined nutritional deficiencies. High incidence of malnutrition-infectious disease synergism. Deleterious food preparation habits. Low food productivity combined with substantial spoilage and losses. Illiteracy.

2. **Low-income small farmers, partially monetized.** Substantial portion of diet comprises local staple, locally milled every day or so. Most purchased foods consist of locally produced vegetables and other products; small expenditures on manufactured products such as salt, tea, and condiments. Farmers have poor food habits and low productivity, but are reached by commercial distribution and mass media information systems. Supply policies may have perverse impact. Low functional literacy. (Small tenant farmers may be less responsive to the price system and productivity-raising programs because of insecurity of tenure and rental arrangements.)

3. **Low-income landless agricultural laborers.** Same as 2 but also socially disadvantaged and less well served by government agencies at the local level. Seasonal underemployment limits impact of general economic progress.

4. **Low-income urban migrants.** Poor food habits. Perverse impact of slightly higher income spent on nutritionally inferior forms of more processed foods. High mass communications exposure. Declining breast-feeding, and high incidence of infant disease from unsterile feeding procedures.

In the simple process of matching previously identified alternatives to the econutrition profiles, [17] many preconceived notions will have to be discarded. This does not mean that a single project must meet the test of practicality for all groups, but at least this filtering process clarifies the potential impact and limitations of a given project. A cereal fortification alternative obviously would be meaningless to a group whose food is not centrally processed. Price policies would have little impact on nonmonetized populations. Nutrition education is of little use if needed nutrients are not available.

To illustrate the kinds of analysis desirable in weighing alternate intervention programs, let us pursue briefly the latter example. In the past, the nutritionist has focused much of his energy and budget on nutrition education because it has been assumed that substantial improvement of deficiencies can be attained through behavorial changes, within the limitations imposed by economic and other external circumstances.[9] There are several implicit assumptions behind a decision to put a country's resources into nutri-

[9] The notion that nutrition education can go a long way toward alleviation of nutritional problems has always been an attractive one. The most recent statement of the attractiveness

tion education programs, which, if made explicit, and examined against the background of the relevant econutritional profile, might lead to useful conclusions about the proper role and character of nutrition education, or at least to some conclusions about alternatives worth researching. First, how much nutritional improvement can actually be obtained merely from specified changes in decisions of the food-buyer and preparer, given the constraints imposed by such factors as income, ecology, and local supply availabilities? Clearly, no improvement results from recommending that people buy foods that are not available, or that require reducing expenditures on the staple caloric source, if calories are an important deficiency.

Second, if people in a given profile were educated to realize the available nutritional benefit, how powerful would such realization be as a behavioral determinant, compared with the esthetic or other aspects of proposed behavioral changes? In addition to the more obvious program costs, changes in food behavior may have costs that seem less "real" from an economic standpoint but that are quite real in the sense that the esthetic or psychic rewards obtained from particular food choices comprise some of the very limited pleasures available to those living in poverty. An example is the linear programming least-cost diet that shows how one can achieve the maximum volume and quality of nutrients within a budget ceiling, given the relative prices of available foods. This approach has been applied successfully to the blending of animal feeds but has not come into widespread use for planning human diets. When tried, this technique typically is applied in ways that overlook the fact that people buy other things besides nutrition when they buy food. These other values, such as taste, bulk, texture, refreshment, and religious proscriptions, are not frivolous. Yet these preferences are not immutable. They do change along with broad changes in dynamic social environments, and they are known to be open to influence through education, mass media persuasion, changes in observed peer or leadership behavior, and so on. To what extent can food habits successfully be changed—and remain changed? And what are the costs?

Third, there are important empirical questions about how best to motivate

---

of this approach—from the view of the planner hard-pressed for resources for competing claims—came in one of the responses to the letters the organizers of this conference sent out to many planners throughout the world soliciting their thoughts on the problems and subjects for this meeting. The correspondent, the Secretary of Finance of a developing country, ended a long and thoughtful letter with the simple question, harking back to his childhood days when he remembered being told that eating some things would be better for him than eating others: "Can't the problem be solved on the cheap by merely telling people what's good for them?"

people to adopt the proposed behavorial changes. Face-to-face applied nutrition education programs have not been very successful. Even when they are successful, they would probably show up poorly from a cost-effectiveness viewpoint. Are there other communication techniques feasible within the context of a specific profiled group?

Comparing the Alternatives
After some potential remedial measures have passed a preliminary screening for relevance and relative probabilities of success, the alternatives need to be compared for (a) cost and relative effectiveness for achieving the nutrition objectives, (b) possible impact on other, nonnutrition, sectors, and (c) some general constraints not easily accounted for in standard economic analysis.
Costs and Benefits
The most important criterion for comparing alternative interventions is the nutritional impact[10] of the interventions relative to their respective costs. An important caution is to avoid the common mistake of stopping short before all costs have been considered. For example, a campaign to encourage longer breast-feeding will involve, in addition to the educational expenses, the cost of the extra food required for the nursing mother, or the cost to her health if her diet is inadequate. In the case of mass fortification projects, per capita cost must be computed on the basis of total outlay. This includes the cost of reaching those who do not need the extra nutrients as well as those who do.

Another case in point is the problem of food waste, which has been highlighted with increasing frequency in both nutrition and agriculture forums. For the urban food buyer, reducing food waste may be an important means of improving nutritional status. Increasing food supplies in this way would lower food prices, increase food intake, and raise real incomes of the poorer consumers who allocate a relatively large portion of their expenditures to food. Some forms of potential waste reduction may appear to be without cost, such as reduction of table waste in the home or use of rice water containing the nutrients boiled out of rice. However, educational efforts needed to effect such behavioral changes are not without cost and must be taken into account. In major causes of food waste—destruction by pests and spoilage in storage and transport—it is assumed that benefits of waste reduction are high compared to costs and should be accorded high priority. In fact, waste in

[10] The analysis would also cover the economic and social benefits of alternatives. Since benefits are being addressed by others in this volume (and elsewhere by the authors; see [6]), the subject will not be discussed here.

agricultural production, processing, and distribution is no different in an economic sense from waste in inefficient industrial, power, or other branches of the economy. In any area, such waste is regarded as a cost of production.

There are two relevant questions here. First, where will the largest increase in supply be obtained for a given expenditure? Will it come from reducing destruction by pests in the field; from reducing losses in storage and transport; from higher initial production through greater investment in seeds, fertilizers, pesticides, or irrigation; from increasing recovery from the milling process, or some combination of these? Second, after these alternatives are ranked by relative effectiveness in relation to cost, how does their economic return compare with the alternative uses of the required resources elsewhere in the economy? Any one country or region, by focusing on waste alone, may be committing the error of nutrient autarchy—that is, of limiting eligible solutions to those depending entirely on domestic production of nutrients. As long as an area or country trades externally, the key question on the waste or supply aspect generally is not necessarily where to get the largest domestic supply increase for a given expenditure, but how to generate the greatest increase in resources given the area's comparative advantages.

Another caution: to restrict benefit calculations to those factors that are measurable also would be a distortion. Good nutrition may improve labor efficiency by preventing blindness or by reducing anemia, and the resulting increased productivity would be measurable. But to stop there would ignore the main benefit, the increased well-being—mental and physical—of those involved. In short, the benefit/cost analysis would not be carried out in terms of actual benefits, but in terms of those benefits that happen to be easy to measure. [18]

Thus, some interventions do not lend themselves to standard quantification of costs and benefits, in part because of severe limitations of data and in part because of the quantification difficulties inherent in programs designed to change human behavior. The planner's contribution here is to narrow down as much as possible what is known about the potential costs and benefits of such interventions and to make clear what is conjecture. Decisions in such instances often must be left to common sense judgments, which will be easier if the planner is honest about assumptions and uncertainties.

There is a battery of other standard considerations included in project analysis, including such issues as whether the project will be self-sustaining. After the initial investment, will the project pay for itself? (Examples would be incentives to encourage the launching of low-cost commercial foods or fortification projects in which the costs could eventually be borne by the consumers.) Also of concern is the nature and source of the needed resource. Some activities, such as nutritional education, might be supported by local monies. Others, such as production of soy isolate, may have significant foreign exchange costs. The costs of some proposed strategies, such as institutional feeding programs, can be covered in part with food commodities readily and gratuitously available from international sources. Similarly, technical and capital foreign assistance may be more easily available for certain projects than for others. This is not to suggest that foreign assistance in nutrition is without its costs—financial, administrative, political, and even psychic. Properly handled foreign aid can be useful in reducing the country's burden, but such considerations must be brought into the cost equation.[11]

Impact in Nonnutrition Sectors

Nutritional activities affect nonnutritional sectors in ways that need to be taken explicitly into account. The number and significance of second-order consequences will vary with the nature of the proposed nutrition intervention. A large nutrition education activity can be viewed in greater isolation than a new policy designed to shift crops. The former will impinge on administrative time and resources otherwise available for other programs, but the latter might necessitate major reallocations of foreign exchange or industrial raw materials.

Some interactions may strengthen efforts to achieve other nonnutrition objectives. One example may be the use of family planning clinics as a distribution outlet for free food supplements for infants. The free commodities may serve as an incentive to draw young mothers to the clinic, and the concern for the young child demonstrated by the clinic personnel may serve to establish a better rapport and enhance chances for the mother's receptivity to family planning practices. Similarly, to a country investing substantial sums in education, student well-being and attendance rates are factors determining learning capability and the returns to education. As a general rule, while activities in harmony with other objectives are preferable to activities inconsistent with such objectives (and are ahead of the game in the competition for resources), nutrition planning should not be subordinated to these other objectives once the nutrition objectives have been sanctioned.

[11] Many foreign assistance agencies, both bilateral and multinational, have recently added, or express interest in adding, nutrition components to their programs. The problem to date has been to identify significant nutritional projects. There is clearly a need for interested countries to propose nutritional projects with the same criteria given developmental undertakings of other types.

Constraints
Besides standard project feasibility questions (like availability of equipment
and other inputs, legal requirements, and so on), there are a number of practical constraints in the developing countries that have hampered nutrition
activities in practice and are worth singling out for special attention. Good
management is one of the scarcest resources in developing countries, and
preference should be given to interventions requiring minimum dependence
on an administrative structure. For example, compared with a health center-
oriented nutrition activity, which requires an army of operatives, a shift in
price policy may require virtually no field staff. In large countries, a conventional nutrition education program, leaning heavily on face-to-face techniques, requires thousands of extension workers whereas a mass media effort
designed to achieve the same end may require only a few dozen employees.
The management requirements of extensive feeding programs may pose
serious obstacles, even where imaginative piggybacking use is made of existing
school, health, and other institutions. If these entities are fully employed, the
added feeding function may appear to have no incremental cost besides provision of the food; but in fact it will incur real costs in terms of reduced time
devoted to the primary functions of the preexisting institutions. For intervention programs not tied to an existing infrastructure, it should be remembered that a heavily administered program also means a claim on limited
talent affecting costs of attaining other national goals.
    Another concern is replicability. If the project's success depends on multi-
plying the impact of an isolated success that is dependent on the personal
initiative and vitality of the initiator—for example, a pilot village applied
nutrition program—the chances of success are more limited than for broad,
sweeping policies creating the same nutritional impact without going
through the replication effort. Too often a successful pilot project loses its
impact in the process of bureaucratization.
    Time is an important consideration, especially with respect to protein-
calorie malnutrition among young children. The criticality of early periods of
growth for subsequent mental and physical capacity requires the planner to
heavily discount those options that will begin to affect a nation's nutritional
status only after a long period of time. For those children passing out of the
critical months impaired by protein-calorie malnutrition, the effects of these
delayed benefits will be very small. Actions such as the development of formulated foods, certain cereal fortification projects, and shifts in price policies—producer incentives and consumer subsidies—can be undertaken immediately and the planner can anticipate a payoff in a very short time period.

267 Nutrition Program Planning: An Approach

At the other end of the spectrum are those activities still in the basic research stage—work on single-cell protein or fish protein concentrate—which, even if technically successful, may not produce a significant nutrition impact for many years. Between these two extremes are projects in varying stages of development, successfully tested in the laboratory and the clinic but still requiring field testing before being exploited on a large scale. The fortification of salt in India and of sugar in Guatemala fall into this category. Thus, alongside his project options, the planner should plot a separate track indicating the time span implied. A long-run strategy might do well to stress measures with immediate impact, with an eye toward development of better substitutes to gradually replace the initial measures over time.

Finally, there are the practical bureaucratic questions. How capable are the people in charge of the alternative proposed programs? Do they have enough commitment and forcefulness (without which approval and allocation mean little) to push their projects through? How many officials are involved in the clearance procedure, and how long will these clearances take?

Factors like these are the real-life determinants of program success or failure. To increase the odds of his program's success, the planner must superimpose these considerations on the purely technical judgments. What emerges is a shorter list of program opportunities. Each time the list is pared down, the planner gets closer to the final shape of his program.

The planning analysis thus far will help determine which set of inputs, or which program, would be likely to achieve the desired target, within the desired time-frame, for the least cost. However, the total cost commonly turns out higher than the resources eventually provided through the budgetary process.[12] After the financial availabilities and policy framework are set, it is then usually necessary to return to the drawing board. Some realignment of objectives, time-frame, and the mix of projects will have to be made, within the limits of the resources actually budgeted. Thus, we return to a point mentioned at the outset, that objective-making is an iterative process involving frequent adjustment throughout the various planning stages. As data are collected and analyzed, the planner's notions may change about the nature of the problem and costs to overcome it. Flexibility to alter objectives is essential.

During the process of adjusting objectives it is important for the planner to

[12] Those interested in promoting nutrition programs will want to distinguish between costs which show up in the nutrition budget and those which do not. Under common circumstances of already overstrained budgets, any new request for a large budgetary appropriation can be expected to encounter resistance from the legislature, special interest groups, and so on.

return to the original analysis. In scaling down an objective resulting from an earlier analysis, it may turn out that what passed the cost-effectiveness test in the context of an ambitious national program may not be the best way to reach more modest numbers.

The Decision

Throughout the above sequence, the nutrition planner, in an attempt to keep his efforts relevant, tries to get guidance or at least clues indicating areas and scope of interest from the policy-level leadership. Now the planner places before the decision-maker[13] the options, alternate objectives, alternate strategies, and, most important, the potential programs and consequences of following alternate strategies. The executive probably is a political figure, and he will add—if it is not there already—a political dimension to the analysis. First, is the overall concept politically attractive? And if so, is it sufficiently visible? How long will it take to see results? Within the specific program and project options, there may be greater political attractiveness attached to one proposal than to another. A massive child-feeding program offers high visibility and many potential votes. A shift in cropping pattern to achieve the same end may go undetected by the electorate; indeed, it may offend some commodity interest groups, which often are notoriously efficient in influencing policy to meet their ends.

Political judgments are also brought to play on the value of creating or encouraging a momentum that could have other nutritional ramifications. In the initial stages of developing support and general public understanding of nutrition, a high-visibility project with relatively minor nutritional impact may still have a useful role in a longer run strategy, by helping develop broad support and momentum that will spill over to the benefit of other activities. In the jargon of economics, one would say that such high-visibility projects have "external economies." Also, since most nutrition programs are forms of income redistribution, certain approaches may be more politically palatable than others. Taxation to feed hungry children is less likely to arouse resistance in those being taxed than a direct money transfer to the poor. There are additional political considerations when other countries are involved. The executive must weigh the cost to the national psyche of being on the receiving end of such assistance, and the cost of potential political embarrassments should they arise.

[13] Complicating the life of the planner is the common absence of an individual who is "the decision-maker." Decisions often result from a far more diffuse process than the generally assumed "centralized decision-making" implied in organization charts.

Decisions result from a complex debate and adversary process among various interest groups, the parliament, and the executive, involving political values and judgments based on emotion, intuition, or the desire to protect one's bureaucratic position. The planner thus becomes only marginally influential in the final decision-making stage. He has, however, been able to systematically discuss, illuminate, analyze, and articulate the options. Clearly, when the executive has some indication of the consequences of various actions, he is in a position to make up his mind more intelligently. As Alice Rivlin notes, on the merits of the planning process: (1) it is better to have some idea where you are going than to fly blind, and (2) it is better to be orderly than haphazard about decision-making. [19]

Now the planner has presented the alternatives to the executive, and selection has been made. The decision should reflect a mix of immediate, intermediate, and long-term payoffs, blending action and research components with greater emphasis on action. A complaint often heard in the past is that nutrition programs are bogged down with irrelevant or duplicating laboratory research. Obviously, attention must be given to scientific research needs, but concentration should be on what social action programs imply—*action*.

Evaluation

Let us assume that the program rides along the bureaucratic and political tracks smoothly: Decisions have been made, policies formulated, programs adopted, manned, and put into operation. The next and final step in the planning process is to determine whether the hypothesis has worked out; with the ultimate measure of activities being their contribution to achievement of the broad objective. (One of the common mistakes of food programmers is the assumption that achievement of the subobjectives—for example distribution of X tons of food through Y thousand schools—implies success.) Evaluation measures the actual performance, informs the planner of weaknesses needing adjustment, assumptions needing alteration or further research, and how costs and benefits are developing under actual operating conditions. Evaluation feeds these important judgments back into the planning process, connecting one planning cycle with the next. For the sake of objectivity the evaluation should be conducted by someone (or some entity) other than the program's planner or implementer.

Evaluation is the element of the nutrition planning process that generally receives the least amount of effort. [20] In principle no one is opposed to evaluation; in practice it rarely happens. (Perhaps one reason funds for evaluation are not included in project budgets is that administrators are reluctant to ask. A request may be interpreted as admission of doubt of the program's effectiveness and therefore may hamper basic funding for the project.) [19] Also, findings of a poorly managed program supported by outside assistance may inhibit future funding from the same source in other sectors. When evaluation does take place, results often are vulnerable to methodological attack. Data may have been collected erroneously, the sample improperly drawn, or interpretations made unsatisfactorily. At the outset, programs must be systematically designed in a way that will generate data for measuring the program's effectiveness.

The Planning Process in Perspective
Although the planning process has earned an enviable reputation in the development business, in practice it is not without its limitations. Asok Mitra, Secretary of India's Planning Commission, once wrote that the planning process is similar to elephant love-making: "It takes the best part of a year to learn one's way about it; the moment of love can be painful and rather hazardous; and anyway one has to wait eighteen months for the result." [21] In addition to the program constraints discussed earlier, there also are analytical constraints. Conclusions depend heavily either on available data, often of uncertain quality, or personal judgments which themselves are subject to human error. A common shortcoming is inadequate recognition of the discrepancy between what logically makes sense and what is operationally realistic.

Also, in a quest for the perfect model planning can be overdone, to the point it becomes a prison to operational movement. (In one of the larger development agencies the lengthy and cumbersome planning procedures prompted one food programmer to retort: "Let them eat plans.") In the beginning, the important thing is not that the bear walk straight but that he walk at all.

Clearly there have been instances in which the promise of planning techniques has been greater than the delivery [22] and instances in which complicated methodological devices have fallen of their own weight. Even though there is now common agreement that "the new planning" has passed the point in its development "which medicine passed in the nineteenth century where it begins to do more good than harm" [12] it is still a fairly new and not yet totally refined art. False starts and blind alleys can be expected as part of the occupational hazards.

Having said this, the planning process, properly scaled to local capabilities and properly action-oriented, can serve a highly useful function for those concerned with better nutrition. If the problem has been clearly defined, the objectives precisely stated, and interventions adequately analyzed, this approach serves as a systematic means of coming up with what will probably be the best possible range of program solutions. Such has not been the common result of the conventional nutrition programming process. Projects now are generally adopted because someone comes along with an idea (the idea commonly reflecting the background of the advocate; thus the medical man sees solutions quite differently from the plant geneticist or the food industry official), with its costs, and with the mechanism to carry it out. In this way a little piece may get done—a commercial formulated food, a fish protein concentrate, a chain of Mothercraft Centers. The piece may or may not be useful if done in isolation. To be effective, perhaps, other actions—extension work, credit provisions, marketing services, food regulation—must take place simultaneously. To the extent that activities exist today in the field of nutrition, they more often than not are the result of the persistence and persuasiveness of the project advocate rather than of a thoughtful look at total needs and alternatives to meet these needs.

This no longer need be so. Today in other fields there are accepted planning approaches that can be adapted for nutrition purposes. Although the answers emerging from such approaches may not have the mathematical precision sometimes available in other aspects of development, the nutrition planner will have a clearer idea than he had before of what will and will not work. At a minimum he will have classified the available activities into those that are clearly useless, those offering the most potential (including possibilities that may not have been considered had the system not been traced), and those that fall somewhere in between.

The making of a nutrition plan could take years—or weeks. Clearly, some good indications of desirable direction are obtainable without elaborately detailed studies. When a government endorses a detailed nutrition planning undertaking, it should not be at the cost of operational delay. Ongoing projects should not be derailed, and new actions can be initiated on the basis of preliminary analysis and best judgments while more elaborate studies are under way. In most instances it is far easier to study and report on the consequences of an operation than to predict these consequences in the abstract.

What all this boils down to is that if malnutrition is a widespread problem affecting a large part of the population, a government interested in attacking the problem in any short-term time-frame will have to think in broader scope than it has to date. In the process, nutrition planning deserves more thoughtful and systematic attention than it has yet received.

References

1. Berg, Alan. Malnutrition and national development. *Foreign Affairs* 46:126, 1967.

2. Berg, Alan, Priority of nutrition in national development. *Nutr. Rev.* 28:199, 1970.

3. Berg, Alan. Nutrition as a national priority: lessons from the India experiment. *Amer. J. Clin. Nutr.* 23:1396, 1970.

4. Berg, Alan. Increased income and improved nutrition: a shibboleth examined. *Internat. Develop. Rev.* 12:3, 1970.

5. Berg, Alan, and Robert Muscat. Nutrition and development: the view of the planner. Paper Submitted to United Nations Panel to Formulate a Strategy Statement on the Protein Problem Confronting the Developing Countries, New York, May 3-7, 1971. *Amer. J. Clin. Nutr.* 25:186, 1972.

6. Berg, Alan, and Robert Muscat. Macronutrition. Proceedings of the Western Hemisphere Nutrition Congress III. Futura Publishing Co., 1972.

7. *Nutrition Research Profile.* U.S. Agency for International Development, New Delhi, 1967.

8. For examples of national nutrition objectives in Czechoslovakia, see Hruby, J., and O. Smrha, Food policy in Czechoslovakia. In *Proceedings of the Eighth International Congress on Nutrition,* Prague. Amsterdam: Excerpta Medica, 1970, p. 570.

9. Bengoa, J. M. Significance of malnutrition and priorities for its prevention. This volume, p. 103. Wilson, Douglas. The economic analysis of malnutrition. This volume, p. 129.

10. Williams, Cicely. Malnutrition. *Lancet* 2:342, 1962.

11. Cravioto, J. Complexity of factors involved in protein-calorie malnutrition. In *Malnutrition is a Problem of Ecology.* Paul Gyorgy and O. L. Kline, eds. Basel, Switzerland, and New York: Karger, 1970, p. 7.

12. Hitch, Charles J. *Decision-Making for Defense.* Berkeley and Los Angeles: University of California Press, 1965, pp. 54, 76.

13. *Commercial Feasibility of Fish Protein Concentrate in a Developing Country.* Vol. I, *The Protein Situation in Korea and the Potential Role of Fish Protein Concentrates.* Report prepared by Sidney Cantor Associates, Inc. for U.S. Agency for International Development, October 1969.

14. *Control of Ascariasis.* Report of a World Health Organization Expert Committee. WHO Technical Report Series No. 379. Geneva: WHO; RNTP/RFNS/19 English, 1967, p. 5; Pollack, Herbert. Disease as a factor in world food problem. *Amer. J. Clin. Nutr.* 21:868, 1968.

15. Rosenberg, Irwin. *Report to Committee on International Nutrition Programs, Food and Nutrition Board, National Academy of Sciences.* Washington, D.C., 1971; Hirschhorn, Norbert. Can small daily doses of antibiotics prevent the cycle of diarrhea, malabsorption, and malnutrition in children? *Amer. J. Clin. Nutr.* 24:872, 1971.

16. Chafkin, Sol. *An Operations Oriented Study of Nutrition as an Integrated System of Tamil Nadu.* Report prepared for Food and Nutrition Division, U.S. Agency for International Development, New Delhi, 1970; Subramaniam, C. Report presented to the United Nations Secretary-General's Panel to Formulate a United Nations Strategy on the Protein Problem Confronting the Developing Countries, 1971. Mitra, Asok. The nutrition movement in India. This volume, p. 357.

17. For a different categorization of profiles see Knutsson, Karl Eric, Malnutrition and the community. Paper presented at the 1971 Dag Hammarskjöld Seminar on Nutrition as a Priority in African Development, Uppsala, Sweden, July 1971.

18. Mathiasen, David. Some comments on nutrition. Internal AID staff memo to author, New Delhi, Feb. 18, 1969.

19. Rivlin, Alice M. *Systematic Thinking for Social Action.* Washington, D.C.: Brookings Institution, 1971, pp. 2, 85.

20. Wray, J. D. Evaluation: everybody talks about it . . . In *Malnutrition Is a Problem of Ecology.* Paul György and O. L. Kline, eds. Basel, Switzerland, and New York: Karger, 1970, p. 144.

21. Letter to author from Asok Mitra, Nov. 3, 1970.

22. Wildavsky, Aaron. Does planning work? *Public Interest.* No. 24:95, Summer 1971.

Additional References

Amir, Shimeon. Multiplying micro-development. *Internat. Develop. Rev.* 12:9, 1970.

Braybrooke, David, and Charles E. Lindblom. *A Strategy of Decision.* Glencoe, N.Y.: The Free Press, 1963.

Bryant, John. *Health and the Developing World.* Ithaca: Cornell University Press, 1969.

Cantor, Sidney M., George E. Shaffer, and Alfred N. Meiss. *Comparison of Alternative Nutritional Strategies: A Study of the Possible Role of Fish Protein Concentrate in a Developing Country.* Report prepared for the 17th meeting of the United Nations Protein Advisory Group, New York, 1970.

Elements of a Food and Nutrition Policy in Latin America. Scientific Publication No. 194. Washington, D.C.: Pan American Health Organization (PAHO), 1970.

Fein, Rashi. Health programs and economic development. In *Economics of Health and Medical Care,* Reprint 83. Washington, D.C.: Brookings Institution, October 1964.

FY 1971 Country Field Submission, Annex O—Nutrition. U.S. Agency for International Development, New Delhi, 1969.

Feldstein, Martin S. Health sector planning in developing countries. *Economica* 37:139, 1970.

Francois, Patrick J. Nutrition—a new operational technique in national planning. *Food Nutr. Africa,* No. 7:65, 1969.

Gish, Oscar. Health planning in developing countries. *J. Develop. Studies* 6:67, 1970.

Joy, J. L. Economic aspects of food and nutrition planning. Paper presented at the First Asian Congress of Nutrition, Hyderabad, India, Feb. 2, 1971.

Klein, David. The planning process of a budget agency: form and content. *Finance and Devel.* 8:20, 1971.

Levinson, F. James. Nutrition intervention in low-income countries: Its economic role and alternative strategies. M.A. thesis, Cornell University, Ithaca, New York, January 1971. Portions of this thesis appear in Levinson, F. James, and D. L. Call, Nutrition intervention in low-income countries: its economic role and alternative strategies. Paper prepared for the United Nations Protein Advisory Group, Document 1. 13/1, 1970.

Meiss, A. N., and S. M. Cantor. Marketing considerations for improved protein foods. *J. Amer. Oil Chem. Soc.* 48:473, 1971. Presented at Symposium on Oilseed Processors Challenged by World Protein Needs, Chicago, September 1970.

Schick, Allen, et al. Planning-programming-budgeting system: a symposium. *Pub. Admin. Rev.* 26:243-310, 1966.

Simm, S. R., F. Cesario, I. L. Kline, and D. M. Yates. *A Systems Approach to the World Protein Problem.* Report prepared by the Battelle Memorial Institute for the United Nations Protein Advisory Group, May 6, 1970.

Schultze, Charles L. *The Politics and Economics of Public Spending.* Washington, D.C.: Brookings Institution, 1968.

Venkatappiah, B. Remarks at Symposium I, Agricultural Development in Relation to National Nutrition Needs, First Asian Congress of Nutrition, Hyderabad, India, Jan. 29, 1971.

Zchock, D. K. Health planning in Latin America: review and evaluation. *Lat. Amer. Res. Rev.* 5:35, 1970.

27 Importance of the Nutrition Component in Economic Planning

Fanny Ginor
Economic Adviser
Bank of Israel, Jerusalem
Senior Lecturer, Tel-Aviv University

Berg and Muscat are to be complimented on their new approach to the nutrition problem, establishing the need for making nutrition an integrated objective in national planning and outlining a conceptual planning framework for this purpose.

This macro-approach may well become a major breakthrough for the solution of the nutritional problems of the developing world, if and when it becomes accepted by those who make the decisions and direct the actions. Let us therefore take a close look at the assumption of the paper, namely, that the decision-maker recognizes the importance of nutrition for national development and is ready for the proposed macro-approach to nutrition and the reordering of priorities that this implies.

This assumption seems to be optimistic at present. The notion that malnutrition is detrimental to the development effort and that the improvement of nutritional deficiencies in itself increases economic growth rates [1] has been gaining ground, but there is still no tendency to make the total change in attitude required for the reallocation of resources, which will allow the quick attainment of solutions to nutritional problems. More efforts will be necessary to convince political leaders and decision-makers of the necessity and effectiveness of an overall approach to nutrition. Apparently quantification is needed to bring about the required change in attitude. The ground has been prepared by developments in economic thought in connection with the human resources concept and the analysis of factors contributing to the increase in productivity. The work done on the economic contribution of education can also indicate the possible ways open to the planner and the nutritionist.

It has long been known that investment in education pays dividends; that, roughly gauged, the more time, effort, and money dedicated to education of an individual, the higher will be his lifetime income. But only recently have calculations been made quantifying the returns on investment in education, and showing the important connection between the rise in productivity and education. [2-5] Comparisons between developed and developing countries, too, revealed that differences in the quality of the labor force were to a large extent responsible for the differences in per capita income.[1] [6,7] Thus "in-

[1] A. O. Krueger attributed 50 to 70 percent of the difference in per capita income between 16 developing countries studied and the United States to differences in the quality of manpower.

vestment in education" has become a legitimate part of any development plan, and resources previously reserved for investment in physical capital assets are now also allocated to educational purposes.

On the basis of what is today known about the impact of malnutrition on the quality of the labor force and the effectiveness of the educational effort, [1,8,9] it should be suspected that some part of the increase in productivity attributed to better education or other factors has to be attributed to nutrition improvement. The question is whether this can be proved and quantified. Can the harm done by malnutrition to learning capacity, alertness, energy, and initiative of the labor force and its longevity be measured in terms of the resulting impact on productivity? And can the outlay on the improvement of nutritional status be termed "investment?" For planners, economists, and policy-makers the term "investment" has its own attractiveness—promising future returns and indicating the impact on the economic growth process.

Regarding good nutrition as the necessary health basis for all occupational activities, the outlay on nutrition could be termed "gross investment" to be divided between "maintenance" of the previous status of nutrition of the adult labor force (comparable to depreciation allowance of tangible assets) and "net investment" in (a) the nutrition of children and youths who will be part of the future labor force and (b) the improvement of the nutritional standard of the adult labor force.

However, there are difficulties. When speaking about maintenance and net investment, can we limit ourselves to the present and future economically active population? What about wives and mothers who work only at home? Their economic importance is beyond all doubt, as homemakers, preparers of food, and mothers who give birth to and rear the future labor force, though their work is not part of the national product in the conventional sense. What about chronically sick and retired people? What about nutrition of children and youth (mainly girls) who will enter the future labor force for only a short period if at all? Hence, the usefulness of terming nutrition of the present and future labor force gross investment, and terming all other nutrition consumption seems questionable, especially as such a division of the family unit and of society into productive and unproductive members with reference to provision of the necessities of life may also be viewed as incompatible with ethical and humanitarian principles.

Furthermore, what about that part of nutritional outlay not necessary for health purposes? Since food is not a medicine, and unless it provides some enjoyment it may not be taken in sufficient amounts, the outlay for taste, esthetic, and other satisfactions may be quite necessary. The enjoyment of food may well be an important factor in the psychological well-being of the labor force. In this case very little of the outlay would represent pure consumption: luxuries in nutrition and, of course, overeating which is detrimental to health and reduces efficiency at work.

Basic difficulties are encountered in the attempt to define certain expenditures which may be termed "investment in the human factor" as investment proper. This difficulty stems from the dual role of the human being in the economy: the goal of all economic activity as the final consumer, and at the same time one of the factors of production.

The inclusion of "investment in the human factor" in the conventional term "investment" in national accounting would require the inclusion of the major part of private and public consumption under this term. Clean and sufficiently large living quarters and sufficient clothing are important for mental and physical health, for successful schooling, and for an energetic labor force. We cannot even be sure whether outlay on luxuries and pure enjoyment is not part of the basis of the high technological standard of the labor force in modern societies. Without the enjoyment derived from consumption and without the desire to acquire it, the labor force, which includes the organizers, the inventors, and the managers, might not function as it does.

As is well known, current expenditure on education is not included in "investment" as used in national accounting, which applies only to outlay on "tangible assets." But discussion of the investment concept in education [10,11] does not prevent the recognition of the strategic importance of education in the development process and of its inclusion under high priority items for resource allocation. In the same way, nutritional outlay does not have to be included in the conventional term "investment" to prove its investment function.

There is, however, an important difference between education and nutrition. While cost/benefit analysis and investment/returns calculations in education may have their implications for private investment decisions and choice of occupations,[2] no such decisions are relevant in the field of nutrition. Only ignorance and lack of means will prevent people from providing themselves and their families with adequate nutrition. Hence, nutrition has usually not been regarded as a matter of public concern apart from situations of famine and extreme food scarcity.

[2] Though private investment in schooling is undoubtedly influenced by expectations of higher life earnings, this is only part of the motivation. [5]

Slowly it is being recognized that public intervention is no less important in
the field of nutrition than in education, since malnutrition caused by ignorance and lack of means seriously retards productivity growth. Social cost/
benefit analysis will not only put nutrition higher on the list of priorities, but
may even open up new sources—such as internal loans to the government
from the public, from pension funds and insurance companies, as well as
from foreign development loans.

In addition to such social cost/benefit calculations it has to be recalled that
the ultimate purpose of the economy is the well-being of the population, and
that the aim of social and economic development is to improve their well-
being. Adequate nutrition being the first and foremost basis of well-being, the
correction of nutritional deficiencies deserves top priority in any development plan, since its goal will be the maximum welfare attainable with the
means available, while providing for future growth. The marginal utility of an
additional dollar spent on the improvement of nutritional deficiencies would
rank higher than most other outlays, while at the same time increasing the
productive capacity of the economy.

Since political considerations are uppermost in the mind of the decision-
maker, a project needs, in addition to "visibility" (as suggested in the paper),
quick success. The impact of good nutrition on children under 5 years today
will bring economic fruits only in ten to twenty years' time when they enter
the labor force. Quicker results on the economic front may be attained by the
improvement of the diet of the present labor force, increasing their alertness,
energy, initiative, and job-learning capacity. Though cost and benefit calculations may show higher returns for the nutritional investment in 5-year-olds
than in the present labor force under a long-range perspective, considerations
(which may be political) requiring quick economic results might lead to preference for the short-term project. In such cases, the addition of humanitarian
considerations may help to give priority to the nutritional needs of children,
and the combination of economic and humanitarian considerations will put
good nutrition for all among the top priorities of national planning. Therefore, it seems to us that a two-pronged approach is necessary—economic and
humanitarian.

The authors emphasize the definition of specific targets at the time of defining national objectives. If the planner is ambitious, as proposed, and the
"macro-approach" is used, should not the broad national objective be total
eradication of malnutrition? Within a certain time period the gradual achievement of this goal can be mapped out in the form of specific targets, with time-

frames as suggested, in an order of priority. If good nutrition for all is the recognized overall target to be attained within a reasonable time period, this in itself requires programs and projects of a scope compatible with the end-target. One of the advantages of the macro-approach is that it can be used to show policy-makers that in most cases the nutrition problem can be solved within a reasonable time period, if it is included among broad national objectives, receives top priority, and efficient solutions are worked out in detail.

A numerical general example may illuminate this. Assumptions are: In a developing economy, one-third of the population are suffering from malnutrition, their nutrient intake on the average being only 75 percent of standard requirements. National product per capita is growing at an annual rate of 2½ percent. Food consumption expenditure of the total population amounts to 30 percent of the gross national product.[3] The food consumption expenditure of the one-third of the population suffering from malnutrition is some 5 percent of the GNP (though their share in disposable incomes is only some 8 percent, their share in total food expenditure is as high as 17 percent). Improvement of their diet to meet standard requirements would require 1.7 percent of GNP. In an economy with an annual per capita GNP growth of 2½ percent this can be accomplished in 3 years' time, when about one-fourth of the *additional* per capita GNP is allocated to the improvement of the diet of the needy, or in 5 years' time, when one-seventh of the additional per capita GNP is devoted to that purpose. Deliberate policies in the direction of income redistribution will be necessary to achieve this, of course, since the increase in the income of the target population stemming from economic growth, even if not smaller than the average, would not reach the desired level for nutrition improvement for some 20 years, while in the poorest sections malnutrition might still continue.

Seeing the magnitude of the problem in "macro" proportions can help the decision-maker to arrive at decisions of resource allocation. But it will also be necessary to devise specific measures that will be effective in bringing about the required nutrition improvement in the target population. Can the systems approach proposed by the speakers provide a framework for working out such detailed and effective measures? The systems approach should make possible the identification of the major factors responsible for malnutrition, the planning of the targets of improvement, and, as there will usually be various possible ways of intervention, the choice of the most effective interventions.

[3] Private consumption equals 70 percent of GNP; food consumption equals 43 percent of private consumption.

A system is defined as "a set of interacting elements," [14,15] and there is no doubt that the nutrition status of a population is part of the economic, social, cultural, political, and institutional makeup and interacts with all these factors. The systems approach requires simplification in order to build a mathematical image of the real system out of the significant factors only, excluding all irrelevant factors. But to single out the factors of a socioeconomic system significant for nutritional deficiencies and their improvement, a large quantity of variables has to be assembled. Since some of the variables are not quantifiable and others are not readily available, in most cases much research will be necessary to provide the variables needed, to quantify qualitative variables, and to trace their interdependencies.

There is danger of too much concentration on research and not enough on action. Research should go hand in hand with action, and incomplete knowledge should not prevent urgently needed action. Will this in practice be possible? Will there not be a demand (by those allocating means and those defending rival or conflicting claims) to await, before acting, final knowledge or at least final results of the research conducted?

But there is no doubt that one feature of the systems approach is vital for quick results, and this is the cooperation of experts from various disciplines—nutritionists, sociologists, economists, and planners. Local experts, though sometimes insufficiently informed about the extent of nutritional deficiencies and their impact on the productivity of the labor force, usually have a good knowledge of the social and economic forces, and can with cooperation relatively quickly identify the main reasons for malnutrition.

It is also very important to ask how much specific country planning can rely on research results of a more general nature. We know that, with all the differences in the developing countries, there are similarities among countries in the same region and countries in the same stage of development. Nutritional problems and their solutions will also be similar for certain groups of countries, and one country can learn from the experiences of others.

References

1. Berg, Alan, and Robert Muscat. Nutrition and development: The view of the planner. Paper submitted to United Nations Panel to Formulate a Strategy Statement on the Protein Problem Confronting the Developing Countries, New York, May 3-7, 1971. *Amer. J. Clin. Nutr.* 25:186, 1972.

2. Schultz, T. W. Investment in human capital. *Amer. Econ. Rev.* 51:1, 1961.

3. Harbison, C. F., and C. A. Myers. *Education, Manpower, and Economic Growth: Strategies of Human Resource Development.* New York: McGraw-Hill, 1964.

4. Denison, Edward F. *Why Growth Rates Differ.* Washington, D.C.: Brookings Institution, 1967.

5. Blaug, M., ed. *Economics of Education.* Penguin Modern Economic Readings, vols. 1, 2, 1968.

6. Krueger, A. O. Factor endowments and per capita income differences among countries. *Econ. J.* 7:641, 1968.

7. Chenery, Hollis B. Growth and structural change. *Finance and Development* (IMF and IBRD) 8:16, 1971.

8. Bengoa, J. M. Priorities in public health nutrition problems. In *Proceedings of the Seventh International Congress of Nutrition,* Vol. 4, Hamburg, 1966.

9. Food and Agriculture Organization of the United Nations. *Freedom from Hunger Campaign: Nutrition and Working Efficiency.* Basic Study No. 5, 1962.

10. Shaffer, H. G. Investment in human capital: Comment. *Amer. Econ. Rev.* 51:1026, 1961.

11. Schultz, T. W. Investment in human capital: Reply. *Amer. Econ. Rev.* 51:1035-39, 1961.

12. Berg, Alan, and Robert Muscat. Nutrition program planning: An approach. This volume, p. 246.

13. World Bank Atlas. *Population, Per Capita Product and Growth Rates.* Washington, D.C.: IBRD, 1970.

14. White, H. and F. Tauber. *Systems Analysis.* Philadelphia: Saunders, 1969.

15. Adelman, Irma, and Cynthia Morris. A systems approach to the study of economic development: Methodological considerations. Paper prepared for the Eleventh World Conference of the Society for International Development, New Delhi, November 1969.

28 Focusing Attention on Nutrition in Development Planning

Robert R. Nathan
President Robert R. Nathan Associates
Washington, D.C.

The paper by Berg and Muscat is a highly useful conceptual and operational document for policy-oriented and responsible leaders and workers in many disciplines. Planners will find it a helpful manual for dealing with the complexities of planning in practically any branch of social science. Further, those concerned with nutrition will be enlightened and stimulated by the specific examples and down-to-earth applications of planning concepts and techniques to the subject of nutrition. It can serve effectively as a bonding agent between planners and nutritionists, with many other specialists benefiting from direct exposure to it as well as indirect fallout.

Particularly welcome is its avoidance of the all-or-nothing approach. Too many, though by no means all, of those concerned with population and family planning are inclined to cease all their efforts unless the rate of population growth is quickly and dramatically reduced throughout the world. Some even argue that development assistance should be stopped unless there is proof of effective population programs, contending that otherwise the aid is totally wasted and even counterproductive. Others have expressed themselves similarly with respect to environment. It would be just about as logical—or illogical—to contend that nutrition is the entire key to development and human progress. Its importance is put into proper perspective in this paper.

There is an urgent need for specialists as scientists, as technicians, as planners, and as programmers and promoters in each sector and in each function. But there is also a need for coordinating and interrelating different disciplines, sectors, and functions. This effort must come from within a specialty as well as from the coordinators or the generalists who are outside the specialty.

Nutrition is an excellent example of an important subject that somehow has not been brought into the main policy streams with those other issues that significantly affect the quality of life. The economists certainly have not given it much attention, nor have many other social or physical scientists. As Berg and Muscat state, too often it is assumed that rising general living standards will inevitably be associated with better nutrition. As with so many generalizations, there is some degree of truth in this conclusion. But as with problems like poverty and health and population growth and pollution, general development alone does not yield solutions. As more resources become available these particular problems may become more manageable but, regrettably, they will not be solved automatically.

Because there is need for efforts on many fronts, the multidisciplinary composition of this conference is gratifying. We all need to learn from one another and to become aware that only coordinated plans and programs can lead to perceptible progress. Notable improvement cannot be expected in nutrition without more and better agricultural output. But expansion in agriculture is no guarantor of better nutrition or even less malnutrition; it depends on what food is produced and how it is distributed and used. This immediately involves not just agricultural production and marketing policies but also research, credit instruments and institutions, price support programs, subsidies for inputs into agriculture, transportation availabilities, education in producing and using foods, and other factors that are tied to a wide range of policies and functions.

Then there are questions of income distribution which affect nutrition. We must concern ourselves with levels and incidence of taxation, with wage policies, with income maintenance programs, with welfare measures and the many other public and private avenues of influencing the distribution of resources. Prejudices and biases and geographic differentials have important impacts on income distribution and on nutrition. Even housing policies and urban-rural relations affect income patterns and have nutritional consequences.

The purpose of repeating these truisms is to say bluntly to nutritionists that theirs is not an independent concern and that solutions to problems in their area cannot be dealt with or solved independently and in isolation. Their contribution must be an input into development planning as well as a beneficiary from good overall planning and wise policies. If they function in an isolated environment, insulated from economic and political concerns, it is less likely that they will succeed in lessening malnutrition and enhancing nutritional standards.

How are nutritionists going to get the issue before the scientists and legislators and policy-makers who can allocate to malnutrition programs the priority they need and deserve? There is no simple answer. It is a matter of developing leadership which can mobilize interest and support. It is a problem of educating those who mold opinion and make policy. It is a task of assembling facts and telling the story both factually and dramatically. It will be necessary to confront political leaders and the public with evidence that we waste billions of dollars of resources on low-priority and even harmful goods and services but fail to spend tens of millions or hundreds of millions to improve nutrition and thereby enhance our health and productivity and quality of life.

An active, positive effort must replace the timid and limited programs that have often characterized the field of nutrition. If nutritionists will take the initiative I am convinced that they will find hosts of allies and supporters in many disciplines.

29 Top Priority Programs in
National Development Plans

Roberto Rueda-Williamson
Regional Nutrition Adviser
Pan American Health Organization
Washington, D.C.

During this conference we have listened to a series of very interesting presentations and discussions. All of them have emphasized the problem of malnutrition, its magnitude, its adverse impact on national development, the characteristics of its conditioning factors, and its detrimental effects on children and adults. We are now aware that malnutrition is the major contributing cause of high mortality and morbidity in the developing areas of the world, that malnourished children who survive pay a high toll in terms of physical and mental retardation, and the malnourished adult, in terms of diminished productivity. Several speakers have emphasized the need for a multisectoral approach to food and nutrition programs, since the factors conditioning the problem are not limited to one single sector of development but simultaneously involve several sectors (agriculture, industry, economics, health, and education). Therefore, if a country is to ensure its population the optimum nutritional status, it must formulate and implement a nationwide coordinated food and nutrition policy.

In their presentation, Berg and Muscat stressed the need for nutrition programs to be carefully planned within the context of national development plans. They discussed the nutrition planning sequences, as well as the importance of a systems analysis approach to the relations between the various subsystems involved and the interrelations of different sets of activities. With such an approach, it is possible to identify, compare, and predict the cost-effectiveness of alternative activities and to ascertain which would yield the highest returns at the lowest cost.

Their discussion of the most important constraints imposed by long- and short-term schemes was very interesting, as were their final comments on the type of factoral information the planner should place before the decision-maker: the options, alternative strategies, and potential consequences of the programs. The fact that, in making the final decision, the policymaker takes into consideration not only the technical aspects presented by the planner but also the political factors, including the attractiveness of the plan, was very much to the point.

At this point, I would like to make some comments on the priorities, costs, and benefits of nutrition programs within national development plans. In assigning an order of priority to health programs, health planners usually take four variables into account: the magnitude and impact of the problem to be solved, its vulnerability, its importance, and the cost of the program. We believe, however, that, in the case of malnutrition, which produces irreversible, adverse effects on the physical and mental development of millions of young children all over the developing world, the fight against malnutrition should be regarded not as a means of development but rather as one of its primary ends.

All newborn children are entitled to the full attainment of their genetic potentialities of physical growth and mental development, but the sad fact is that most of them cannot and do not exercise this human right because of environmental deficits during the first 5 years of life. Today nobody questions the right of freedom of speech. Yet, because the intellectual capacity of the malnourished children who survive is diminished, their freedom of thought, which is a precondition for the freedom of speech, is abridged.

We must recognize, however, that unfortunately this rationale will not by itself convince policymakers in the developing countries to assign high priority to nutrition protection for young children and to allocate the necessary budgetary funds to insure its immediate application. In establishing priorities in a national plan of development, policymakers will be more interested in programs usually considered to yield better rates of return and higher profits in monetary terms. Nevertheless, we should still try to measure the present primary cost of malnutrition and its consequences in the region, in order to convince planners to assign nutrition programs the high priority they deserve.

By applying to Latin America the corresponding death and birth rates of the United States, the Pan American Health Organization estimated that 768,000 more children under 5 years of age died in Latin American countries in 1968 than would have died had their mortality rates been similar to that of the United States. [1] This excess mortality amounts to about 2,000 preventable deaths every day, the result of the synergistic action of malnutrition and infection. In a recent study, [2] Cook estimated the immediate cost of the wastage of a child's life due to malnutrition (cost of childbirth, cost of rearing a young child, and even the cost of the funeral). In Jamaica, in 1968, this cost was estimated at U.S. $110 for a child dying in infancy, and U.S. $190 for a child dying at the age of 1 to 5 years. On this basis, the cost of the excess mortality of preventable deaths of children under 5 would total $110 million per year in Latin America and the Caribbean area.

The very heavy economic burden on the national health services due to the prevailing excess morbidity in the malnourished population should also be roughly estimated. The annual cost of pediatric beds in hospitals in Latin America and the Caribbean area, taking as a basis the conservative assumption that 50 percent of them are occupied by children suffering from the combined effects of malnutrition and infection, amounts to $170 million per year. This is how much could be saved on hospital pediatric treatment in the region if the child population at risk was protected through supplementary feeding programs, immunizations, and environmental sanitation projects. The estimated cost of such programs is less than half the present economic burden represented by late, costly, and less effective types of treatment, not to mention the concomitant suffering, pain, and social dissatisfaction.

We can even try to estimate the cost of the present wastage of educational efforts in the region. Most countries assign a high priority to education and devote from 5 to 25 percent of their national budget to it. Nevertheless, their efforts to expand and upgrade their school systems are being in part defeated, because the children who survive severe mulnutrition reach school age with diminished intellectual and learning ability. They are unable to take full advantage of the educational programs because we failed to protect their intellectual potentialities at the right time. Although it is very difficult to estimate the actual cost of this educational wastage, there is no doubt that it adds several million dollars to the accumulated cost of the other types of wastage mentioned above.

We are therefore depleting our economic resources. We have the money, but it is not allocated to the right type of activities, such as nationwide comprehensive maternal and child health programs, providing full and opportune protection for the most vulnerable groups.

A study by Selowsky [3] showed how a milk distribution program for 100,000 children during the first two years of life would have an accumulated cost of between $2.5 and $5 million, a present value of benefits of between $25 and $40 million (the increased earnings of the adults generated by the supplementary feeding program during the first two years of life), and a *net* present value of benefits ranging from $20 to $37.5 million. The estimated rates of return range from 19 to 25 percent. Based on assumptions derived from our present knowledge of the effects of malnutrition on the mental development of a child and "the empiric evidence" of diminished productivity in adult life, Selowsky advances the hypothesis that, for the less developed countries, the probable short-term bottleneck in the process of human capital formation is a deficit in preschool types of investment in human capital, infant nutrition being one of the sources of preschool human capital formation. He also argues that early deficits in human capital formation can rarely be made up by later types of investment in human capital.

To sum up, I am absolutely convinced that, in establishing a national development plan, a country should assign top priority to nutrition programs designed to give dietary and nutrition protection to the most vulnerable groups of the population, namely, pregnant women and children under 5 years of age, through comprehensive maternal and child health services. Investments in human capital formation will yield very high rates of return by speeding up social and economic development in developing areas of the world.

There is an increasing awareness by governments of the need to give nutrition programs high priority in national development plans. Some countries in Latin America, such as Cuba and Chile, have already significantly expanded comprehensive maternal and child health programs and have established a policy of free distribution of milk to all pregnant women and nursing mothers and to all children under seven years of age. Other countries, such as Colombia and Venezuela, although they have not as yet formulated a universal policy in this field, are progressively expanding their supplementary feeding programs for mothers and children and obtaining a significant coverage of the groups at risk.

Furthermore, at a number of international meetings, the ministers of health and of agriculture of the region of the Americas have officially recognized the need for national food and nutrition policies and have recommended that special action be taken on this matter. In accordance with those recommendations, PAHO/WHO, FAO, UNICEF, UNESCO, and ECLA are currently conducting a regional project to promote the formulation and implementation of food and nutrition policies by the countries. A permanent secretariat headed by a general coordinator has been established in Santiago, Chile. It will organize and conduct four subregional conferences, the first of which will be held in Lima in 1972 for the Andean countries (Bolivia, Chile, Colombia, Ecuador, Peru, and Venezuela). The participants will be high-ranking officials of the national planning agencies and of the ministries of health, education, agriculture, industry, development, and economic affairs. The proceedings of this conference could serve with great advantage as one of the basic documents for the Regional Project on National Food and Nutrition Policies in the Americas, as well as for similar projects in other regions of the world.

References

1. Pan American Health Organization. *Health Conditions in the Americas, 1965-1968.* Sci. Pub. No. 207, 1970.

2. R. Cook. The primary cost of malnutrition and its impact on a society. Paper presented at the Third Western Hemisphere Nutrition Congress, Miami, Fla., August 30-September 2, 1971.

3. M. Selowsky. An attempt to estimate rates of return to investment in infant nutrition programs. Paper presented at the Conference on Nutrition, National Development, and Planning, Cambridge, Mass., October 1971.

30   Some Conceptual and   In Sang Song
Administrative Difficulties   President, Korean Development
in Nutrition Planning   Association, Seoul

Population in Chinese is spelled with the two characters denoting "human" and "mouth." Literally, population is "human mouths" to feed. For an ancient ruler whose responsibility it was to rule his subjects, the most crucial task was to feed his people. If this reflected an Oriental philosophy that emphasized the importance of food, set against it is a common Korean proverb which affirms that in a living mouth a spider cannot spin a cobweb. The proverb is often used to encourage a person who has become jobless. How do we reconcile these rather opposing views on the importance of food? To me they are a reflection of the basically important and yet most intricate nature of food in a human society.

People must eat, and indeed they do eat, but the range of food consumed is so wide—from grass roots to peacock tongues—that it makes all the difference between eating for mere survival and eating like a gourmet. This brings us to what Mr. Berg calls "buying up." And it is on this issue that one encounters an initial problem in nutrition planning, because the practice of buying up implies, at the same time, the capability of "buying down." If income decreases, one may buy down from rice to barley, from barley to millet, and so on. Where do we set the minimum floor below which one cannot survive? In terms of calories or of specific nutrients it may be easy to answer, but in terms of foodstuffs the problem is not at all simple. So one has to fall back to the more common practice of employing a national income concept, saying that per capita income below so many dollars constitutes starvation level. But we all know that GNP calculation is particularly weak when it comes to measuring the self-supply of food to the rural population. In other words, it is conceptually clear as to what constitutes the starvation level, but it is not so easy to define who belongs to the starvation class.

Pioneers in the field of nutrition planning have made it clear that malnutrition is a direct impediment to economic development, and therefore nutrition constitutes an important branch of investment. This, in turn, implies that nutrition planning and economic planning could, and in fact should, go together, employing basically the same investment criteria. But one cannot lump together all investment for the improvement of nutrition. Improved nutrition for children will yield results in a decade or so, but a subsidized food program for the aged does not promise any future yield—food bills for the aged cannot be anything but consumption. Nutrition planning that is indifferent to ages, therefore, cannot counter the proponents of the "growth only" policy, because at least a part of it will have a negative effect on saving. So nutrition planning ought to start with the sphere where the spending is apparently an investment, that is, the child feeding programs.

Child feeding may have another desirable side effect, namely to change habitual preferences for specific food items. Traditional preference for a particular type of food, such as a predominant preference for rice in the Orient, poses a serious problem in designing an efficient and economical nutrition improvement plan.

The next question relates to the proposition that the better fed persons are invariably better suited to contribute to economic growth through their labor. I am afraid such a position has many weaknesses, particularly when the argument is used to imply that the better fed children are physically taller and heavier than the less fortunate ones, and that the physical superiority measurable in terms of weight and height is prima facie evidence for their economic superiority. This statement may hold true for a single race with the same physical characteristics, but I wonder to what extent it can be applied to interracial comparisons on a global basis. Even the proposition that the better fed are more physically fit is not particularly revealing. In fact it is a tautology, because better fed—and not necessarily expensively fed—implies by definition a diet adequate to maintain physical fitness. Moreover, just as there is a level of nutrition below which one cannot properly perform normal economic activities, there would seem to be an upper limit above which an additional nutrition input would not have a significant effect on an individual's output. If there are acknowledged difficulties in setting an operational minimum nutrition level, defining the upper limit is equally evasive when one actually attempts to measure it.

As much as I would like to subscribe to the idea that proper nutrition is an absolute must in economic development, I can see why this proposition is not going to be particularly popular among the less developed countries striving to attain economic self-sufficiency. It is one thing for an economist to claim that poor countries are poor because they started poor, but it is quite another to say that the poverty of the nation is related to undernourishment of the people in it. For, in development planning, an inflow of foreign capital and belt-tightening measures for national saving are accepted as effective measures for breaking the vicious circle within a tolerable time span. But if malnutrition is taken as a basic reason for underdevelopment, the period required to alleviate it is simply too long to be politically acceptable, and the resources too enormous to be within the reach of poor countries. Moreover, the belt-tightening measures, which may even involve a degree of restraint in food consumption, will usually run directly counter to the nutrition planning arguments.

There is one more point of an administrative nature that should not be taken lightly in adopting nutrition planning in a country with a free market system. The administrative difficulty in rationing is well known. Hence any practical and long-run nutrition program in a free society has to rely on a price mechanism, that is, to make foodstuffs available at an artificially reduced price level, lower than the real demand and supply for foodgrains warrant. A low price for foodgrains, however, may attract users of foodgrains for other purposes than daily meals—makers of rice wine, for example—and the entire purpose of adopting a cheap grain policy will be defeated.

I have raised, in random fashion, some of the points that occurred to me in connection with nutrition planning in order to call attention to the many conceptual and administrative pitfalls that need to be much more closely scrutinized and carefully considered before advocating implementation of a nutrition improvement program.

31 National Nutrition Survey in Japan

Sadao Orita
Chief, Nutrition Section
Ministry of Health and Welfare, Tokyo

Because of the development of various kinds of public health services, backed by remarkable economic growth, the national health status of Japan has much been improved and the people's interest in their own health has proportionately increased. The change in dietary habits accompanying the considerable rise in the average national nutrition status has given rise to new problems in the present phase of national nutritional improvement. Especially noteworthy is the sharply rising incidence of those chronic diseases closely associated with dietary habits, such as cardiovascular diseases, diabetes, and other disturbances of the nourishment metabolism. There is increasing need to recognize these facts accurately and to promote positive interventions for nutritional improvement aiming at a higher national health level.

The influence of nutrition improvement is far-reaching. It leads to the betterment of physique and physical strength, prevention of diseases, promotion of health, better working efficiency, and even to the nation's higher economic growth. In fact, it is a basic requirement if people are to live healthy and enjoyable lives. In this sense, the role to be played by the administrators of nutrition improvement is immense. What is important is to determine how to carry out efficient activities with limited resources. To begin with, it is necessary to collect as much information as possible on the national health status, food consumption, and socioeconomic factors affecting the people's dietary habits, then to anlayze it, and finally to initiate effective nutrition program planning.

We have been engaged in a national nutrition survey for more than twenty years, since 1946, collecting relevant data to aid in the administration of nutritional improvement. The following describes the actual circumstances of the survey and indicates those points requiring improvement in the future.

History of National Nutrition Survey

Historically the national nutrition survey may be divided into two stages. The first stage began at the close of World War Two, when Japan was extremely short of food and the majority of its people were undernourished, some to the point of starvation. To collect the basic data necessary for instituting emergency measures, the first nutrition survey was conducted in Tokyo in December 1945, in which the caloric intake and the physical condition of the inhabitants were surveyed. From the following year onward, the scope of the survey was enlarged every year and by 1948 covered all Japan. The data collected in these surveys pointed out the importance of establishing policies to ensure food supply and bring about nutritional improvement, which gave birth to various interventions such as importation of food, the start of school feeding with food supplied by foreign aid, the determination of nutritional requirements and the food composition standard, and a number of nutritional improvement activities. A Nutrition Section was eatablished in the Ministry of Health and Welfare to control the national nutritional improvement, and at least one nutritionist was stationed at each health center in Japan (one center for every 100,000 people) to guide local inhabitants toward nutritional improvement. In this way, the national nutritional survey paved the way for systematic nutritional improvement and further served as an impetus to the enactment of the globally unprecedented Nutrition Improvement Law.

The second stage began in 1952, when the Nutrition Improvement Law was enacted to legally support the national nutrition survey. This law stipulates that the government shall conduct a national nutrition survey in order to clarify the national health status, the caloric intake, and the relation between the caloric intake and the economic burden as basic data for establishing interventions for nutrition improvement.

In the late 1950s the Japanese economy showed rapid progress and technical innovations in the food industry helped to diffuse various kinds of processed food, leading to changes in Japanese dietary habits. A diet which until then had centered on cereals gradually incorporated other items into a complex food pattern. Information gathered through the national nutrition survey, and the nutrition interventions based on such information, contributed much to this change.

While the average national nutrition level was thus much elevated, various new problems emerged—such as the differing nutrition levels among regions and income classes, and irrational dietary behavior such as overeating or going without a meal. The survey method was partially modified in 1964 so as to collect new and necessary data as a preliminary step to cope with these new problems in nutrition improvement. With the ever progressing urbanization, lack of exercise, and increasing stress in daily life in recent years, the necessity arose of pursuing the interrelation between caloric intake and health on an individual basis, and study is now under way aiming at remodification of the survey method from 1972 onward.

Outline of the National Nutrition Survey

1. Subjects of Survey

In conducting the national nutrition survey, the census districts are taken as sampling units, and the survey is conducted with all the households (16,500) and their household members (68,000) of a specific number of districts (346) randomly selected. (The figures given above are those for 1966.)

2. Items of Survey

a. Caloric intake survey: Number of meals not taken, number eaten out, and the quantity of food taken during a given 5 consecutive days of mid-May.

b. Economic survey: Retail price of food in and around the survey districts.

c. Physical conditions survey: Physique (height, weight, chest circumference, and sitting height), blood pressure, and other routine medical examination.

3. Method of Survey

a. Caloric intake survey: The enumerator (who is a nutritionist) visits the households to be surveyed at least once a day during the period of the survey to check and guide the filling of the questionnaire.

b. Physical conditions survey: All the subjects of each district are made to gather in a conveniently located place for medical examination by doctors and physique and physical strength examination by public health nurses.

4. Period of Survey

Once a year, for a period of 5 consecutive days in mid-May.

Characteristics of the National Nutrition Survey

Few other countries are conducting nutrition surveys on a nationwide scale; the features of Japan's national nutrition survey may be summed up in the following two points.

1. The survey does not merely aim at outlining food consumption statistics but at grasping, from a medical standpoint, how foods are being taken, caloric intake, physical symptoms resulting from over-intake or insufficient intake, the influence of food habits on physique and physical strength, and, further, the relation between food habits and the household economy.

It is noteworthy that, in the disturbed period immediately after the end of World War Two, a survey was made not only of food intake but of body height and weight and the development of beriberi, anemia, and a number of other nutritional diseases. In the second and subsequent surveys, the survey items regarding health and physique increased in number. Valuable data gathered through these repeated surveys are serving as indicators for promoting interventions designed to improve the national health status and to better the younger generation's physique.

2. The actual circumstances of food consumption are surveyed not by an indefinite method—such as an estimate based on the suppliable quantity, or the household income and expenditure, as in the case of a food balance sheet— but by a factual scaling of food at each household surveyed prior to its being taken.

In any country, such a scaling-based survey may theoretically be conducted with a very limited number of subjects, but such a survey being conducted by the government and involving as many as 70,000 people is unique. One major reason why such a complex survey is feasible in Japan is that there are enough human resources to make it possible. In Japan, nutritionists engaged in the nutritional improvement of regional inhabitants existed even in prewar days, and they are now stationed at 832 health centers throughout the country. (Japan has about 160,000 registered nutritionists, of whom about 50,000 are in activities directly related to nutrition.) Another reason is the high interest in nutritional improvement on the part of the general public.

Proposed Improvement of the National Nutrition Survey
1. The unit of the current survey is not individuals but households. The adoption of such a household unit system resulted from the fact that the Japanese intake of animal protein, calcium, and vitamins was generally insufficient from 1945 through the 1960s, and consequently the emphasis was placed on raising the average nutrition level. It has so far not been particularly necessary to collect information on the distribution of the intake of nutrients, qualitative information, and information on food consumption from individual persons. Hereafter, however, in order to grasp the true picture of the ever diversifying national food pattern and to promote nutritional improvement interventions suitable to this changing era, it will be necessary not only to conduct surveys on an individual basis but to add such new items as a physiological examination, a biochemical examination, and an exercise test so as to clarify the interrelation between the intake of nutrients and health.

2. Since the social environments related to food habits—such as urbanization, rise in national income, and nucleation of family structure—have been undergoing remarkable changes in recent years, future nutrition surveys will require

information on those socioeconomic factors affecting diet as well as information on food consumption and health conditions.

3. Directly or indirectly related to the government's nutrition administration, in addition to the national nutrition survey, are such other surveys as "Study of Farmers' Nutritive Intake"; "Family Income and Expenditure," collecting data primarily on the urban household economy; and the "Food Balance Sheet," based on the FAO formula. The trouble is that these surveys are not well coordinated with each other, thereby hindering effective consolidation of the data for better and wider use. It is thus necessary to maintain good liaison among those organs in charge of the respective surveys.

Future Objective of the Nutrition Improvement Administration
It is acknowledged among the world's nutrition experts that the nutrition improvement administration in Japan played a major role in the nation's postwar rehabilitation and economic growth. And the national nutrition survey was the foundation of that administration. The future objective of Japan's nutrition improvement administration is to implement steadily those interventions satisfying the requirements stemming from socioeconomic changes of the times. This calls for further substantial development of the nutrition survey in order to identify new nutrition problems emerging with the changing times, and also for establishment of a nutrition information system making it possible not only to process necessary information speedily and properly but to obtain relevant information whenever it is needed.

The technique of systems analysis is considered a useful means for effective implementation of nutrition improvement. In Japan, too, interest is rising in the use of this technique and an analytical case study is under way at various ministries. Rather a long time, however, will be required to introduce this technique into the nutrition improvement administration because a number of basic problems require solution beforehand—such as arousing the understanding and interest of the administrators, training and securing expert personnel, and perfecting the technique itself.

It is hoped that the above description of the national nutrition survey in Japan is suggestive in one way or another for the nutrition administrators of those countries which are currently suffering from malnutrition problems in conditions similar to those that Japan experienced after the war.

References

Nutrition Section, Japanese Ministry of Health and Welfare, *Nutrition in Japan.* Tokyo, 1964.

Kaneko, Taro, comp. *Basic Knowledge of PPBS.* Japanese Ministry of Finance, 1969. (In Japanese.)

Resources Council, Japanese Science and Technology Agency. *Recommendation on the Modernization of the Marketing System of Foods with a View to a Systematic Improvement of the Nation's Food Life.* Tokyo, 1966.

Chairman: Dr. Martin J. Forman (USAID, Washington); Dr. Joy; Dr. Jan
Drewnowski (Institute of Social Studies, The Hague, The Netherlands); Dr.
deVries; Mr. Berg; Dr. Myron Brin (Hoffman-La Roche Inc.); Dr. Robert Cook
(Caribbean Food and Nutrition Institute); Dr. Latham; Dr. John Wyon
(Harvard University, Center for Population Studies); Mr. E. O. Obayan
(Central Planning Office, Nigeria); Dr. Sai; Dr. Vahlquist; Mr. Peter Greaves
(British Nutrition Foundation); Dr. Venkitaramanan

Joy   The question of the practicability or the feasibility of the use of a systems approach is a matter of very great concern to me at the moment. I am
involved currently in a planning operation in which we are trying to use essentially what would be called a systems approach; indeed it is completely consistent and compatible with what the paper has offered.
   When we try to translate our findings into working briefs for each of the
ministries or for the econometricians or the nutritionists involved in any
particular stage, it is quite a job. There is a very large pile of homework and
when we get the homework back we are going to have to return it for all sorts
of corrections. It doesn't worry me that we cannot complete anything like a
perfect job by our deadline, but what does worry me is that the evident inability to give equal consideration to all choices is going to allow people to
hold that the arguments we have so far mustered are not conclusive and therefore should not be listened to. We will still be very much at the mercy of
politicians because we won't have a sufficiently well-documented case. However, I present this as a practical consideration, not as any argument that the
approach is wrong. What I hope is that we can invest enough at this stage to
have something to build upon when we continue with the planning process.
   One has to translate the systems analytical approach into what is currently
being called communications support terms. In order to reconcile the various
inputs that are being fed into this decision process, a secretariat is required
which can prompt the process, set the homework, return it for corrections,
reprocess it, and coordinate it. That doesn't exist either, but clearly we are at
the beginning of an organic process and, with any luck, we shall have something very much better than could otherwise have been the case.
deVries   I think the econutritional profile is a very good term to use, but the
paper implicitly considers a country as a closed system. It isn't so. In addition
to a food balance sheet, as FAO introduced the concept, I would propose a
nutritional balance sheet to see what nutrients are imported and exported, for

the country as a whole and for regional areas within a country.

In the rural areas you find that consumption is determined largely by local production and that trade doesn't add or subtract very much from it. Therefore, to alter the nutritional status in rural areas we need not income redistribution but productivity redistribution; and in those areas where trade is not very important, it has to come from the people living in the area.

I made some of these nutritional balance sheets in Indonesia before the war and found them very rewarding on a regional scale. Recently in Zambia we had to use much smaller areas, encompassing a population of half a million or 200,000 people. We found very different econutritional profiles in different districts and provinces of Zambia.

Berg We share your concerns, and warn against the dangers of what in our paper we have called "nutrient autarchy."

Obayan I am a planner (who has learned something about nutrition in the last three days); I am confronted by a nutritionist in my office who comes to tell me that he has a program and he wants me to allocate resources to it. I must say that I have not been convinced yet how to go about it. The message hasn't reached me.

Also, the objective has not been made clear. We talk about malnutrition; immediately it appears to me we are talking about agricultural development, food production, health, educational development, human capital, all sorts of things put together in a package I can't understand. It is so difficult to point to a single program which does not have a connection with many other sectors. To improve nutrition in one area, you begin to think of how to reach the people; you must build roads, you must build schools, you must build hospitals, there must be a ministry of information to inform the people. So many projects are tied in with a particular nutrition item. How can I be convinced that I should allocate resources to that particular project; the cost-benefit analysis, the regression analysis—they haven't convinced me. The facts are still very meager.

This comprehensive systems analysis approach does appeal to me, but it has one weakness I have found difficult to overcome. Within any program there are several projects. We have to distinguish between programs and the projects that make up the program. The problem of the planner is to decide whether a particular project will qualify. He must find evidence to say I accept this, I reject that, I accept this, I reject that. I have not yet seen here that acid test that will enable me to say: I accept A, B, C projects in the nutrition program and this is what it will mean in terms of resourses which I have to allocate to it.

Sai I think that my last colleague has made exactly the point that we have been trying to make all along—tackling nutrition problems is not a simple issue which can be solved with a needle and micronutrients. People want to eat food, not simply absorb nutrients.

One difficulty in systems analysis application in our situation is how to integrate the psychosocial milieu and its contribution with the content and the method of delivery of our programs and projects. Nutrition should be not only an input of various foods into the system but also should influence and be influenced by other parts of the system. If you have a choice of building a road just for the sake of building a road or building a road to a food production area, by all means put in a road to the food production area so food can move.

Another thing that hasn't been clearly delineated is the influence within a nation's nutrition program of external aid food. Supplementary feeding usually refers to foods coming from outside the country. If this is the case, the systems analysis should show clearly what the contribution of this is going to be, both in positive terms in the nutrition cost and in possible negative terms in depressing local production of certain types of food.

Greaves Mr. Obayan remarked that, although he had heard a lot of talk these last three days about "nutrition," it seemed to him that what people were talking about were agricultural production programs, food production programs, health programs. He might have added community development programs, and so on. I submit that this is precisely the point, or at any rate a major part of it. All such programs have nutritional implications, but these have to be made explicit and the programs in consequence possibly modified. This should be a continuous process. Maybe this is the way to think about nutrition policy—not in terms of something special called a "nutrition program." Good nutrition, like happiness, is best pursued indirectly.

I am reminded of what a very senior official said to me last year in a country in the Middle East: "We are a very poor country. We can't afford luxuries like 'nutrition.' We have a more basic problem—just to produce enough food." But there are obvious nutritional implications in this. Man's primary nutritional need, in physiological terms, is for energy-calories. Thus, if energy supplies are limited for adults, either body weight will fall, or activity will be decreased, or both of these will happen. So I agree with the delegate from Ethiopia who suggested on the first day of this conference that emphasis might have to be placed in certain circumstances on cereal production. Governments should be prepared to spend money on defining, by surveys and

other means, the nature and extent of the nutritional situation in their countries. But I believe that nutritional components will be brought into government programs only if there is someone strategically placed with the government apparatus who has an interdisciplinary awareness of nutrition and is
qualified to identify nutritional implications and opportunities, and who is
indeed consulted by colleagues at the policymaking level.

Vahlquist This conference should create an awareness among planners and
economists of the seriousness of the nutritional situation among children in
the developing countries; but it is important that such an awareness and the
novelty of a new concept, the systems approach, does not, through its exact-
ing demands for figures, partially paralyze traditional nutrition intervention
programs.

I would offer a concrete proposal: since it may on occasion prove very hard
to produce cost benefit figures convincing enough to assure a reasonable share
of scarce budgetary means, would it not be reasonable to accept something
like the following rule of thumb. In countries with a prevalence of severe
malnutrition—say a prevalence of protein-calorie malnutrition in the zero-to-
five-year age group of 10 percent or more—there should automatically be
allocation of a minimum fixed percentage of the health ministry's budget. A
similar rule of thumb should also be applied by bilateral international agencies.

Drewnowski It has been said here that the main task of the conference is to
build a bridge between the nutritionists and the general economic planners.
My contention is that the greater part of that bridge has to be built by economists. Economists need to reappraise their methods, to improve them in
such a way that they will be useful for increasing the welfare of the people.

That reappraisal should take place in two stages. First, the planner should
understand that planning in terms of national accounting variables such as
GNP, income per capita, and rate of growth is not enough, because those
variables are different from the real conditions in which people live. Therefore, if we plan in terms of these variables, we stop planning halfway. What is
needed is improvement in the actual situation of the people, and for that,
national income is only a stage, albeit an important stage.

The first problem in proceeding from national accounting variables to the
welfare situation is distribution. The plan should include targets for changing
the distribution in a desirable way; of course, in traditional economic thinking the market mechanism takes care of that. But we should realize that the
planner must take care of it. In planning the use of resources he must be

aware of the consequent social changes as well as the political dimensions of his choices. Only if planning is approached in that way can it serve to improve nutrition and education and housing and all the other components of the level of living.

The second stage follows from the first. Planners formulate a plan (to use planning jargon) by maximizing something—by using specific criteria for making their decisions. What do they maximize? Usually they maximize national income or the rate of growth of national income. But if what I have just said is correct, they should maximize instead a set of variables referring to conditions in which people actually live. This makes it necessary to find quantitative expressions for various aspects of social conditions. But such a methodological advance is quite possible, given the planner's awareness of the need to alter the traditional approach to planning.

Although the economist's task is the larger one, nutritionists, who have to build from their side the smaller part of the bridge, should remember that improvement in nutrition cannot be tackled on a sectoral basis; it is a part of the whole national economy and the whole social change and should be coordinated into an overall economic and social plan. Only then may the cooperation develop in a fruitful way.

Venkitaramanan Any nationwide effort directed to the nutritional improvement of children and vulnerable segments of the population must be based on a better understanding of nutrition systems than is now available. To this end, a comprehensive, operationally oriented survey of nutritional systems operating within Tamil Nadu has been developed in cooperation with the government of Tamil Nadu and the Central Food Ministry.

Tamil Nadu has had a long-standing concern for nutrition and is known for its extensive and successful experience in child feeding. The nutrition project, which evolved through the joint efforts of AID and central and state governments, represents the desire on the part of the Tamil Nadu government to broaden its ongoing nutrition programs. Significant participation by state personnel plays an important role. Side by side with the "strengths" in Tamil Nadu, one may note that the state is a low-income area with substantial need for nutritional improvement. The diet of many small children appears to be quite inadequate. This is a crucial nutritional problem in India and it is hoped that experience gained from the project in Tamil Nadu will be applicable in other regions as well.

This is the first time a systems approach to the study of nutrition has been utilized in India, or in any other country. Upon completion, the concepts developed will be utilized, with modifications, throughout the nation in planning an All-India Children's Nutrition Program.

Objectives of the Project

1. To identify, describe, and analyze a nutrition system—those conditions and forces in Tamil Nadu which appear to be the principal determinants of the diets of preschool children in selected family income classes

2. To identify possible points or elements in the system which appear to be susceptible to modification in order to achieve significant changes in these diets and therefore in the survival rates of the children; and to describe the kinds of action programs needed for this purpose

3. To identify the possible points or elements in the system that can sensibly relate nutrition, via increased survival rates, to socioeconomic areas such as (a) family planning, (b) general economic development, and (c) quality of life

4. To limit the foregoing analysis to those parameters most relevant to proposed solutions to nutrition problems in Tamil Nadu

5. To propose, as they emerge during the course of the project, specific action programs related to solutions of nutrition problems in the state which could be undertaken by the state government, private Indian organizations, or bilateral assistance organizations

The Setting: Tamil Nadu

Tamil Nadu is situated at the southeast extremity of the Indian peninsula with an area of 129,901 square kilometers. The population of this state accounts for 7.51 percent of India's population. The decennial censuses of Tamil Nadu have shown that its population has increased from 33.7 million in 1961 to 41.1 million in 1971, an increase of 22 percent over the decade. The state ranks second in the literacy rate within the Indian Union. The percentage of literacy had risen to 39.4 percent in 1961. The percentage of urban population has also increased from 26.7 in 1961 to 30.3 in 1971. This population lives in 443 towns and 14,124 villages.

Concern and past efforts for nutritional improvement in Tamil Nadu are known to have existed for quite some time. It is widely recognized that Tamil Nadu is a relatively low-income area with urgent needs for nutrition improvement. Table 1 illustrates (within certain margins of error) the nutritive "gap" existing in the state. To discover ways and means of closing this gap is the main objective of this study.

Table 1. Availability of Calories and Selected Nutrients per Capita per Day in Tamil Nadu, 1968-1969

Nutrient	Recommended allowance	Foodgrains	Other foods	Total	Index (all India)
Calories (no.)	2400-3900	1386	266	1652	87.6
Proteins (gm)	55	34.0	6.0	40.0	73.0
Iron (mg)	20	7.8	0.9	8.7	67.4
Vitamin A (IU)	3000	180	518	698	78.6

Source: Monthly Commentary, *Health and Nutrition.* New Delhi: IIPO, 1969.

"In Madras City alone, out of the total 30,938 deaths, 44 percent of all deaths (13,647) occurred in children below 6 years. Most of these are due to malnutrition and preventable infection. All available nutritional survey statistics and the overwhelming clinical impression among preschool children show that they lack in their diet enough protein, calorie-giving foods like carbohydrates and fats, vitamins, especially A and B group, sometimes Vitamin D and E, and [there is] also [a] deficiency in iron-containing foods." [1]

The Approach: Systems Analysis
The effort to build an integrated system model for nutritional improvement is intended to answer a wide range of questions relating to aspects of agriculture, food processing and distribution, and business and consumer needs and preferences as they affect nutritional intake of the target groups. It is assumed that the analytical model will make it possible to test hypothetical interventions by computer programming, without initiating the actual intervention in the real world. The model will then identify the consequences of the proposed intervention for the entire nutrition system and will permit testing of combinations and variations as well. Actual test or demonstration projects can be limited to interventions that appear to offer the greatest benefits for a given investment. Demonstration projects to be carried out in the Tamil Nadu study will be chosen by this method.

The implementation of any nutrition-related policy amounts to an intervention at some point within the integrated system: accuracy in predicting the results of specific interventions is a measure of the model's utility. Accordingly, the study is designed to include examination of the effects of a substantial number of past interventions in order to (1) test efficiency of the model; (2) identify gaps or inconsistencies in data included; (3) define modifications and refinements in model and data that will improve predictive value.

The study team has been struck by the variety of nutrition-related private and public activities in which little attention has been paid to measurement and appraisal of performance results, other than numbers reached. It is likely that some action projects to be recommended, or to be implemented by the study team in cooperation with state and private agencies, will be modifications of ongoing fortuitous interventions, suggested by earlier study of results of these interventions. The study design allows for this possibility. It also provides for flexible allocation of resources for identification and study of these fortuitous interventions, during the study period, which will be most useful for testing and refining the integrated system.

The development of the integrated system is logically prior to some of the action-oriented demonstration projects that will also be part of the study. The likely payoff from varying price policies, for example, can be estimated from the relationships that merge in development of the total system and this will affect the nature and design of possible price-related projects. There are, however, other areas in which available information is less adequate for establishing relationships to be incorporated in the total system. The entire subject of the impact of nutrition education is obscured by the absence of useful results data. In this and similarly clouded areas the need for demonstration projects is immediate, in order to complete and improve the integrated system as well as to test the costs and benefits of specific interventions.

The study approach necessarily involves the reservation of manpower and other resources for some action projects that cannot be specified until initial returns from the integrated system are available, while simultaneously providing for immediate implementation of other projects determined to be critical to yielding high potential payoffs. The model will begin with delineation of relatively unambiguous and generally understood relationships, adding more obscure and complete ones as analysis and further investigation suggest them.

Possible Outcome

The proposed study is designed to collect and build a comprehensive data bank around three major subsystems critically related to the availability and consumption of nutrients within the state of Tamil Nadu. The conceptual approach and the methodology adopted for the analysis of nutrition systems are believed to be capable of answering a large number of questions. The study is carefully designed to be able to respond to cost-effective and cost-benefit considerations of alternative nutritional improvement programs.

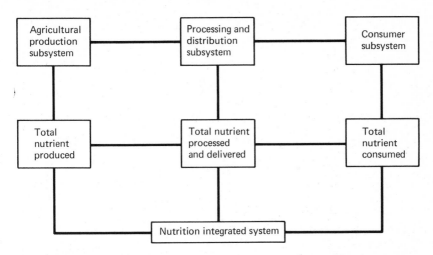

Figure 1. Diagram of Systems Approach. This diagram is an oversimplified presentation of our systems approach. Clearly, complex economic, social, cultural, and organizational interrelationships and consequences are implicit in this model. The analyst will continuously seek to discover the relationships existing between and within the subsystem.

Some of the questions to be answered by this study are:

(1) What are the nature and extent of major nutritional deficiencies in Tamil Nadu with special reference to preschool children and pregnant and lactating mothers? To what extent: (2) does increase in per capita income of family lead to an increase in the amount spent on food? (3) is increase in income of the family related to nutritional improvement, particularly of the child in the family? (4) is it possible to evolve an acceptable program of agricultural production and cropping most adequate to the nutritional needs of the population? (5) is it feasible to develop and recommend a price policy for agricultural commodities responding to the nutritional and consumer needs in the region? (6) is the range of policy alternatives for subsidies and incentives to farmers to adopt crops and practices advantageous for improved nutrient availability effective? (7) are nutritious foods commercially viable and what is their elasticity of demand? (8) is there a new emerging pattern of consumption for goods and services in rural areas due to improved agricultural incomes? (9) is it possible to modernize and introduce new food processing capabilities for improved quality and quantity of nutrient availability? (10) is it feasible to recommend new marketing and distribution practices for foods and food products involving significant improvement in nutrient delivery for

the population? (11) does good nutrition bear on reduced fertility and morbidity rates? (12) What combination of improved nutrition, health, and
hygiene programs provides the best cost-benefit advantages with respect to
"healthier and fewer babies?" (13) What economic benefits for the state,
and India as a whole, can be expected from an investment in nutrition
improvement?

Cook I want to comment very briefly on two points which arose from Dr.
Rueda-Williamson's paper.

First, I would like to explain how the wastage figures that he quoted were
derived. Following are the expenditures, per child, in Jamaica in 1968-1969:
the cost of child birth, $12; the cost of clothing and cot, $24; cost of funeral
and wake, $30; cost of 10 percent more food in pregnancy, $7; cost of breast
milk and food for a child aged 7 months, $37; cost of breast milk and food
for a child, average age 1 year 9 months, $115. Total for a child dying in
infancy, $110; average total for a child dying between ages 1 and 4, $190.

This refers to the wastage from deaths due to malnutrition or malnutrition
and infection. Where these figures fit in an economic balance sheet I do not
know, for I am no economist. But the expenditure on a child who dies in
infancy or before the age of 5 must be a dead loss somehow. The grand total
of the figures Dr. Rueda-Williamson quoted for Latin America was $300
million; this may in fact be a rather small sum in comparison with the gross
national product of all Latin America, but I would be happy to see the day
when Latin America spent even a quarter of that sum on the prevention of
malnutrition.

Dr. Rueda-Williamson put his money, so to speak, on a strengthened and
improved and extended program of maternal and child health, and I certainly
agree with him. What other program fulfills the two very important criteria
put forward in this meeting; that is, that a program be politically acceptable
and that it carry a fair guarantee of success?

Latham Dr. Rueda-Williamson works for PAHO and among the countries
that he visits is Cuba. He has said that serious problems of protein-calorie
malnutrition and of growth and development in children have greatly improved in Cuba. How has Cuba achieved this? Is it attributable to the spread
of medical services away from the cities to the rural areas? Has a better distribution of food, for example animal products, reduced the prevalence of
PCM among the poor, and coronary heart disease among the wealthy? I
would like to have heard some comments on this kind of thing.

It seems to me that examples of practices in some other countries deserve consideration here and haven't received it. Not too many people know that China, a rice-growing country, a rice-eating country, is exporting large quantities of rice because rice is more expensive on the world market than is wheat; China buys wheat at a cheaper price than rice and has somehow persuaded its people to eat wheat. How have they done this? Does this not hold some important lessons for other countries?

Wyon   Several people have asked me to say a little about some of the findings from the Khanna Study carried out in Ludhiana district in Punjab between 1953 and 1960. We visited every household every month over a period of 4 years and collected data on births, deaths, and migrations as well as information related incidentally to nutrition.

We were able to measure birth rates and birth intervals to show the influence of long lactation, which prolongs the birth intervals. We were able to show the differential death rate by sex—only about 800 females survived for every 1,000 males in the population.

We established the importance also of migration, not only rural to urban but also rural to rural; in other words, rural India is still not full. When we compared these parameters on a village-to-village basis we found villages extraordinarily comparable; but when we broke them down into different caste groups, we found that these distinct social groups had their own ways of practicing birth control, of allowing more females to die than males, of migrating and, of course, of earning their living. Within the individual villages these groups have their own particular ways of responding to population problems and of making use of the nutrients available to them. All of them, however, know too little about the importance of feeding children and how much food children need in the crucial period from 6 months to 2 years.

Brin   Dr. Muscat asked why one cannot design programs with eventual results that can be seen and measured—for instance, such as when malaria is eradicated. To me this implied that although great strides have been made to increase protein availability at the international level, it may be difficult to see the improvement at the level of the individual. We should now direct part of our attention to micronutrient deficiencies as these are evidenced by vitamin A deficiency blindness, various anemias including that of pregnancy, pellagra, riboflavin deficiency, and so on. These clinical diseases can all be prevented and some successfully treated by micronutrient supplementation. We therefore need to develop appropriate delivery systems for remedial micronutrient supplementation in order to reach remote villages as well as urban centers. Suitable effective delivery systems have been suggested, such as Nutricube®, but remain to be proven under all field conditions. A good family nutritional delivery system would also be capable of distributing protein foods, when available, and would combine suitable education with nutrient delivery. Such remedial programs should not displace efforts to improve protein nutrition, but rather run parallel to them. Furthermore, they should be considered as only *interim intervention* systems which can be discarded when other developmental programs become successful in raising nutritional status to levels compatible with normal productive health. My experience in clinical nutrition and in the laboratory suggests that even marginal micronutrient deficiency modifies man's behavior. Correcting these deficiencies, therefore, might make a population more receptive to socioeconomic developmental programs.

Berg Maybe too many of us have been looking for a magic wand to suddenly help us find the answer to nutrition problems; that's just not possible. Our paper is an attempt to say, first, that there are no valid answers unless we look at nutrition within the context of a given situation; and second, that we have to look far more broadly than in the past at all the interconnections to try to come up with answers. The case studies to be presented this afternoon are designed to set nutrition problems in the relevant context.

We are not saying that planning, per se, is the answer. All we are saying is that it is probably more effective to think systematically about a problem than to think about it piecemeal. Nutrition has had a history of ad hoc-ism, of snatching here and snatching there. If we can think in a logical, sequential way about this problem, it's possible that we just might come up with something resembling a solution of a different order of magnitude.

Forman The purpose of this conference was to open up a dialogue between people who traditionally have not been talking to one another, in the hope that a continuing dialogue and increased understanding will result in more effective programming. Therefore the apparent wish of several participants to continue the discussion augurs well and indicates that the conference has achieved its purpose.

Reference

1. Raju, V. B., et al. *Report of the Committee on Supplemental Feeding Programs for Preschool Children.* Madras, 1970.

Part VI   Case Studies

33 A Historical Perspective

Michael C. Latham
Professor of International Nutrition
Cornell University, Ithaca, New York

Although we may look with alarm on the current nutritional problems of the nonindustrialized countries, and we are appalled at infant mortality rates which are 100 or 300 per 1,000, we need to remember that there have been changes and there have been vast improvements.

Infant mortality rates in Ithaca, New York—a thriving university and film town fifty years ago, a backwater today—were 94 per 1,000 in 1921. That is a time when many at this conference were born, and that figure is similar to the infant mortality rate (IMR) in many Latin American cities today. In that same year, 1921, Lackawanna, another small New York town, had an infant mortality rate of 274 per 1,000, [1] which is as bad as almost any city in the developing world today.

In New York City the IMR in the summer months of 1892 was 340 per 1,000, and diarrhea accounted for half these deaths. By 1902 the figure had dropped to 215 per 1,000 and the mortality from diarrhea was 85 per 1,000. A publication by McCleary [2] suggests that a number of programs introduced in the administrations of Mayors Strong, Van Wyck, and Low influenced this marked improvement. These included the sterilization and inspection of milk, improvements in street cleaning and refuse disposal, a diphtheria antitoxin program, improved treatment conditions, and the establishment of recreation piers and small parks.

Much of what we have heard over the last three days has tended to be pessimistic. Very serious nutritional problems exist in the world and vast numbers of people are affected. I am particularly concerned that the gap between rich and poor, both nations and people, is widening. This is something that politicians and economists can end. The problem is equally one for India, where the Green Revolution favors the big landowner and creates new problems for the peasant, and for the United States, where vast agricultural subsidies are given to large farming corporations while no minimum wage and appalling standards of life exist for many of those who harvest the crops—the 2,500,000 migrant workers and their dependents. [3]

It is appropriate, therefore, to use some historical perspective, to view what has been done in the past and to see if there are some good lessons to be learned from both successes and failures. No one can dispute that very important nutritional diseases have been eliminated from, or greatly reduced in, countries or regions where once they were endemic. It is also true that scientific knowledge has advanced to a point where we can, if the political will existed, greatly reduce the incidence of most of the serious nutritional diseases that plague the population of the world. The lessons learned from looking at the means of control and possible reasons for reduction of certain deficiency diseases might have relevance to devising a strategy for the fight against other forms of malnutrition which concern us today. In this respect, a gathering of case studies from around the world, some dealing with success stories and others with failures or partial failures, would add significantly to the literature of nutrition. My role today is to examine certain nutritional conditions in a historical perspective and to suggest the relevance of their control to current problems. We will then hear four case reports, from Czechoslovakia, from Colombia, from India, and from Japan.

Nutritional Politics
Nutritionists, physicians, and scientists in general shun politics. Economists are probably less shy in this regard, but they too have not used much political muscle. I do not believe that the nutritional problems of the world can be solved outside the political arena. [4] I believe that nutritionists, physicians, and others have to operate within that arena if their objective is to improve the nutritional status of people. Research workers can, I suppose, undertake laboratory research of great importance to nutrition, entirely outside of politics. But even the directions that research takes and the money available for it are controlled by "politics." The application of its results is often largely decided by governments.

In recent testimony before a committee of the U.S. Senate I described how undernutrition, like other conditions confined to minority groups or to the poor, tended to be shortchanged in the United States. [5] As examples I cited lead poisoning and sickle-cell anemia. I mentioned the pitifully inadequate efforts made to control these serious diseases of minority groups compared with the large national and state campaigns to control poliomyelitis and phenylketonuria (PKU), conditions that are less prevalent but are not confined to the poor or to minority groups. Similarly, undernutrition and malnutrition related to poverty received scant attention in the United States until they recently became hot political issues. Sadly, it was not nutritionists or physicians who really put these problems on the political map. In all countries malnutrition and its control are related to politics. I do not think that we can afford to ignore this fact of life.

I turn now to consider why the prevalence of some selected nutritional diseases has declined, and to suggest certain parallels between these conditions and some of the serious problems of malnutrition that remain important causes of morbidity and mortality in nonindustrialized countries.

Rickets and Kwashiorkor

Homer's *Iliad* is claimed by historians to contain the first description of rickets. In the second century A.D. Soranus of Ephesus, in a treatise on "Diseases of Women," gives a description of the condition and discusses its epidemiology and prevention. Stephen Locknes' painting of the "Adoration of the Child," which is dated 1470, and several other paintings of the period show the bowlegs, the Harrison's sulcus of the chest, the protuberant abdomen, and several other features typical of the rachitic child. [6]

In 1650 Francis Glisson, professor of medicine at Cambridge University, published the first detailed monograph on and classic description of rickets. [7] However, it was almost two hundred years later, in the 1860s, that Armand Trousseau, another great physician who was working at Paris' famous hospital, the Hôtel Dieu, published his remarkably correct views on the etiology and treatment of rickets. [8] Trousseau set out to prove that rickets, then rampant in Europe, resulted from a combination of a poor diet and a sunless environment; he suggested that the disease was made more acute by rapid body growth, and he demonstrated that it could be successfully treated with fish liver oil preferably accompanied by exposure to sunlight. Cod liver oil had been rather empirically, but successfully, used for rickets at Manchester Infirmary in England from 1789, but Trousseau went further by demonstrating that other fish liver oils were equally effective, that certain meat fats were slightly effective, and that vegetable oils were ineffective in preventing rickets. Trousseau was heretic enough to postulate that the beneficial effects of cod liver oil came not from its action as a specific drug but rather from an unknown beneficial food factor in its fat.

A recent paper on Trousseau [9] points out that it is indeed strange that these extraordinarily modern precepts he put forward were by 1900 being completely ignored. This is not because Trousseau had gone unheard, but rather because Pasteur's germ theory of disease had overshadowed and completely eclipsed other possibilities of cause. Cod liver oil became an old-wives' remedy and most people regarded rickets as a chronic infectious disease. The medical profession pointed out that it was endemic, because of its infectious nature, in the children of crowded city slums. They called for the development of a vaccine against rickets.

Despite the hodgepodge of fact and fiction, of correct and incorrect observation, we entered the twentieth century and even World War One with no accepted consensus on the etiology of, and no agreed medical treatment for, rickets. Thus in 1917 Findlay wrote: "In spite of the most varied and intensive research we have practically no real knowledge of the nature of the causation of rickets. Bad housing, unhygienic conditions and industrialization might explain its distribution," he said. [10]

It was Edward Mellanby who made the first comprehensive investigation of the role of nutrition in rickets. His research was to have world wide effects on the knowledge and treatment of the disease. Beginning with reports on puppies in 1919, Mellanby, using controlled diets, proved conclusively that rickets was a dietary deficiency disease and that certain fats could both prevent and cure the disease. Within a few years Harriet Chick, working in Vienna, demonstrated the beneficial effect of sunlight on rickety children, and McCollum and his colleagues at Johns Hopkins demonstrated the presence of a second fat-soluble factor which was named vitamin D. They proved that it was different from fat soluble vitamin A. [11] There followed the work on irradiated sterols which led to our present knowledge.

Throughout the early part of this century rickets was an extraordinarily prevalent disease not only in Europe but also on other continents. It was especially common among, though not confined to, the children of the poor in large urban centers. Findlay in his 1918 survey of Glasgow wrote that it was only with the greatest difficulty that the medical team could find sufficient nonrachitic children for the needs of his research among those attending the dispensary of Glasgow Royal Hospital for Sick Children. Is this not reminiscent of protein-calorie malnutrition in the slums of some developing countries today? Rickets had been aggravated and made worse by industrialization and by changes in the life and conditions of those who moved to the city. This has similarities to the nutritional marasmus-weanling diarrhea syndrome of the septic fringes of large tropical cities, where lack of sanitation, a decline in breast-feeding, and changes in child-rearing practices have had disastrous effects on child health.

Although there are references to the condition in the literature, for example in the Irish Famine of 1848, [12] it was not until modern times that an assortment of physicians in Africa, Asia, and Latin America accomplished the scientific recognition of kwashiorkor. And yet this is a very common disease, a very serious disease, a very widespread disease, and one that has a very high mortality. Seeing case after case as I did working in four different hospitals in Africa, and as one would do in similar hospitals over half the globe, I often wonder how anything so distinctive and destructive as kwashiorkor could have been missed by the organized efforts of medicine for so long. This lack of recognition becomes even more surprising when one finds that the largely illiterate population in many parts of the world had recognized the disease and in many cases had their own name for it.

It was only in 1931 that Dr. Cicely Williams, working in Ghana, gave her classical description of the disease and in 1935 introduced the Ga name kwashiorkor into written medical literature. [13] However, for the next ten to fifteen years there was much dispute in regard to these findings. One of Dr. Williams' principal antagonists was Dr. H. S. Stannus, an eminent British physician and an authority on pellagra. He published an article in the *Lancet* objecting to a West African "native" word and stating that from a study of the pictures he was convinced that the disease was pellagra. [14]

Trowell and Brown, who had been working in East Africa on the disease, including its pathological features, visited Stannus in London in 1937. They were convinced by him that the childhood disease they were studying was indeed pellagra with certain anomalous features—edema, anemia, and fatty liver. Trowell published his material on "pellagra in infants" in 1937 and shortly afterward received a cable from the United States offering to send a substance called nicotinic acid. No one in East Africa had heard of nicotinic acid and its remarkable success in the treatment of blacktongue in dogs by Elvehjem and his colleagues. The nicotinic acid arrived in East Africa and was tried. Nearly all the children died. [15]

Meanwhile many descriptions of the disease had come from Asia, Africa, and Latin America. This, however, was the era of vitamins and bacteria, and medical scientists were reluctant to accept a new syndrome whose cause was due neither to avitaminosis nor to an infection. Thus Castellanos in Cuba [16] called the disease pellagroid beriberi—an attractive concept, pellagra accounting for the skin changes and beriberi for the edema. He did not explain the fatty liver.

It was not until 1939 and the outbreak of the Second World War that work in several parts of the world began to coalesce. Cicely Williams had moved to Malaya and had described cases of kwashiorkor there. She was in correspondence with Trowell who, disappointed with the treatment of the disease with nicotinic acid, now accepted that this was not pellagra. Within a few weeks of his publication of an article stating his belief that the edema syndrome was due to protein deficiency, Malaya and Singapore were overrun by the Japanese. Cicely Williams became interned as a prisoner of war and for four years herself experienced the effects of dietary deficiencies. When she emerged in 1945, research had resolved many of the points of disagreement and kwashiorkor was an accepted clinical entity well separated from pellagra. Kwashiorkor was recognized as resulting from a protein deficiency.

Rickets was an extremely prevalent and a devastating disease in Europe and elsewhere in the early part of this century, just as protein-calorie malnutrition is in many parts of the world today. Both diseases occur in infants and preschool-age children, and both may result in permanent sequelae. Rickets, fifty years later, at least in its serious forms, has almost disappeared from the dingy industrial cities where it was so prevalent, while protein-calorie malnutrition remains our number one nutritional problem.

The incidence of rickets began to decline before its nature was fully evaluated, and this was due to social and economic improvements affecting the poor. Similarly the incidence of kwashiorkor will be influenced by social and economic change. However, it was only when the etiology of rickets was accepted scientifically and was made known to the general public that successful prevention became feasible. People became aware that improved diets could prevent the "English disease." Attempts to control rickets led to the widespread use of cod liver oil, and this led to the development and extension of child health services as a vehicle for rickets prevention. In 1911 there were fewer than 100 infant welfare centers in Britain and in 1931, just twenty years later, there were over 1,400. These clinics flourished because of national concern about rickets, but they served and they continue to serve other useful purposes. Thus although it was probably unnecessary, once home diets had improved, for many of those attending the clinics to take cod liver oil, nevertheless it is still valuable for these children to attend a clinic with their mothers for advice and for health education. We saw in France and the United States during the same period the development of *gouttes de lait* and of milk depots, all stimulated by a concern about rickets and the high infant mortality rates. [2]

In Zambia ten years ago there were no under-five clinics; today there are over 400. Their principal objective is to instill in the mother a positive attitude toward the growth and development of her child, that is, to prevent protein-calorie malnutrition. During my eight years in Tanzania a major effort was made to get women to bring their children to various maternal and child health clinics where UNICEF dried skimmed milk was provided, but where prevention and treatment of various other diseases could be practiced. The dried skimmed milk power (DSM), the CSM, the Incaparina, the other protein-rich supplements used in the prevention of kwashiorkor are analogous to the cod liver oil of fifty years ago in relation to rickets. The benefits from such programs will be much wider than just the advantage gained from the dietary supplement, because the habit of clinic attendance, the ability of the clinic to immunize and to educate, and the understanding by the mother that her actions can influence the growth and health of her child will all have far-reaching effects.

But I should not leave the impression that medical and public health measures have been the only or even the most important factors in conquering rickets, or will be the only weapons in controlling protein-calorie malnutrition. Not only was rickets affected by other measures, but the scourge of rickets and public attention to it resulted in major social changes. Slum clearance, smoke abatement, the suburban house with a garden, the development of parks and playgrounds, even the perambulator or baby carriage all allowed the infant to get more exposure to sunshine, and all were part of overall programs to control rickets. Improvement of living conditions for the poor was a major factor in the rapid decline in rickets in industrialized Europe and North America. Another factor was better wages, allowing an improved diet. Lives have changed, in fact, because of attention to and concern for this one disease. The mother who puts her child in the playpen in the sunshine, or who tells her son to drink his milk, or who goes to the infant clinic for a checkup, often does not really know why she is doing these things or what disease she is preventing by so doing; her actions have become everyday routines in her life.

In the future it may be unnecessary for the Zambian mother to get a protein-rich supplement from the clinic, and it may become everyday practice for her to add dried fish or pounded beans to her child's maize gruel. The reason for doing these things may be forgotten, but kwashiorkor will then be a rare disease. Left behind will be a tradition of child welfare, a clinic system where immunizations will be routine, and the benefits of accumulated knowledge of child care.

The actual elimination of rickets required major social and economic changes; it was accomplished by government action, by planned change, by public health measures, and by popular cooperation. Together these elements were successful in the conquest of this disease, which affected more than half the children in some areas of the world, which had a high mortality, and which left its survivors maimed for the rest of their lives. These same elements can be successful in the control of protein-calorie malnutrition in its endemic foci today.

It is realized that rickets is still a public health problem in some parts of the world, for example, Ethiopia, and that a small recrudescence of the disease has recently occurred among the immigrant population in Britain. However, the disease as a major crippler and as a principal source of public health concern has disappeared.

The purpose of providing a historical outline of the incidence of rickets and kwashiorkor is that there are important similarities in their medical recognition, and that the story of the decline of rickets has, I believe, important lessons to teach those who are trying to reduce the prevalence of kwashiorkor, marasmus, and other forms of protein-calorie malnutrition. Analogies of this kind are useful both for planners and for nutritionists.

It is striking that both in rickets and kwashiorkor there was an accumulation of scientific knowledge and yet a reluctance, not of the public, but of the medical profession to accept the evidence; this reluctance was largely because of prevailing medical fashion. Thus physicians like Trousseau and Guérin clearly demonstrated that fish liver oils and even butter in the diet, and sunshine on the skin, could cure rickets, findings which were widely publicized in medical journals, and yet their evidence was not generally accepted. In the nineteenth century physicians had the fixed, stubborn belief that diseases of this kind were due to an infection, to an organism. They rejected experimental evidence in favor of circumstantial observations such as the prevalence of rickets among the poor and in the crowded slums. Scientists were so obsessed with the findings of Pasteur that they refused to think about dietary deficiency as a cause of disease, despite the work of Lind on scurvy. It was not until the discovery of vitamins, followed by new experimental studies on rickets, that the overwhelming evidence proving rickets to be a deficiency disease would be accepted.

As for kwashiorkor, in 1930s deficiency diseases were in vogue but the medical fashion was vitamins; new ones were constantly being discovered. Therefore, if kwashiorkor was not due to a tropical infection, it must be a vitamin deficiency. Despite the very great differences from pellagra, eminent physicians right up to 1945 [17] were still describing the disease as infantile pellagra. One also sees in the history of kwashiorkor the very common barrier often placed in front of the medical innovator.

It is significant too that both diseases can be reduced by the use of a dietary supplement, that the provision of this has stimulated the establishment of child health clinics, and that planned social and economic changes have been features in the control of both diseases.

I shall turn now to a short review of other important deficiency diseases in which some success has been achieved in their control.

Pellagra

Pellagra, a deficiency disease characterized by the three D's—dermatitis, diarrhea, dementia (some add a fourth D for death)—is also historically very interesting, and its control has some relevance to the control of other kinds of malnutrition. It is a disease primarily of those who subsist on a diet mainly of maize, although important outbreaks have been recorded in wheat eaters in Newfoundland [18] and sorghum (jowar) eaters in India. [19] The work of Goldberger and his colleagues between 1913 and 1930, when they proved that the disease was due to a vitamin deficiency, and showed in humans and dogs that it could be cured by nicotinic acid and niacin, is one of the most exciting thrillers in modern medicine. It was a classic work in epidemiology.

Although pellagra was first described in northern Spain by Casal in 1735, the history of the disease and of its control occurred mainly in the New World. In the first thirty years of this century pellagra was a major disaster in the southern United States. Like so many forms of malnutrition, it was in the United States a disease of the poor, the underprivileged, and the deprived. While rickets was especially an urban disease of Europe and a temperate sunless environment, pellagra was mainly a rural disease of warm sunny climates. Where rickets occurred in the children of worker victims of industrialization, pellagra in the United States was a disease of those whose livelihood depended on inadequate remuneration from their labors in the Southern cotton plantations. There was a peculiar dependence on cotton as the only cash crop, and there was a minimum cultivation of foods by poor workers for their own consumption. Corn was the cheapest food, and its nutritive value was made worse by so-called technological advancement in the milling process.

In 1928 there were almost 7,000 deaths attributed to pellagra in the United States, and the state of Georgia alone had around 20,000 cases of pellegra per year. By 1948 the disease was relatively rare, and by 1958 it had been virtually conquered in the southern United States. [20] The prevalence of pellagra was influenced by ignorance of its cause, by a peculiar and patronizing agriculture including the odious system of sharecropping, and by poor economic circumstances for an oppressed segment of society. Its remarkable conquest resulted from ingenious scientific work proving its etiology and the application of this knowledge; but also from agricultural changes and from improved economic conditions. Goldberger's work led to concrete agricultural extension activities to combat pellagra, and there developed a greater attention to food crops with a reduction of the acreage under cotton.

It is significant here that in the world in general, and in developing countries in particular, agricultural research has devoted more of its energies and talent to cash crops than to food crops. This was especially so in the colonial territories. In Tanzania prior to independence there were agricultural research facilities concerned with coffee, with cotton, with sisal, and with tea, but none for cereal crops, legumes, or any other important food products. Undoubtedly this agricultural obsession with cash crops for the world market has contributed to malnutrition. It is good to see the comparatively recent surge of activity in the field of agricultural research in tropical food products including the cereals, legumes, and root crops.

There has been an important decline in pellagra in many countries in which endemic foci existed. These include Rumania, Italy, Yugoslavia, and to a lesser extent Egypt and some countries in tropical Africa. One of the most important endemic foci of pellagra in the world today is in South Africa. It is not purely chance that this is a country where industrialization has benefited mainly one segment of the population, where black laborers are treated much as they were in the southern United States fifty years ago, and where oppressive legislation results in major disruption of families. Pretorius in 1968 [21] reported that it was not unusual to see pellagra in 50 percent of patients attending certain Bantu clinics. It has also been reported that a majority of black patients admitted to mental hospitals in the capital city of Pretoria have pellagra.

Pellagra will disappear wherever predominantly maize diets give way to a more varied diet, where knowledge of the causation of the disease can be translated into preventive action, and where economic and agricultural conditions change for the better. In areas where some temporary phenomenon threatens to result in an extensive outbreak of pellagra it is easy to adopt procedures whereby nicotinic acid tablets are prescribed for whole communities, as we found in Tanzania, [22] or where the disease is endemic it should be possible to enrich maize with niacin. Pellagra has been largely controlled, and with some political will and public health ingenuity it could become a rare disease everywhere.

Beriberi

While pellagra is a disease of maize eaters, beriberi is associated almost exclusively with a rice diet. Beriberi became a scourge as the milling industry marched across Asia producing polished rice, deprived of its thiamine content. This rice became available at a cost no more than home-pounded rice but at a cost of many millions of lives lost or made miserable by beriberi.

It is interesting, perhaps frightening, in this regard to consider how many nutritional deficiency diseases have been adversely affected by industrialization, by so-called technological advancement. Although beriberi is the classic example, because of its association with milling which removed some protective nutrients, there are similar associations between rickets and the growth of cities, pellagra and the cotton industry, scurvy and long nautical journeys, and now nutritional marasmus and the availability of prepared milks to replace more desirable breast-feeding. As a corollary here, it is worth remembering that the pernicious practice of bottle-feeding infants, which has spread from industrialized to industrializing societies, is having disastrous public health effects (in increased marasmus and gastroenteritis) and could have very damaging economic consequences. In 1963 I estimated that 40 million gallons of human breast milk were produced in Tanzania each year. The value, based on the retail price of milk, was U.S. $22 million at a time when the budget of the Tanzanian Ministry of Health was about U.S. $5 million per year. [23]

Where the history of pellagra is associated with maize and the New World, the history of beriberi is linked with rice and with Asia. Although Eijkman first proved that there was a nutrient present in the outer coat and germ of rice that can prevent neuritis in chickens and cure beriberi in his patients, it was Takaki in Japan who first showed conclusively that beriberi was a nutritional disease. In 1878, 30 percent of sailors in the Japanese navy developed beriberi each year, and according to Williams the disease had virtually disappeared from the Japanese navy less than a decade later. This was accomplished by provision of a mixed diet and before we had any knowledge of vitamins.

But it took careful experimental work, all of which contributed to our knowledge of vitamins, to prove that beriberi resulted from a vitamin deficiency and to show ways in which it could be prevented and cured. It was not until we had this scientific knowledge and began to apply it that beriberi began to markedly decline as a public health problem. The disease had been a major cause of illness and one of the commonest causes of death in many Asian countries and, although not eradicated, its importance as a cause of both morbidity and mortality has greatly declined. We really do not know how to apportion the credit for this remarkable reduction, despite extensive writings such as R. R. Williams' *Towards the Conquest of Beriberi.* [24] Undoubtedly important factors have included a public awareness of the cause of the disease as a result of nutrition education; an increase in the variety of food eaten even by the poor in Asian countries; deliberate programs of rice treatment such as parboiling and thiamine enrichment; and public health measures, including prophylactic consumption of thiamine tablets and early treatment of cases of the disease. Technology in a sense brought on a huge epidemic of beriberi when milling of rice became popular, and technology allied with science, with economic development, and with public health measures has led to its decline. A measure now being tested is amino-acid fortification of cereals as a means of combating PCM. Again it is Japanese technology that has produced the cheapest synthetic amino acids.

Endemic Goiter
Perhaps the best example of a disease that can be easily controlled is endemic goiter due to iodine deficiency. This provides an example too of a disease that can be virtually eliminated without social, economic, or health changes in the population. But it is a preventable disease which has not been adequately tackled. Kelly and Snedden, writing in a 1958 WHO monograph, [25] provided a comprehensive review of the known geographic distribution of endemic goiter; they estimated that there were 200 million goitrous people in the world.

There are areas in all the continents of the world where goiter is endemic and, in some of these foci, cretinism, deaf-mutism, and retarded mental development occur in the children of iodine-deficient women. New areas of high goiter prevalence are still being discovered. In 1964 in the Ukinga highlands of Tanzania we found that 75 percent of more than 300 persons examined had goiter. [26] This was in a country where goiter had not previously been considered a public health problem.

We have good evidence of striking success in goiter control from using iodine in salt. Switzerland, with its high prevalence of goiter, was the first country to adopt this measure. New Zealand too has had a successful program. In the United States and India salt iodization is not mandatory but has been successfully used in certain areas, for example in Michigan and in the Kangra Valley of the Himalayas, respectively.

A developing country where a very successful program has been in operation is Colombia. A survey of 180,000 schoolchildren in 1945 showed that 53 percent had goiter. In the 7 most affected *municipios* in the state of Caldas, 83 percent of the children had goiter when salt iodization was introduced in 1950; the goiter rate had dropped to 33 percent by 1952 and, when the area was resurveyed in 1965, only 2 percent of the children had thyroid enlargements. [27] This kind of success can be expected with salt iodization where iodine deficiency has resulted in endemic goiter. Where salt iodization is not feasible, injections of iodine in oil have proved successful in goiter control and in reducing the incidence of cretinism. [28]

Nutritionists and planners alike should be a little ashamed that many countries, including the United States, have not introduced mandatory salt iodization programs, despite the fact that goiter still occurs and that this measure is both cheap and effective. It is true that social and economic development, which leads to a greater movement of foods and less dependence on locally grown products, does serve to reduce goiter prevalence by increasing consumption of foods grown in soil providing adequate iodine.

Dental caries, although it cannot be prevented by fluoride, can be greatly reduced. Undoubtedly the fluoridation of water supplies must be included among nutrition success stories. Dental caries is one of man's most prevalent and universal diseases; it is also an economically extremely expensive disease and one that is disabling. A cheap and simple means of reducing dental caries by 60 or 70 percent exists with fluoridation. [29] Yet few countries have adopted this measure in all their cities and towns. In areas without suitable water supplies it would be possible to achieve similar results using fluoride in table salt. The use of salt as a vehicle for nutrients other than iodine and fluoride deserves more attention than it has received; it is possible that other minerals, vitamins, and even amino acids could be provided in this way. [30]

This review is far from comprehensive—there are many other deficiency diseases for which there are positive success stories. The important subject of nutritional anemias has not been discussed; vitamin A deficiency is still a significant cause of blindness in some countries, and its control requires measures similar to those required for the prevention of protein-calorie malnutrition; there are some B vitamin deficiencies such as ariboflavinosis that, while not serious public health problems, nonetheless are prevalent; there is scurvy, which is not a major cause of morbidity in any country; and there are the oft-mentional deficiencies of minerals such as calcium, which have not convincingly been shown to cause serious disease in large groups of people anywhere, but which may play a role in osteoporosis and periodontal disease.

Conclusion

If I am propounding one thesis—and I hope I am doing more than that—it is that control of malnutrition has had a major influence in the past both on economic development and on planned social change. Nutritional deficiency diseases have caused much human suffering. Their prevalence was influenced by poverty and often also by technological change. The diseases caused misery and some social unrest. Their control was often planned both to reduce morbidity and also to alleviate a social ill. The eradication of these diseases was an integral part of development, it significantly influenced this development, and it had marked beneficial social consequences.

In one sense both pellagra in the United States and rickets in Britain had a positive influence, once there was the scientific knowledge concerning their cause and enough public and political outcry to allow their control. I am convinced that public funds expended on their eradication was money well spent because it brought dividends in terms of desirable changes that contributed both to national development and to the quality of life. A broad attack on protein-calorie malnutrition today—an attack combining public health measures, agricultural innovation, educational means, and social development including poverty control—will bring similar benefits both in terms of national development and of control of the condition itself, which affects not only health but, as noted by other speakers, future productivity.

If there really is such a thing as an "economic takeoff point" or, as I prefer to see it, a "quality of life takeoff point," then I would venture to predict that it will be reached when protein-calorie malnutrition is no longer a major health problem and when infant mortality rates have fallen below about 75 per 1,000 and toddler mortality rates to a much lower level.

Although I use here the analogy of pellagra and rickets with kwashiorkor and marasmus, similar analogies are valid with other deficiency diseases, for example, between beriberi and vitamin A deficiency. With keratomalacia it should be remembered that there is no world vitamin A gap, just as there is no thiamine gap, in the sense that there is a world protein gap. But keratomalacia is essentially a disease of the very poor and it emanates from conditions of life that should not exist at this time. It would virtually disappear if either the division between rich and poor was substantially narrowed or if we devoted a little more effort to its public health control (and we can "immunize" against vitamin A deficiency in childhood).

Investments in broad programs to deal with the sometimes complex causes of malnutrition are likely to have benefits far beyond the reduction of deficiency diseases. The lesson of history is that they may form the springboard for urban and rural development projects and may be the catalyst for a general improvement in the quality of life.

References

1. *Ithaca Journal.* Ithaca, N.Y., 1921.

2. McCleary, G. F. *Infant Mortality and Infant Milk Depots.* London: King, 1905.

3. Nelkin, D. *On the Season.* Ithaca: Cornell Industrial and Labor Relations Series, 1970.

4. Latham, M. C. Starvation of politics or politics of starvation. *Lancet* 2:999, 1969.

5. Latham, M. C. The edibility gap: differences between promise and delivery in the family food commodity program. U.S. Senate, Select Committee on Nutrition and Human Needs, *Hearings.* Washington, D.C.: G.P.O., 1971.

6. Hess, A. F. *Rickets Including Osteomalacia and Tetany.* Philadelphia: Lea and Febiger, 1929.

7. Glisson, F. *De Rachitide Sivo Morbo Puerili que Vulgo.* London, 1650.

8. Trousseau, A. *Clinique Medicale de l'Hôtel Dieu de Paris.* Paris: Baillère, 1861.

9. Mayer, J. Armand Trousseau and the arrow of time. *Nutr. Rev.* 11:321, 1957.

10. Findlay, L. The aetiology of rickets. *Lancet* 1:825, 1922.

11. McCollum, E. V. *A History of Nutrition.* Boston: Houghton Mifflin, 1957.

12. Woodham-Smith, C. *The Great Hunger: Ireland 1845-1849.* New York: Harper and Row, 1962.

13. Williams, C. D. *Archives of Diseases of Childhood.* 8:423, 1933; *Lancet* 2:1151, 1935.

14. Stannus, H. S. Kwashiorkor. *Lancet* 2:1207, 1935.

15. Trowell, H. C., J. N. P. Davies, and R. F. A. Dean. *Kwashiorkor.* London: Edward Arnold, 1954.

16. Castellanos, A. Pellagroid beriberi. *Bol. Soc. Cubana Pediat.* 7:5, 1937

17. Gillman, J. and T. Gillman. *Perspectives in Human Nutrition.* New York: Crune and Stratton, 1951.

18. Davidson, S., and R. Passmore. *Human Nutrition and Dietetics.* Edinburgh: Livingstone, 1963.

19. Gopalan, C. Possible role for dietary leucine in the pathogenesis of pellagra. *Lancet* 1:197, 1969.

328   Michael C. Latham

20. Davies, J. N. P. The decline of pellagra in the southern United States. *Lancet* 2:195, 1964.

21. Pretorius, P. J. The clinical nature and extent of protein malnutrition in South Africa. *S. African Med. J.* 42:956, 1968.

22. Latham, M. C. Nutritional studies in Tanzania. In *World Review of Nutrition and Dietetics* 7:31, 1967.

23. Latham, M. C. The use of dairy products and eggs in increasing production of protein-rich foods in developing countries. In *Proceedings of Seventh International Congress of Nutrition.* Hamburg, 1966, p. 61.

24. Williams, R. R. *Toward the Conquest of Beriberi.* Cambridge, Mass.: Harvard University Press, 1961.

25. Kelly, F. C. and W. W. Snedden. *Endemic Goitre.* WHO Monograph Series No. 44, 1960.

26. Latham, M. C. A goitre survey in Ukinga, Tanzania. *Transactions of Royal Society of Tropical Medicine and Hygiene* 59:342, 1965.

27. Pardo, F., R. Rueda-Williamson, and J. O. Mora. Le efectivad de la sal en la prevención del bocio endemico en Colombia. *Archivos Latinoamericanos de Nutrición* 18:7, 1968.

28. Pharoah, P. O. D., I. U. Buttfield, and B. S. Hetzel. Neurological damage to the fetus resulting from severe iodine deficiency during pregnancy. *Lancet* 1:308, 1971.

29. Latham, M. C., R. B. McGandy, M. B. McCann, and F. J. Stare. *Scope Manual of Nutrition.* Kalamazoo, Michigan: Upjohn, 1970.

30. Levinson, F. J., and A. Berg. With a grain of fortified salt. *Food Technology* 23:71, 1969.

34 The Czech Experience in Nutrition Improvement

L. Křikava
Head, Division of Metabolism and Nutrition
Institute of Human Nutrition, Prague

J. Mašek
Director, Institute for Clinical and
Experimental Medicine, Prague

P. Malek
Institute of Human Nutrition, Prague

To illustrate the nature of our national nutritional problems in Czechoslovakia, which were resolved by a reasonably oriented national food and nutrition policy, it is necessary to look into the past. All efforts for improvement started in 1945, almost without a national tradition. Nutritionists, research workers, food policy makers, and so on were scattered all around the world during the years of World War Two.

The situation at that time was as follows: On the one hand, the population, who had been living for many years on a meager ration of foodstuffs, was critically aware of practical problems with regard to feeding; and on the other hand, the government had to face many serious problems of economic relief and rehabilitation in all sectors. The importance of improving nutrition as part of the total health picture of our population attracted not only public attention and interest, it was also immediately recognized by the authorities as a matter crucial to the national interest and it received first priority in national development planning. The government assumed the initiative in establishing a national food policy and in agricultural development.

The First Period (1945-1950)

Because basic data on food consumption and on the nutritional status of the population were lacking, an empirical economic approach was used. Some guidelines were given by a plan developed by the government-in-exile. Rationing, production incentives, and price controls were the principal approaches employed to regulate supply and distribution of foodstuffs. Special attention was directed to vulnerable and to some productive groups of the population.

Central planning bodies recognized that nutrition problems call for cooperation, collaboration, and the concerted action of many ministries. Special commissions in agriculture, the food industry, trade, health, social welfare, and labor were established. Their aim was to prepare precise departmental objectives and programs and to specify their responsibilities in preparation of a carefully planned national food and nutrition policy adopted to local conditions. A central food and nutrition commission was composed of top-ranking representatives and experts from all ministries concerned.

First information from health services as well as data from small-scale surveys on food consumption and the nutritional state revealed insufficient intake of calories and of all nutrients, especially proteins, which were far below requirements. Undernutrition, subclinical deficiencies, and failure in growth in children were reported.

Generally it was known that because of wartime disruptions the country had serious infant feeding problems. An alarming fact was the very high mortality in young children. Table 1 illustrates infant mortality in some countries of Eastern Europe from 1937 to 1969.

The authorities gave highest priority to preventive pediatric measures in the fight against malnutrition in children and in development of safe milk supplies. Better facilities for medical care and a decline of mortality from infectious diseases resolved the problem in a short period of time. To fight such deficiencies as avitaminosis D or anemia, health services initiated large-scale operations to supply deficient nutrients for vulnerable groups of the population.

The Second Period (1950-1960)

The second period saw expanded activities of the commissions mentioned above. To ensure fundamental research and to provide scientific foundations for the food and nutrition policy, some research institutes were created and the existing establishments started their work. Funds and adequately trained personnel at all levels were available. Countrywide surveys of production, distribution, and consumption of food, of socioeconomic changes in a changing society as well as of the nutritional state were accomplished. [1] An

Table 1. Infant Mortality: Number of Deaths before One Year per 1,000 Live Births

Country	1937	Average 1945-49	1960	1965	1969
Czechoslovakia	117	100	23	25	23
Bulgaria	150	127	45	31	30
Yugoslavia	141	102	88	72	–
Hungary	134	114	48	39	36
Poland	136	111	55	42	–
Rumania	174	159	75	44	55
USSR	184	81	35	28	26

Source: Federální statistický úřad, Český statistický úřad, Slovenský statistický úřad. *Statistická ročenka ČSSR 1970.* Praha: Státní nakladetelství technické literatury, 1970.

increasing amount of information was being made available. The mechanism for exchange of data and information was established.

The revision of provisional recommended nutrient allowances was based this time not only on data from nutrition surveys, but also on more detailed investigations of the metabolism of various nutrients and was compared with data from animal experiments. The data thus obtained have not represented an optimum value but a desirable level of intake. [2] Recommended food allowances [3] were translations of biological findings on human nutrition into economic reality [4] and were used as a basis for planning food production.

Rapid economic development, increasing industrialization, and a new agricultural policy resulted in rising food production, and the system of food rationing was abolished in 1953. The effect of the availability of foodstuffs and of an increase in income in a fairly homogeneous society is demonstrated in index numbers in Table 2. Trends in food consumption from 1936 to 1968 in kilograms per year and per person are shown in Table 3, and the nutritive value of food consumption in Table 4.

There were some applied nutrition programs. The main attention was focused on group feeding at children's establishments such as schools and day care centers and on communal catering for workers employed under varying conditions and in different environments and in centers of the State Labor Reserves. [5,6,7]

The rise in the standard of living of the population has been manifested in a generalized stabilization of caloric intake and in increased consumption of

Table 2. Indices of Trends in Food Consumption (1936=100%.)

	1948-49	1954-58	1959-63	1964-66	1967-69
Meat	91.2	142.4	169.1	178.8	197.6
Fats and oils	79.4	120.6	141.1	143.3	142.8
Milk	90.0	96.9	83.3	87.6	94.3
Eggs	92.0	121.0	129.7	160.1	180.0
Cereals	96.7	106.3	98.5	97.6	90.9
Potatoes	99.2	101.4	89.3	90.9	96.0
Pulses	62.5	40.0	32.5	37.5	25.8
Vegetables	128.2	115.3	123.4	122.4	130.7
Fruit	126.8	112.8	111.9	101.2	98.4
Sugar	105.2	146.6	160.3	161.2	164.2

Source: Federální statistický úřad, Český statistický úřad, Slovenský statistický úřad. Statistická ročenka ČSSR 1970.

332   L. Křikava, J. Mašek, P. Malek

Table 3. Food Consumption (kg. per year per person).

	1936	1948	Average 1950-52	Average 1960-62	Average 1967-68
Meat	34.0	31.5	42.1	58.0	65.6
Fish	2.1	4.2	2.5	4.7	5.0
Milk	205.4	173.1	221.9	172.6	192.0
Eggs	138.0	114.0	168.0	181.0	247.0
Fats	14.1	10.5	14.2	20.2	20.5
Sugar	23.2	22.4	28.2	37.7	38.0
Potatoes	118.9	113.5	129.7	103.0	115.8
Pulses	4.0	2.6	2.1	1.4	1.1
Vegetables	65.5	92.2	73.0	81.8	86.4
Fruit	42.9	55.0	43.9	49.7	42.1
Cereals	121.1	120.4	139.4	128.6	123.5

Source: Federální statistický úrad, Ceský statistický úrad, Slovenský statistický úrad.
Statistická ročenka CSSR 1970.

Table 4. Nutritive Value of Food Consumption (per day per person)

	1936	1948	Average 1950-52	Average 1960-62	Average 1967-68
Calories	2545	2194	2717	3138	3113
Total protein in grams	72.6	64.9	74.5	87.3	90.9
Animal protein (grams)	32.2	27.2	31.6	42.3	47.7
Fat (grams)	79.0	60.5	73.8	103.1	108.3
Glycids (grams)	395.5	361.4	443.0	472.2	450.5

Source: Federální statistický úrad, Český statistický úřad, Slovenský statistický úřad.
Statistická ročenka CSSR 1970.

fats and proteins. In persons with deficiency signs, qualitative deficiencies prevailed over the quantitative deficiencies found formerly. The main cause of inadequate nutrition was insufficient consciousness of nutritional factors in diet.

In this coordinated effort several research institutes and laboratories—of high schools and of the Academy of Sciences and the Academy of Agricultural Sciences—were engaged. Very important work has been done by the group of experts joined in the Society for Rational Nutrition, which promotes information exchange between individuals at various levels. The annual meeting brings together not only top-level planners, economists, nutritionists, and agriculturists but also those working directly in the field as dietitians, home economists, health educators and so on. The journal of the Society provides a source of sound and current information for nutrition education.

In development of an integrated nutrition program, the health educators played a leading role in nutrition education. A long-term, comprehensive nutrition education program, directed by the Institute of Health Education, uses all channels available in its operations. Various approaches to educating children and adults among all socioeconomic levels of the population have been tried, involving governmental agencies and services related to health, education, community development, social welfare, and so on. [8,9]

The Third Period (1960-present)
At present there are no difficulties with regard to quantity. A concerted effort for nutrition improvement has won this struggle.

The golden age of food consumption and nutritional status surveys has been long gone. An annual evaluation of food consumption based on global data, food balance sheets, and household budgets gives the picture of a high caloric diet, characterized by a high consumption of animal fats, cereals, and sucrose, and with an evident seasonal deficit of vitamin C. A so-called signaling system for nutritional problems was established with the aim of obtaining continuous information on the diet and nutrition of the population and is directed by the hygiene services. [10]

A comprehensive research project called "Ways to Ensure Sound Nutrition of the Population" has been finished, and a new one, "Rationalization of Nutrition," is directed now to the struggle for quality. Future projects are (1) problems of obesity [11] and iron deficiency anemia; (2) research into factors involved in the mechanism of metabolic effects of infrequent feeding and their interactions; [12] (3) problems of digestion and utilization of nutrients; (4) interaction of environmental factors influencing the relationship of nutrition and behavior. The recommended nutrient allowances will be revised in response to changing conditions of modern life and changing labor conditions. [13] Main attention will be concentrated on the effect of industrial food preparation, and on the hygienic properties and the preservation of the physical and nutritional value of conventional and new foods and their enrichment.

References

1. Křikava, L. Náš postup při vyšetřování stavu výživy obyvatelstva ČSR. *Acta Inst. Aliment. Hum. Pragae* 1:19, 1956.

2. Mašek, J. The present work of the Institute for Human Nutrition in Prague. *Acta Inst. Aliment. Hum. Pragae* 2:6, 1958.

334   L. Křikava, J. Mašek, P. Malek

3. Hrubý, J. and O. Šmrha. Food policy in Czechoslovakia. In *Proceedings of the Eighth International Congress on Nutrition*, Prague. Amsterdam: Excerpta Medica, 1970, p. 570.

4. Hrubý, J. *Příspěvek ke koncepci vývoje výživy v ČSSR*. Studie ČSAV č. 7. Praha: Academia, 1971.

5. Mašek, J., S. Hejda, and J. Kaucka. Communal catering. *Acta Inst. Aliment. Hum. Pragae* 4:20, 1969.

6. Mašek, J. Activities of the Institute of Human Nutrition, 1962-1968. *Acta. Inst. Aliment. Hum. Pragae* 4:7, 1969.

7. Křikava, L. The trend of the nutritional status of our population. *Acta Inst. Aliment. Hum. Pragae* 2:13, 1958.

8. Adamec, Č. Nutrition education of adults in Czechoslovakia. Paper presented at the Eighth International Congress of Nutrition, Prague, 1969, pp. A 1-2.

9. Traufrová, M. Health education of the population in selected ecological units. *Zdravotni Vychova* 23:3, 1971.

10. Hejda, S. Epidemiological investigations of the nutritional status of the population. *Acta Inst. Aliment. Hum. Pragae* 4:17, 1969.

11. Mašek, J. Recommended nutrient allowances. *Acta Inst. Aliment. Hum. Pragae* 4:15, 1969.

12. Fabry, P. Multiple effects of the food intake pattern in man. Paper presented at the Eighth International Congress of Nutrition, Prague, 1969, pp. F 1-2.

13. Kaucká, J. and E. Horáčková. *Versuch die Ernährung der Nachtarbeiterzu rationalisieren*. Téze II. Symposia o společném stravování v K. Varech. Praha: SRV, 1967, p. 19.

35 The National Nutrition Program in Colombia

Jaime Paez-Franco
Director of Nutrition
Colombian Institute of Family Welfare
Bogotá

Introduction

Colombia, as a developing country, faces a serious nutritional and feeding problem which undoubtedly has slowed down its economic and social development. In view of this situation, the various Colombian governments have made great efforts to progressively consolidate a program of nutrition and feeding, directed to the most susceptible groups of the population, with the active participation of the different sectors of development. This program of national scope started with isolated activities of an experimental character in demonstration areas, and has been converted in the course of recent years into a wide-ranging national plan. [1]

The Colombian experience is a positive example for the planning and development of this type of program, which may serve to inform and encourage other countries having similar nutritional problems. Therefore, what follows is a report on the outstanding features of its nutritional problems, the different programs constituting the national plan, and some of the results achieved, particularly in terms of changes in the nutritional status of special groups of the population.

Basic Information on Colombia

Colombia, a country with 21 million inhabitants and a territory of 444,000 square miles (1,138,914 square kilometers), is situated in the northwestern part of South America. With a yearly growth rate of 3.2 percent, its population is predominantly young (46 percent under 15 years). It has a population density of 18.4 inhabitants per square kilometer, with a slight predominance of urban population (54.2 percent). The average number of persons per family is six, the population in the productive age group (15 to 64 years) is 51 percent, and the work force has been estimated at 30 percent of the total population. [2,3]

The gross national product growth rate reached 7 percent in 1970. For the same year, the per capita income was around U.S. $300, the monthly family income for 51 percent of the population being lower than U.S. $25, and the unemployment index stood at 14 percent. The principal contributions to the gross national product were made by: agriculture, 29 percent; manufactures, 19 percent; trading, 16 percent; and transport, 6 percent. [4] In the educational field, according to the 1964 census illiteracy amounted to 27 percent—38 percent in the rural population and 14 percent in the urban population. For the period between 1961 and 1966, the school dropout rate was 78 percent at the primary school level, 73 percent at the high school level, and 55 percent at the university level.

Nutritional Status of the Colombian Population

From an analysis of the different direct and indirect indicators of nutritional status it may be concluded that Colombia faces serious nutritional problems. During 1968 the infant mortality rate was 65 per thousand, that of the preschool population was 9.7 per thousand and the ratio between the above mentioned rates was 6.7. The number of deaths in children under five years of age represented 43.7 percent of the general mortality, and the specific mortality rates from measles and diarrhea reached 9.0 and 95.0 per 100,000 inhabitants, respectively. These rates are rather high compared to those of the countries which have reached an advanced level of development. [2,3]

Studies carried out by the Department of Nutrition of the Colombian Institute of Family Welfare (National Institute of Nutrition up to 1969), demonstrate that the general prevalence of protein-calorie malnutrition in children under five years of age, belonging to families of a low socioeconomic level (70 percent of the whole population), was at the level of 66.6 percent in 1967. [5] For the same year, the mortality rate due to avitaminosis, other deficiency diseases, and anemias was 9.9 per 10,000 inhabitants, and the morbidity rate due to the same illnesses was 33.4 per 1,000 inhabitants. [3] Other indicators show that in 1966 the prevalence of iron deficiency anemia was 133 per 1,000 inhabitants and that of endemic goiter was 3.6 percent of the total population. Likewise, dental examinations showed a DMF score of 15.4 in the population older than 5 years.

The feeding status of the population refers essentially to the adequacy of calories and nutrients per capita per day, available for consumption, as well as to food supply. The information is based on different nutritional surveys—the food balance sheets, the recommended dietary allowances, and the goals for food availability—formulated by the Department of Nutrition of the Colombian Institute of Family Welfare. Marked deficits can be seen, particularly in the consumption of calories (83%), proteins (72%), calcium (46%), and vitamin A (56%) (see Table 1). In relation to the adequacy of the food available in 1966, similar deficits for proteins (92%) and vitamin A (68%) are noted.

Table 1. Percentage Adequacy of Family Dietary Intake of Calories and Nutrients, per Capita per Day in Ten Urban and Rural Areas, by Socioeconomic Levels, Colombia, 1963-1966

Area and socio-economic level	No. families	Calories	Proteins	Calcium	Iron	Vitamin A	Thiamine	Riboflavin	Niacin	Vitamin C
Urban										
Very low	44	76	67	39	109	56	82	47	77	91
Low	9	80	80	43	108	54	67	55	87	101
Middle	16	93	106	69	112	107	77	92	102	148
High	20	114	126	87	165	135	110	110	124	200
All levels	89	88	87	56	126	86	85	71	93	127
Rural										
Very low	94	77	64	40	108	50	81	54	89	174
Low	47	90	82	54	125	68	77	68	94	192
Middle	15	87	82	49	140	56	88	60	93	161
High	10	98	97	66	124	84	98	74	95	216
All levels	166	83	72	46	115	56	83	61	90	178

Building a National Nutrition Structure

The government of Colombia, with the cooperation of the Interamerican Cooperative Service of Public Health (SCISP), created the Laboratory of Nutritional Studies of the National Institute of Hygiene in 1943. The first National Institute of Nutrition was founded in 1947 as a branch office of the Ministry of Hygiene. This institute and the preceding organs dedicated their major efforts to the study of endemic goiter in the country and the iodization of salt on a national scale, as well as to the development of some applied nutrition activities for experimental purposes. In January 1963 the Congress approved a law creating a true National Institute of Nutrition, with its own budget and administrative autonomy. Its financing came from a proportion of the sales of iodized salt for human consumption, a state monopoly. [5]

The institute oriented itself toward the organization of a national plan of nutrition, to include recruitment and training of personnel from all levels, research, nutritional education, supplementary feeding, agricultural extension, treatment of malnourished children, technical assistance to medical schools and other educational centers for the establishment of a curriculum in the science of nutrition and, finally, technical assistance to institutional food services for improving the diet provided to specific groups of the population.

As a consequence of an administrative reform designed to regroup and reinforce the work of the different agencies of the health sector, in order to develop an integrated program of protection to the mother, child, and family, and to devote increasing resources to the national program of nutrition, the Congress approved Law 75 of 1968, [6] which established the Colombian Institute of Family Welfare (CIFW), incorporating in it, among other agencies, the National Institute of Nutrition, now the Department of Nutrition. Following formation of the new organization, the national budget for nutrition programs went up from 6 million Colombian pesos (approximately U.S. $300,000) to 86 million (approximately $4,300,000) in 1971 by means of a considerable increase in the share of the sales of iodized salt and in the contributions of the national government through the Ministry of Public Health and the Ministry of Education.

The Colombian Institute of Family Welfare is represented by a board of directors, presided over by the wife of the President and including the ministers of public health, education, agriculture, and justice, the general commander of the police, a representative of the church, and two of the national Congress. It has a general director, three technical directors and an administrative director. The Director of Nutrition is one of the three technical ones, working on the following areas: coordination of applied nutrition programs; supplementary feeding and food services; nutritional education and nutritional investigations. [7] The coordinating structure of the applied nutrition program is organized in 16 administrative sections (one for each of 15 states and Bogotá D.E.) for the execution of the programs at the state level. The Institute has 38 public health physicians trained in nutrition and 159 nonmedical nutritionists of whom 18 physicians and 122 nonmedical nutritionists work at the state level (see Table 3, p. 344).

Coordinating Structure of Nutrition Programs in Colombia
The complex factors determining the nutritional situation have necessitated the establishment of the Integrated Program of Applied Nutrition (PINA), a governmental mechanism of coordination among the sectors of health, education, agriculture, social assistance, and community development, which are the most directly involved in the solution of the problem. The institute organizes, directs, and gives financial help to this program, whose purpose is the coordination of the activities and resources of the entities executing actions intended for the improvement of the nutritional and feeding situation of the community.

The Colombian Institute of Family Welfare has a sectional coordinator, in the states where PINA is operating, who is a public health physician trained in nutrition. The coordinator is the executive secretary of a departmental coordinating committee, which includes the governor and his secretaries of education and agriculture, the chief of the Sectional Health Service, the regional director of the institute, and representatives of other governmental agencies and of semiofficial and private ones involved in the program. [8] This committee is responsible for planning the nutrition programs to be carried out in the state and for ensuring the technical and economic resources for their development. The technical orientation and the execution of the different programs are the responsibility of technical groups drawn from the entities represented in the coordinating committee, so no new governmental structures need be set up to execute the programs. [8] PINA has an operating fund in each state, financed by national (CIFW), state, and local contributions.

The National Nutrition Program in Colombia
The following nutrition and feeding programs are executed through the coordinating structure of PINA.

National Program of Nutritional Education and Supplementary Feeding (PRONENCA) To use the nutritional resources of national and foreign origin in the most efficient way, the government organized a National Plan of Food for Development (PLANALDE), in which the resources and actions directed to mothers and infants constitute PRONENCA. The major sources of nutritional help for PRONENCA are (1) the Agency for International Development (AID), through the voluntary agencies, CARE and CRS/CARITAS; and (2) the World Food Program (WFP) of the United Nations. PRONENCA is intended to protect the most susceptible groups against malnutrition (children under 5 years of age, schoolchildren, and mothers in the periods of pregnancy and lactation). These groups are covered through the governmental services of health and welfare and through the primary schools. [9]

The basic feature of this program is general nutritional education, given simultaneously with a supplementary feeding of significant nutritional value, by means of which a high proportion of the protein requirements for the above mentioned groups is covered. These supplements are mainly powdered milk, oil, meat, fish, cheese, wheat flour, and corn flour. In addition, a locally produced vegetable mixture of high nutritional value is included in the family supply. [10] Some details about the different subprograms and their accomplishments are presented in Table 2.

Treatment of Malnourished Children
The Nutrition Education and Rehabilitation Services (SERN) constitute an economical and effective method to treat advanced malnutrition at the level of the health organizations and to impart a practical education to mothers about aspects of nutrition and feeding. Simultaneously with these, service units of Nutrition Education and Food Demonstration are operating in numerous health agencies to develop preventive measures and take care of the moderate and mild cases of malnutrition. Special guidelines have been designed for the operation of these services and units. [11] At present there are 35 SERNs and 140 units of Nutrition Education and Food Demonstration operating in Colombia. In addition, routine treatment of malnourished children is carried out through the 1,120 health centers in the country.

Assistance to Institutional Food Services
Because adequate nutrition considerably affects not only the health status of a person but also his working capacity, [12] the institute has given a high priority to organizing and operating food services for population groups in institutions such as hospitals, educational institutes, factories, sport and youth organizations, armed forces, and other types of public and private

Table 2 Achievements in the WFP Areas and in the AID (CARE, CRS/CARITAS) Areas, during the second quarter of 1971, National Program of Nutritional Education and Supplementary Feeding.

Groups	WFP areas[a]			AID-CARE-CRS/CARITAS areas[b]		
	Population in the group[c]	Beneficiaries No.	%	Population in the group[d]	Beneficiaries No.	%
Schoolchildren	3,175,905	758,884	23.9	3,259,722	779,074	23.9
Preschool and infants	1,537,576	294,864	19.1	1,578,155	302,690	19.1
Mothers	459,959	90,142	19.6	472,098	92,531	19.6
Total	5,173,440	1,143,890	22.1	5,309,975	1,174,035	22.1
Total Population	10,951,398			11,240,420		

[a] Antioquia, Bolívar, Caldas, Huila, Tolima, Valle del Cauca, Bogotá D.E.
[b] Atlantico, Boyacá, Cauca, Cesar, Córdoba, Cundinamarca, Chocó, Guajira, Magdalena, Meta, Nariño, Norte de Santander, Quindío, Risaralda, Santander, Sucre and National Territories.
[c] Estimated population on July 1, 1971 on the basis of numbers from Department of Statistics.
[d] For the AID areas an estimate was made of the number of beneficiaries applying the same percentages of achievements obtained in the WFP areas.

enterprises. This assistance is complemented by supplying manuals of nutrition and buying guides to facilitate the planning, control, and spending of the respective budgets.

Nutrition Education

Nutrition education has received particular attention because of the generally low level of knowledge on nutrition and the insufficient training about feeding and diet imparted in the different professional centers. Courses have been established from the primary school to the university level, [7] along with promotion and development of educational programs for the general population. Besides this formal education, the program includes in-service training of field workers (multipliers) in basic aspects of nutrition and feeding. Abundant educational material and teaching guides are distributed for the different levels. The educational program is considered as a common denominator of all the other programs. [7]

Extension Programs—Agriculture and Animal Husbandry

Within the coordinating structure of PINA, the national agencies for agricultural extension are playing a fundamental role in achieving at the family level, particularly in rural areas, production of better quality food containing the nutritive substances most lacking in the region. For instance, the program aimed at production of concentrated feed for animals, sponsored and directed by the institute with the help of WFP and UNICEF, seeks to transform foods which by themselves are deficient in nutrition (cereals) into proteins (meat, eggs, milk) of a high nutritional value. The following subprograms deserve to be emphasized: (1) organization of community groups for training in the different techniques of agriculture and animal husbandry; (2) organization of PINA farms in the states to supply selected species of animals and vegetables to the poorest peasants; (3) production of concentrated feeds for animals, to be supplied to poor peasants; [13] and (4) supervised credit for farmers and cattle raisers, based on funds generated by the sale of the abovementioned concentrated foods, and directed to low-income peasants with the purpose of stimulating the establishment of small agriculture and cattle projects. [14]

Nutrition Research

The purpose of the research projects is to provide up-to-date knowledge of the magnitude and characteristics of the nutritional and feeding problems of the country and of their causes and, furthermore, to determine the most adequate means to contribute to their solution. Research enables the nutrition programs carried out by the institute to respond to the real needs of the country and to be implemented as efficiently as possible. New sources of proteins that can reach the most needy groups of the population are looked for constantly, and techniques for their better utilization are studied.

For the development of research programs the institute has received economic help and technical assistance from important universities and foundations. Among those helping have been Harvard and Cornell Universities, the Rockefeller Foundation, and the Food and Agriculture Organization of the United Nations (FAO).

Results of the National Nutrition Plan
The results are presented in terms of *efforts* (activities) and of *changes* observed in the nutritional status of specific groups of beneficiaries. There are serious difficulties involved in this second type of evaluation. The first difficulty arises from the fact that the nutrition programs in the country are basically a part of the National Health Plan. [15] Therefore, at a given moment, it is difficult to isolate the effects of the programs on the nutritional status of the population. For instance, in a health center where nutritional education and supplementary feeding are carried out, medical care, immunizations, and so on are provided simultaneously; these will of course contribute indirectly to the improvement of nutritional status. But we cannot and would not, for ethical reasons, constitute control groups of individuals who do not receive the benefits of the health and nutrition programs. Furthermore, the national scope of the programs considerably limits evaluation on a large scale, because its cost would take a large part of the operational budget. If we add to this the fact that a number of the underdeveloped countries do not have computer facilities to handle the information derived from these programs, it is easy to understand why comprehensive evaluation frequently is not possible. In view of these difficulties, evaluation is performed in Colombia on the basis of representative samples, utilizing some experimental designs.
Evaluation of Efforts
What follows is an evaluation of actions carried out in the development of the National Nutrition Plan during the period 1963 to 1971.
1. **Technical and economic resources.** The increase in technical and economic resources for nutrition programs in Colombia between 1963 and 1971 is presented in Table 3. As can be seen, these resources significantly increased, allowing a large expansion of the program.
2. **Nutritional education and supplementary feeding.** The actions carried out in the development of PRONENCA are included under this heading. Table 2 shows the coverage of this program in 1971 in relation to the vulnerable

344   Jaime Paez-Franco

groups (preschool children, schoolchildren, and mothers) in the two areas (WFP and AID) into which the country was divided on the basis of the origin of the supplements. In the WFP area a total of 772,830 beneficiaries received supplementary feeding (14.9 percent of the total susceptible groups); the coverage in the AID area was similar.

Table 3. Distribution of Economic Resources for the Implementation of PINA and PRONENCA According to the Financing Source, Colombia, 1970 and 1971

	1970		1971	
Financing source*	Col. $	%	Col. $	%
Central government (CIFW, Education Ministry)	10,648,748	32	15,571,096	26
State governments (municipalities, secretaries of health and education)	11,638,375	35	14,798,391	25
Community participation	7,367,674	22	19,624,314	33
Others	3,554,233	11	10,224,852	16
Total	33,209,030	100	60,218,653	100

*U.S. dollar exchange rate: 20.40

Table 4. National Program of Nutrition Education and Supplementary Feeding (PRONENCA), Colombia 1971. Percent of Dietary Recommended Allowances Supplied to Beneficiaries of the Different Subprograms.

Subprograms	Calories	Proteins	Fats	Carbohydrates
Children under 5				
SERNs*	46	99	91	22
Health centers	40	92	67	21
Day care centers	46	79	88	24
Hospital pediatric beds	26	48	26	22
Pregnant and nursing mothers				
Health centers	25	41	38	14
Schoolchildren				
Urban primary schools	17	38	13	16
Rural primary schools	6	18	9	4
Vacation camps	33	61	49	20
School hot lunch	17	31	25	10

*Nutrition Education and Rehabilitation Services

345 The National Nutrition Program in Colombia

Table 4 shows the percent of dietary recommended allowances supplied to the beneficiaries of the different subprograms of PRONENCA. The adequacy of calories for preschoolers oscillates between 26 percent in children from pediatric beds and 46 percent in children in the day care centers and in the Nutritional Education and Rehabilitation Centers. The adequacy of proteins for the same group ranges between 48 percent in children from pediatric beds and 99 percent in those in the Nutritional Education and Rehabilitation Centers. Simultaneously all the mothers and children included in the program received education on food and nutrition. The national budget for PINA and PRONENCA almost doubled in 1971. Increasing domestic contributions will facilitate the future phasing out of foreign aid, eventually making the program self-sufficient.

3. **Nutritional education.** The program of nutritional education has been developed at three basic levels: (1) the *professional level,* which includes activities carried out in the medical schools, nutrition and dietetics schools, nursery schools and others, directed at incorporating and assisting in the teaching of nutrition in these schools; (2) the *middle level,* which encompasses the activities involved in training teachers, auxiliary nurses, and other subprofessional personnel; and finally (3) the *community level,* which includes actions aimed directly at the population in general, through mass media communication.

In-service training achievements at the professional level in the period 1963-71 are presented in Table 5. A total of 2,887 professionals received the above-mentioned training in 2,868 hours of instruction. Table 6 shows what

Table 5. In-service Training on Food and Nutrition at the Professional Level, Colombia, 1963-1971

Professional Personnel	No. students	No. groups	Average students per group	No. hours	Average hours per group
Physicians	2,014	93	21	1,527	16
Agronomists and veterinarians	253	14	18	354	25
Dentists and bacteriologists	162	22	7	167	8
Nurses	204	17	11	236	13
Nonmedical nutritionists	20	1	20	36	36
Public health instructors	18	4	5	89	22
Home economists	10	1	10	40	40
Other professional personnel	206	11	18	419	38
Total	2,887	163	17	2,868	17

Table 6. Formal Training on Food and Nutrition at the Professional Level, Colombia, 1963-1971

Professional Schools	No. students	No. groups	Average students per group	No. hours	Average hours per group
Medicine	1,964	69	24	2,693	39
Dentistry	167	7	24	21	3
Nutrition and dietetics	492	29	16	3,971	130
Nursing	200	13	15	508	39
Biochemistry	128	5	25	168	33
Physical education	71	3	23	64	21
CRECENA*	107	4	53	1,180	590
Total	2,859	130	21	8,605	66

*Regional Center of Applied Economics and Nutrition

was carried out in formal teaching at the university level. A total of 2,859 students were instructed during 8,605 hours. At the middle level a total of 18,512 students were instructed during 11,659 hours. The in-service training at the middle level is summarized in Table 7; a total of 27,256 persons were trained, during 25,352 hours.

Finally, at the community level, 883,098 persons in 41,291 groups received education on food and nutrition, during 330,316 hours. In addition, 1,492 radio programs and 850 different short messages were repeatedly broadcast, 299 programs were televised, and 800 newspaper articles were written; furthermore, 938 different educational aids were prepared for use in the educational programs.

4. **Agricultural animal husbandry and extension.** The community extension groups organized from 1963 to 1971 are presented in Table 8. A total of 1,388 organizations was established, including 36,017 participants. At present, 80 percent of the established organizations are still functioning. In developing this program, 7,997 cattle projects, 10,911 agriculture projects, and 7,605 artisan projects were organized, a total of 26,513 projects. The production of concentrated food for animals reached 6,154 metric tons at a value of U.S. $550,000, of which U.S. $250,000 have been put into the revolving credit fund.

5. **Nutrition research.** A number of nutritional surveys and studies have been carried out, covering the following subjects: physical growth, in order to establish Colombian standards of weight and height; the prevalence of endemic goiter in the country and the iodine content in salt at the consumer level;

Table 7. In-service Training on Food and Nutrition at the Middle Level,
Colombia, 1963-1971

Type of personnel	No. students	No. groups	Average students per group	No. hours	Average hours per group
Supervisors, directors, and teachers	19,369	566	34	12,709	22
Sanitary inspectors	1,641	79	20	1,463	18
Auxiliary nurses	3,820	247	15	7,345	29
Community development leaders	239	14	17	478	34
Auxiliary nutritionists	30	4	7	86	21
Agricultural extensionists	190	23	8	3	35
Cooperative officers	240	1	240	24	24
Agricultural officers	193	5	39	84	17
Rural home economists and social workers	403	46	9	1,214	26
Peace Corps volunteers and Dutch volunteers	202	15	13	376	25
Other	929	44	19	770	19
Totals	27,256	1,044	26	25,352	24

Table 8. Associations of Agricultural Extension Organized by the Applied Nutrition
Program, Colombia, 1963-1971

Type of association	Organized 1963-71		Existing 1971	
	No. associates	No. members	No. associates	No. members
Farmers	148	2,326	105	1,591
Housewives' clubs	624	16,734	604	20,989
4 - H Clubs				
Agricultural cooperatives	356	7,082	246	4,144
Community development	30	1,960	31	2,796
Other rural organizations	58	3,901	51	4,000
Parents' clubs	21	1,563	11	312
School clubs	19	474	14	344
Adult education clubs	36	93	6	93
Others	96	1,884	22	298
Total	1,388	36,017	1,090	34,567

methodological aspects of nutrition surveys; acceptability of protein-rich foods, particularly vegetable mixtures; dietary management of malnourished children; iron deficiency anemia and the malabsorption syndrome. There have also been studies on recommended daily dietary allowances and food consumption for the Colombian population. As a complement to the above-mentioned studies, goals have been established for the production of foods required to meet the nutritional needs of the population in a reasonable time. These goals are evaluated yearly on the basis of the food balance sheet, regularly drawn up by the Department of Nutrition.

Current studies are: the project on malnutrition and mental development in cooperation with Harvard and Cornell Universities; a study on the acceptability of recipes using opaque-2 corn, which is being carried out with the economic collaboration of the Rockefeller Foundation; a study on diets of maximum nutritional value for the low-income Colombian population, with the aid of the Colombian Fund of Scientific Investigations (COLCIENCIAS); and a study on the design of vegetable mixtures to be utilized in the expansion and extension of PRONENCA. Finally, it should be noted that experimental designs are being drawn up for evaluating the effects of some programs on the nutritional status of the beneficiaries.

Evaluation of Changes

Under this heading are included the evolution of indirect indicators of nutritional status in the period between 1960 and 1968; the changes observed in the prevalence of endemic goiter; the changes in the nutritional status of a group of preschoolers covered by PRONENCA in 1970; and finally, the changes observed in basic knowledge on food and nutrition in a sample group of mothers who received nutritional education through the health centers.

1. Evolution of indirect indicators of nutritional status. Infant and preschool mortality rates decreased sharply from 100 and 17.6 in 1960 to 65 and 9.7 in 1968, respectively. Nevertheless, these rates continue high as compared to those of industrialized countries. The mortality rate of children under five years of age as a percentage of the general mortality shows a significant reduction, from 51.8 percent in 1960 to 43.7 percent in 1968. Finally, the mortality rates for measles and diarrhea in the period 1960-68 do not show an important reduction, remaining markedly higher than those of developed countries.

2. Prevalence of endemic goiter. The prevalence of endemic goiter in 183,000 students studied in 1945 was 52.6 percent; [16] in seven localities of the state of Caldas the prevalence was 83 percent. The prevalence dropped to 34 percent in 1952, after two years of experimental distribution of iodized salt in these localities. [17] A national program of salt iodization for human consumption was started in 1960 under the supervision of the National Institute of Nutrition. In order to evaluate the results of this program after three years of operation, a third survey was carried out in these seven localities, using the same methodology as in the previous studies. The prevalence of endemic goiter showed then a dramatic drop to 1.8 percent (Table 9). [18] Recent studies carried out by the Ministry of Public Health and the Association of Medical Schools reported the general prevalence of endemic goiter in the general population as 3.6 percent. [19] By means of the iodized salt program, endemic goiter has been eradicated as a public health problem in Colombia.

3. Changes in the nutritional status of children covered by PRONENCA. To overcome the methodological problem arising from the fact that no control groups were constituted to accurately measure the effect of the supplementary feeding on the nutritional status of the beneficiaries, in the present evaluation the weight and height increments achieved during the supplementary feeding program are compared with those observed in the high socioeconomic class of Bogotá. [20] If the beneficiaries of PRONENCA, who belong to a low socioeconomic class, achieve weight and height increments equal to or higher than those of the upper class children, under conditions in which the only change introduced is the supplementary feeding, one might assume that the increases are attributable to the program.

The previous comparison was made using the Mann Whitney Test. [21] Similarly, this evaluation shows the initial and final distribution of the children according to the classification of their nutritional status. This classification was carried out on the basis of standards of weight expected for height, as elaborated by the Department of Nutrition of the Colombian Institute of Family Welfare. [20] Infants under 1 year of age constituted 9.3 percent; 79 percent were children from 1 to 4 years; and 11.7 percent were children over 4 years of age. The same proportions of boys and girls were studied. The distribution of children according to their nutritional status, by type of service providing the food supplement, at the outset and at the end of the program, is presented in Table 10. Important changes in nutritional status can be noted; 13.4 percent of the children moved from a malnourished to the well-nourished status.

The evaluation of the effect of the supplementary feeding on the nutritional status of the beneficiaries is, of course, incomplete and not very sensitive

350   Jaime Paez-Franco

Table 9. Effect of Salt Iodization Program on Endemic Goiter Prevalence in Schoolchildren of Seven Municipalities of the State of Caldas, Colombia, Before and After Consumption of Iodized Salt.

Municipalities	1945[a]			1952[b]			1965[c]		
	Examined	With goiter	%	Examined	With goiter	%	Examined	With goiter	%
Aguadas	1,067	958	89.8	618	174	28.2	980	15	1.5
Aranzazu	357	312	87.4	391	110	28.1	1,087	20	1.8
Chinchiná	503	431	85.7	649	178	27.5	1,059	7	0.7
Manizales	4,380	3,418	78.0	3,278	1,229	37.4	5,252	127	2.4
Neira	487	445	91.3	412	153	37.2	1,044	8	0.8
Pácora	656	614	93.5	901	317	35.2	1,048	19	1.8
Salamina	612	528	86.2	262	43	16.4	1,696	26	1.5
Total	8,062	6,706	83.1	6,511	2,204	33.9	12,166	222	1.8

[a]First National Goiter Survey, 1945.
[b]After two years of experimental consumption of iodized salt, 1952.
[c]After three years of nationwide iodization of salt, 1965.

Table 10. Nutritional Status* of Children Who Received Food Supplementation, at the Outset and at the End of Program; Preliminary Evaluation of the National Program of Nutritional Education and Supplementary Feeding, 1971.

| Type of service providing supplement | Normal | | Malnutrition | | | | | | | | Total | |
| | | | First degree | | Second degree | | Third degree | | | | | |
	% outset	% end	% outset	% end	% outset	% end	% outset	% end			% outset	% end
Health centers	52.1	65.2	17.4	16.1	13.3	9.4	17.2	9.3			47.9	34.8
Nutritional rehabilitation centers	- -	29.3	13.2	17.9	28.3	19.8	58.5	33.0			100.0	70.7
Day care centers	66.1	86.2	15.6	7.4	11.9	5.5	6.4	0.9			33.9	13.8
Other services	46.6	64.4	20.1	18.2	12.8	11.9	20.5	5.5			53.4	35.6
Total	51.6	65.0	17.4	16.1	13.5	9.5	17.5	9.4			48.4	35.0

*According to classification based on the comparison of current weight value against that expected for height.

since it only shows the evolution of those children who really succeeded in passing from one category to another in the classification. Nevertheless, a number of chronically malnourished children having marked deficiencies in weight and height did not succeed in reaching the "normal" zone in the classification, appearing then as malnourished children, in spite of adequate clinical and biochemical gains and sustained progressive increases of weight and height. [22]

Under these conditions, it is more accurate to evaluate these effects by comparing the weight and height increments achieved by the children to those observed in a control group or to those expected according to local standards. [20] Applying this second alternative, the analysis of the increments was carried out, grouping the children into normal and malnourished categories according to the weight for height classification. [22] In Table 11 the comparison between the weight and height increments of the initially normal and those observed in normal children of the high socioeconomic level of Bogotá is presented. There were no statistically significant differences between the abovementioned values, demonstrating that the normal supple-

Table 11. Comparison Between Weight and Height Increments of Initially Normal Children Who Received Food Supplementation and Their Expected Increments Using the Colombian Standard; Preliminary Evaluation of the National Program of Nutritional Education and Supplementary Feeding, 1971, Using the Mann-Whitney Test.

		Weight Increments			
Type of service providing supplement	Number	Sum ranks observed weight increments	Sum ranks expected weight increments	Z	P
Health centers	4,571	20,747,447	21,045,207	1.18	.23
Day care centers	72	5,118	5,322	.41	.68
Other services	102	10,131	10,779	.77	.44

		Height Increments			
Type of service providing supplement	Number	Sum ranks observed height increments	Sum ranks expected height increments	Z	P
Health centers	4,571	20,757,540	21,035,114	1.10	.27
Day care centers	72	5,026	5,414	.77	.44
Other services	102	9,713	11,197	1.76	.07

mented children had similar increments to those observed in children from a high socioeconomic level.

The comparison between the weight and height increments of the initially malnourished children and those observed in the upper-class children of Bogotá is presented in Table 12. In relation to weight increments, the comparisons showed statistically significant differences in favor of the supplemented children. Regarding height increments, all the differences were statistically significant in favor of the children benefited by PRONENCA, with the exception of those serviced by health centers; there the increments favored the Bogotá samples.

4. Changes in basic food and nutrition knowledge. Using a sample of 10.6 percent of the mothers who took part in the regular PRONENCA educational talks during 1970, at the end of the program 83 percent of their answers to nutrition questions were right as compared to 59 percent at the outset—an increase of 24 percent resulting from this educational program (Table 13).

Table 12. Comparison Between Weight and Height Increments of Initially Malnourished Children Who Received Food Supplementation and Their Expected Increments Using the Colombian Standard; Preliminary Evaluation of the National Program of Nutritional Education and Supplementary Feeding 1971, Using the Mann-Whitney Test.

		Weight Increments			
Type of service providing supplement	Number	Sum ranks observed weight increments	Sum ranks expected weight increments	Z	P
Health centers	4,195	18,110,396	17,086,751	4.59	.001
Nutritional rehabilitation centers	106	13,480	9,098	4.91	.001
Day care centers	37	1,723	1,052	3.62	.001
Other services	117	14,895	12,600	2.22	.02

		Height Increments			
Type of service providing supplement	Number	Sum ranks observed height increments	Sum ranks expected height increments	Z	P
Health centers	4,195	16,972,494	18,224,653	5.63	.001
Nutritional rehabilitation centers	106	12,381	10,197	2.40	.02
Day care centers	37	1,589	1,186	2.10	.03
Other services	117	11,708	15,787	3.90	.001

Table 13. Evaluation of Nutrition Knowledge in a Sample Formed by 10.6 Percent of the Mothers Covered by the Health Services During 1970*; Preliminary Evaluation of the National Program of Nutritional Education and Supplementary Feeding, 1971

States	No. selected mothers	No. answers	Initial evaluation No. right answers	Initial evaluation %	Final evaluation No. right answers	Final evaluation %	Increase achieved by education (%) in no. right answers
Antioquia	1,986	19,860	13,821	70	17,011	86	16
Bogotá	1,616	16,160	9,388	58	12,271	76	18
Bolívar	1,092	10,920	6,123	56	9,000	82	26
Caldas	147	1,393	925	66	1,294	93	27
Huila	212	2,120	1,135	54	1,681	79	25
Tolima	447	4,470	2,642	59	3,649	82	23
Valle	1,116	11,160	5,054	45	9,719	87	42
Total	6,616	66,083	39,088	59	54,625	83	24

*Total number of mothers assisted: 62,414. Sample selected for the study (10.6%): 6,616.

Summary

The geographic, demographic, educational, economic, and health conditions of Colombia which have been presented demonstrate that Colombia has one of the highest growth rates in the world, simultaneously with a low income per capita, a low educational level, a high unemployment index, and high morbidity and mortality rates from controllable diseases, elements constituting the relevant components of underdevelopment. There is a high prevalence of malnutrition in children under five years of age belonging to the low socioeconomic level, and the diet is low in calories, proteins, and other essential nutrients. The National Nutrition Program developed under the direction of the Colombian Institute of Family Welfare has as its purpose to alleviate the deficiencies described, and this paper has indicated what measures have been taken and what results have been achieved.

References

1. Rueda-Williamson, R. El programa de nutrición aplicada base del plan nacional de nutrición. Bol. Ofic. Sanit. Panamericana 68:187, 1970.

2. Departamento Administrativo Nacional de Estadistica. El Pais en Cifras. 4th ed. Bogotá: Imprenta Nacional, 1968.

3. Ordonez, A. Informe al Honorable Congreso de la Republica, Agosto 1966-Julio 1970. Bogotá, 1970.

4. Colombia Information Service. Colombia Today. Vol. 6. New York, 1971.

5. Instituto Colombiano de Bienestar Familiar (ICBF), Dirección de Nutrición. Informe sobre Siete Años de Programas de Nutrición en Colombia, Enero de 1963 a Enero de 1970. Publicación DIR 70-01. Bogotá, 1970.

6. ICBF. Ley 75 de 1968. Bogotá, 1968.

7. Paez, J. Los programas de nutrición del Instituto Colombiano de Bienestar Familiar. Paper presented at Primera Conferencia Nacional sobre Familia, Infancia y Juventud, Bogotá, March 2-7, 1970.

8. ICBF, Dirección de Nutrición. El Programa Integrado de Nutrición Aplicada (PINA). Bogotá, 1970.

9. Paez, J. El Programa Nacional de Educación Nutricional y Complementación alimentaria (PRONENCA) en el Plan Nacional de Alimentos para el desarrollo. Paper presented at Congresos de Pediatría IX Panamericano, II Latinoamericano, y IX Colombiana. Bogotá, July 25-30, 1970.

10. Paez, J. Situación Actual de las Mezclas Vegetales en Colombia. Recursos Proteínicos en America Latina. Publicación INCAP L-1 Guatemala, 1971, pp. 493-503.

11. Paez, J. Nutrition education and recuperation services in Colombia, organization and operation. Paper presented at the Conference on Nutrition Rehabilitation and Mother-craft Centers, Bogotá, 1969.

12. Tavera, J., et al. Nutrición y desarrollo socioeconomico. Paper presented at Primera Conferencia Nacional sobre Familia, Infancia y Juventud, Bogotá, March 2-7, 1970.

13. ICBF. Plan de Operaciones del Proyecto: Programa Mundial de Alimentos—Colombia—191.

14. ICBF. Reglamento Prestamos des Crédito Agropecuario Supervisado.

15. ICBF. Minsalud. Información sobre Nutrición y Alimentación para el Plan Nacional de Salud.

16. Parra, H. Bocio simple en Colombia y yodización artificial de la sal. Revista Colombiana de Pediatría 8:176, 1948.

17. Gongora, J., et al. Dos años de tratamiento del bocio simple con sal yodada en el Departamento de Caldas. Rev. Med. y Cir. 16:357, 1952.

18. Rueda-Williamson, R., et al. La efectividad de la yodación de la sal en la prevención del bocio endémico en Colombia. I. Resultados en escolares de Caldas. Archivos Latinoamericanos de Nutrición 16:65, 1966.

19. Ministerio de Salud Pública y Asociación de Facultades de Medicina. Estudio de Recursos Humanos para la Salud y Educación Médica en Colombia; evidencia clinica. Bogotá, 1969.

20. Rueda-Williamson, R., H. Luna, J. Ariza, F. Pardo, J. Mora. Estudio seccional de crecimiento, desarrolla y nutrición en 12,138 niños de Bogotá, Colombia. I. Tablas de peso y talla en niños Colombianos. ICBF Publicación TRI-31. Bogotá, 1968.

21. Snedecor, G. and W. Cochran. Statistical Methods. 6th ed. Iowa City: Iowa State University Press, 1969, p. 130.

22. Mora, J., F. Pardo, and H. Luna. Métodos simplificados para la evaluación del crecimiento y del estado nutricional en niños menores de seis años. ICBF Publicación TRP-97. Bogotá, 1970.

36 The Nutrition Movement in India

Asok Mitra

Secretary Planning Commission, New Delhi

I

At the beginning of 1971 the *Economic and Political Weekly* of Bombay published a monograph called *Poverty in India* by V. M. Dandekar and Nilakantha Rath. The authors produced two tables purporting to show, state by state, the percentage of rural and urban populations with inadequate intake of calories in 1961-62. For all India, 30 percent of the rural population and 46.5 percent of the urban population were estimated to be below the desired calorie intake of 2,194 for rural areas and 2,159 for urban areas. Even allowing for the defects of the original consumption surveys—inasmuch as a large amount of homegrown vegetables or locally raised animal proteins perhaps did not go into the accounting, for example in Kerala—the dimensions were alarming by any standards. The authors projected estimates for 1980-81 of the per capita consumption of different sections of rural and urban populations, concluding that if the past trend continued in the coming decade, the overall growth in income and consumption would be smaller than that assumed in the plan perspective. The consumer expenditures of the poorest 10 percent in the urban area might well be at the level of the corresponding sections of the rural population. For another 40 to 50 percent of the urban population, though their consumer expenditures would be somewhat higher than those of the corresponding section of the rural population, the difference might not always be enough to compensate for the higher cost of urban living. Thus even in 1980 there could still be a serious food gap, caused by continuing lack of purchasing power.

The magnitude of the problem is illustrated in another way; at present there are about 27 million families, totaling roughly 110 million people, who operate between 5 to 30 hundredths of an acre of land per capita. Any program of land distribution that would give these families half an acre of land per capita to enable them to become self-sufficient and to raise enough food for themselves, and, some to spare for other necessities, would require a transfer of 42 million acres of land now held by families who own more than, say, 20 acres. The 1971 census put the number of agricultural laborers in India at 47 million. Assuming that a family of agricultural laborers would consist of an average of five members and that the wife works in 50 percent of the families, the total population subsisting on agriculture, without land, would be about 150 million.

This group at any rate, and perhaps those of slightly higher status and income, cannot afford to pay for any food but what is grown on the spot and processed locally. This explains why most farmers in India store their cereals in the shell and bring out only those quantities from their small bins that they will eat during the week. It is unrealistic to expect that such a population will adopt new, sophisticated, unconventional foods whose consumption would involve processing, packaging, transport, warehousing, and wholesale and retail outlets that the traffic would not bear. These populations will have to rely on their own resources of processing food and conserving as much of its nutritional value as possible.

The problem boils down to a deficiency in calorie intake, and this is of great significance. Protein intake through cereals and small quantities of pulses and vegetables and very occasionally other proteins, which otherwise would be considered adequate, becomes inadequate in the face of this calorie insufficiency, as the protein is used for the purpose of providing energy. For if the food intake is deficient in the amount of calories needed for the body, the protein in the food is called upon to provide the calorie deficiency before it can start performing its legitimate function. Protein malnutrition in India at many levels, particularly in the earlier age-groups, is conditioned to a considerable extent by the inadequate level of calorie intake.

Appreciation of this fact has an important bearing on the approach toward control and prevention of protein-calorie malnutrition. A large and rapid increase in protein availability for a population of India's size is something out of India's present economic reach, particularly if it is imagined in terms of processed and marketed food with a profit ratio at wholesale and retail points. It has, therefore, been argued that crash programs for the invention of protein foods will remain only programs on paper, possibly diverting attention from the more modest but more practicable things that can be done by gradual development, and that the way of closing the protein gap must be first to close the food gap.

The first and most important program in this country in the field of nutrition will thus continue to be the Green Revolution, including multiple cropping and the intensive cultivation of high-yielding varieties of cereals. The major investment will continue to be on the inputs of the Green Revolution and its extension machinery. This program has achieved a breakthrough in wheat, and it has achieved reasonable success in coarse grains and shows promise in rice; these three will continue to be the main sources of calories and proteins for a long time.

The crucial ingredient in a multiple-cropping program will be evolving short
duration varieties of seeds for different crops containing high nutrition content. The success of this program will depend on ground water mobilization
and rural electrification. The number of harvests of vegetables, pulses, and,
more recently, short-duration soyabean can all be multiplied many times
over, with a gain to nutrition. Some of the more important research and extension programs center on pulses and oilseeds, commodities neglected so far
or unresponsive to research investment, but which carry the key to nutrition
for the poor people. It is now increasingly realized that apart from the agricultural and agronomic investment in these areas, a suitable pricing policy will
have to be brought to bear.

Simultaneously, research effort has been stepped up on the breeding of new
cereal varieties, especially wheat with high protein content. It also seems
possible to extend the genetic enrichment of cereal protein with lysine and
pulse protein with methionine. Milk, eggs, fish, and animal products are receiving attention in research and extension on the one hand and field endeavor on the other. They are encouraging signs that more and more peasants
find it more and more profitable to divert land to ruminant husbandry and
poultry farming, although these are still limited to specific tracts.

II

Attention has lately turned to improving the blue-collar worker's nutrition
through food served at workers' canteens, even as the realization grows that
productivity per worker in Indian factories could optimally increase with
steady reinforcement of his diet not only with calories but carefully selected,
conveniently priced proteins. Here malnutrition plagues productivity even as
the lack of protein-calorie-balanced school meals contributes to human and
economic wastage because of the many dropouts in primary and secondary
schools. Fortunately, the quest is on not only for least-cost solutions but also
for the development of cheap unconventional foods. With respect to low-cost
protein, considerable progress has been made in recent years on processed or
extruded foods from groundnut flour and soyabean products. The Protein
Foods Association of India, in collaboration with the government, is making
experiments in low-cost protein foods and weaning foods; experiments on
cottonseed flour protein isolates and protein isolate toned milk have had
measures of success. Emphasis has been directed to semiconventional foods
through fortification of wheat products, salt, and bread with requisite levels
of calcium, iron, vitamins, and proteins. Spectacular results have been ob-

tained by the administration of iodized salt in endemic goiter areas. In the production of Balahar and low-cost protein foods there have been intensified experiments on their quality and consumer acceptability as well as their keeping properties. The scheme for the production of cottonseed flour has concentrated on extracting human nutrients from cottonseed. In the quest for least-cost solutions, attention has veered to an integrated systems approach in an effort to relate the world of agriculture to that of food processing and distribution and to the social and economic milieu of the consumer. A rather unique systems study has been undertaken by the government of Tamil Nadu (see p. 303). This analysis holds the promise of revealing relationships hitherto overlooked and suggesting answers to some of the questions raised in this paper.

III

On any showing, the national emphasis must continue to be for a long time on raising the per capita income and consumption of the lowest 40 percent of the population by such programs as will enable them to produce, buy, and consume more food each day of their lives. This means that the major purpose of the plans must be not only to intensify and enlarge those sectors of national development that have already been identified and are being supported, but to provide more employment and assure more purchasing power at least to the lowest 40 percent of the population in rural and urban areas. This will call for a rapid and extensive expansion of employment opportunities, sustained and augmented from year to year through large programs of rural public works, the extension of the Green Revolution, and expansion of rural and urban jobs and services in the primary, secondary, and tertiary sectors, supplemented by construction programs in the public and private sectors. While it is by no means suggested that the current nutrition programs should be anything but augmented, subject to availability of resources, the obvious direction for future effort is a rapid expansion of employment and income opportunities, which alone can provide the most enduring base for any worthwhile national program of nutrition.

The second major goal—which is likely to yield results more substantial than even direct investment programs for expectant and nursing mothers, infants, and preschool children—is the improvement of environmental sanitation in villages and towns, the safeguarding and assurance of a drinking water supply, safe and proper disposal of sewage and wastes, and a universally enforced immunization program against tetanus for expectant mothers and against smallpox, the enteric diseases, diphtheria, and tuberculosis in infants and very young children.

These preventable diseases take a bigger toll of human efficiency and human lives than the gravest malnutrition, and their prior removal is bound to reduce the incidence of malnutrition sharply and bring the eradication of malnutrition within the realm of practical politics. A determined and effective potable water supply program for the 3,000 urban areas and 550,000 villages will mean immeasurably more enduring nutritional dividends than the most assiduously pursued feeding program. Rigorous enforcement of the adulteration laws will be a cheap way of assuring nutrition, beside which many of the current programs must appear rather "precious" and far less rewarding. The unfinished public health revolution deserves to be completed to confer the full benefits of the positive nutrition programs. Incidentally, it is on the instrumentality of the public health and sanitation machinery and the immunization network that the worthwhile nutrition programs of the country can be made to ride piggyback with the greatest economic efficiency and the maximum economy of human effort.

IV

But these measures by themselves will not cater to the special needs of several particularly vulnerable categories of the population that are almost defenseless against malnutrition. Nearly two-thirds of expectant mothers belonging to the poorer sections of the community suffer from malnutrition—in fact, mortality continues to be high. For the prevention of critical malnutrition damage, the nutritional needs of infants in the womb and in the first year of life, of young children of preschool and school age, also must be looked after. These are the most important target populations, whose nutritional needs will have to be reinforced by an adequate program of immunization and the removal of deficiencies in vitamins and minerals. The Fourth Five-Year Plan (1969-74) recognized these areas and underlined several requirements designed to match administrative efficiency with better nutritional delivery.

First, resources being limited, it was necessary to establish priorities with reference to age-groups, classes, and areas. Second, it was important to improve the efficiency and existing coverage of the organizations and delivery systems which serve the needs of priority age-groups, classes, and areas. Third, programs of distribution were to be invariably reinforced by specially assisted programs of handling, production, processing, and supply.

Among the specific measures addressed to special target groups and geographical areas, the major ones are (1) feeding programs for schoolchildren administered by the state governments; (2) special feeding program of the Department of Social Welfare for (a) preschool children, (b) tribal areas throughout the country, and (c) slum areas of metropolitan cities; (3) feeding programs of the Department of Social Welfare for preschool children of ages 3 to 6 years; (4) Applied Nutrition Program of the Department of Community Development (which started during the Third Five-Year Plan period with the help of UNICEF); (5) Composite Nutrition Program of the Department of Community Development in conjunction with state governments for women and preschool children; (6) prophylaxis against nutritional anemia in mothers and children of the Ministry of Health and Family Planning; and by (7) the program of the Health and Family Planning Department for the control of blindness in children caused by vitamin A deficiency.

V

The most critical target needing direct intervention is composed of the expectant and nursing mother and the infant up to 6 months of age. A number of experiments at the National Institute of Nutrition at Hyderabad and at Safdarjang Hospital, New Delhi, have demonstrated that a special nutrition intervention program in the last trimester produced babies with significantly higher birth weights and improved health records. More than 17 percent of births in India are premature, and this high incidence is caused partly by malnutrition. Premature babies have a lower rate of survival, and all children who experience fetal undernutrition are born with inadequate physical reserves of stored nutrients. Deficient birth stores of vitamins A and B12, iron, and folic acid can seriously impair the child's resistance to infection since these nutrients are not fully provided in breast milk.

At any one time in India there are at least 5 million expectant mothers in their last trimester. This is the critical point at which programs should begin, and statistically this presents a manageable and identifiable target. It is possible to provide proper food through the health system, under controls. The actual program, which will depend upon the efficiency with which the maternity and child welfare clinics work, must concern itself with the mother and consequently with the health delivery system. It can work if the 25,000 health centers throughout the country are staffed and equipped to deliver a useful package of benefits including supplemental precooked food and medical attention, including immunization of mother and child. Such a program would also serve to put the rural mother firmly on the road to family planning.

The most important task is to deliver adequate quantities of vitamins A and B12, iron, and folic acid to the expectant mother and fetus. Ideally, this program ought to be reinforced by serving a small quantity of food to the expectant mother in addition to the nutrient. Paul Cifrino has calculated that a program reaching three-quarters of all the five million mothers with 200 grams of food per day would require 270,000 tons, which happens to be the amount of foodstuffs used in the school midday meal program, which reaches only 10 percent of the children of school age.

The Khanna study, made by John B. Wyon and John E. Gordon, has demonstrated that there is a compelling difference in the death rate beyond 6 months between those children who do not receive any solid food and those who do—even where the food causes digestive difficulties and weanling diarrhea. Any solid food during these months is immensely better than none.

Shanti Ghosh of Safdarjang Hosptial, New Delhi, has argued that the answer to the problem of malnutrition in this age group lies partly in the more effective use by the village community of the locally available inexpensive foods in proper combinations. Education, rather than the physical availability of food, is the most effective instrument in this field because the infant at this stage cannot take more than 75 to 100 grams of cooked solids. Contrary to popular notions, knowledge of how to use easily available foods is largely lacking even among the middle and upper and educated classes. The best results may be achieved when this education is reinforced by a universal program of immunization of the expectant mother and the infant child against tetanus and the communicable diseases, supported by programs of combating intestinal pests and parasites.

Although the use of processed, high protein foods is a tempting alternative, there are inevitable problems of transport, storage, and acceptance. It has often been debated whether the solution to the problem of preschool-child malnutrition in India—where 80 percent of the population lives in rural areas and under economic conditions in which they can hardly afford the type of food they need—lies in the dissemination of processed foods, and whether these can be provided in the right quantities and their intake sustained to the point of making a significant impact on the nutrition situation. Another important reality which interferes with delivery systems even in village communities is the differences in levels of income and status between sections of the population, which can make nonsense of the original intentions and result in most of the food going to the richer segments. Instruction on how to feed solid foods of local origin to infants and preschool children should therefore receive high priority, along with a program informing people of the greater nutrition value in rice gruel, coarse-milled cereals, and other local products that have tended to go out of fashion by a kind of Gresham's Law in the world of the poor man's food.

VI

An associated area that promises to yield enduring results is family planning. The Khanna study [1] and studies by other authors, particularly Carl E. Taylor, [2] of several villages in Punjab show that, among the programs likely to make a profound impact on the health and nutritional status of pre-school children in the long run, the family planning program, which aims at limiting the family size to three children, is extremely important. The level at which births are limited is largely determined by the felt need of a surviving son. This level has been high because 30 percent of the children did not survive the first two years, the single most important cause of child mortality being malnutrition; the crisis period could be clearly identified as between the child's sixth and twenty-fourth month.

C. Gopalan, [3] in an analysis of admissions to pediatric wards, shows that of several hundred cases of severe protein-calorie malnutrition only 39 percent of the stricken children belonged to birth orders 1 to 3, as against 61 percent belonging to birth orders 4 and above. It was significant that although a greater proportion of children of the earlier birth orders were among *general* admissions to the hospital, most of the cases of malnutrition were in children in the later birth orders.

In another field study covering 1,400 preschool children, Gopalan [4] found that while 32 percent of the children belonging to birth orders 4 and above exhibited various signs of malnutrition, only 17 percent of the children of earlier birth orders showed such evidences. The heights and weights of preschool children showed a negative correlation with family size. Even allowing for normal distribution of children in the two birth order groups in the community these data would show that 62 percent of all nutritional deficiency states in preschool children are encountered in children of birth orders 4 and above. This would suggest that even under the current economic and living conditions, mere limitation of family size to three children could bring down the incidence of malnutrition in preschool children in India by about 60 percent. The prospect would improve still further if one took into account the possible impact of countrywide family planning on the nation's general economic status and the supply of food resources.

The rapidly growing concern for nutrition and matching action programs for enriching the quality of life are but a reflection of the problems of economic and population growth and of the requirements of distributive justice. Health, nutrition, and family planning are now viewed as facets of a single task of preventing waste and improving the nation's human resources and productivity. Of these three, nutrition will continue to demand the most pervasive attention and to challenge our organizational and administrative ingenuity for a long time to come.

References

1. Wyon, John B., and John E. Gordon. *The Khanna Study: Population Problems in the Rural Punjab.* Cambridge: Harvard University Press, 1971.

2. Taylor, Carl E. Population trends in an Indian village. *Sci. Amer.* 223:106-114, 1970.

3. Gopalan, C. Nutritional status: Needs and services. Paper presented at Seminar on the Preschool Child, December, 1970.

4. Gopalan, C. Nutritional status: Needs and services (rev. 1971).

37 Nutrition in National Development: The Japanese Experience

Toshio Oiso
Director, National Institute of Nutrition, Tokyo

Planning the nutritional improvement of a nation is a problem of fundamental importance. I have found it extremely difficult to make people realize that importance; and even when it is recognized, there are still many barriers lying ahead that hinder establishment of a national policy on nutritional improvement.

There are two main reasons: first, national improvement of nutrition takes time. Government and political leaders do not consent to this long-run plan, but insist on an effective policy that can be accomplished within a short period so that their services can be visible to the voter. As votes cast from special groups are guaranteed, politicians tend to bestow favors on such groups and to show less interest in achievements that are broader and that contribute to the benefit of a nation but that do not produce votes.

Second, politicians have the impression that raising the national economic level will naturally result in better nutrition and thus they always yield the priority to economic development. The financial circles of the government are fascinated by figures indicating short-term benefits, and at the same time are concerned with self-preservation, so that a basic, long-range policy like improvement in nutrition is overlooked. Even members of the medical profession, closely concerned with the health of the people, are very keen on dramatic therapeutics and show less interest in unglamorous nutritional improvement.

In industry, businessmen employing many laborers are likely to resist improving the nutritional status of their employees on the ground that it may bring about rising expectations as to living standards, leading to demands for a raise in wages.

Another decisive group concerned with improvement of nutrition is composed of entrepreneurs engaged in the production and distribution of food. They tend to work up a production plan that will maximize the producer's advantage. With regard to importation of food they first take care not to exert pressure on the producer and thus seem to neglect the benefit of the consumer. From the standpoint of nutritional improvement it is therefore exceedingly difficult to attain impartial allocation of precious resources.

Food shortages in Japan started in 1941, and the situation yearly became more grave. Up to around 1947 the nutritional status of the nation was very low and Japan suffered severe damage: physical development of the younger generation was suspended and malnutrition caused adults to lose their will to work. Such a deplorable food situation, experienced for the first time in this country, called attention to the importance of nutrition and gave us who are engaged in improving the nutritional status of the nation a very good opportunity to make the politicians realize the importance of nutrition. In spite of the gravity of the nutrition problem, however, the concept of economic priority usually still prevailed.

Looking back to the prewar period, a National Institute of Nutrition was established in 1920, which conducted fruitful studies concerning nutritional improvement and acted to upgrade community nutrition on a small scale. From this experience we clearly recognized the necessity of a specialist—the nutritionist who educates the public, instructs people on the balance of nutrients, and prepares recipes for special purposes. In 1924, a training school for nutritionists was first established. Junior high school graduates received special education for one to two years; a few graduate nutritionists commenced activities in 1925. They were qualified as nutritionists by the government and training facilities of this kind rapidly increased. In order to raise the social status of the nutritionist it was important to educate the public whenever there was an opportunity, as their level of knowledge on nutrition was low. The basic importance of this policy was clearly shown, and training of specialists spread throughout the nation. With an increase in specialists in nutrition, the next problem was to secure employment for them.

In 1946, the National Nutrition Survey was first conducted, to locate and acquire food for the population. In the same year the Nutrition Section was set up in the Public Health Bureau of the Ministry of Health and Welfare in order to execute a unified nutrition policy, which provided a strong background for national development. The Council on Food and Nutrition, headed by the prime minister, was established in the Economic Stabilization Board, under the Office of the Prime Minister. Though this council was considered appropriate to contribute to national development, the conception was too broad and the time was not ripe. Accordingly this organ ceased to exist after a period of two years. During this period, however, the diets of hospitals, factories, and other mass feeding facilities were improved.

Community cooking in the rural farming districts had already been practiced in the busy harvest season. Improvement of meals provided in the boarding houses of cotton mills lowered morbidity and absence rates of the workers, resulting in an increase in production. Businessmen came to realize the value of nutritional improvement in raising profits.

The school lunch program came into practice on a wide scale; the physical status of children subsequently soon improved. This program was started by the Ministry of Education as an aid to parents who could not provide lunch to be taken to school, because of the shortage of food. The program was thence expanded to educate both parent and child on proper nutrition.

In 1952, we requested politicians to enact a law authorizing a nutritional improvement agency. Although the government at that time did not give consent, a strong movement throughout the nation led to the cooperation of a large number of politicians. Finally the Nutrition Improvement Law, [1] a rather unusual law, was passed. The establishment of a Food and Nutrition Committee, prescribed in this law, gave an opportunity for many scientists, other experienced and knowledgeable people, and prominent governmental officials to participate in discussions of national nutrition problems.

The aims of this committee were: first, to set up a section to scrutinize nutritional requirements of the Japanese [2] in order to decide the amount of nutrients necessary to improve physical status and fitness; second, to estimate the amount of food required to furnish these nutrients; third, to make the results public.

Government officials in charge of food production and allocation first thought these objectives only scientists' academic theories. But by demonstrating standard values of nutrients to the public we tried to gain their approval by education through the media. It was proved that the consumer can be given the incentive to make demands concerning the production and importation of food, influencing the producer to change his policy and produce food suitable to meet the consumer's local food habits.

Consequently, nutrition gradually became a consideration in planning food allocation at the national level. The increase in the intake of various nutrients, especially the quality and amount of protein foods, is surprising. Along with improvement of the nutritional value of foods, changes in the kinds of foods and in dietary patterns were seen. This improvement was followed by an abrupt drop in the mortality rate from beriberi and tuberculosis and in the infant mortality rate. [3]

Though all of this cannot be attributed to nutritional improvement alone, the physical status of the Japanese population has attained a high level over the postwar period. [4] During this period the nation's economic status has also risen. We cannot clearly say whether elevation of national health is attributable to the rise in the economic level or whether nutritional improvement first contributed to raising the economic level. Generally speaking, improvement in nutrition cannot always be achieved by economic development alone. People must be educated on the rational use of food resources. In the sense that health and the will to work are basic to man's happiness and welfare, planning in nutrition is linked to national development policy.

References

1. Nutrition Improvement Law. National Law No. 248. July 31, 1952.

2. *Recommended Nutritional Allowances for Japanese.* Japanese Agency of Science and Technology, National Resource Council. February 24, 1952. *Recommended Nutritional Allowances for Japanese* (revised). Japanese Ministry of Health and Welfare. August 18, 1969.

3. Oiso, T. Recent annual changes in nutrition in Japan. *Exc. Med.,* International Congress Series No. 221. *Diabetes Mellitus in Asia, 1970.* Proceedings of a Symposium, Kobe, Japan, May 24, 1970, p. 234.

4. Insull, W., Jr., T. Oiso, and K. Tsuchiya. Diet and nutritional status of Japanese. *Amer. J. Clin. Nutr.* 21:753, 1968.

38 General Discussion

Chairman: **Dr. Max Milner** (Protein Advisory Group, New York); **Dr. Ginor;**
Dr. Santos; Mr. K. V. Natarajan (Planning Commission, India); **Dr. M. S.**
Randhawa (Punjab Agricultural University, India)

Ginor   After the establishment of the state of Israel there were signs of malnutrition in various sectors of the population owing to supply difficulties and
mass immigration. The immigrants, coming from all parts of the world with
different cultural backgrounds, brought with them different food habits,
which had to be adapted to local conditions. Since then nutrition has gradually improved, and there is at present no serious malnutrition even in the
poorer sections of the population.

A comparison of food balance sheets shows an increase in the intake of most
nutrients per capita from 1949-50 to 1969-70 (Table 1). Family consumption
surveys reflect improvement in the nutrition of the wage-earning urban and
semiurban population, mainly with regard to animal protein intake (Table 2).[1]

The distribution of families by expenditure per capita in the dietary survey
showed that only in the lowest 10 percent of the urban population was the
intake of calcium, thiamine, iron, and vitamin A still inadequate and in need of
correction in 1968-69, and the intake of riboflavin and calories at a level not
providing adequate margins of safety (Table 3). The intake of animal protein
and niacin, which had no adequate safety margin in 1951, had improved. The
second lowest 10 percent of the population showed only insufficient margins
of safety for five nutrients in 1968-69.

While nutritional deficiencies were largest in the lowest income groups, the
survey in 1963-64 revealed some nutritional deficiencies in families at all
economic levels. Even for nutrients with quite satisfactory average intakes
(such as calories, animal protein, riboflavin, and ascorbic acid) there was still
inadequate intake among 6 to 19 percent of all urban families, while inadequate intakes of calcium, iron, and vitamin A (the average intake of which
was in need of correction) prevailed among 20 to 32 percent of all urban
families (Table 4). While 1963/64 represents an improvement in comparison
with previous years, there was further improvement in 1968/69, especially
among large families and low-income groups.

The following factors contributed to the improvement in nutrition, in addition to the rise in incomes and the standard of living: (1) special clinics for

[1] Based on dietary surveys made by Dr. Sarah Bavly once every five to six years.

Table 1. Food Balance Sheets, Israel, 1949-1970

Per capita per day	1949-50	1954-55	1969-70	Change in % from 1949-50 to 1969-70
Calories	2,610	2,860	2,988	+14.5
Protein (grams)	83.9	88.8	91.5	+ 9.5
(Animal protein, grams)	(32.2)	(29.8)	(44.3)	+37.6
Fat (grams)	73.9	82.2	104.3	+41.1
Vitamin A (I.U.)	3,195	3,603	4,212	+31.8
Thiamine (Vit. B_1)	1.92	1.92	1.68	−12.5
Riboflavin	1.79	1.41	1.42	−20.7
Niacin	13.4	13.7	16.8	+25.4
Ascorbic Acid (Vit. C)	126	134	130	+ 3.2
Calcium	850	926	722	−15.1
Iron	15.0	16.0	16.3	+ 8.7

Source: Statistical Abstract of Israel, No. 22, 1971.
Note: When comparing food balance sheet figures with survey figures the following should be taken into account: (1) The food balance sheet is based on data at the wholesale level and does not take into account spoilage at the retail trade level, in transport, and in the homes, or loss of vitamins by cooking. (2) The food balance sheet covers the total population, including rural population, people in the army, hospitals, and other institutions, while the survey covers only the urban and semiurban wage-earning population, and in 1968-69 the total urban population.

Table 2. Comparison of Nutrient Intake per Capita in Various Urban Dietary Surveys

	1951	1956-57	1963-64
Calories	2,150	2,240	2,220
Protein total (grams)	76	76	75
Animal protein (grams)	31	33	37
Fat (grams)	70	64	71
Calcium (mg)	1,006	857	819
Iron (mg)	11.4	11.9	12.1
Vitamin A (IU)	7,200*	4,700	4,460
Thiamine (mg)	1.20	1.28	1.22
Riboflavin (mg)	1.44	1.52	1.43
Niacin (mg)	9.6	12.5	12.7
Ascorbic acid (mg)	181*	108	87.4

Source: Sarah Bavly, Levels of Nutrition in Israel 1963/64, Urban Wage and Salary Earners. Jerusalem: Ministry of Education and Culture, 1966.
*This large intake of vitamin A and ascorbic acid was a seasonal phenomenon, as in 1951 the survey did not cover the whole year. These two figures can therefore not be used as a basis for comparison.

Table 3. Comparison of Intake of Nutrients per Unit in Lowest Income Decile of the Population (in percentage of recommended allowance per unit[a])

Nutrient	1951[b]	1963/64	1968/69
Calories	86	81	87
Total protein	102	100	119
Animal protein	89	86	116
Calcium	69	65	63
Iron	86	76	67
Vitamin A	107[c]	66	56
Thiamine	101	120	77
Riboflavin	77	82	84
Niacin	75	152	126
Ascorbic acid	167[c]	81	100

Source: 1963-64: S. Bavly, Levels of Nutrition in Israel 1963-64, Urban Wage and Salary Earners. Jerusalem: Ministry of Education and Culture, 1966.
1951: S. Bavly, Levels of Nutrition in Israel 1951. Jerusalem: Central Bureau of Statistics and Economic Research, 1952.
1968-69: S. Bavly, Dietary Survey. Jerusalem, 1972.
[a]Intake per capita per day translated into quantities per unit by expressing the recommended allowance for each member of the family according to age and sex as factor of the recommended allowance of the reference man, aged 18 to 34 years. Based on recommended allowances of the U.S. Research Council (changed every five years), which have a high margin of safety. Therefore 80% is still adequate, though the margin of safety is not quite adequate, 60 to 79% is inadequate and in need of correction, below 60% is grossly inadequate and in urgent need of improvement.
[b]Lowest 4% of survey population. Since the survey did not include single persons, pensioners, and families without earners, this may well reflect 10%, if not more, of the population.
[c]Seasonal phenomenon, not comparable (see note to Table 2).

mother-child care, which give also nutritional advice, now reach 80 percent of pregnant women and young children; (2) school lunches give the school-children of all strata of the population, especially the poorer ones, one good meal at low subsidized prices, assuring the supply of sufficient nutrients to the children of the needy. This arrangement is especially important for the children of working mothers who cannot prepare a warm meal for their children during the day; (3) comprehensive health services, allowing the early diagnosis of diseases and early treatment, increasingly prevent malnutrition as a result of disease; (4) education in nutrition and food preparation is offered in most elementary schools, in all vocational schools for girls, and in all junior high schools; (5) agricultural development, especially improved storage facilities have increased the periods of supply for vegetables and fruits, eggs, meat, poultry, and fish. These foodstuffs are therefore available during the whole

Table 4. Levels of Nutrient Intakes for the Urban Population of Total Number of
Families (1963-1964)

	Total (%)	Levels[b] A	B	C	D
Calories	100	57[a]	27	13	3
Protein total	100	73	23	3	1
Animal protein	100	88	6	4	2
Calcium	100	48	28	16	8
Iron	100	57	23	14	6
Vitamin A	100	51	17	16	16
Thiamine	100	90	6	3	1
Riboflavin	100	67	21	10	2
Niacin	100	98	2	–	–
Ascorbic acid	100	70	11	8	11

Source: S. Bavly, Levels of Nutrition in Israel 1963-64, Urban Wage and Salary Earners.
Jerusalem: Ministry of Education and Culture, 1966.
[a]This figure is composed of 43% A+ (i.e., overconsumption of calories) and 14% A.
[b]A= 100% or more of recommended allowance, B = 80-100%, C = 60-80%,
D = below 60%. See note to Table 3.

year at reasonably stable prices; (6) in the realm of government policy, imports of frozen meat and fish make possible an orderly supply to the population during the whole year; subsidies for milk, eggs, and bread assure low
prices for essentials; and nutritional enrichment of food is effected by the
addition of vitamins A and D to margarine, of calcium and riboflavin to
flour.

Santos I would like to report our experience in setting up a food and
nutrition policy in the state of São Paulo and in establishing priorities.

We started by making an assessment of (1) the natural resources for food
production, including geographical situation, ecological conditions, size, soil
condition, and so forth; (2) human technological and financial resources,
population and growth rate, population by age group; (3) the social and cultural patterns of the different regions, mainly the educational levels of the
population; (4) the institutional system and its level of efficiency; (5) the
condition of the infrastructure of food supply—storage, transportation, processing, marketing system, and so on; (6) the stage of socioeconomic development of the different regions and the growth rate of each; and (7) the existing
conditions and plans for integrating social and economic development, particularly in relation to agricultural development.

Although conditions for each country differ with respect to food policy, I believe that the principles we adopted for diagnosing and establishing priorities may be applicable to other nations.

We first diagnosed the food and nutrition situation, taking into consideration all the available data and supplementing them with additional research. We then assessed the resources available and established a correlation between the food and nutrition situation and the available resources, identifying also the many obstacles in the way of plan implementation.

Next we made an evaluation of the patterns and levels of food consumption, of nutrient consumption, and set targets for improving the existing conditions: short-term, medium-term, and long-term targets, for the whole population, with a high priority accorded the lower income and especially vulnerable groups.

Then we established a base plan, with sectoral programs and specific projects; to implement such a plan we established an integrated multisectoral system for evaluation, supervision, and readjustment of the plan.

Natarajan India's fourth five-year plan has a separate chapter on food and nutrition for the first time, briefly setting forth a coordinated nutrition policy. It takes into account the multidisciplinary nature of nutrition problems, covering nutrition, agriculture, health, education, economics, and sociology; such a policy would also include food production, storage, marketing, distribution, consumption, extension, education, feeding programs, and the like.

We have also briefly stated in the plan that priorities have to be laid down in nutrition, keeping in view three considerations. One, since resources are limited, priorities have to be established with reference to needs, classes, and areas. Two, the efficiency of the existing programs has to be improved and their coverage has to be extended, while at the same time strengthening the organizations that serve the needs of priority classes and areas. This is an important plank in our plan to improve the supervisory machinery for women's programs. Three, programs of distribution should be supported wherever necessary by programs of production, processing, and supply. This includes wheat processing as well as modernization of rice mills.

I would like to briefly refer to a number of issues this conference might consider. One, can a suitable strategy be evolved to optimize returns from investment on government-sponsored nutrition feeding programs with reference to the most vulnerable classes and vulnerable areas? Optimization in this regard will mean not merely following the path of humanitarian assistance but also getting the best return in terms of the physical efficiency of the working force.

The second issue concerns decisions on the relative roles of home feeding and institutional feeding.

Third, are there guidelines available for resolving such fundamental questions as the relative priorities to be accorded in feeding programs as between current working force and potential working force? We really have not solved this problem yet.

The fourth issue is the shift of crop emphasis, which the development of high-yielding varieties of cereals implies, from coarse grains to rice and wheat; it will mean perhaps that calorie and protein yields per acre will rise less than if the incentives and improvements were concentrated on coarse grains.

The fifth issue is how to provide the necessary infrastructure for nutrition education. There should be an adequate reservoir of trained workers at various levels. In fact we have a big manpower problem with respect to nutrition functionaries at various levels—national, federal-state, and district and lower levels.

And finally, in view of the high and rising share of useless cattle, especially in our country, and taking into account the low calorie and land ratio implied in animal husbandry programs, should there be any continuing emphasis on such programs? Do they really represent a high priority? Does such an emphasis reflect merely the priorities of predominantly middle-class representatives, the planners, based on their urban diets?

Randhawa   The cry of despair from Abyssinia moved me greatly, and reminded me of the plight of India in 1966. But since then we have made many changes. The problems of food and nutrition are closely bound up with the problems of agricultural development. In this case the experience of India, particularly the state of Punjab, is unique. It can be of interest to many people here.

Food production in India rose from 74 million tons in 1966 to 104 million tons in 1970. But for this increase in production we wouldn't have been able to face the problem of feeding nine million refugees from East Bengal. In terms of food production I find one very bright spot in India; that is the state of Punjab, where the production of cereals rose from 2.4 million tons in 1960 to 6.7 in 1970, a 300 percent increase. An increase of this magnitude has never taken place in this country before, and that is why I offer a few thoughts on the Green Revolution in that area and the problem of malnutrition.

The first step we took in Punjab was the consolidation of fragmented holdings of land under a new law, thus laying the basis for agricultural development. Formerly the land was divided in very tiny strips, and now the pieces of land are large enough to be economically workable.

The next important development was establishing the agricultural university. Although American aid in food was very helpful in a crisis, it is the aid in creating institutions for agricultural development that has been most effective, and an important link was the development of the agricultural universities on the pattern of the land grant universities in America. My own university, Punjab Agricultural University, was modeled on this very pattern and has played a pivotal role in the Green Revolution, in the sense that for the first time research and extension activities were tied together. Formerly they were disparate, and were not making a significant impact.

In addition to the colleges of agriculture, veterinary sciences, and engineering, we have colleges of home economics to teach women about food and nutrition. The village women are brought in large numbers to be exposed to these programs, and that has proved very useful. Radio can also play a very important role in disseminating information. Our own agricultural program is broadcast usually late in the evening, and when I go out on my walks I see that some of the farmers have hung their transistor sets from the branches of trees and are listening intently while they dig potatoes.

Probably the most important factor in the Green Revolution has been rural electrification. In Punjab the use of electric power in agriculture rose from 15 percent in 1960 to 25 percent in 1970. This has enabled us to tap ground water; the number of wells run by electricity has increased manyfold and at the same time a number of operations have been mechanized. At present 95 percent of the crop in Punjab is mechanically threshed, thanks to electricity and tractors.

The use of tractors has a direct connection with the problem of malnutrition. Not only can land be plowed rapidly but so much time is saved that it is possible to insert a third crop, a legume crop, between wheat and maize during the monsoons. In our university, not only have we developed high-yielding varieties of wheat and rice, but we are giving the same attention to the pulses; we have a 60-day crop that can be sown right after the harvesting of wheat and then can be harvested before the other cereal crop is to be planted. This is possible only with rapid means of cultivation and power in agriculture. Here the affluent countries can play some useful role, allocating with a greater sense of responsibility such natural resources as fuels, linking them to food production, and thus contributing to the solution of the world's nutrition problem.

There was reference earlier to the problem of roads. Roads have played a very important role in agricultural development and in reaching the people. We started a crash program to build rural roads; already more than 70 percent of the villages have been joined with market towns, and we propose to join the remaining 30 percent in the next 3 years.

All these things are important in the sense that ultimately the impact of research, development of new varieties with high protein contents, and development of high-yield pulses is felt in the lives of the people.

39 Summation

Derrick B. Jelliffe
Director
Caribbean Food and Nutrition Institute
Kingston, Jamaica

During the last few days an immense number of complex ideas have flowed
through our minds. Rather than trying to package them neatly, the purpose
here is to outline the main themes that have emerged and to attempt to give a
satellite's-eye view of the conference as a whole—and how it fits into developments and trends in nutrition and national planning in the last two decades.

This conference has been of historic interest, and the organizers deserve
congratulations for the foresight, energy, and support that have made it possible. Fifty-five countries have been represented here in an important pioneer-
ing dialogue, an interchange of views and experience between development
planners and nutritionists.

The conference has endorsed the idea that, in all aspects of nutrition and of
economics, the level of accurate information is imperfect and there is still a
great need for further investigation on every conceivable front. Nevertheless,
there *is* sufficient information already available to make practical judgments
and to move ahead into new types of programs, conjointly.

The main question has been: *Should nutrition logically have a major emphasis in national development plans all over the world, especially in the lower
income countries of the Third World, for economic as well as for humanitarian reasons, bearing in mind the other very great claims on limited resources of all types?*

This, of course, is a question of the greatest importance affecting the well-
being of millions of people, and it seems likely that the present conference
will have a tremendous impact, probably after an indeterminate gestation
period.

It seems, in fact, that a turning point has been passed concerning the relationship of nutrition and national planning. During this conference there have
been problems of linguistics, of jargon, of code words. Occasionally one won-
dered whether it might not be more profitable to have interpreters in the two
languages of "econolingo" and "nutritionish." Nevertheless, participants from
the two subcultures were able to overcome their tunnel-vision to a considerable extent and to understand, at least peripherally, what the other was
talking about. There were also considerable problems of a philosophical and
metaphysical nature in relation to the definition of such terms as national
development, national growth, and the quality of life.

Interactions of Nutrition and Economic Development

Nutritional Perspectives

A great deal of attention has been given to nutritional perspectives. The biological impact of malnutrition has been amply stated, especially its devastating effect on the physiologically and culturally vulnerable mother-child complex, as well as on the economically deprived and on the productively important wage earner or food producer.

It has also been stressed that nutrition is only one part of the complete ecology that surrounds man anywhere, and it is necessary to consider all the different interacting variables in development plans.

The immediate effects of this biological impact, especially on mothers and young children, have been emphasized fully, including the high rate of malnutrition of all degrees of severity and of consequent, often lethal, infections. The later effects, physical and mental, have also been discussed. The stunting of physical growth appears to have more significance for women, in relation to subsequent maternal mortality from difficulties with the birth process.

With regard to the later effects of childhood malnutrition on mental development, the evidence resulting from experimental animal studies is absolutely clear. Also, *the evidence with regard to human subjects has reached the level of clarity and assurance that puts it beyond reasonable doubt.* This impairment of mental development—this interference with what have been called the primary tools of modern culture: reading, writing, learning, communication—affects the least privileged in all genetic groups. Not only in so-called developing countries, but in underprivileged communities everywhere, are found the biologically, socially, and psychologically handicapped survivors of childhood malnutrition.

In recent years the scope of nutrition has changed very considerably, as nutritionists have come to realize more and more that their role is much wider than previously imagined. The era of the nutritional ecologist has now arrived, bringing an awareness to the nutritionist of his wider responsibilities and also of the impingement of all aspects of the ecology on nutrition, including the economic level of the community.

The nutritionist has also become much more aware of the financial burden of malnutrition to the community, especially through the drain on the health services, and of the need to consider cost-benefit implications of alternative programs.

Economic Perspectives

The economic consequences of nutritional status, or malnutrition in particular, have been emphasized. The costs of malnutrition—the educational loss, the effect of high child mortality rates, the decreased productivity of the worker—all of these have been mentioned. Some are quite clear and definite; others are exceedingly probable but need the support of more evidence before they can be presented with complete assurance.

Obviously, the role and priority of nutrition have been changing in plans for national development. In recent decades there seem to have been two main schools of planning philosophy, which may perhaps be termed the "early development" school and the "modern development" school.

Early Development School

In the first two decades after World War II this school predominated, with major emphasis on national economic expansion, rising GNP, capital production, and so forth. Human resources were regarded as an end but not as a means, and consequently nutrition, health, and the like were minor considerations, or were classed as welfare issues.

This approach was based on the assumption that ultimately the rise in GNP would be spread throughout the population, producing general benefits, including nutritional improvement. This has not come about as hoped. In some countries the GNP has not risen as dramatically as anticipated, and, when GNP has increased, the distribution of benefits through the population has been much more difficult and slower than hoped. Also this approach has had an inadequate effect, if any, on the overwhelming problems of employment, education, and nutrition.

Likewise, it has become apparent that economic improvement is not necessarily related automatically or immediately to nutritional improvement. Examples include the peasant farmer who raises cash crops and subsists on a worsening diet, and the transitional culture of the urban shanty-town, with bottle-feeding supplanting breast-feeding.

Reconsideration of the approach of the "early development" school has also been called for because of a general dissatisfaction with the outcomes and values of industrial economic development in the western world itself, paralleled by worldwide trends toward more social relevance and community involvement.

Modern Development School

Be that as it may, a modern school has developed in economic thought, which relates development more to standards of living—to human happiness perhaps—rather than interpreting it in exclusively economic terms. This has led to a mixed approach, with the planner of this school defining goals to include *both* an increase in the GNP of a country (but with a greater emphasis on income distribution and more attention to agriculture, employing intermediate technology) and, at the same time, a greater concern for social benefits, for improvement of the quality of life, at least in such material terms as living standards, employment, adaptive nonformal education, housing, health, and, very definitely, nutrition.

This change seems to have come about partly for humanitarian reasons and partly as a way of reaching people in the community directly, thus circumventing the obstacles to attempts to distribute increased national income to the groups most in need. In other words, it is an indirect economic distribution mechanism, an attempt to break the cycle of poverty and misery by getting to its roots.

Goals: Conflict into Confluence

In the last two decades nutritionists and planners have often been in conflict. But the discussion that has come out of this conference illustrates that many of their problems are shared. For example, each discipline appreciates the very complex interacting network of systems or pathways that need to be considered in dealing with their particular problems. There is also dissatisfaction, soul-searching, and rethinking in both fields. There is new knowledge and the beginning of mutual education, leading to confluence rather than conflict.

This flowing together of the goals, objectives, aims, and actions of the development planners and the nutritionists is both logical and necessary for various reasons. First, the planner is certainly concerned with the improvement of human resources—that is, people. Second, the modern development planner is much concerned with the quality of life and with social benefits, and is now demanding from the nutritionists and others advice on programs. Third, the national planner realizes that his decisions can affect nutrition and that, in effect, he is a nutritionist without realizing it, because many of the things that he does affect nutrition in one way or another.

As for the nutritionist, he appreciates more and more the cost-benefit realities of his work. He also understands that contributions to nutritional improvement may often lie outside traditional, classical nutritional fields. For example, nutritional betterment can sometimes be achieved by means of improvement in communications, transport, storage, price policies, and so on.

Also, the nutritionist is increasingly aware that programs have to be considered in relation to economic benefits as well as to direct effects.

This mutual reexamination is leading to a changing and a widening of the roles of these two groups and, in turn, to a more systematic approach to the whole question of nutrition planning.

Wider Roles and Systematic Approaches

The conference agreed that a nutrition program is both a separate entity and also an important theme running through many aspects of national development plans. For example, agricultural projects need to be evaluated with an eye to nutrition implications.

There will be a choice of different alternative projects which can go to make up the development program, and the question is how to make this selection. In the course of this conference a most valid and logical approach has been emphasized, which appeals particularly to someone trained originally in medicine and who is familiar with the need to make a diagnosis based on varying sources of information. There is a general consensus on the need for a systematic, analytic type of approach, based on community data.

Two questions that came up during the conference were: Do we know enough to go ahead now? Do we need much further detailed information? The answer to both seems to be "yes."

There is enough information already available to go ahead with some programs; in particular, the idea of relating the degree of investment in a national development budget to the amount of serious malnutrition in young children in a country as a priority is appealing and urgently needed.

At the same time, more information is required to facilitate a more rational selection of choices than in the past. Agreement on the desirability of a collection of information leading to an "econutritional profile" is one of the most important results to come out of this meeting; it is a new conceptual approach, merging the nutritional with the planning approach. The ecological variation of programs from one part of the world to another has been much stressed. There is no universal panacea for malnutrition; details vary greatly in different nations and some type of systematic approach is required. This may be on a limited basis or, in some circumstances, a full systems analysis approach. However, many things are not known about the latter. What subsystems of information should be included? The range may vary from place to place. How are these measured?

However, a beginning has been made, and systems analysis, or at the least a systematic approach, is the correct and logical tool if priorities are to be established. It will provide information to evaluate programs, to test their cost-benefit ratio, and also can become a continuing process that will give returns not only for a period of a year or two but in decades to come.

In other words, there is a need for diagnosis of the nature, the scope, and the trends of nutritional problems, and for assessment of the determinants of the problems in a particular area. From this one can go on logically to select from the alternative approaches that are required. Everywhere, the blend, the mix will vary. There is no doubt of the need for an integrated program, combining macro and micro elements, and, indeed, "super-macro" approaches, to take into consideration the global influence of trading policies, of the prices of agricultural products, of international food aid, and the like.

The need, then, is for a logical program mixture based on the facts as they actually exist. The selection will be determined by the magnitude of the problem, its cost, and the likelihood of being able to deal with it, together with the effect of the program on population dynamics, economic advancement, ruralization of population, and also on its political appeal.

Two programs of a non-nutritional type were mentioned during the conference—the space program and the malaria eradication program. Both have their messages. The moon program and the rest of the space program were "impossibilities" realized only through a systems analysis approach. Surely some of this technology can be applied to other problems of a more pressing nature. Conversely, the malaria project may have been less successful than hoped because it did *not* take into account many aspects of the local ecology, because it started some decades back before the systems approach became prominent.

Conclusions

In summary, there is a need for change in the roles of the development planner and of the nutritionist. The modern planner should have a major role in improving nutrition. In fact, the econutritionist, or the nutritionally oriented planner, can have immense relevance, perhaps being even more significant in improving nutrition than the classical nutritionist. Seminars, conferences, and interchanges between nutritionists and planners will be very helpful in this regard and certainly deserve much further attention.

The contemporary nutritionist also has a much wider scope and vision than in the past. One of his roles is to inform the planner and to give technical advice, and the training of nutritionists should take this into account. There is a need, for example, in the training program to study political science, the techniques of decisionmaking and policymaking, modern managerial meth-

ods, and the like. Similarly, education in some aspects of nutrition will help
the planner too. Everybody has stated clearly, and this of course is fundamental, that nutritional policy has to be made on an intersectoral, interdisciplinary basis. How easy to say and how difficult to do. A key figure in the
future in this regard is going to be the informed planner, who will play an
important role in the difficult task of coordinating intersectoral activities.

Will the papers and discussions presented exist in a vacuum or are they going
to mean something? It seems certain that they are going to mean a great deal,
although this can be visualized as only the beginning of an organic process. A
great deal of information is still needed on either side. Not all of us are completely convinced about all points, and there are disagreements. But there is a
beginning of a confluence, forming part of a world trend.

For example, in such international agencies as WHO, PAHO, FAO, UNICEF
a key priority is an emphasis on nutrition in national planning. In the next
two years, five seminars are going to be held in various parts of the Americas
that will be jointly attended by members of the nutrition and of the national
planning fraternities. The emphasis given to this approach by U.N. agencies is
also indicated clearly by the fact that this technical problem came up before
the U.N. General Assembly, leading to the publication of *International Action to Avert the Impending Protein Crisis.* [1] Likewise, in the U.N. Second
Development Decade, planners at an international level are concentrating on a
mixed or balanced approach to development, emphasizing *both* economic
advancement and social benefit.

This trend also is visible in some individual countries, notably India. Also, a
recent conference on Nutrition and National Development in Africa, held at
the Hammarskjöld Foundation in Uppsala, indicates the concern of the
Swedish government, combined with the fact that within the Swedish International Development Authority (SIDA) there is a considerable emphasis on
nutrition as a component of national development. [2]

Major changes in emphasis have shown up in a variety of other organizations
and institutions. This trend, this confluence, this interaction, this joining
together of the forces of the development planner and the nutritionist is
already proceeding, although undoubtedly there will be problems of mutual
understanding. Many of the points made in the course of this conference need
further factual backing, but there is no doubt that this trend is on us now. It
represents a tremendously valuable opportunity for trying to bridge the
"application chasm," the gulf between scientific knowledge and its application
in the community, especially among rural and urban peoples in less developed
countries.

In conclusion, it is appropriate to quote from the 1971 McNamara Report, which briefly and lucidly summarizes the points covered above: "In the end development is like life itself—complex. The danger is to oversimplify. Development has for too long been expressed simply in terms of growth and output. There is now emerging the awareness that the availability of work, the distribution of income, and the quality of life are equally important measures of development.

"Although this is gradually being accepted in theory, it has as yet to be translated into practice by either the developing countries or the suppliers of external capital. It is towards this broader concept of the entire development process that the World Bank is moving.

"If we are to meet our mandate to our member countries and, indeed, to man himself I believe that we must move even faster." [3]

References

1. United Nations. *International Action to Avert the Impending Protein Crisis.* U.N. Publication E/68/XIII.2. New York, 1968.

2. Michanek, E. *The World Development Plan: A Swedish Perspective.* Uppsala: Dag Hammarskjöld Foundation, 1971.

3. McNamara, R. S. Address to the Board of Governors of the International Bank for Reconstruction and Development. Washington, D.C., 1971.

40 Closing Remarks

Jerome B. Wiesner
President, M.I.T.

I have been living in this cybernetic institution for thirty years or so, and during this period I have seen systems analysis become almost a way of life here; many people use these concepts regularly in their work. The concepts that we have been working on and trying to understand are relatively easy to apply in creating models of physical systems. But in the much more complex social systems you have been considering here, though you will almost certainly get very useful insights, you may get into trouble if you take the quantitative lessons derived from models too seriously.

Nonetheless, I think these social questions are very important and we should be investigating them with all possible means. I have come to believe that what we are all doing—as we work with technologies on these development problems and make efforts to improve the quality of life for the individual—is really to extend the old biological evolutionary process by direct intervention. We have intervened by using our brainpower, our augmented muscle power, and our abilities to collaborate in the creation of very large systems. But we have to keep in mind, it seems to me—and this is the thought I would leave with you—that like biological evolution, the social evolution we are engaged in remains an experimental process.

It is not possible to make a model, in my view, even if you could measure and find all the relevant values, that would allow you to predict the long-term behavior of a social system or even a subsector of a social system. Therefore, one can't expect that the nutritionists or physical planners or economic developers are going to lay out for us—for any society or any subsection of the society—a long-range plan that will be very close to right. The important thing is that at every stage they can help us bring together the best information and the best judgment and so indicate the most probable next right steps. But we must be aware that the next steps are always much more likely to be at least partially in the wrong direction and so we should be extremely careful to seek those indicators which would tell us what the next right step is. I have always believed that if politicians and planners and other people who have to face the public had this point of view and were rewarded for being quick to admit that things needed to be changed, we would make more rapid progress. Instead, they frequently are not even allowed to admit that anything is wrong with a plan; there has to be a very, very large error signal, as we would call it, before a corrective action can take place.

Another important aspect of the assessment and analysis problem is the ability of the various contributors to a plan—to its creation, to its execution, to its funding—to talk the same language, and that is why a conference such as this is so important.

But I believe that the need is much greater. I don't believe a conference, even one involving people who start with a great deal of common understanding, is an adequate means of providing the kind of interdisciplinary education that is needed. Many institutions like ours feel that one of their most important roles in the decades ahead is to provide young men and women with a broad enough background so that regardless of whether they are professional nutritionists or economists or planners, they will have an understanding and a cognitive style that is flexible enough to encompass the points of view and cognitive styles of other people engaged in their common enterprise.

Nonetheless a conference such as this can move us forward in our efforts to interact, to be sensitive to the broad range of problems that must be confronted as we struggle to make man's lot on this earth a little better.

Name Index

Subject Index

Academy of Agricultural Sciences (Czechoslovakia), 332
Academy of Sciences (Czechoslovakia), 332
Advisory Committee on the Application of Science and Technology (ACAST), 120, 156
Aflatoxin, 177
Africa
exports, 25
malnutrition effects, 23, 43, 155
OAU, 157
See also specific countries
Age
Colombia nutrition program, 340
and malnutrition effect, 4, 9-11, 156
and nutrition priorities, 44, 46, 124-125, 146-147, 290-291, 361-363
and size studies, 7-9
See also Preschool children
Agency for International Development (AID)
Colombia nutrition program, 340, 344
Tamil Nadu project, 303
Agriculture, 248
cash crop *v.* food crop, 25-26, 31-32, 223, 321-322, 375
credit, 342
and economic development, 31-32, 247-248
and education, 376
electrification effect, 376
extension programs, 342, 346, 376
Green Revolution, India, 313, 358, 360, 375-376
land reform, 376
mechanization, 376
price control effect, 180-182
research, 151-152, 183-184, 358-359, 376
sharecropping, 321-322
transportation effect, 377
See also Animal husbandry; Cereals; Dairy production; Food production; Legumes; Poultry production
AID. *See* Agency for International Development
All-India Children's Nutrition Program, 304
American Public Health Association, 104
Amino acids, 15-16, 186, 241, 324. *See also* Protein

Anemia, 105, 171, 295, 309, 317, 336, 362
Animal husbandry, 176-178, 375
Colombia nutrition program, 342, 346
Animal protein, 94, 121, 176, 370. *See also* Protein
Applied Nutrition Programs (ANP), 187, 220, 231, 362
Argentina, food fortification, 182
Ariboflavinosis, 105, 325
Ascorbic acid, 370
Asian Congress of Nutrition, 23
Asian Nutrition Conference, *1971,* 11
Association of Medical Schools (Colombia), 349
Atherosclerosis, 105
Avitaminosis, 336

Baby foods, 179
Bangladesh, employment, 71
Bayley technique, 9
Beans, 213. *See also* Legumes
Beriberi, 105, 295
research on, 323-324
Biafra, malnutrition effects, 145
Binet-Simon scale, 10
Birth weight: malnutrition effect, 124, 147, 362
Blindness, 105, 158, 325. *See also* Vitamin A
Bolivia, maternal-child health programs, 288
Brazil
food fortification, 185-186
nutrition research, 373-374
processed foods, 179
Breast-feeding
encouragement need, 122, 257
and family planning, 75
and industrialization, 170, 323
and malnutrition, 146-147
milk quality, 171
and supplements, 124
Burma, sale of food commodities in, 182

Caesarean section, 9, 41-42
Calcium, 325, 370
Carbohydrates, 4, 26
CARE, 340
Cattell technique, 9
Casava, 97

Cell development, and malnutrition, 34-37, 42
Central America, 179. *See also specific countries*
Cereals, 22
consumption and income level, 167-168
fertilizer effect, 25
fortification of, 184
high-yield, 120, 151, 358
v. legumes, 176
v. oilseeds, 208
v. poultry production, 97
protein research, 183-184
v. pulse production, 230-231
See also Agriculture; Food production
Chicken, 97, 176-177
Child-feeding programs, 94-135, 191-193
in Czechoslovakia, 331
in India, 303, 362
tradition effect, 291
See also Day Care centers; Preschool children; School feeding programs
Chile, 108
food fortification, 185-186
malnutrition effects, 15
maternal-child health programs, 288
China, as rice exporter, 308-309
Chloroquine, 186
CIFW. *See* Colombian Institute of Family Welfare
Cinema. *See* Communications media
Cod liver oil. *See* Fish oil
Colombia, 314
Candelaria, 46
food fortification, 185
food supplements, 288
Incaparina use, 213-214
nutrition program, 335-355
salt iodization, 325
Colombian Fund of Scientific Investigations (COLCIENCIAS), 348
Colombian Institute of Family Welfare (CIFW), 336, 338-339, 349, 355
Commodity price
control effect, 169, 180-182, 259, 292, 329, 359
and subsidy, 373
supply-demand function, 168-169, 174-175, 202
unconventional foods, 213-214
Communications media
and food habits, 235-237
and marketing, 217-222, 235
nutrition effect, 88-89, 189, 232, 234-237, 239-240, 260, 345-346, 376
and traditions, 187-189, 220

Composite Nutrition Program (India), 362
Consumer expenditure survey, 251
Corn, 46, 189, 240, 321-322
enrichment, 184-195
opaque-2, 348
Cornell University, 343, 348
Corn soy milk (CSM), 180
Costa Rica
food fortification, 185
size study, 114
Cotton, 321-322
Cottonseed, 186, 360. *See also* Oilseeds
Council on Food and Nutrition (Japan), 367
Credit
for agriculture, 342
for food production, 178
Cretinism, 324-325
Cuba, 288, 308
Culture. *See* Tradition
Cystic fibrosis, 233
Czechoslovakia, 314
nutrition program, 329-333

Dag Hammarskjöld Seminar on Nutrition as a Priority in African Development, 116
Dairy Production, 176-178
Danish International Development Agency (DANIDA), 212
Dar-es-Salaam, University of, 118
Day care centers
in Czechoslovakia, 331
and food supplements, 226-227
and unconventional food, 224
See also Preschool children
Death rate, 74
birth trauma, 9
fertility effect, 25, 76-78, 132
health services effect, 100, 132
and malnutrition, 109-113, 124, 286, 305, 336
nutrition programs effect, 348
Dementia, as characteristic of pellagra, 321
Dental caries, 325
Dermatitis, as characteristic of pellagra, 321
Diarrhea, 170-171, 321, 336
Diphtheria, 361
Direct feeding, 140. *See also* Child-feeding programs; School feeding programs
Dominican Republic, rice enrichment in, 185
Dwarfing. *See* Size

Immunization programs (continued)
in India, 360-361
and nutrition programs, 191, 259-260
Incaparina (processed food), 179, 213-214, 241-243, 319
Income level
and economic development, 70-73
and food consumption, 167-168
and food expenditure, 72, 95, 97, 131, 167, 168, 251
and food supplements, 26, 140-141
and low weight gain, 4-5
and marasmus, 93
mental performance, 12
and nutrition, 17-18, 31, 70, 92-95, 100, 167-169, 172-174, 210, 247, 349, 352-353, 370
and population growth, 207-208
price control effect, 180-182
redistribution effect, 96, 98, 134-135, 200-201, 238-239
and size, 7-9
subsistence, 56, 261, 357-358
Tamil Nadu study, 307
urban migrants, 261
India, 91, 145, 159, 199, 314
birth weight study, 37
All-India Children's Nutrition Program, 304
Applied Nutrition Program, 220, 231
communications media, 239-240
economic development, 83, 92-93
family planning, 74, 77-79, 309
food consumption, 168, 174-176
food fortification, 184
food production, 121
Green Revolution, 313, 358, 360, 375-376
health services, 82, 84
Khanna study, 309, 363
malnutrition effects, 13, 37
nutrition programs, 160, 220, 231, 304, 357-365, 375-377
pellagra, 321
population growth, 207-208
price controls, 174-175, 182
salt fortification, 267
salt iodization, 324
school feeding program, 160
Tamil Nadu project, 193, 260, 303-308, 360
transportation, 259
Indonesia, 10, 300
Industrialization
breast-feeding effect, 170, 323
and rickets, 316, 323
Infants. See Maternal-child health care;

Preschool children
Infection, and malnutrition, 170-171, 189, 259-260, 287, 360-361
Institute of Health Education (Czechoslovakia), 333
Integrated Program of Applied Nutrition (PINA), 339, 342, 345
Intelligence. See Mental performance
Interamerican Cooperative Service of Public Health (SCISP), 338
International Action to Avert the Impending Protein Crisis, 120
International Federation of Agricultural Producers (IFAP), 89
International Labour Organization (ILO), 90
International Rice Institute, 183
International Union of Nutrition Sciences, 46
Iodine deficiency. See Endemic goiter
Irish famine, 1848, 316
Iron deficiency anemia. See Anemia
Israel
food fortification, 184
nutrition study, 370, 372-373
nursing leave, 257
Italy, decline in pellagra, 322

Jamaica, cost of high child mortality rate, 286
Japan, 314
beriberi, 323-324
food production, 121
labor productivity, 96
nutrition policy, 208-209, 366-369
nutrition survey, 293-297
population growth and income level, 207-208
rice research, 185, 224
size study, 42, 114
Joint FAO/WHO Expert Committee on Nutrition, 106

Keratomalacia, 326
Khanna study, 309, 363
Korea, seasonal food shortages, 259
Kwashiorkor, 23, 45, 98, 145, 149
and age, 146
defined, 4
features, 107-108
and infection, 171
and mental performance, 9-11, 15, 38
research on, 34, 316-321

Labor productivity
and education, 275-286

396   Subject Index

Labor productivity (continued)
and food production, 119-120
and health service ratio, 81-86
and nutrition, 54-58, 65-66, 96, 119-120,
131-133, 136-142, 201, 359
Laboratory of Nutritional Studies of the
National Institute of Hygiene (Colom-
bia), 338
Lactation. *See* Breast-feeding
Land reform, 376
Language. *See* Learning; Mental perform-
ance
Latin America
economic development, 83
malnutrition, 109, 287
See also specific countries
Latin American Society of Nutrition, 237
Laubina (processed food), 179
Lead poisoning, 233, 314
Learning
and malnutrition, 12-18, 37-38, 112,
145-146
and size, 14-15
See also Mental performance
Lebanon, commercially processed food, 179
Legumes, 177, 240
consumption and income level, 168
v. high-yield cereals, 120, 151, 176
PAG study, 120-121, 151
research need, 151
Livestock production. *See* Animal hus-
bandry
Lower class. *See* Income level
Lysine, 183, 241

Maize. *See* Corn
Malaria, 100
Malaya, birth weights, 37
Malnutrition
in Africa, 23, 43, 155
and age, 4, 9-11, 156
and agricultural reform, 31-32
awareness of, 30, 156-157
and breast-feeding, 146-147
and birth order, 364-365
and birth rate, 124
and birth weight, 44, 147
causes of, 116-119, 255
community planning, 3-4, 32-33
costs of, 155, 286-288, 308
and death rate, 109-113, 124, 286, 305,
336
defined, 3-4, 129-131
diagnostic criteria, 154-155

and economic development, 65
education effect, 16-17, 286-287
v. education allocation, 59-60, 63
and employment, 70-71
and environment, 3, 7, 29-32, 44-45, 50,
56, 117-119, 145
epidemiology study, 146-148
and family planning, 65
and food expenditures, 131
and food production, 119-121
and health services, 122, 155, 162, 189,
191
human aspect, 43-44, 58, 64, 66, 148-
149, 278, 381
and income level, 17-18, 56-57, 70, 98, 336
and infection, 110, 170-171, 189, 259-
260, 287, 360-361
international planning, 22-25, 156-157,
160-161
kwashiorkor features, 107-108
and labor productivity, 131-133, 145
and learning process, 12-18, 37-38, 112,
145-146
macro *v.* micro approach, 31-33, 43-46
marasmus features, 107-108
and mental performance, 9-11, 36-39,
59-60, 132, 147, 379
mild and moderate, 105-108, 129, 147-
148
mixed forms, 105-108
and motivation, 16-18, 145
and natural disasters, 118-119
and political system, 30-31, 42-43, 50-
51, 145, 148-149, 155-157
priorities, 23-24, 104-105, 146-149
psychosocial effect, 16-18, 156
regional planning, 157
and resource limits, 3, 33, 38
size studies, 7-9, 41-42, 109-116, 130,
145-146, 156
time factor, 27, 33
and trade effect, 157
and weaning, 146-147
See also Kwashiorkor; Marasmus
Mann Whitney test, 349
Marasmus, 23, 45, 79, 145, 149
and age, 147
and breast-feeding, 323
and cell growth, 36
defined, 4
features, 107-108
and income level, 93
and learning, 15
and mental performance, 9